T0373373

DIVIDED AMERICA on the WORLD STAGE

BROKEN GOVERNMENT
and
FOREIGN POLICY

HOWARD J. WIARDA

Potomac Books, Inc.
Washington, D.C.

Library of Congress Cataloging-in-Publication Data
Wiarda, Howard J., 1939–
  Divided America on the world stage : broken government and foreign policy / Howard J. Wiarda.
    p. cm.
  Includes bibliographical references and index.
  ISBN 978-1-59797-290-1 (hardcover : alk. paper) — ISBN 978-1-59797-293-2 (pbk. : alk. paper)
  1. United States—Foreign relations—Decision making. 2. United States—Foreign relations—1989– 3. United States—Foreign relations administration. 4. Political culture—United States. I. Title.
  JZ1480.W5 2009
  327.73—dc22
                                        2009015022

Printed in the United States of America on acid-free paper that meets the American National Standards Institute Z39-48 Standard.

Potomac Books, Inc.
22841 Quicksilver Drive
Dulles, Virginia 20166

First Edition

10 9 8 7 6 5 4 3 2 1

Contents

Illustrations

Preface

Divided America on the World Stage is the fourth general book I've written on American foreign policy;[1] I've written other books on more specialized subject areas or regions such as Asia, Europe, and Latin America.[2] Inadvertently or no, each of these books has tended to become a little more cynical, a little more pessimistic, a little more discouraged and discouraging about the present course and future direction of foreign policy. Only two explanations are possible, and both, doubtless, have some validity. Either I'm getting more cynical and pessimistic as I grow older, or else American foreign policy is in fact becoming worse, more disjointed, and less functional. I believe the second explanation is the more accurate one, but I'll leave it up to my faithful readers to decide.

The title of the first general book I wrote in 1987–88 on American foreign policy, *Foreign Policy without Illusion: How Foreign Policy Works and Fails to Work in the United States*, already hints that I felt American foreign policy did not work very well or as intended. When I returned to writing about American foreign policy some years later, I titled the book *The Crisis of American Foreign Policy: The Effects of a Divided America*. Its cover features a picture of the Philadelphia Liberty

---

1. Earlier books were *Foreign Policy without Illusion: How Foreign Policy Works and Fails to Work in the United States* (Glenview, IL: Scott, Foresman/Little, Brown Higher Education, 1990); *American Foreign Policy: Actors and Processes* (New York: Harper Collins, 1996); and *The Crisis of American Foreign Policy: The Effects of a Divided America* (Lanham, MD: Rowman & Littlefield, 2006).
2. *U.S. Foreign and Strategic Policy in the Post–Cold War Era: A Geopolitical Perspective* (Westport, CT: Greenwood Press, 1995); *On the Agenda: Current Issues and Conflicts in U.S. Foreign Policy* (Glenview, IL: Scott, Foresman/Little, Brown Higher Education, 1990); and *Dilemmas of Democracy in Latin America: Crisis and Opportunity* (Lanham, MD: Rowman & Littlefield, 2005).

Bell with its focus, symbolically, on the large crack in the bell. In the present book the main theme is breakdown or brokenness, specifically, divided America and its broken government. So if we think of these titles as a progres-sion, I've gone from what works and what doesn't to "crisis" to "divided" and "broken." That development pretty much sums up my view of what has happened to American foreign policy over the years.

I think we are in bad shape in terms of foreign policy. Things are not work-ing. Our main institutions—Congress, the presidency, the Defense Department, the State Department, FBI, Homeland Security, and so on—are not functioning very well or as intended. Dysfunction, gridlock, indecision, paralysis, incom-petence—all are setting in or becoming worse than before. Not just one president or one administration is at fault; rather our whole governmental system seems to be breaking down. And now it turns out the country is broken as well, making it difficult for Barack Obama's administration to implement new policies. Hence, my subtitle's inclusion of *Broken Government*.

When I did the first edition of my textbook on foreign policy, along with serious analysis I filled it with insider stories and gossip about Washington policymaking. After all, I had lived for long periods in Washington, had seen it from the inside, and had participated in the foreign policy process at some high levels. Students loved the book because it shared so much insider knowledge, but faculty members (who make the decisions to adopt a book or not) were more skeptical, perhaps not believing that American foreign policy worked in such a haphazard way. So for the second edition the publisher asked me to tone it down, cut back on the stories, and provide a more institutional analysis. The book sold well, but readers missed all the fun gossip and "insiderisms" of the first edition.

This completely new book seeks to capture the spirit and liveliness of the first edition of the textbook referred to above while maintaining the solid institu-tional analysis of the second. It contains some wonderful, amusing, entertaining stories and gossip. It is full of Washington insiderisms. After all, I am writing from my Washington perch at the Center for Strategic and International Studies (CSIS), one of Washington's most prestigious think tanks and the only one devoted entirely to foreign policy. Every day at this institution and others in the nation's capital that I visit regularly, I am thrown in with foreign ministers, defense ministers, prime ministers, and visiting heads of state. I am frequently able to ask them questions, engage them in conversations, and, with some, become friends and on a first-name basis. I concluded, why not include this information in the book that I write? And in the best of all worlds, why not combine this insiderism with a clear, readable, straightforward analysis of how American foreign policy works or fails to work?

That is what this book does. First, it is well organized, well written, clear, and devoid of academic jargon. Second, it is a fun book, full of wry observations and stories, and entertaining as well as enlightening. Third, it is also a serious book, probing deeply into the American psyche and political culture, examining how our institutions work or fail to work, and exploring the roots of our foreign policy malaise. And fourth, while aimed at a general, informed reading audience, the book could easily be adapted for classroom use, either as a main text or as supplemental reading. It covers all the main subject areas, albeit from a somewhat selective perspective; it has about the right number of chapters to fill a whole semester; and it is certain to stimulate classroom discussion and controversy.

I have spent the last twenty-five years working in the Washington think tank and policy worlds. Most often these positions have been combined or alternated with a university academic position. So I know both the academic and the policy worlds, from inside and out. At different times in my career I have worked for the State and Defense departments and consulted for the CIA, the White House, and other government agencies. Four U.S. presidents have sought my advice, and my writings on foreign affairs have (sometimes) influenced policy—hopefully for the better. Now I have captured some of this insiderism for this book.

This book could not have been written without the assistance over the years of a number of institutions and individuals who have strongly supported my work. These include the Center for International Affairs (now the Weatherhead Center) at Harvard University, the Department of Political Science at the University of Massachusetts, the Washington think tank American Enterprise Institute for Public Policy Research (AEI), the National War College in Washington, the School of Public and International Affairs (SPIA) at the University of Georgia, and my Washington "home" for the last sixteen years, CSIS.

Among individuals, Dr. Iêda Siqueira Wiarda has been my wonderfully supportive spouse through all of these years and many projects; Doris Holden for almost as long has been my faithful word processor, editor, and friend; and Kathryn Johnson also helped prepare the manuscript and has excellent editorial skills. Cynthia McMeekin and Annie Kryzanek are the most recent of an extraordinary line of research assistants; at Potomac Books, Inc., Hilary Claggett and Claire Noble have been extraordinarily pleasant, helpful, and able. Many thanks for all your help. However, all these persons and institutions are absolved of responsibility for any mistakes of fact or interpretation that remain; those are mine alone.

Howard J. Wiarda
CSIS
1800 K Street NW (but not one of the so-called K Street bandits)
Washington, D.C.

1

Introduction:
Crisis and Calamity in
American Foreign Policy

Americans are optimistic people. We usually have a positive, forward-looking out-look on life. We're a can-do people who like to take charge and want everyone to be as well off and democratic as we are. From an early age both our parents and our advertising tell us not to dwell on the past but focus on the future. That advice helps us get ahead, avoids negativity, and keeps us happy, hopeful, and prosperous.

But recently our faith and optimism have been severely tested. The surprise attacks of September 11, 2001, led many Americans to ask, "Why do they hate us so?" Since 2003 we have been enmeshed in the terrible Iraq War seemingly without a way to win the war or to get out with any degree of honor. Then came Hurricane Katrina and the terrible destruction in lives and property it wrought in New Orleans and along the Gulf Coast, and we witnessed the almost complete incompetence of government at local, state, and national levels in dealing with the problems. President George W. Bush was denounced in many quarters as "the worse president we've ever had" while the reputation of Congress and other institutions dipped even below that of the president. Name an agency—the CIA, FBI, the Department of Homeland Security, the Food and Drug Admin-istration, the Immigration and Naturalization Service—and it seems to be dys-functional. And in 2008 the nation's economy slid toward disaster.

Something in America is not working. Or not as well as it should. Or maybe quite a few things are not working. Other countries are starting to surpass us in educational as well as economic, social, and political achievements. We all sense that there are problems afoot, even though we're not quite sure precisely what it is that's not working. Or why it's not working. Was Bush the problem or Congress or some combination of the two? If this poor leadership is all that's wrong, presumably it can be corrected at the election time. But many observers think the country's problems run deeper. They believe that as a nation maybe we've lost our way, our can-do attitude, and that we're confused, uncertain, and deeply divided over the country's future direction, including over foreign policy. And if the voters and the general public are confused and divided, then why in a representative democracy would we expect our elected leaders to be any clearer in their policy decisions than the general public is? All of this uncertainty spells trouble for them and for Barack Obama's administration as well.

This book takes the position that our country, including our foreign policy, is in considerable trouble and that the causes of our difficulties are deeply rooted. They cannot be changed quickly or overnight. They are not just the result of one president or one Congress; therefore, they are not amenable to easy change. Instead, our problems are the result of profound shifts in American culture, society, and politics over, let us say, the last half century.

All this is paradoxical in many ways. Here we are, the richest country in the world or very close to it. Our gross national product (GNP) and competitiveness ranking place us at number one or at least in the top five. American culture, movies, styles, freedom, and upward mobility are widely admired throughout the world. The American private economy is, or was, the most dynamic and one of the wonders of the world. Our universities are widely considered the world's best, and Americans have won more Nobel Prizes than other nations' citizens. Yet by contrast, our political system and institutions, and by extension our foreign policy, do not seem to be keeping pace. They are in decline or dysfunctional—and widely despised abroad—even while our accomplishments in other areas continue to be impressive. So why does this disjuncture exist? Why is our political system, and now our economy, not working? Why does our foreign policy go astray? *Divided America on the World Stage* wrestles with these questions.

Causes of Our Foreign Policy Troubles

Two themes dominate the discussion right at the beginning. First, our foreign policy problems go back a long way. They did not arise yesterday with the wars in Iraq and Afghanistan. And second, there are multiple causes involved. Just as I believe no one president, Congress, or administration is to blame for the country's foreign policy problems, similarly there is no one single cause. Our foreign policy crisis was a long time abuilding, and the web of causation that helps explain it is complex.

Here are some of the main social, cultural, and political causes of our foreign policy decline. Later the chapter discusses how these and other causes have altered the workings of our foreign policymaking institutions as well.

VIETNAM WAR

The Vietnam War (1965–75) was a terribly divisive period in American history. Similar to the rifts the Iraq War has caused, the Vietnam War split America between pro- and antiwar factions as no previous war had done. People led street protests and violent demonstrations. To avoid military service, many young American men cheated or lied about their health or personal circumstances while others fled abroad to avoid being drafted and sent to Vietnam. Universities and other groups mobilized against the war, with families as well as faculties split down the middle. There were marches on Washington, and some called for the overthrow of the government. The Vietnam War opened up a political divide, a generational gulf, a split between pro- and antimilitary factions never before seen in America. Many of the era's conflicts were nasty, confrontational, and mean spirited. Neither the divisions nor the scars of that war have healed to this day. The Iraq War has reopened these ancient wounds.

NIXON AND WATERGATE

Democrats John F. Kennedy and Lyndon Johnson initially involved the United States in Vietnam and accelerated the war, but it was the Republican administration of Richard Nixon that prolonged the war and drew the brunt of the public's criticism. Many Democrats harbored a knee-jerk hatred of Nixon anyway. Then, in 1972, a group of Republican operatives broke into Democratic Party headquarters located in Washington's Watergate apartment complex, apparently hoping to dig up some dirt on the Democrats, and got caught. The White House and Nixon himself were implicated, if not in the crime then in the cover-up. Thus the country polarized once again. Under threat of impeachment, Nixon was forced to resign the presidency, again leaving deep wounds that are still with us.

STREET POLITICS: THE DEMOCRATIZATION OF FOREIGN POLICY

The civil rights movement of the 1960s, the assassinations of Martin Luther King

Jr. and Robert F. Kennedy, the Vietnam War, and Nixon and Watergate brought people into the streets for protests, marches, and demonstrations. Meanwhile, older and more conservative Americans, believing the ballot box was the only expression of politics, were appalled at the dissidents' violence, their oftentimes filthy language, and their confrontational style. Foreign policy issues that used to be decided among small coteries of well-informed professionals in the State and Defense departments, the CIA, and the White House were then being debated and even decided in the nation's churches, town meetings, and universities, to say nothing of the street demonstrations. In these forums the debate was often raucous, shrill, ill informed, and sometimes fierce and dangerous. In the similarly polarizing debates over policies regarding Central America in the 1980s and Iraq more recently, the same characteristics were present.

This is what we mean by the "democratization" of foreign policy. Everyone got into the act. Now most of us, including this author, tend to think that democracy is a good thing and the more of it the better. But that does not hold true in the realm of foreign policy. There, real knowledge and expertise about other countries and issues are necessary. Can you really have foreign policy made by a "committee" of 535 congresspeople, 435 in the House and 100 in the Senate? Can it be made by thousands of protestors in the streets or demonstrating faculty members or activist local politicians who often have a partisan ax to grind and, at the same time, lack not only knowledge but also access to intelligence information? Regardless of whether we think it is a good or bad thing, the democratization of U.S. foreign policy has served to further alienate a population that is already divided over other issues.

Changing Cultural and Social Values

America has a very different culture and society than it had in 1960. These changes are also reflected in its foreign policy.

1. We are more diverse and multicultural. Among other things, this development means it is harder to form a consensus on foreign policy and other issues. Also, more of our diverse citizens have an interest in U.S. policy toward their native countries.

2. We are more urban, better educated, and wealthier. One would think that these changes would increase our interest in and knowledge about foreign affairs, but that has not proved to be the case. Many Americans seem more

interested in shopping or tending their outdoor grills than in learning about other countries and issues.

3. We are less religious than we used to be. Thus we share fewer values, have more diverse beliefs, and again face greater difficulties when seeking to forge consensus. Harvard political scientist Samuel P. Huntington has characterized America historically as an "Anglo-Protestant" country. Is that still true, and what are the implications if it is no longer so?

4. We are a nation of immigrants. Now, however, America seems to have lost control of its borders. Widespread immigration is changing the face, culture, and society of America. Whether we think that is good or bad, we must acknowledge the reality.

5. We are interdependent. America is now more interdependent with more and more countries on a host of issues: trade, drugs, energy resources, tourism, investment, finance, immigration and labor supplies, manufacturing, services, agriculture, and the economy in general. All this interdependence complicates our foreign policy, making us less independent and more reliant on other countries and what they do.

THE END OF THE COLD WAR

While the Cold War was being waged from 1947 to 1991, we had one clear enemy and one clear threat—the Soviet Union and the possibility of its thirty thousand nuclear missiles raining down on our heads. Now with the Soviet Union gone and the threat of nuclear annihilation greatly diminished, we have no clear enemy and no clear threat. Is it China, Iraq, a revived Russia, Osama bin Laden, the Taliban, druglords, Iran, the flood of immigrants, terrorists, or what? Without a clear foe or threat, American foreign policy has floundered, losing its unity and its focus. As a former Soviet high official, Georgi Arbatov, said in 1998, "We will deprive you of an enemy and then what will you do?"

POLITICAL DIVISIONS

Look at the country today. We are almost exactly evenly divided between red states (Republican) and blue states (Democrat). The electoral college is similarly equally divided, with only one or two states often able to determine presidential elections. The Senate and Congress in general rank low in popularity, play politics with the issues, and almost never get much accomplished. The last three presidential elections were extremely hard fought and too close to call right up to the end. Polls tell us that the electorate is split: 45 percent Republican and 45 percent Democrat with only 10 percent left as independents, or swing voters.

Can anything be more evenly divided than that? Moreover, these divisions may well continue long term and well into the future. And if the electorate is evenly divided, in a democracy where elected officials listen closely to their constituents, why would we expect our political leaders to be any more clear of purpose than the electorate is? Foreign policy is in large part a reflection of domestic values and politics, so if we are divided in our values and political loyalties, we should not expect a clear and consistent foreign policy.

CULTURAL DIVISIONS

Americans are deeply divided over cultural issues. Gay marriage, the role of religion in our public life, gays in the military, drug policies, and sexual liberation have all become deeply divisive issues. It could once be said of America that it was a Christian and "God-fearing" nation. But it is doubtful if the same thing, or with the same degree of conviction, could be said today. Americans are inclined not to dwell on sin and damnation, we do not want government interjecting itself in the bedroom, religion has been all but banned from public expression, and, with widespread divorce, in vitro fertilization, and arguments for same-sex households, we are not quite certain what the family unit looks like anymore. The divide between a religious and a secular society is wide and getting wider. And all this differentiation makes it harder for us to carry out a successful foreign policy, for the president to lead, and for the country to fall in behind.

Institutional Divisions

The discussion above focused on values; culture, particularly *political* culture; and voting returns. Now it turns to the changing nature of American institutions and how they also reflect and reinforce the deep and basic divisions in society. Each topic is discussed more fully in the chapters that follow.

Chapter 2 explores models of foreign policy decision making. Most foreign policy books suggest that there are three such models. The "rational actor model" conforms to what most of us think of as foreign policymaking: a list of options is presented to the decision maker—or, in President George W. Bush's term, "the decider"—be it the president, secretary of state, or whomever. Each option is carefully evaluated, the pros and cons of each are rationally (hence the term "rational actor model") weighed, and then the decision maker decides.

But we know it doesn't always work that way. The process is not always rational. Oftentimes bureaucratic rivalries (between the State and Defense departments, for example, or between the CIA and the FBI) get in the way. The policy is not so much rationally developed but is the result of bureaucratic or institutional rivalries and infighting over power, budgets, and turf. Hence we call this the "bureaucratic politics model," quite different from the rational actor one.

A third model has to do with the internal or organizational standard operating procedures (SOPs) *within* each of these bureaucracies. Each agency has its different SOPs, or what we might call its own "political culture." For example, the CIA consists mostly of foreign policy analysts and operatives while the FBI is made up of mostly lawyers, and that fact alone is sufficient to make them think and operate completely differently. In another example, the State Department consists of people typically from elite, liberal, Ivy League universities while Defense Department (DOD) personnel are predominantly Southern, Protestant, and more conservative. You do not need to be an Einstein to figure out those two agencies will think differently and have contrasting views of the world. We therefore call this the "organizational model" based on the fact that distinct cultures and sociologies within the U.S. "family" of foreign policy agencies make them think and behave in divergent ways. And then the question becomes, how, when, and with what implications does the rational actor model also get influenced, or even overwhelmed, by the bureaucratic politics or the organizational models?

As if these three models did not make things complicated enough, I wish to add two more models, or explanatory paradigms, to the list. The first I call the "political process model." Although all presidents and politicians of all kinds prefer to say that politics never enters into their foreign policy considerations, in fact politics and most particularly the president's or congressperson's reelection calculations are *always* at the forefront. Politicians, we know, do what they do to get reelected; therefore, almost never does one vote against his or her constituents' wishes. There are few "profiles in courage"—members of Congress who vote in the best interests of the country over their reelection possibilities—out there. Some scholars argue that these narrow, partisan, parochial, political, and reelection calculations trump the rational actor calculations of the country's best interests. So we need to take this political process model, which suggests that foreign policy is subject to the same kinds of political deals, logrolling, and partisanship as is domestic policy, into account when we talk about foreign affairs.

A fifth model is what I call the "self-aggrandizement model." It suggests that representatives, senators, and other politicians at all levels get into politics not, as they say, for public service but for private gain. In this regard (and it should not be surprising), politicians are just like the rest of us: they are looking out for number one, numero uno, themselves. The facts are that congressional salaries are very comfortable, congresspeople can supplement their salaries in all kinds of ways (including dipping into leftover campaign funds for their own private use), and the perks are wonderful: free foreign travel, a short work week (Tuesday afternoon to Thursday morning), long vacations, huge staffs, available hard-working interns, free haircuts, the country's best health care, pension plans equal to those of professional football players, numerous investment opportunities, and so on.

These perks and high incomes are why representatives and senators are so reluctant even if defeated to leave Washington and why they fight so hard to stay there, usually reincarnated as high-priced lobbyists. Folks in Congress (and other politicians) of course deny these self-interested motivations, but they exist nonetheless and may be more important in explaining congressional voting behavior and foreign policy decision making than any of the other models presented here. The self-aggrandizement model is summed up in the familiar Washington phrase that you "do well [for yourself] by doing good [for others, your constituents]."

Chapters 3 and 4 focus on political culture and public opinion and particularly on the recent changes in these factors. For example, American political culture used to be based on a broad consensus: we saw ourselves, and were seen by others, as a white, Western, Christian, Protestant, honest, hardworking, ethical, and moral (according to the Ten Commandments) nation. Whatever your own present-day adherence to any or all of these adjectives, plainly this description of the United States needs to be seriously modified. Is the United States still considered a "white" nation, or is it now multiracial? Are we Americans still viewed as Western, or are we multicultural? Are we Christian and Protestant or now mainly secular or indifferent to religion? Are we honest and hardworking or self-interested (as above) and over-the-hill? Are we ethical and moral or, after the Enron, AIG, and other scandals, interested in just making a buck? And how does this changing political culture, now in all its pluralism and diversity, affect our foreign policy—which is similarly hard to specify or pinpoint?

Much the same applies to public opinion: it is divided, fragmented, and difficult to find a basis for consensus. First of all, the American Republic shows a three-way divide: one-third is isolationist (opposed to foreign entanglements like the wars in Iraq or Afghanistan unless we are directly attacked), one-third is liberal internationalist (strongly in favor of the United States pushing human rights and democracy), and the other third is conservative internationalist (supports a strong defense and military). Not only is the country evenly divided between these three positions, but if one of the factions proposes something, it usually provokes the other two to gang up against it. Again, competing public opinions result in paralysis and gridlock.

Or take public opinion on the issues. America is almost evenly divided on the Afghanistan war and other foreign policy issues. It is exactly evenly divided on whether the president is doing a good job on foreign policy. The split is 50–50 on whether the United States should pursue a national policy that actively promotes democracy and human rights in other countries. On virtually every issue the same splits that we saw in the presidential elections of 2000, 2004, and 2008—evenly divided and too close to call—are present. And if public opinion, the electorate, and Congress are so evenly divided, why should we expect our foreign policy to be free from these same divisions? In a democracy, after all, policy ultimately reflects the people's will, and if the people are uncertain and divided, so too will be their foreign policy.

Moving from political culture and public opinion, chapter 6 looks at the organized expression of these views through interest groups. And here we find much the same phenomena: deep divisions, increasing polarization, and the inability to get policy enacted. Labor and business groups are evenly divided over trade policy and globalization, and no candidate wants to antagonize either of these two groups. Both the strong defense and the strong pro–human rights groups have powerful lobbies that speak for them and defend their interests. Almost every ethnic group in the United States now has a lobby organized to defend its interests, but they are facing challenges too. The Israeli lobby is one of the most powerful, but it is being increasingly challenged by pro-Arab groups; the anti-Castro Cubans in Miami have long had a hammerlock on U.S. policy toward the island, but that is changing as the generations change; the Irish and Greek lobbies have long been strong, but now we also have organized Hispanic, Asian, and African (and, within these, lobbies for individual nations) lobbies.

How do you fashion a coherent U.S. policy if all these powerful special interests are weighing in with their own preferences?

A special concern in this book is what has come to be called the "privatization of foreign policy." A relatively new phenomenon, the privatization of foreign policy is part of a trend that began almost thirty years ago under President Ronald Reagan to privatize areas of government that were previously considered public responsibilities. The privatization of foreign policy, takes place at several different levels. Agencies like the State Department or DOD now routinely farm out many of their functions (not just food or janitorial services but, in the Defense Department's case, many aspects of security as well) to private contractors, which are not accountable for the funds spent and have no responsibility to the electorate.

Privatization also means we citizens have allowed private interest groups to influence whole regions of foreign policy—again without much accountability or responsibility—for their own purposes rather than for the good of the nation as a whole. I once heard a senior State Department diplomat sum this situation up neatly, if a bit oversimply: "We have given Latin America to the Miami Cubans, turned over Middle East policy to the Israeli lobby, given the Caribbean to the congressional Black Caucus, let big business dominate China policy, and given Africa to charitable and religious NGOs [nongovernmental organizations]." Not only are these private groups largely unaccountable for their actions, but they have no responsibility to the electorate for what they do. Moreover, when playing such a strong role in policymaking, they have their own interests mainly in view and not necessarily those of the United States.

Chapter 7 discusses political parties. Historically our political parties have been domestically oriented, have not talked much about foreign policy, and have been structured to secure their candidates' election rather than to give voice to foreign policy issues. But now all this is changing. Foreign policy issues—trade, immigration, globalization, jobs, and conflicts such as Iraq—are much more on the front burner than before. In addition, the two main political parties have set up foreign policy action arms, ostensibly to promote democracy abroad, but also to promote the parties' own international positions. I will have more to say on these party-affiliated international affairs institutes later on, not least because if you're a partisan *and* interested in foreign affairs, these are interesting places to work or to serve an internship.

The huge gaps between the parties on foreign policy and other issues are best illustrated by those large electoral maps that show the United States as "red" (Republican) and "blue" (Democratic) states. Blue states are in the Northeast and along the West ("Left") Coast while red states are mostly in the South, West, and Southwest. Since 2000 the presidential election has been decided by a handful of Midwestern states (and Florida) that are still up for grabs. These electoral regions reflect the intensely partisan divisions that exist nationwide and between the parties in Congress. Moreover, these partisan divides geographically also reflect the cultural divisions referred to earlier: voters in the South not only tend to be Republican but also more conservative and more religious, while those on the East and West coasts are not only more apt to be Democratic Party supporters but also more liberal and more secular.

What may be even more astounding is that people are more likely to locate and even move for job purposes, families, and politics to those states and regions where they feel more comfortable culturally, religiously, and politically. Conservatives in the North and East tend to move to the South, conservative Californians are moving to the mountain states of the West, and liberals in the South migrate North or to the East or West coasts. So the red states are becoming even redder and the blue states even bluer. Can the country survive these increasingly geographic-cum-religious-cum-political divides that are increasingly polarizing the nation? Or is our society becoming what it was before the Civil War, with two distinct geographic and cultural areas so far apart that they are unable to live together anymore?

The book now turns to two innovative chapters on the role of the media and think tanks in foreign policy. Chapter 5 emphasizes the increasing political biases within the media, the growing political polarization between liberal media and conservative talk shows, the growing concentration of ownership of the media, and the declining coverage of foreign affairs news. The conclusion is that the media are not just neutral, objective reporters of the news but participants in it, often with their coverage driving and shaping policy rather than simply reporting on it.

The think tank discussion in chapter 8 is fun for readers because these institutions are not just important influences on foreign policy but also fascinating places to work, especially for young people. The American Enterprise Institute for Public Policy Research (AEI), the Brookings Institution, the Center for Strategic and International Studies (CSIS), the Heritage Foundation, the Council on

Foreign Relations, the Carnegie Endowment, the Center for American Progress (CAP), and numerous other smaller "tanks" do the government's "thinking" for it. They do the background research, write speeches and policy papers, and provide the intellectual and ideological arguments on which policy is based. They also serve as "transmission belts" between more academic, university-based research and the policy arena and as revolving doors through which their scholars go in and out of high government positions.

Chapter 11 covers the main government institutions involved in policy-making and their rivalries. We call this "bureaucratic politics." First, we deal with the agencies that most of us think of as the most important in foreign policymaking: the Department of State, the Department of Defense, and the Central Intelligence Agency. Two themes are especially important in this discussion: first, the longtime rivalry among these main institutions for dominance in foreign policymaking; and second, the increasing dominance among these three of the Defense Department as it increasingly expands its power and encroaches on the turf (diplomacy and intelligence, respectively) of the other two.

These rivalries and turf battles have been made even more complicated by the rise and emergence of other large Washington bureaucracies on the foreign policy scene. Since the late 1980s, as international trade, international markets and commerce, and globalization have all expanded, the Treasury, Energy, and Commerce departments have all come to play a bigger role in influencing foreign policy, as have the Office of the U.S. Trade Representative (OTR), the Environmental Protection Agency (EPA), and the international divisions of the Labor and Agriculture departments. With the war on terrorism, the FBI has taken on a greater foreign policy role (that often overlaps with the CIA). In 2002 the government also created the Department of Homeland Security, which incorporates some forty-three other agencies in a bureaucratic tangle that has yet to demonstrate coherence and functionality. And three years later, in an effort to bring central direction to what is by now sixteen separate intelligence agencies (plus additional numerous military intelligence agencies), the government established the Office of the Director (or "czar") of National Intelligence, whose office still performs its coordination functions feebly and incompletely.

Chapters 10, 12, and 13, respectively, review the top of the foreign policy-making system: Congress, the National Security Council (NSC), and the presidency. To many observers of foreign policy, Congress has become a dysfunctional participant in foreign policy. Most of its members are far more interested in and knowledgeable about domestic policy than they are foreign policy (being able to deliver the goods back home is what gets them reelected). When they do delve into foreign policy issues it is usually their own narrow, parochial, partisan reelection possibilities that they are interested in and not necessarily good policy. Although the president leads on foreign policy, an activist Congress can hamstring and frustrate executive leadership. Particularly when the Congress and president are of two different parties ("divided government"), the entire political system may face paralysis and gridlock. When the situation gets too bad, it forces us to question whether our historic checks and balances and the separation of powers are really still good things.

The president is, of course, the focal point and the center of this entire, cumbersome decision-making apparatus, so I have saved consideration of the presidency and his personal foreign policy staff (the NSC) for last. Several large questions concern us here. The first is how and why the NSC, which is supposed to be objective and professional, has become so partisan, so political, and so ideological in recent decades. The answer, I suspect, is that the NSC and its appointments process have changed, just as every other institution considered here, and become more intensely partisan, more driven by political extremes, less pragmatic and centrist, and more ideological.

The second question concerns the presidency. Since Richard Nixon resigned in disgrace in 1974, we have had seven presidents: Gerald Ford, Jimmy Carter, Ronald Reagan, George H. W. Bush, Bill Clinton, George W. Bush, and now Barack Obama. Of the seven, six were almost entirely inexperienced in and were woefully undereducated in foreign policy. Only George H. W. Bush had extensive foreign affairs experience, having served as a congressman, the head of the CIA, the ambassador to China, and vice president before coming to the presidency. It is probably no accident therefore that Bush is widely thought of as running the best U.S. foreign policy of recent decades, ending the Cold War without the loss of a single American life, waging the first war with Iraq but without getting lost in internal Iraqi politics, and laying the groundwork for a new, post–Cold War international order.

So other questions pertaining to the presidency are: Why does the American system so often so ill prepare our presidents for leadership on foreign policy? What is there in the career pattern of politicians that leaves them without the opportunity to obtain foreign affairs experience? Why must our presidents so often learn about foreign policy, dangerously, after they come to office and while "on the job"? And then, of course, we must also deal with why the relations between presidents and Congress are so poisonous, why the system so often produces conflict and paralysis, and why the U.S. political system is in a state of gridlock.

Could it be that Americans actually prefer it that way, that is, gridlocked so that no one branch emerges dominant and new policy initiatives are stymied? The answer is yes: the polls show that many American voters prefer paralysis over concerted action. That option, of course, serves to limit the damage that a dysfunctional government—either Congress or the president—can do in any one, single policy area, but it also means a preference for ineffective government. And isn't that inclination toward deadlock over effectiveness a sad commentary on American politics? We will have to wait and see if the Obama administration and its Democratic-controlled Congress can overcome these barriers.

In the chapters that follow we learn about how American foreign policy works—and what's wrong with it. In the conclusion we pull together all the diverse themes presented in this introductory chapter and make sense of it all. The questions we wrestle with at the end are these: Can the American system still be salvaged? What can we do to change and reform it, or is it so dysfunctional that we need to start over again? And if we do the latter, what would the system look like? Would it be a parliamentary system, one with fewer checks and balances, something more streamlined, efficient, and less bureaucratic?

But there is an even more basic determination to make. Ultimately, in a democracy, the political system is a reflection of the electorate, or, in the United States, of our own people. It may be uncomfortable to contemplate, but in most countries people tend to get the government that they deserve. In this regard our data suggest the American people are ill informed on foreign policy, don't know much about other countries, and often lack basic knowledge about the world in which they live. So maybe the problem is not the system. Maybe it is we the people. As Shakespeare said, "The problem is not in the stars, it is in ourselves." And if that is the case, then we are *really* in bad trouble. Read on!

Suggested Reading

Chollet, Derek, Tod Lindberg, and David Shorr, eds. *Bridging the Foreign Policy Divide: Liberals and Conservatives Find Common Ground on 10 Key Global Challenges.* New York: Routledge, 2007.

Destler, I. M., Leslie H. Gelb, and Anthony Lake. *Our Own Worst Enemy: The Unmaking of American Foreign Policy*. Rev. ed. New York: Simon & Schuster, 1985.

Dougherty, James E., and Robert L. Pfaltzgraff. *American Foreign Policy: FDR to Reagan*. New York: Harper & Row, 1986.

Dull, James W. *The Politics of American Foreign Policy*. Englewood Cliffs, NJ: Prentice Hall, 1985.

Franck, Thomas M., and Edward Weisband. *Foreign Policy by Congress*. New York: Oxford University Press, 1979.

Godwin, Jack. *The Arrow and the Olive Branch: Practical Idealism in U.S. Foreign Policy*. Westport, CT: Praeger Security International, 2008.

Hartmann, Frederick H., and Robert L. Wendzel. *America's Foreign Policy in a Changing World*. New York: HarperCollins College Publishers, 1994.

Hoff, Joan. *A Faustian Foreign Policy from Woodrow Wilson to George W. Bush: Dreams of Perfectibility*. New York: Cambridge University Press, 2008.

Hollander, Paul. *The Survival of the Adversary Culture: Social Criticism and Political Escapism in American Society*. New Brunswick, NJ: Transaction Books, 1988.

Huntington, S. P. "The Democratic Distemper." *Public Interest* 41 (1975): 9–38.

Kluger, Richard. *Seizing Destiny: How America Grew from Sea to Shining Sea*. 1st ed. New York: A. A. Knopf, 2007.

Lovell, John P. *The Challenge of American Foreign Policy: Purpose and Adaptation*. New York: Macmillan, 1985.

Manela, Erez. *The Wilsonian Moment: Self-Determination and the International Origins of Anticolonial Nationalism*. New York: Oxford University Press, 2007.

McConnell, Grant. *Private Power and American Democracy*. 1st ed. New York: Knopf, 1966.

Nathan, James A., and James K. Oliver. *Foreign Policy Making and the American Political System*. 3rd ed. Baltimore, MD: John Hopkins University Press, 1994.

Quester, George H. *American Foreign Policy: The Lost Consensus*. New York: Praeger, 1982.

Rosati, Jerel A. *The Politics of United States Foreign Policy*. 4th ed. Belmont, CA: Wadsworth/Thomson Learning, 2006.

Spanier, John W., and Eric M. Uslaner. *American Foreign Policy Making and the Democratic Dilemmas.* 6th ed. New York: Macmillan, 1994.

Wiarda, Howard J. *Foreign Policy without Illusion: How Foreign Policy-Making Works and Fails to Work in the United States.* Glenview, IL: Scott, Foresman/ Little, Brown Higher Education, 1990.

Wittkopf, Eugene R., and James M. McCormick, eds. *The Domestic Sources of American Foreign Policy: Insights and Evidence.* 4th ed. Lanham, MD: Rowman & Littlefield, 2004.

Zakaria, Fareed. *From Wealth to Power: The Unusual Origins of America's World Role.* Princeton Studies in International History and Politics. Princeton, NJ: Princeton University Press, 1998.

———. *The Post-American World.* New York: Norton, 2008.

2

Models of Foreign
Policymaking

Chapter 1 offered an introduction to some of the main problems in American foreign policy. We are more divided as a country; our values and political culture are changing rapidly, making it difficult to form a consensus; the country is both fragmented and polarized along sharp political and religious divides; we have intense and worsening bureaucratic rivalries among the main foreign policy agencies; Congress and the White House are often at each other's throats; the media and the main think tanks reinforce and perpetuate the political and ideological divides that already exist; our leaders are often inexperienced in foreign policy; and, on the part of Congress especially, the main and often virtually only goal is to get oneself reelected and not necessarily work for what's best for the United States. We now need to start sorting out these various issues and see if we can find some patterns and order in them.

The fact is foreign policy seldom works according to the way we think it does or the way we think it should. The process is usually much more complex than we think it is. We tend to assume (and this idea is reflected in much writing and theory about international relations) that the nation's leaders make foreign policy decisions on the basis of the best information possible. We believe our leaders weigh all this information carefully, consider the pros and cons of the various policy options, and then make their decisions based on what they think is best for U.S. national interests. This process sounds rational; indeed, for that reason we call such careful weighing of the options the "rational actor model."

But we already know that policy development seldom works that way. If it did, foreign policy would certainly be more coherent and rational than it actually is. If it really were as simple as this process, we would be justified in saying, as journalists and television commentators still do, "Washington did this," or "London did that," or "Moscow's policy is such and such." But when we say, "Washington did this or that," what do we mean by "Washington"? Do we mean the White House or Congress? Do we mean the State Department or the Department of Defense? As soon as we start asking these questions, we get into a much murkier, more complicated, and more interesting explanation than we would if we just said, "Washington's policy is . . ." That simplistic statement is far too monolithic an interpretation than is in fact the case in this complex, pluralistic country of ours.

Foreign policy is seldom so neat and coherent as the rational actor model implies. It is usually messy, partisan, and political just as other aspects of policy are. Only in rare instances—for example, President George W. Bush's immediate decision after the 9/11 terrorist attack to launch an offensive against Afghanistan and Iraq—does foreign policy work with the unity of purpose that the rational actor model suggests. Maybe, given the fiasco that the Iraq War has become, we are better off if it does not work with such single-minded purpose in the hands of a president who is weak on foreign policy credentials (as are most presidents). It's a tough choice: if a president and his foreign policy team are experienced in international affairs (Eisenhower, Nixon, George H. W. Bush), then the rational actor model may work well. But if a president is inexperienced in foreign policy (Kennedy, Johnson, Ford, Carter, Reagan, Clinton, George W. Bush, Obama), then maybe it is better to have all the checks and balances of the American political system come into play.

This book proceeds on the assumption that the rational actor model is only one among several models of foreign policy decision making. It may work in the right circumstances, but then again it may not; and in the wrong, inexperienced hands, we may not want it to work. Hence, we need to be informed about alternative models of decision making that are also influential. These others may emerge as alternatives to the rational actor model, or they may be used in addition to or alongside it. In most foreign policy decisions, several or all of these models may be operating at once.

In addition to (1) the rational actor model, the other models of foreign policy are:

2.   The "bureaucratic politics model," which indicates that agencies at the State and Defense departments, FBI and CIA, or Treasury and Justice

departments, for example, oftentimes have rival, overlapping, and competing bureaucratic interests that they try to protect and enhance.

3. The "organizational model," which suggests that each agency has internal norms and procedures that govern its behavior and are often different from, and maybe conflicting with, other agencies' standard operating procedures.

4. The "political process model," which describes how partisanship, logrolling, and calculations about reelection possibilities affect decision making.

5. The "self-aggrandizement model," which suggests that politicians are not necessarily serving the country's national interests (rational actor model again) or even their own partisan political advantage (political process model) but are trying to advance their own career goals.

Each of these models is considered in detail in this chapter. But first, a discussion of the term "model"—what it means and why we use models—is helpful.

Models of Foreign Policy—Why Useful

When we use the term "model," we are not referring to attractive men and women parading the latest fashions on a catwalk. We are also not seeking to bias the discussion by implying that the term as we use it carries approval or that we're in favor of what is presented in the model.

No, as used here and in the social sciences generally, "model" is a neutral term. It does not imply approval or disapproval. In the social sciences a model is an intellectual construct, a phrase, a clause, or a longer statement used to summarize, put in organized form, and simplify more complex processes. A model is a shorthand tool, a simplification of reality. It helps us give meaning to events and interpretations of them that otherwise would be so complex and multifaceted that they would not make any sense. If we say the United States is a "liberal democracy" or a "pluralist democracy," those labels are models: shorthand, simplified terms that describe what we all understand is a more complex underlying situation.

A model, therefore, is not an exact mirror of reality. Instead, a good, useful model simplifies reality, approximates it, and breaks it up into smaller and more manageable components that make it easier for us to understand. Reality itself, in all its complex, multifaceted dimensions, is always more complicated than can be presented in a few pages. Reality may involve so many layers of motivations and behavior that we can never comprehend it completely. No one single model—

evolution, for instance, or the big bang theory—or even a combination of several models can completely capture all of reality. Hence, we use models to present parts of reality and simplify it somewhat for the sake of making explanations easier and more understandable. Models, as seen below, are useful devices in the social sciences (including foreign policy analysis), but they are not to be confused with the even more complicated kaleidoscope that is reality itself.

Why then do we employ models in the social sciences—and in this book?

1. Models help us organize, highlight, and give coherence to complicated events.
2. Models help put events in a larger and more understandable context, enabling us to see the big picture. They provide perspective.
3. Models enable us to think clearly about social and historical processes that are otherwise very complicated.
4. Models help us organize our data, see patterns and relationships, and order our thinking.
5. Models are heuristic devices; that is, they show or teach us things we might not otherwise understand.
6. Models give us a handle on complex, multifaceted events and point to relationships among various explanatory factors.

Models are thus useful devices for observing reality, but they ought not to be confused with reality itself. They should be viewed pragmatically as useful devices, but they should not be seen as ultimate truth. To the extent they are helpful and enable us to see complex issues more clearly, let us use them. But models are not to be worshipped, reified, or employed beyond their usefulness. New events and new facts (as seen here in the addition of two new models and the role of new actors in the process) may force us to alter our interpretations and to either revise the models we use or scrap them altogether in favor of a new model. The issue is a utilitarian one: we use models where and to the extent they help in our understanding, but we should not hesitate to replace them when they have outlived their usefulness.

The Rational Actor Model

The rational actor model, as the name implies, is based on a notion of foreign policymaking that is orderly, coherent, and rational. None of the messiness of politics or partisan wrangling enters into it. Political parties and interest groups are not involved in this model. Nor is the idea that a president may choose a policy, nor a congressman cast his vote, on the basis of reelection considerations. That is what we mean by a model simplifying reality: the rational actor model is a useful way of thinking about some aspects of foreign policymaking, but it also leaves out a great deal.

The rational actor model assumes that nation-states have clearly defined geostrategic and national interests that can be identified (without the tug-of-war over political differences over these issues) and that these interests can be advanced by a rational, singular, and unified foreign policy. It assumes that states speak with a single voice and have one definable and clear foreign policy position. In the rational actor model, the decision-making process proceeds according to the strict canon of logic, merit, and rational choice. Foreign policy is based on coolly calculating the national interest, devoid of partisan considerations and isolated from the political process. It may be that such a nonpartisan decision-making system existed in the far distant past, but since the Vietnam War, the end of the Cold War, and the beginning of the Iraq War, it is hard to believe that it exists now.

Typically the rational actor model presumes the president and his close advisers make a choice from among carefully weighed and considered alternatives. In this idealized view of foreign policy, the alternative choices are set forth and are carefully weighed and evaluated by the Department of State, the National Security Council, and the president. The president makes the final decision, often by checking one of the options and signing off on the decision. Once the president makes his decision, then presumably the entire U.S. government helps implement it.

The process, however, seldom works this easily, smoothly, or "rationally." One can think of many reasons why it wouldn't. Suppose, as in the decision to launch the war on Iraq, the intelligence information the president received as to whether Iraq had weapons of mass destruction (WMDs) is wrong. Suppose both the State Department and DOD, because their staffs don't know Arabic or have much knowledge about the Middle East, have underestimated the difficulties involved. Suppose the big U.S. oil companies were involved in the decision, and it was made on the basis of benefiting the companies and not necessarily U.S. national interests. Suppose the president lied to the American people or maybe that a small group in the U.S. government wanted to overthrow Saddam

Hussein for its own private reasons. Or, once the war started to go badly, perhaps both the president and Congress began looking for a way out, an exit strategy that benefited them electorally but could be a disaster in terms of long-term U.S. national interests. Questions such as these make it clear that foreign policy seldom operates according to the strict requirements of the rational actor model.

It is doubtful that U.S. policy has *ever* been completely divorced from partisan, political, and special interest considerations or that it *ever* conformed exactly to the rational actor model's requirements. But it comes closer at some times than at others. For example, partisan posturing and the usual interest group struggle were largely suspended for the duration of World Wars I and II. During some periods of the Cold War and even with George W. Bush's decision to wage war on the terrorist Taliban in Afghanistan (but not on Iraq), the rational actor model operated at least in part. When the nation is attacked as it was on September 11, 2001, we like to think that we can set aside partisan differences and that the president will act rationally to defend the nation's interests.

A major dividing line was the Vietnam War of the 1960s and 1970s. Until that time, department officials have told this author, the State Department operated on most issues largely autonomously from partisan politics or the domestic interest group struggle. They made their recommendations on the basis of the best available information; they passed them on to the White House, which coordinated with the Pentagon and other agencies; and the president made the decisions. They didn't have legions of lobbyists pounding on their doors, congressmen interfering in their decisions, or students staging protest movements in the streets. In this era, the rational actor model more or less operated.

But no longer. The Vietnam War era began the process of politicizing U.S. foreign policy. In short order we witnessed the Martin Luther King Jr. and Robert Kennedy assassinations, the burning of major American cities, anti-war demonstrations, Nixon's Watergate scandal, the "power to the people" move-ment, conflicts in Central America, and now the war in Iraq. These events brought people out into the streets, "democratized" our foreign policy, and led to foreign policy being made in churches, synagogues, local town councils, and college forums, not just in the State Department or White House. Policy was not just influenced by a variety of interest groups, as in classic interest group theory; it was literally made by and sometimes turned over to private interests. Similar changes happened with Congress. It not only held hearings—the usual practice—on foreign policy decisions made by the administration, but, sensing a weakened president, it sought itself to make foreign policy. These changes helped spell the decline, and maybe the end, of the rational actor model of foreign policy decision making.

Here's how the rational actor model works or is supposed to work. The example we use comes from the situation that arose in the former Yugoslavia in the early 1990s (the difficult Iraq case is reserved for a later discussion). The former Yugoslavia in the early 1990s was disintegrating and dividing along religious and nationalistic lines into separate countries. This development was accompanied by extensive hatred, violence, human rights abuses, armed conflict, and even genocide. The main aggressors seemed to be the Serbs while the main victims were Bosnian and Kosovar Muslims. What was the United States to do? Several options were under review:

1. Do nothing, and let the locals resolve their own problems.
2. Let the Europeans handle it; it's their continent.
3. Send humanitarian aid.
4. Work to establish a peace process.
5. Arm the Bosnians and others to resist the Serbs.
6. Send in United Nations (UN) peacekeepers.
7. Send in North Atlantic Treaty Organization (NATO) military forces.
8. Bomb the Serbs to stop the genocide.
9. Send in U.S. ground forces to pacify and occupy the country.

Note that the options are listed, from top to bottom, in increasing com-mitments of U.S. force and troops.

At first, then–secretary of state James Baker favored option 1, doing nothing. As he put it, "We don't have a dog [a U.S. strategic interest] in this fight." But the continued television coverage, mainly by Christiane Amanpour of CNN, of this bloody genocide aroused the public. Americans could not just stand by while the Bosnians were being raped and massacred on our television screens. The next option was to get the Europeans to police their own neighborhood, but when they couldn't get their act together, the burden fell back on the United States. We then tried humanitarian aid and establishing a peace process, but the violent genocide continued. Option 5, arming the Bosnians, was rejected by Congress, the media, and the public because, it was said, it would only make the bloodshed worse. Meanwhile, the State and Defense departments were in disagreement.

Those at the State Department wanted to intervene, citing humanitarian grounds, while DOD officials were reluctant to do so, fearing "another Vietnam" in which the military itself would be discredited.

Eventually, under mounting congressional, media, and public pressure, more forceful action had to be taken. That involved cajoling European and U.S. forces under NATO and UN auspices to send in military forces. But because the United States didn't want to involve itself in a ground war in southeastern Europe (shades of Vietnam), it resorted to air strikes instead. Although that way, from twelve thousand feet, the resultant carnage and bloodshed would not be shown on American television, the air strikes did raise UN charges of human rights abuses and even war crimes.

We use this example for several reasons. First, it shows how a policy options paper can be structured to gradually raise the stakes, from doing nothing to waging a full-scale bombing campaign. Next, it demonstrates over time that if one action doesn't work, you may have to go to stronger and stronger measures. Finally, and most important for our purposes here, it shows how the model can break down and rationality goes out the window as Congress, the public, the media, European allies, to say nothing of the conditions on the ground in Yugoslavia itself, are constantly changing, and U.S. agencies disagree (see bureaucratic politics model below) about what to do.

Similar options papers are regularly prepared for other foreign policy issues where tough choices need to be made. Such options papers constitute the essence of the rational actor model. But notice how quickly, in this case and others, the choice among options is influenced, and sometimes overwhelmed, by other considerations: the public and State Department officials who at first are reluctant to get involved, graphic and bloody images on television that force them to change their minds, differences between the State and Defense departments over what should be done, and the difficulty of getting allies to see the issue in the same terms.

At some levels the rational actor model does in fact operate. On many noncontroversial issues, for example, the president is presented with a series of options from which to choose without the issue becoming the "stuff" of national headlines and partisan conflict. At lower levels, in the State and other departments, numerous routine issues are similarly framed in terms of the policy options of the rational actor model. Finally, in times of genuine crisis such as immediately following 9/11, the president may be able to make clear decisions based on a rational choice among options without Congress, the media, public opinion, and various interest groups getting into the act. But with the end of the Cold War and with Iraq policy being debated, it is likely that foreign policy decisions will be the result of more partisan squabbling and of more involvement of the media, public opinion, the interest groups, and so on in the process.

The main problem with the rational actor model is that it fails to take all the factors at play into account. The rational actor model therefore cannot be the sole basis for our understanding of foreign policy. Very often, the orderly, rational processes implied in that neat model are overwhelmed by other considerations, including changing and often fickle public opinion, partisan wrangling, bureaucratic turf rivalries, electoral calculations, interest group competition, media images, the desire for career advancement, and so forth. While we strive for foreign policy that is orderly and rational, we must recognize that other factors (and other models) that may force the careful and rational calculations of that model into the background are simultaneously at work.

The Bureaucratic Politics Model

The main foreign policymaking agencies in Washington—the State Department, DOD, the CIA, and the NSC; increasingly the Treasury, Commerce, and Justice departments and the Office of the Trade Representative; and now the FBI and Department of Homeland Security—are not well-oiled cogs in a smooth-running, foreign policy machine. In fact it rarely works that way. Instead, these agencies are competitive—mainly with each other. They compete for budgets, perks, turf, power, and prestige. Often their efforts while in competition with each other are greater than those they wage against their enemies. As one State Department official told the author during the height of the Cold War, "Dealing with the Russians is easy. The hard part is dealing with a certain five-sided building that lies across the Potomac River."

That remark illustrates what we mean by "bureaucratic politics," or the competition over foreign policy among big bureaucratic agencies that is often as hard or harder to deal with than are our real enemies. All these agencies are competing for the same scarce budgetary dollars; all of them vie for the prestige that accompanies foreign policy triumphs. At the same time, all of them are jealous of each other's prerogatives and power and want a greater share of it for themselves. Thus the State Department may compete with the Defense Department, both of them compete over intelligence gathering with the CIA, the

Treasury and Commerce departments both want a greater share of international economic policy, and the FBI and Homeland Security do not get along. On top of this competition between agencies, competition within agencies—for example, in the Defense Department, competition among the U.S. Army, Navy, Air Force, and Marines—is often intense.

All this competition and bureaucratic rivalry are oftentimes terribly frustrating to Congress, the public, and even the president, who is nominally the commander in chief. The observers' attitude is, why can't these agencies just get along, present a united front, and become more effective? Why can't the president just bang heads until he gets these agencies to act together in support of our policies? He could, but it's not so easy. For one thing, these agencies are very good and experienced at bureaucratic infighting. They know all the rules, they know how to bend them to their wishes, and they know how to deal with Congress and the media. For another, these agencies will endure longer than any "mere" elected officials. While each president is elected to a term of only four (or maybe eight) years and congresspersons to only two or six years, DOD, the State Department, the FBI, and so on are institutions that will be around forever. Any adept bureaucrat can outmaneuver an elected official any day of the year, if by no other technique than outlasting him or her.

What makes these bureaucratic competitions so intense, and at the same time so difficult to resolve, is that they often have overlapping and at the same time perfectly legitimate responsibilities. For example, State, DOD (and each of the services), Treasury, Energy, FBI, Justice, CIA, Homeland Security, and others all have intelligence services that compete and overlap with each other. The Pentagon has an office of political-military affairs, and so does the State Department. As the Commerce and Treasury departments and the OTR went more and more into the areas of international trade and commerce, the State Department also created an office of international commerce. If you add them up, it turns out that no fewer than forty-three offices of the U.S. government have responsibilities for counterdrug policy. In a difficult country like Iraq, so many U.S. agencies have representatives there that even the ambassador cannot keep track of, let alone coordinate, them all. And many of these agencies do not report through the ambassador at all: they prefer to deal directly with their agency headquarters in Washington, bypassing the ambassador and thus forfeiting any hope of policy coordination.

Most often this bureaucratic battle is limited to fights for turf, power, and money, but sometimes it gets nasty or even violent. In one case the author knows of, the head of the FBI mission in a certain country told the U.S. ambassador he wanted to print in the newspapers the names of three hundred of that country's officials who were suspected of involvement in drug trafficking and request that they come in for questioning. Since the list included cabinet heads and chiefs of the armed forces, and since questioning by the FBI is tantamount to being found guilty, the ambassador, wanting to have good relations with that country, said he didn't think publishing the officials' names would be a good idea. The FBI agent responded that if the ambassador didn't cooperate, *he* would be indicted for obstruction of justice. Wow! That's nasty stuff. While bureaucratic politics usually involves interagency battles for turf, money, and prestige, sometimes it sinks to the level of one agency taking on or even suing another in a full-scale "war."

Bureaucratic competition for foreign policy influence has not gotten better but in fact much worse—and more complex—over the last several decades. In the late 1980s, during the Cold War, the main competing agencies in foreign policy were the State Department, the Defense Department, and the Central Intelligence Agency. But then in the 1990s, with the Cold War over and international economic issues and globalization becoming increasingly important, the Treasury and Commerce departments and the Office of the Trade Representative gained increased influence. At this stage, therefore, there were three main arenas of bureaucratic competition: (1) the usual one, which pitted State, DOD, and the CIA against each other; (2) a new one with the foreign and strategic policy agencies (State, DOD, the CIA) posed against the economic ones (Treasury, Commerce, OTR); and (3) another new one involving the economic agencies competing with each other.

Since the 9/11 attacks this problem of bureaucratic competition and rivalry has become even more intense. Some persons who work within the system believe it is now completely out of hand, hampering not just the U.S. government's ability to carry out foreign policy but also its capacity to protect the country from additional terrorist attacks. Among the newer changes:

1. Previously limited to doing domestic criminal investigations, the FBI is now authorized to investigate international crime as well, thus involving it in conflicts with the CIA.

2.   The CIA is now authorized to do previously prohibited domestic intelligence, thus conflicting with the FBI and local, county, and state police forces.

3.   The Treasury Department, Energy Department, Justice Department, Secret Service, Environmental Protection Agency, and many others have all beefed up their intelligence units, thus conflicting with both (1) and (2) above.

4.   The new Homeland Security Department, which consists of a mishmash of twenty-two formerly independent agencies, is woefully disorganized, uncoordinated, and in conflict at multiple levels with all of the agencies above.

5.   The new Office of the Director of National Intelligence and its director, referred to as the intelligence czar, are supposed to coordinate all these new and old agencies in the fight on terrorism. But that office is still disorganized and weak, and the various military intelligence agencies have refused to share all their information or their functions with the czar's office.

After absorbing this information, it is easy to see why U.S. foreign policy and our intelligence agencies were unable to coordinate their information and strategies and prevent the attacks of 9/11 from happening. And the United States remains vulnerable today.

Besides the war on terrorism, other foreign policy issues are made much more complex or even impossible to resolve by our inability to get our bureaucratic act together. Take the other "war," the war on drugs, for example. No fewer than forty-eight U.S. federal agencies are involved, to say nothing of state, county, and local authorities. The list includes the State Department, Defense Department, Coast Guard, Justice Department, Drug Enforcement Administration (DEA), and a host of others. No one person or agency is in charge of all these myriad antidrug operations, and some of their policies are contradictory. The Drug Enforcement Agency, for example, a division of the Justice Department, is a law enforcement agency. Its function is to arrest drug traffickers wherever they are, even if that means on occasion arresting persons who are not American citizens in their own countries, kidnapping them, and bringing them to the United States for trial. By contrast, the State Department, whose function is to foster good relations with other countries, doesn't think arresting and kidnapping other countries' citizens is the best way to maintain good relations with them.

The media tend to personalize these conflicts, but doing so usually disguises a deeper conflict underneath. When reporters focus on former secretary of state Colin Powell's conflicts with former secretary of defense Donald Rumsfeld, or on former secretary of state Condoleezza Rice's disagreements with Defense Secretary Robert Gates, they overlook the real conflict between two large and powerful bureaucracies, both of which have a legitimate role to play in foreign policy. What bears reemphasis is that both have overlapping and equally legitimate roles to play, and thus they are inevitably prone to conflict. In times of crisis, the president can set aside or override many of these rivalries. But in normal times—and even in times of conflict such as the Iraq War—and with the proliferation of old and new agencies playing foreign policy roles, we can expect that these bureaucratic conflicts will only become deeper and more widespread.

The Organizational Model

Not only do the main foreign policy agencies of the U.S. government have interests and responsibilities that are uniquely their own, they also have their own methods and procedures for doing things. We refer to these as standard operating procedures or SOPs, and each agency has its own set. Moreover, each agency has its own culture, or its own internal expectations and ways of behaving. The problem for foreign policy is that one agency's SOPs or political culture may conflict with another agency's SOPs or culture, or the SOPs of a particular agency may run contrary to a presidential order, or the cultures of two agencies—State and DOD, for example—are so at variance that they can hardly work together or even talk the same language.

One almost has to work for or have a career in each of these agencies to appreciate fully their distinct cultures and their different views of the world and of how best to operate. Consequently, these agencies' views lead them to very different policy responses. For example, the Justice Department and the FBI consist mainly of lawyers whose orientation is law enforcement. Their job is to arrest people, put them on trial, and throw them in jail. That stems both from their training as lawyers, and from the organizations' SOPs and their cultures as law enforcement agencies; and, assuming the proper procedures have been followed, that is also their responsibility. But at the State Department, where the emphasis is on diplomacy, getting along with most nations is unlikely to be served if Justice or the FBI, in the case offered earlier, insists on throwing the citizens of other countries, including allies, in jail.

Or take the Treasury and Commerce departments or the OTR. These agencies consist mainly of economists, accountants, or specialists in finance and trade who tend to see the world through the lenses of an economics major. But suppose the State Department declares, with regard to third world debt, for example, that if a country declares it can't pay its own debts, then the economics and trade issue becomes a political issue (who *will* pay?), and that's part of the State Department's turf. Or take the case of the North American Free Trade Agreement (NAFTA) with Mexico and Canada. It is almost always discussed as an economics, or jobs, issue, and therefore is often seen as the responsibility the Department of the Treasury or maybe of Labor. But then the State and Defense departments say that no, the trade agreement is only a means to an end and that NAFTA's real purpose is to stabilize Mexico. Then it becomes a political (State) and security (Defense) issue and moves to their turf. Thus we can see how these overlapping responsibilities and the distinct orientations of the different agencies toward the issues can lead to conflict and turf battles over who's in charge.

Perhaps the competing State and Defense departments provide the best cases of how these differences in SOPs and cultures lead to foreign policy conflicts. The differences here are at multiple levels. First of all, the Defense Department personnel, especially at their officer corps levels, tend to be Southern, lower middle class, Republican, Christian, and conservative. That is the department's political culture. By contrast, the State Department staff tends to come from the East Coast and is upper middle class, heavily Democratic, less religious, and more liberal. The two departments thus have very different views of the world. Often given these vast dissimilarities, they are far apart and often actively dislike each other. Second, while the military is oriented toward the use of or the threat of force, the State Department is oriented toward diplomacy. The State Department often loves to have its diplomacy strengthened by the presence of military force (even while not knowing much about military weapons, resources, or deliverability) while the Defense Department, since Vietnam and now during the Iraq War, is often reluctant to see its forces and equipment squandered in useless wars. On many foreign policy issues these two agencies think and behave so differently that they are almost irreconcilable.[1]

1. The author of this book taught for a time at the National War College in Washington, D.C., which is the highest-level U.S. training institution for military officers. About one-fourth of the class is civilians from the State Department and other agencies. The program's goal is not only to provide good relations between State Department officials and military officers (they

Sometimes a situation arises where two very different cultures exist within the same agency. The best example is the CIA. On the one side are the tweedy, pipe-smoking (oops, you can't smoke inside the CIA anymore), sports jacket–wearing, former college professor types who make up the analytic branch. On the other side are the gung ho, action-oriented, Wild West guys who make up the operations branch. The operations guys look on the analytic guys as effete while the analysts look on the ops staff as "crazy cowboys" who are often out of control. With two very different cultures operating in the same agency, how can they possibly be reconciled?

A classic case of how the internal culture and SOPs of the different agencies work at cross-purposes (and almost led to World War III) is provided by the Cuban missile crisis of 1962. Those who have seen the movie *Thirteen Days* as well as those who know the "bureaucratic politics" literature will recognize this scene. President Kennedy had given the U.S. Navy specific instructions on how to blockade the Soviet ships headed toward Cuba with nuclear missiles aboard. But the Navy had its own way of organizing a blockade, which went back to John Paul Jones and the War of 1812, that ran the risk of igniting nuclear war. When he heard what the Navy was doing, Kennedy was livid. Here is a wonderful illustration of how the standard operating procedures of one agency—in this case, the Navy—can result in risking a nuclear holocaust in the eyes of another—the White House.

As the discussion highlights, many crucial aspects of foreign policy decision making and implementation are based on organizational routines and practices particular to that agency and not on clear choices among competing options. These routines or SOPs are increasingly important as the government becomes larger, more specialized, and more dependent on having rules, regulations, and procedures governing the functioning of the organization. For the fact is, the Navy, the State Department, DOD, the FBI, the CIA, and all other agencies have their own ways of doing things, or their own SOPs. Foreign policymaking must recognize and operate within these organizational norms if it is to be effective. And that means decision makers must know the internal political culture and

often start off disdaining each other), but also to educate the officers about diplomacy's uses and the diplomats in how to employ military force in support of diplomacy to the best advantage. After all, if you're a diplomat engaged in negotiations with a foreign power, it's nice, and adds to your bargaining power, to have a full Navy battle group just offshore with several thousand Marines on board. At the end of this one-year course, the two groups had a much better understanding of each other.

the SOPs of each of these agencies. Hence, the organizational model needs to be taken into account along with the bureaucratic politics and rational actor models in the making of foreign policy.

The Political Process Model

The political process model views foreign policy as emerging from the interactions of hundreds or even thousands of influences, pressures, and interest groups operating on foreign policy issues. It is not just the preserve of handfuls of experts in the State Department, Defense Department, White House, and other agencies, but is a complex, often convoluted, complicated political system and process. It is Political Science 101 but applied to foreign policy.

In this model, foreign policymaking is not much different than domestic policymaking. It is not the product of a pure rational actor model but of the American political process in all its dimensions. Logrolling, interest groups and partisan politics, and political deals are all involved; therefore, the outcome is not entirely predictable. On some issues, interest groups and partisan pressures will line up one way and on others in another way. Some of these interests will have more power than others, and the relative balance among them will vary over time and from issue to issue. Some groups are strong on human rights issues and others on business or labor concerns; some focus on Latin America and others on Asia or the Middle East. The configuration of all these political forces is never quite the same.

The many actors and interest groups involved in foreign policy try to build coalitions of like-minded groups to be more effective in advancing their cause—just as in domestic policymaking. They often involve themselves in the hurly-burly of politics: election campaigns, fund-raising, congressional hearings, lobbying. These groups may occasionally get all of what they want, but often they have to settle for compromise. Plainly this emphasis on politics and the policy process is not in accord with the rational actor model. Foreign policy, therefore, is seldom "pure" in an absolute or idealistic sense, any more than domestic policy is. Diverse interests, lobbies, and points of view must be satisfied. The end of the Cold War diminished the threat of a Soviet nuclear attack and therefore ushered in even more "playing politics" with foreign policy issues than before. Then with the war on terrorism and the threats of terrorist attacks, the president again enjoyed greatly enhanced presidential authority and the ability, for a time, to make foreign policy decisions in defense of the nation above the usual political fray. But that was also problematic: if the normal checks and balances and interest group politics had been operating in the war on terrorism, we probably would have made fewer mistakes in the Iraq War. By 2007, as the Iraq War began to run out of steam and wind down, the usual partisan politics reasserted itself.

The political process model of foreign policy encompasses the same log-rolling, or trading of votes, that goes on in domestic policy. These processes may have little to do with the issue of the moment or even with foreign policy, for most members of Congress have little interest in foreign policy except as their votes affect their reelection chances. They may become involved in the issue of the moment only for vote-trading purposes: I'll give you my vote on this issue in return for your vote on the next issue. The vote may also involve voters' pressures on members of Congress to vote a certain way in return for campaign funds or support later on for their pet issues or may stem from the White House's or the political leadership's pressure to vote a particular way in return for pork.

For example, when Speaker of the House Nancy Pelosi introduced a motion opposing the war in Iraq and setting a date for the American troops' return, she found herself twenty to thirty votes short. Quite a few members mainly from Pelosi's own Democratic Party feared that by opposing the war they would be accused by their constituents of undermining the troops. Their votes could come only at a price. So one by one the recalcitrant representatives were brought into the Speaker's office, asked what they wanted, and found themselves loaded with pork: a bridge here, a highway program there, tariff protection in one place, special earmarks in others. In the end Pelosi got the votes to pass the legislation, but it was a close call, and many found the trading of pork for votes on a national security issue unseemly. Like it or not, however, that's how the system works.

The political process model is based on the assessment that foreign policy, like domestic policy, is shaped by powerful forces, interests, and actors in the broader political system and cannot be separated from it. Politics no longer "stops at the water's edge," to use Senator Arthur Vandenberg's oft-quoted phrase; instead, it is subject to the same political crosswind that buffets health care or social security. In Vandenberg's Cold War days, and briefly during the war on terrorism, allowing foreign policy to be subjected to partisan political pressures was thought too dangerous to the country, but now foreign policy is no more immune from political calculations than are other kinds of policymaking. Interest

groups, lobbies, think tanks, political parties, and individual politicians now regularly seek to make propaganda and mobilize public opinion on foreign policy as
much as on domestic issues. Members of Congress now routinely "play politics"
with foreign policy; both they and the White House regularly seek to use foreign
policy to gain partisan advantage. Foreign policy *is* domestic politics to a degree
unheard of in the past. When we say, "All politics is local," we mean foreign
policy has to pass muster in the political arena just as domestic policy does.

Foreign policy has been increasingly politicized and has become the product of domestic political and partisan considerations. Both political parties,
Congress, and the White House have contributed to the increased politicization
of foreign policy. They routinely treat votes on foreign policy issues as "candy" to
be traded for votes on other issues: a Defense Department base built or kept in a
congressperson's district, protection for sugar growers in Florida or corn growers
in Iowa, start-up funds for a favored company, earmarks for special projects dear
to a members' (or the voters') hearts, and even the infamous "bridge to nowhere."
When Bill Clinton needed votes for NAFTA in the 1990s, he gave so many
patronage plums away that people started to make jokes about it: truckloads of
White House cufflinks, overnights in the Lincoln bedroom, presidential visits to
various districts. George W. Bush had a Republican-dominated Congress for his
first six years and didn't have to worry so much about congressional votes, but
after 2006 the president used the same techniques to keep Congress as much
in line as possible: threats of a withdrawal of congressional reelection campaign
funds, generous earmarks for the congressional districts, rides on Air Force One.

The political process model is an important and useful framework for
thinking about foreign policy issues. Few things are automatic in Washington
anymore: a president has to lobby, use the bully pulpit, and build support for his
program if he wishes it to succeed. All of these strategies are preeminently political acts. Although this maneuvering should not surprise us, in some quarters it
is still thought (or wished) that foreign policy takes place in a political vacuum
and is the special preserve of a handful of State Department and NSC advisers.
That portrayal is no longer accurate, however; since Vietnam and the politicization of foreign policy, international affairs are as much a matter of partisan
politics and political logrolling as is domestic policymaking. That is not to say the
organizational model, bureaucratic politics model, and even rational actor model
are unimportant in understanding politics, but we now need to add a fourth, the
political process model, to the other three.

The Self-Aggrandizement Model, or Looking Out for Numero Uno

The self-aggrandizement model, some say, represents a quite cynical way of understanding American foreign policy. We have the most trouble convincing young students and idealistic readers of this model's relevancy. This model suggests that members of Congress and the executive branch alike are in the foreign policy "game" not necessarily from self-sacrifice or to serve the public interest, as the usual campaign rhetoric suggests, but mainly to garner prestige, power, perks, career opportunities, and money for themselves. Politics is an ego trip, and if you make it to the upper levels, it's a very nice life. Or, even if you start off as idealistic, eventually you get caught up in the same ego-inflating perks, the sense of self-importance, and the desire to make it big financially as everyone else does. Politics is thus a career path to money and power as much as banking, commerce, or real estate is. If the public interest also gets served in the process, well and good; but it happens often as a by-product of the pursuit of private interests. At a minimum, it is fair to say, politicians look for policy initiatives that serve both their private interests and the public interest.

A rich literature exists in political science and political psychology on those themes of public- versus private-regarding behavior, on egoism in politics, and on self-interest as a primary motivation. The political science subfield of rational choice is built entirely on this notion of calculating, self-centered, self-interested politicians and institutions seeking in the political process to increase or aggrandize their power, perks, and wealth. This literature indicates foreign affairs as much as domestic politics are strongly shaped, if not determined, by the self-centered and career-oriented goals of both elected and appointed politicians. The literature and much evidence suggest that politicians are only rarely the selfless, public-spirited defenders of the public interest that their own language and our elementary civics texts suggest. Politicians behave and vote in order to maximize their personal election or reelection possibilities. Politicians therefore make their private career goals their first priority and try to calculate their votes and positions accordingly. But to do so they must couch their rhetoric in language that appears to be serving the public interest.

Harold Lasswell was one of the twentieth century's greatest political scientists and a pioneer in the psychopathology-and-politics school. He writes, "Political man is a deceptive creature. He imposes his private motives on public objects but he does so in a manner that few can see through." Some believe

Lasswell is too cynical about politicians while others say he is just realistic. He calls politicians "actors in disguise" because they say they are serving the public when in reality they are serving their own self-interests. Politicians, he says, engage in "ritual displacements of motives," by which he means that they say one thing when they really mean or intend to do another. In short, according to Lasswell and many others in this school, politicians seek to advance their own private careers and agendas, but they cover up their schemes with the language of serving the public.

Lasswell wrote his pathbreaking analysis some time ago, but many students of Washington policymaking, using either Lasswell's psychopathology or more recent rational choice theory, believe the situation now is even worse—more self-serving, less public spirited—than a few decades ago. For one thing, beginning in the 1970s party discipline in Congress began to break down, allowing members to be individual, calculating, self-interested political operators far more than possible in the past. For another, for both legislative and executive branch members, their government salaries, the perks involved (free transportation, the world's best health care, the ability to dip into campaign funds to augment a salary, one of the world's most generous pension systems, endless supplies of interns to do your bidding, many more), and the lifestyle of Washington, D.C., became much more attractive and worth holding onto at all costs.

There are so few contested seats and so little turnover in Congress because members love it in Washington. They would not trade their life for any other, have taken elaborate pains to all but guarantee their continuous reelection, and do not want to go "back to Peoria" (or Grand Rapids or North Platte) anymore. Besides, even on the remote chance a congressperson is defeated during the next election, that member can become a lobbyist and combine a high salary, generous commissions, and the already generous government retirement. Not a bad life. Plus politicians are invited to appear on such television shows as *The NewsHour with Jim Lehrer,* the evening news, and the numerous talk shows and thus become political stars like former secretary of state Henry Kissinger, Speaker Pelosi, former White House chief of staff James Baker, or Representative Lee Hamilton. Either on the job or in "retirement" (upon the unlikely event of electoral defeat), members of Congress as well as former State Department or DOD officials do very well.

Hence, when public officials at the federal level complain about their pay or long working hours, we should be skeptical. An overwhelming majority of them love their jobs and their life in Washington and would not do anything else—unless they could trade up for an even higher position. Salaries are high and can be nicely supplemented, the perks are wonderful, the power and influence are great, and the privileges and opportunities unmatched. After all, Washington is seen as the most powerful city in the most powerful country in the world, and who would want to walk away from that? Answer: no one. We should therefore not feel very sorry for those who occupy policy positions in the executive or legislative branches; they are well taken care of, mainly by themselves. More than that, as students of politics, we need to acknowledge their self-centered and self-aggrandizing motives as a powerful factor in explaining why they act or vote as they do.

The self-aggrandizing model and motivations as explained here should not be carried too far. There are genuinely public-spirited members of Congress and civil servants who are dedicated to serving the public interest. We need, however, to recognize the motives of self-interest—money, power, prestige, perks, influence, media attention—discussed here and how, in this egocentric age when naked self-promotion and looking out for number one have become not only acceptable but the norm, politicians are no more exempt from self-promotion than are celebrities. At the same time, the precise weight to assign to self-interest calculation versus more altruistic impulses is not entirely clear. At the least we should conclude that foreign policy (and other) officials only rarely advocate a position that does not benefit them electorally or in other ways. Few politicians are willing to commit political suicide and vote against their self-interests; there are few "profiles in courage" in Washington, D.C. In the end, while we should take politicians' self-centered motivations into account when assessing foreign policymaking, we should not assume that those are their only motivations or that we can ignore other factors. For most politicians a middle position, which also enables them to sleep better at night, is that they do well for themselves while also doing good works for their constituents or their country.

Conclusion

Various explanations of the policy process may be used in studying American foreign policy. No one explanation provides a full and complete understanding of the process by itself. At the same time, all the approaches set forth here have some useful insights to contribute.

In foreign policy and doubtless other fields, we should be wary of all-encompassing, single-cause explanations. Those who advocate such single-cause explanations, or seek to elevate one particular model—however useful—as the sole one permitted or utilized, usually have some ideological, methodological, or partisan ulterior motives. We should be wary of and careful with such private agendas. At the same time, an approach that emphasizes too many models or vantage points tends to lose us in the mishmash and complexity of its explanations.

When reviewing policy motivations, we need an approach, therefore, that is multifaceted enough to account for the complexities involved but simple enough that it can be efficiently utilized. The five interrelated models set forth here seek to strike a balance between these two extremes. Each of this chapter's models—which are woven into the chapters that follow—provides insight into the workings of foreign policy. At the same time, no one of them offers a sufficient and complete explanation by itself. The best strategy is to be eclectic and employ the most useful aspects of each of these models while at the same time examining the relations among them. For example, on some straightforward and noncontroversial issues, the rational actor model may apply, but other, more complicated issues are likely to be made more complex by bureaucratic turf fights, organizational and process issues, political calculations, and self-interest (electoral or monetary) considerations.

The five models presented here—rational actor, bureaucratic politics, organizational, political process, and self-aggrandizement—should be seen as complementing and not competing with each other. Where one model is useful in offering an explanation of the issues, we should use it; but where other factors need to be brought in, we must be willing to use other models to advance our understanding too. Foreign policy is like an onion: once you peel back one layer, you will usually find more layers underneath that also need to be peeled back to arrive at the core issues. The decision about which model to use in reviewing foreign policy processes should be based on pragmatic criteria rather than personal, partisan, or ideological bias. Our approach here will be to weave all these models together to give us the best explanations of foreign policy that we can muster.

At the same time we need to recognize that not all explanations are equally relevant for all times and places. The balance of explanatory power of the several models may be altered over time. The rational actor model still applies in some cases, but over the last few decades as foreign policy has become more politicized, it has lost some of its explanatory power. As government has become bigger and more bureaucratized, and as new agencies like Homeland Security have been added to the mix, the bureaucratic politics and organizational models have figured more prominently in our explanations. The political process model is useful not just because foreign policy has become more politicized but also because that model encompasses so much: public opinion, the interest group struggle, political party competition, and so on. And finally, in this era of Jerry Seinfeld–like narcissism and looking out for number one (oneself), who can doubt that the self-interest/self-aggrandizement model is relevant?

As we proceed with our analysis of foreign policymaking and how it works, we need to keep these models and approaches in mind as ways of organizing our thinking and exploring patterns. In the next chapters we return to American political culture and public opinion as major influences on foreign policy.

Suggested Reading

Allison, Graham T., and Philip Zelikow. *Essence of Decision: Explaining the Cuban Missile Crisis.* 2nd ed. New York: Longman, 1999.

Art, R. J. "Bureaucratic Politics and American Foreign Policy: A Critique." *Policy Sciences* 4, no. 4 (1973): 467–90.

Bendor, Jonathan, and Thomas H. Hammond. "Rethinking Allison's Models." *American Political Science Review* 86, no. 2 (1992): 301–22.

Drezner, Daniel W. "Ideas, Bureaucratic Politics, and the Crafting of Foreign Policy." *American Journal of Political Science* 44, no. 4 (2000): 733–49.

Halperin, Morton H., Priscilla A. Clapp, and Arnold Kanter. *Bureaucratic Politics and Foreign Policy.* 2nd ed. Washington, DC: Brookings Institution, 2006.

Hermann, Charles F., Charles W. Kegley Jr., and James N. Rosenau. *New Directions in the Study of Foreign Policy.* Boston: Allen & Unwin, 1986.

Hilsman, Roger, Laura Gaughran, and Patricia A. Weitsman. *The Politics of Policy Making in Defense and Foreign Affairs: Conceptual Models and Bureaucratic Politics.* 3rd ed. Englewood Cliffs, NJ: Prentice Hall, 1992.

Ikenberry, G. John, ed. *American Foreign Policy: Theoretical Essays.* 4th ed. New York: Longman, 2002.

Krasner, Stephen D. "Are Bureaucracies Important? (or Allison Wonderland)." *Foreign Policy* 7 (Summer 1972): 159–79.

Neustadt, Richard E. *Alliance Politics.* New York: Columbia University Press, 1970.

Piper, Don C., and Ronald Terchek, eds. *Interaction, Foreign Policy and Public Policy.* Washington, DC: American Enterprise Institute for Public Policy Research, 1983.

Rosati, Jerel A. *The Politics of United States Foreign Policy.* 4th ed. Belmont, CA: Wadsworth/Thomson Learning, 2006.

Wiarda, Howard J. *Foreign Policy without Illusion: How Foreign Policy-Making Works and Fails to Work in the United States.* Glenview, IL: Scott, Foresman/ Little, Brown Higher Education, 1990.

3

Who Are We?
American Political Culture
in Transition

Other nations, friends, and allies, as well as enemies, have long considered the United States unique, different, and often peculiar, and that opinion extends to its foreign policy. All nations are distinctive, of course, with their own histories, cultures, and ways of doing things; but America, with its power, wealth, and globalized culture, is something special. Since colonial times, Americans have seen themselves as a "beacon on a hill," a nation endowed with a special moral mission to bring the benefits of its civilization, culture, political system, and economic accomplishments to other, poorer, less richly endowed lands. Our foreign policy from the beginning has been imbued with a sense of missionary fervor for democracy, human rights, the environment, and so forth as well as for a hardheaded defense of our national interests.

When America's sense of moral purpose and its more narrowly defined defense of the national interest are in harmony, American foreign policy often works pretty well. When they diverge, our foreign policy tends to fragment, come under criticism, and break down. A good example of the former is the U.S. response in World War II: we not only opposed Nazism and fascism (moral purpose), but we also opposed the unification of Europe under a single, hegemonic, German or Axis power (national interest). In the Cold War, we opposed both "godless communism" (moral purpose) and Soviet aggression and expansionism (national interest). But see how U.S. foreign policy breaks down regarding the Iraq War: the goal to bring democracy to Iraq (moral purpose) was laudable albeit probably not very realistic; but with no evidence of weapons of mass destruction or of Iraqi links to al Qaeda, where was the hardheaded national interest behind our occupation? When moral purpose and national interest are not in harmony, American foreign policy gets in trouble very quickly.

In this chapter we look at the political culture undergirding American foreign policy. Political culture has already been defined as the values we hold as a nation—our belief system, or the moral, religious, and political beliefs we value as a nation. Much of American political culture is shaped and determined by our geographical location, our history, our colonial experience as an offshoot of Europe, and what political scientist Samuel P. Huntington calls our "Anglo-Protestant" tradition. Public opinion, the topic of chapter 4, is simply the organized, systematic, measurable expression of our political culture. Because in talking about political culture we need to avoid simplistic assertions or stereotypes of national character (all Germans are this, all Italians are that, all Americans are such-and-such), we rely as much as possible on good public opinion survey data, which can be used to give a more scientific, measurable, and accurate statement of contemporary American political culture.

And that brings us to the main theme of this chapter. What exactly is American political culture? Are we still the Anglo-Protestant nation that Huntington described? Who are we and what do we stand for as a nation? Do we still have much unity of purpose? Or, in this era of greater diversity and multiculturalism, are we so diverse as a nation that we no longer have a single political culture? Are we instead, as many interpretations suggest, becoming a nation of multiple, smaller ethnicities, regions, factions, and cultural identities with little attachment to a central core of beliefs? And if we are that divided and fragmented, how can we have a single and coherent foreign policy? The issue is one of the biggest underlying American foreign policy today.

A Digression: Funnels, Circles, and the Plan of the Book

We owe it to our readers to make a brief digression here to explain the book's plan, logic, and organization. Chapter 1 provided a brief introduction to the main themes, and chapter 2 covered the distinct models used to explain foreign policy decision making. This chapter deals with the substance of foreign policy, focusing on American political culture and public opinion. This and the following chapters are arranged not just randomly but in logical sequence.

This book emphasizes the domestic influences on American foreign policy. And in doing so it proceeds from the broadest and most general influences—

American political culture and public opinion and the impact they have on foreign policy—to the narrowest and most specific ones. Successive chapters then detail the impact of organized groups and interests on foreign policy: the mass media, interest groups, political parties, and think tanks. The focus then narrows still more, concentrating on ever smaller groups and institutions in the policy process: Congress and such executive agencies as the State Department, the Defense Department, the CIA, the FBI, and the Department of Homeland Security. Finally, becoming more narrowly defined and specific, the book looks at the people who actually decide foreign policy issues: the National Security Council, the White House staff, and the president himself.

Two visual images illustrate how this system works. The first, in figure 3.1, is a "funnel of causation." Think of the funnel used in a science lab to pour liquids from one vial to another or the funnel you might use in your car to put oil into the engine. The funnel is wide at the top to catch the broadest popular influences: political culture and public opinion. Then the funnel narrows to capture numerically smaller and better-organized groups: the mass media, interest groups, political parties, and think tanks. The funnel narrows some more to take in Congress, executive government agencies, the NSC, and, at the narrowest point, the president. Out of the funnel at the spout's end flow official decisions and policies.

Figure 3.2 similarly helps organize our thinking about foreign policy. In the set of concentric circles, the outer circle represents the most general influences on foreign policy: political culture, public opinion, and the mass media. In the next, smaller circle are more focused, organized groups: political parties, interest groups, and think tanks. The third circle includes Congress and the various government agencies. Finally at the core of the concentric rings are the NSC and the president, the ultimate source of foreign policy decision making.

Either of these two images, the funnel of causation or the concentric rings, can be used to organize your thinking about foreign policy. Of course, neither of these two images is to be taken literally: policy does not flow out of the bottom of a funnel. But both of these models or images help us to order our materials, provide logic and organization to the discussion, and show how policy in the American democracy flows from the broadest and most general sources (that is what democracy is all about); through several intermediary stages, or "filters"; and to the focal point of the American system—the president.

Figure 3.1 Funnel of Foreign Policy Causation

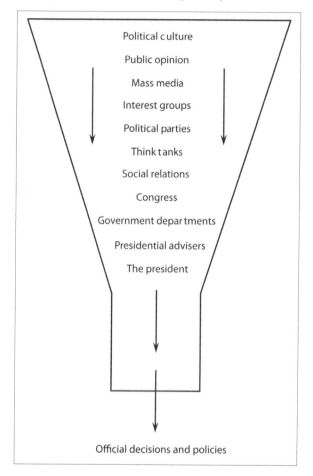

Official decisions and policies

The Unique American Experience

America is a funny country. By "funny" I mean it is unique, different. Not only is the United States the most powerful nation in the world, it is virtually the only one with a moralistic foreign policy. No other country in the world has the advancement of human rights, democracy, and free-market capitalism among its chief foreign policy goals. No other country thinks of itself—and has the power to reinforce its stance—as a moral exemplar, or a model for the world on economic and political issues, a beacon on a hill. No other country seeks so vigorously to export its institutions to the rest of the world, not because of imperialistic motives, but because it really believes its institutions are the world's

Figure 3.2 Concentric Circles of Foreign Policy Influences

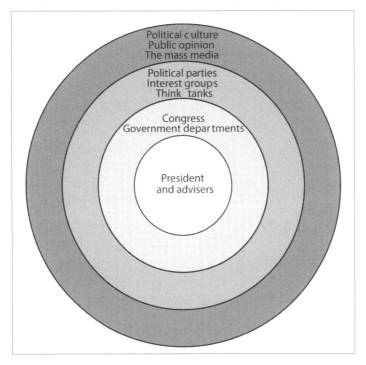

best, that other countries should follow its example, and that they would be far better off if they did imitate the United States.

Isn't this a lot of nerve, or chutzpah, on our part? Who gave us the right to be the world's moral arbiter and to back it up when necessary with overwhelming military force? Why should we be able to tell the rest of the world not only what's best for them but also how they should order their lives? Isn't this arrogant and ethnocentric, meaning that we view the rest of the world not on their own terms or in their own cultural conditions but through our own rose-colored lenses? Such a moralistic foreign policy sometimes drives friends and allies, as well as enemies, absolutely crazy. At the same time, in our standing for democracy and human rights, our policy can be an inspiration for countless others. That is the dilemma, the paradox, we must deal with.

Let us start with some preliminaries about the American experience. First, the United States is relatively inexperienced in foreign affairs. As a nation, we are rather young compared to our European allies, and we have not practiced foreign policy all that long. In his farewell speech George Washington warned against foreign entanglements, and throughout the nineteenth century the United States—smartly because we were still a relatively weak power—concentrated on domestic expansion, consolidation, and national development rather than on many international adventures. The main exception was the country's forays into Latin America, which we considered "our" neighborhood. In World Wars I and II, the United States intervened reluctantly, quickly demobilized its troops after each conflict, and assumed after the war that it could return to peace, normalcy, and isolation from troubling world conflicts. The Cold War (1947–91) changed that posture, bringing the United States into the world arena really for the first time and making us a global superpower. So the United States has been a serious, global, foreign policy "player" for little more than sixty years, a relatively short time by world standards.

Second, most European countries see U.S. foreign policy as terribly naive. They think our belief that we can change the world is unrealistic. When America goes off on crusades thinking we can bring democracy, human rights, or women's rights to countries—such as Iraq or Afghanistan—that have no tradition, history, or culture supportive of freedom and democracy, it drives our European allies crazy. At the same time the smarter of them recognize that without U.S. leadership, there would be little global progress on democracy, human rights, land mines, corruption, transparency, and other issues. Many of our European friends are therefore torn: they admire America for its leadership on democracy and human rights, but they lament when our sometimes excess enthusiasm for such causes backfires, as in Iraq, or runs amuck and causes difficulties for themselves.

A third point to emphasize, implied in the preceding discussion, is how vast the differences are between the foreign policy of the United States and that of other countries. The United States operates from the basis of moralism, or of doing good in the world, in its foreign policy, which it then seeks to combine with a less moralistic defense of its national interests. Most other countries in the world operate from a perspective of national interest alone. For example, when the French navy blew up a Greenpeace boat, killing a photographer, as it impeded French nuclear tests in the South Pacific, the French government justified its actions by citing "reasons of state" or "national interest." To these rationalizations there was nary a peep of objection from French citizens. Now contrast this reaction with what would occur in the United States if the Department of Defense blew up a boat belonging to an environmental group and killed someone during a peaceable demonstration. It is the difference between a country operating purely from motives based on national interest (reasons of state) and one that must constantly justify its actions in moral terms. The moralism and sometimes holier-than-thou attitude of American foreign policy makes us lovable or at least admirable to some but drives others to despair and destruction.

A fourth element of the American experience has to do with the pluralism of American society and hence its impact on our politics and our foreign policy. This characteristic is especially true of the forty years since the democratization of American foreign policy. The question now is, who speaks for American foreign policy? During President George W. Bush's second term, was it the president, Speaker Nancy Pelosi, antiwar congressman John Murtha, or pro-war senator John McCain? Was it the State Department, DOD, Homeland Security, the FBI, the CIA, or maybe some governor in the Southwest carrying out his own foreign policy in dealing with Mexican immigration? Or was it ex-president (and moralist par excellence) Jimmy Carter? It drives our allies (and foes too) mad that the United States speaks with so many voices on foreign policy because they can never tell which one is the voice of leadership on foreign policy. But that situation reflects America's incredible pluralism and diversity as a society, which most of us think is one of the great glories of American democracy, particularly since the democratization of American foreign policy—one of the recurrent themes in this study—began in the late 1960s. By contrast, most European and other foreign ministries are much more insulated from public opinion than our State Department is, are far more immune from democratizing and pluralist pressures, and therefore can speak with one voice in ways that we cannot.

America's problems and difficulties in carrying out a serious and coherent foreign policy have deep, historical origins. They are also the result, for good or ill, of the kind of society and culture we have become and are impacted by our geography, our history, and our values. While this book is not about diplomatic history and cannot relate the entire background of U.S. foreign policy, we do need to understand the most important features from the past and from our special situation to better comprehend our current foreign policy and how it works—or fails to work.

GEOGRAPHY AND GEOSTRATEGIC POSITION

The United States is a product of geography—as are other nations—and American foreign policy has been strongly shaped by the country's location. To the east we have about four thousand miles of ocean separating us from other powers, to the west more than five thousand miles of ocean. To the south are mainly small, weak states (except Mexico, which chiefly affects us through immigration), and to the north is Canada, a fellow English-speaking (for the most part, except Quebec) country. The public opinion polls tell us that Americans believe English-speaking countries are more friendly and trustworthy than any other kind!

During most of America's formative period in the eighteenth, nineteenth, and early twentieth centuries, therefore, the nation was largely insulated by natural frontiers that kept hostile foreign powers at bay. Contrast that experience with that of Europe, where the larger powers—France, Germany, Great Britain, Spain, Austria, Russia—live right next to each other, share borders, and have been at each others' throats in war for hundreds of years. America's geographical isolation also shaped the strong political tradition of *American isolationism*. Still with us in attenuated form (30 percent of the population supports it), this policy argues the United States should stay out of foreign affairs, throw up protectionist (economic) and security (military) barriers, and stay out of most foreign conflicts. Geographic distance also enabled the United States to concentrate on its internal social and economic development and to expand its frontiers from the Atlantic to the Pacific until it could become powerful enough, in the Spanish-American War and World War I, to play a major power role.

But is traditional isolationism still a viable basis for policy? Probably not. When Japan attacked Pearl Harbor in 1941 and threatened the U.S. Pacific Coast, it meant the end of America's ability to use the oceans as a defense perimeter. Modern, long-distance bombers; intercontinental ballistic missiles equipped with nuclear weapons; and spy satellites circling overhead, which may similarly carry lasers, chemical weapons, or nuclear materials, mean that geographic distance doesn't provide natural protection anymore. In addition, satellite television, personal computers, jet travel, the movies, and all modern means of communication and transportation have further broken down countries' traditional isolation worldwide. The globe is now smaller and more interdependent than ever before. Under these conditions, it doesn't seem possible that a U.S. isolationist and go-it-alone policy could work anymore. Whether we wish it or not, the United States is part of an interdependent world, and we need to adjust our foreign and strategic policies accordingly.

WEALTH AND RESOURCES

A second major contributing factor in the development of American foreign policy is the country's natural wealth and self-sufficiency. The United States is a richly endowed nation. It is one of the world's most productive countries agriculturally. It has, or had, abundant coal and iron ore, located in juxtaposition, for the smelting of steel, which is the essential ingredient for industrialization. It has oil and natural gas, though we are no longer self-sufficient petroleum producers, making us vulnerable to foreign pressures. In addition, the United States had abundant forests and timber and still has some of the richest farm land on earth, a wealth of minerals and other natural resources, and, in the Great Lakes and river networks, one of the world's greatest inland transportation systems. This abundance of natural resources helped make the United States one of the richest nations on earth. The only comparably endowed countries are Argentina, Brazil, China, France, Germany, Great Britain, India, Mexico, and Russia. (Japan, the second richest country in the world, is absent from the list because it has few natural resources.) All of these countries are either past, present, or future major world powers.

America's sheer wealth and self-sufficiency have bred in the public a number of attitudes that also affect our foreign policy. First, if we are self-sufficient, or at least used to be, then we don't need other countries or to pay very much attention to them—hence isolationism again. Second, if we're self-sufficient, then we don't need to study foreign languages, foreign cultures, or international relations, which helps explain many Americans' appalling lack of knowledge of the rest of the world. Third, our abundant wealth as a nation has helped instill in Americans an attitude that America is a special nation, superior to others, ordained of God, and with a special, missionary-like obligation to bring the blessings of our culture and democracy to other, less fortunate countries. Fourth, our affluence and self-sufficiency have led us to conclude that we can go it alone in the world, thumb our noses at the multilateral initiatives or the interests of other nations, and follow our own pursuits regardless, or even disdainful, of what other countries think.

But is that a responsible or even viable and workable position to take? First, we are no longer self-sufficient regarding oil, among many other things, so we do need to pay attention to other nations. Second, 9/11 showed us that we are woefully deficient in Arabic speakers and knowledge of Islamic culture; recently the U.S. government has launched a crash campaign to train students in such critical languages as Arabic, Chinese, Urdu, Russian, and others. Third, since 9/11 we have begun to realize that not all the world loves us, that anti-Americanism is on the rise, and that we need to be more modest and circumspect in imposing our institutions on other countries. And fourth, such issues as acid rain, global warming, and resource depletion, which are by their nature international in scope, have forced us to recognize that we cannot just go it alone anymore. On at least some issues we must pay attention to what other nations and multinational agencies are doing.

RELIGION

America was founded on a Christian and predominantly Protestant basis, with strong Puritan and Calvinist beliefs, especially in New England, New York–New Jersey, Pennsylvania, and the South. By the time the nation was founded and the Constitution written in 1787, there was already considerable religious diversity; but it was still diversity within an overwhelmingly Christian context. This tradition, which Samuel P. Huntington calls the Anglo-Protestant tradition, lies at the heart of the American cultural and political experience. By Anglo-Protestant, Huntington means that not only has the United States been a Christian nation historically but that virtually all our law and political traditions, including limited government, the rule of law, political freedom, trial by jury, habeas corpus, separation of powers, representative government, the Bill of Rights, and democratic governance, have come from Great Britain. Not from France, Germany, or Latin America.

This early history and the religious basis of many U.S. institutions help explain America's (more than other nations') longtime concern with doing good in the world and its still widespread belief that America is a special nation blessed by God, with a special obligation to bring the benefits of our God-favored country to less-favored lands. It helps us understand the strongly moral basis of our foreign policy, our notion of ourselves as a shining beacon to others, and our efforts to act with ethical purpose in a world that is often anarchic and immoral. This strong religious tradition may also explain our inability to treat other nations as equals, our tendency to look down on foreign or non-Christian (think Islamic) cultures, the sense of moral righteousness that the United States brings to its policy, and the powerful belief in America that other countries can learn from us whereas we have little to learn from them.

Over the course of its history and particularly since the 1960s, the religious foundation of the United States—if it even still has a religious foundation—has changed enormously, with major implications for foreign policy. First, America has become much more religiously pluralist than before with a far greater variety of religious (and nonreligious) groups—Jewish, Buddhist, Hindu, Confucian,

Islamic, Mormon, Wiccan, atheist—and sects, factions, and breakaway groups within the dominant Christian tradition. It is doubtful that we can identify the United States as a "Christian" country anymore. Second, the United States has become much more secular, with the Supreme Court over the last five decades strictly segregating church from state, with religion being discouraged in public discussion and school prayers, with less than half the population attending church services regularly, and with no one single set of moral and religious values (such as the Ten Commandments, which have also been banished from public buildings) governing personal and individual behavior. And finally, in the absence of a single, dominant set of national beliefs (for shorthand purposes, let us use Huntington's phrase of Anglo-Protestant), the American purpose and our foreign policy have also become less certain, more fragmented, without clear purpose, and confused over our direction and goals. There are other reasons for our foreign policy confusion, of course, but clearly lacking a single set of unifying moral, ethical, and religious beliefs is one of them.

Huntington not only laments the passing, or at least decline and shunting aside, of this Anglo-Protestant tradition, but he also sees in it dire consequences for the nation and our foreign policy. Others are less convinced by Huntington, arguing that our current pluralism and multiculturalism reflect present-day realities and are beneficial for the nation, that in the name of religion we have not always done good in the world, and that one does not have to be a Christian to believe in democracy, human rights, or checks and balances and to act ethically in the world. One must admit, however, it is probably harder to keep a nation together and act with unified purpose in foreign policy on a secular-pluralist basis than on the basis of a policy grounded in a single set of moral-religious principles. But that, as they say, is water under the bridge. In the present circumstances and given all the changes in American society since the late 1960s, it is no longer possible to go back to that single, Christian, Anglo-Protestant way of life, even if we were sure we wanted to do so.

Other historians have carried Huntington's argument further. Gertrude Himmelfarb, who has written a wonderful book on the subject titled *One Nation, Two Cultures*, argues that, in place of the earlier, dominant, Anglo-Protestant tradition, America is dividing into two distinct and often warring cultures. On the one side is the traditional Anglo-Protestant culture, with people who still believe in the Bible's teachings, the Ten Commandments, and the ethical goodness of America and its institutions, and that we should export these values to other nations. On the other side is a growing, secular, nonbelieving, nonreligious America, whose adherents are doubtful and cynical about America's moral purpose or even character and unconvinced, under the doctrines of religious and political relativism, of our quasi-religious campaigns to export our institutions to other countries.

But look what Himmelfarb, other historians, and sociologists, to say nothing of the U.S. census bureau data, do next. They locate the continuing, core religious tradition of America in the South, Southwest, Rocky Mountain states, and the Midwest and among those who are rural, less well educated, and conservative. The secularists are mainly located in New England and along the East and West coasts and engage in such professions as the media, entertainment, teaching, and highly educated governmental and other elite positions. These secularists tend to be quite liberal in their thinking. Now, a moment's reflection will lead us to realize this grouping is precisely the lineup of red and blue states—with the South and West being red, the two coasts blue, and the Midwest a swing area—in presidential elections since 2000. It also reflects our two political parties, with the Republicans being identified chiefly as the party of religion and traditional values and the Democrats as the party of secularism and liberalism. To the extent our political party differences are now being hardened and the country polarized by these reinforcing religious and ideological differences indicates how deeply our society is now divided. And, as we started off the book, if the country is divided and polarized, we cannot expect our foreign policy to show a coherence and unity of purpose that the nation as a whole does not. It is an important theme to which we will return in other chapters.

The American Historical Experience

History has the capacity to be either a unifier or a divider of countries. In Iraq, where we have seen a virtual civil war between the Shiites and the Sunnis, and in the former Yugoslavia, where Robert D. Kaplan wrote his book *Balkan Ghosts: A Journey Through History* about the ancient hatreds and long memories of the region's people, history has a tendency to divide. But in America, where we have the Founding Fathers, our glorious Constitution, Abraham Lincoln and the freeing of the slaves, and heroic victories in World Wars I and II and the Cold War, history has been a unifying factor. It has given us an underlying belief system, values, and a mythology that helps hold the country together. The question is, does history do that still? Or has history become in the United States, as it has in other countries, a divisive force?

The thirteen colonies, protected by oceans and great distances, had little need of foreign policy. The colonies traded with Europe, Africa, and the Caribbean, but they were largely immune to European great power rivalries and the marauding pirates of the Caribbean. Their colonial master, Great Britain, protected them from the French in Canada and Louisiana and from the Spanish in Florida and the Southwest. Nevertheless, in Protestant-Calvinist New England, the sentiment was already well established that foreign as well as domestic policy would have to show the credentials of morality and religion.

The new nation's position did not change much after it declared its independence. George Washington famously warned against foreign entanglements. Thomas Jefferson sent U.S. naval forces to the Mediterranean to ward off the Barbary pirates, but that show of force was mainly a police action. The War of 1812 was essentially a defensive struggle, and the famous Monroe Doctrine of 1823 was limited in its effects only to our weak neighbors in the Caribbean. The so-called Indian Wars of the 1820s were aggressive actions against weak forces. In 1836 and then again in 1846 the United States defeated Mexico and seized Texas and the Southwest as part of our westward expansion; today Mexico dreams of recovering these territories through migration.

America's primary preoccupation during the nineteenth century was with internal, continental development—that is, achieving its "manifest destiny" with coast-to-coast expansion and consolidation—and not with foreign wars. Plus, the United States at this stage was too weak to play a big-power role. But after the Civil War, as the population rapidly increased and as the United States emerged as an industrial power, it acquired more aggressive designs to go along with its newfound economic power. In the 1880s we acquired Hawaii, gained Puerto Rico and the Philippines in the Spanish-American War of 1898, and repeatedly intervened in the Caribbean and in Central America during the first three decades of the twentieth century.

World Wars I and II, the Korean War in the 1950s, and the Cold War were unifying wars in American history. So, initially, was the war on terrorism. Almost all Americans accepted the justifications for these wars and supported both the troops and their government's actions. But the Vietnam and Iraq wars were unpopular, and public enthusiasm for fighting a protracted war on terrorism also faded over time. All three of these wars divided the public and led to bitter internal debate. With the public divided, the government was often uncertain, vacillating, and ineffective in carrying out the policy too. All three of these unpopular wars became metaphors in our public discussion for what's wrong, or right, with America.

For purposes of this book, the Vietnam War deserves special attention. First, along with the Civil War, it was the most divisive war in American history. Second, with people out in the streets marching and demonstrating against the war; with universities, churches, and town councils taking sides on the war; and with families, groups, and civil society divided but also mobilized against the war, Vietnam was instrumental in "democratizing" American foreign policy, for good or ill, really for the first time. Everyone became involved.

Finally, the Vietnam War broke down the consensus that had heretofore existed over foreign policy. From this point on, American public opinion was about equally divided three ways: one-third of the population was still isolationist in the way much of the country had been before World War II, one-third was conservative internationalist and believed in maintaining a strong military to protect us, and one-third had become liberal internationalist, committed to democracy, peace, and human rights and no longer to war or a strong defense. It became increasingly difficult after Vietnam to build a working foreign consensus on almost any specific issue.

The consensual basis of American governmental authority similarly broke down during this period. Think of our presidents prior to that era. Franklin D. Roosevelt carried us through the trauma of World War II and is regarded as a great leader, Harry Truman is acknowledged by both Democrats and Republicans to have been one of our better presidents, Dwight Eisenhower was elected twice and enjoyed widespread popularity as a president, and John F. Kennedy enjoyed similar popularity until he was cut down by an assassin's bullet. But both Lyndon Johnson and Richard Nixon, mainly because of Vietnam, were divisive presidents whose policies polarized the country.

Jimmy Carter came out of the post-Vietnam, liberal-internationalist wing of the Democratic Party committed to human rights, peace, and a mushy inter-nationalism; he is widely considered to have been a failure as a president. By contrast, Ronald Reagan took a tough, conservative-internationalist position that polarized the country as much as Carter's policies had. George H. W. Bush was a moderate who tried to skate between these two polarized positions. While he is widely credited with having run a successful foreign policy at the end of the Cold War, he lacked vision, was not a good campaigner or politician, and was defeated on economic policy grounds ("it's the economy stupid") after only one term in office. With Bill Clinton, foreign policy returned to idealistic, Carter-esque, liberal internationalism, and George W. Bush adopted a hard-nosed, Reagan-esque, conservative internationalism. With Barack Obama, romantic idealism à la Jimmy Carter appears to have returned.

You have to know how Washington works. When a liberal administration like Bill Clinton's or Barack Obama's comes to power, it is staffed almost exclusively with ideas and personnel from the earlier and similarly liberal Democratic administrations, those who worked for them during the campaign, and members of the liberal establishment in Washington—those think tanks (the Brookings Institution and the Center for American Progress), law firms, and nongovernmental organizations closely linked to the Democratic Party—who had been waiting impatiently to return to government policymaking after long years of Republican administrations. Likewise, when a conservative administration like George W. Bush's comes to power, it is staffed almost exclusively with ideas and personnel from the earlier, conservative administrations; the campaign; and the conservative establishment in Washington—those think tanks (AEI, Heritage Foundation, Hoover Institution, and Hudson Institute), law firms, and NGOs closely affiliated with the Republican Party—who had been waiting out the preceding Democratic administration.

In this way, a liberal-Democratic administration largely repeats the policy agenda from its party's past while a conservative-Republican administration also repeats its party's policy agenda from the past. The same ideas and personnel, with newcomers always being added, of course, are repeated from one administration to the next. And the same interest groups and NGOs, which often have their own private agendas that they seek to carry out, persevere from Democratic to Democratic and Republican to Republican administrations (see chapter 6). Thus since the Vietnam War, the same divisions and conflicts in the body politic have been perpetuated over a thirty-five-year period with largely the same groups and interests involved, and as they have become institutionalized in the respective Republican and Democratic parties, think tanks, and interest group supporters and lineups, these divisions have also become deeper, meaner, and more entrenched.

FOREIGN POLICY BEHAVIOR

In the 1970s it was fairly easy to draw a picture, or at least an idealized version, of what the U.S. population looked like. We thought of ourselves, and were often thought of abroad, as a white, European, Christian, Anglo-Saxon nation. We lived in the richest nation on earth (giving rise to the still-widespread notion abroad that "all Americans are rich"), and our democracy and free enterprise system were the envy of the world. I used to work as a trainer for the early Peace Corps, teaching the volunteers about the countries and cultures they would experience overseas, and I remember that if the Peace Corps sent out a volunteer who didn't correspond ethnically or racially to the image above, people in the host country would often say, "He/she didn't look American to me!" That means racism and national stereotyping are practiced in other countries as well as in the United States.

When not long after my stint with the Peace Corps I wrote my first book about American foreign policy, I tried to characterize American society in terms of the traits I thought were intrinsic to American culture and therefore of major importance in understanding its foreign policy. Among the traits I emphasized were isolationism, moralism, idealism, a religious basis to policy, and so on. Looking back on that list today, however, I am uncertain how many of those traits still apply or if they apply to the same degree. Are we still a "white, European, Christian, Anglo-Saxon nation"? And if not, then what are we as a nation? What principles, if any, do we stand for? Or, as in the title of the book by Huntington referred to earlier, "Who Are We?"

If we cannot answer those questions, then it is easy to see why we are in trouble as a nation. If we can no longer identify a set of traits that define us, then it should not be surprising if our foreign policy is also confused. And if we are divided or disagree about who we are or if we've lost our identity, then it should not come as a shock that our foreign policy is similarly adrift, fragmented, and confused. For ultimately in a democracy, foreign policy reflects who we are as a nation. So let us revisit the traits I once used to describe our society and see which, if any of them, still apply and to what extent. Keep in mind that if we are unclear, divided, or fragmented on the issues of who we are and what the United States stands for, we should not expect our foreign policy to clarify these matters for us.

ISOLATIONISM

With secure borders historically on all sides and with abundant land and resources, the United States seldom in the past felt the need for a vigorous foreign policy. Until World War II the United States was an isolationist country, content to stay out of most international conflicts. The war and the consequent Cold War changed all that. The United States emerged as a global superpower and then, after the Cold War, as the only superpower.

But even at the height of the Cold War, 30–35 percent of the electorate expressed isolationist sentiment. The isolationists would prefer that the United States not play such a strong international role; stay out of entangling alliances like NATO; have a strong defense but not serve as a global policeman or fire-man, putting out brush fires wherever they occur; avoid trade pacts as well as international organizations like the UN; and not engage in "missionary camp-aigns" to bring democracy to unlikely countries. Currently, in the aftermath of the frustrating Iraq War, isolationist sentiment has climbed to more than 40 percent.

Two comments may be offered at this point. First, the United States is so big and powerful, our economy and culture historically so strong, and the forces of worldwide globalization now so robust, that it is impossible to revert to the isolationism of the past. We are a major player in the world whether we wish to be or not; we cannot just bury our head in the sand and hope the world's problems will go away. It is a legitimate issue, however, to ask if the United States at this stage should reduce some of its large-scale and very expensive commitments. Second, it is very difficult in the United States to conduct a successful foreign policy if 40 percent of the population wants nothing to do with it and is against everything that the administration wants to do. Imagine yourself as president having to deal with genocide in Darfur, global warming, China's threatening posture, al Qaeda, the Taliban, and global terrorist threats, and four out of ten persons are automatically against all your policies. Additionally, on each of these issues, for different political or ideological reasons, another 20–30 percent are going to oppose you on partisan grounds. It is easy to see, therefore, how almost any international action on your part will result in 60–70 percent, or two-thirds, of the electorate disapproving whatever you do. For these reasons alone, it is very difficult for the United States or its president to conduct a serious foreign policy.

Idealism

Americans want their foreign policy to be moral, ethical, and idealistic. It is not enough for the United States to stand only for the national interest; we have always believed in a higher moral purpose—democracy and human rights, for instance—and not just in what the Europeans call "Realpolitik." Hence, in the two great world wars of the twentieth century, it was not enough for us to prevent German hegemony in the heart of Europe; we also had to make the world safe for democracy and defeat evil fascism. Similarly, during the Cold War, it was not sufficient for us to contain the Soviet Union; we also had to vanquish "godless communism." In the First Gulf War (1990–91), George H. W. Bush not only wanted to force Saddam Hussein out of oil-rich Kuwait, he also sought to roll back Hussein's "naked aggression." In the same vein, we cannot be allied with an apartheid regime in South Africa that represses blacks, military regimes in Latin America that violate human rights, or Islamic regimes that marginalize women.

Usually America is able to keep pursuits of its national interests and its moral purpose in close harmony. For instance, we not only defeated the Axis powers but also strengthened democracy and snuffed out fascism, and we not only prevented a Marxist takeover in Central America but also engineered transitions to democracy there that greatly improved human rights. But what if idealism and hardheaded national interest diverge? For example, we may be against "godless communism," but we have to acknowledge China's rising power and our need to trade with the country. Saudi Arabia does not have a democratic regime, but we desperately need its oil to keep our economy going. Egypt's ruler is also authoritarian, but we need to tolerate that government for the sake of Middle East peace and Israel's security. Saddam Hussein was an SOB, but at least he maintained stability and kept terrorism under control, which is more than we can say for his successors. The trouble with having a moralistic foreign policy is as long as it serves our national interest too, the public will support it. However, when the policy is moralistic but not realistic (bringing democracy to Iraq) or is realistic at the expense of idealistic goals (giving aid to military dictators who support our interests but are gross violators of human rights), American policy usually founders.

Practicality and Impatience

The United States is not a notably patient country. Americans want quick results and are often impatient with policies that don't produce fast outcomes. Our electoral cycle feeds into that eagerness: members of Congress or presidents campaigning for reelection and their opposition insist on speedy outcomes and certainly by the end of the politicians' terms. Otherwise, we vote them out of office.

America is also impatient with protracted conflicts (Iraq, Afghanistan) or diplomacy that drags on and on. Who remembers what the Doha Development round or Strategic Arms Limitation Talks (SALT) are all about? We want to solve the problem or resolve the conflict quickly and get back to our normal lives. But in many areas of the globe, conflict is endemic, the problems are intractable, and there are no quick solutions. For example, after the Soviet Union collapsed and the Cold War ended, our stated goal was to bring democracy and free markets to Russia. But in a country where the underlying values (political culture) and institutions are not democratic, this process would take three or four generations, not three or four years. Similarly in Iraq, Afghanistan, and elsewhere in the developing world, creating a democracy, building institutions and civil society, and fashioning modern, functioning economies will require a hundred-year commitment on our part, not just a decade. But plainly the public has no patience for such a long-term commitment, it cannot be sustained politically, and the political parties, caught up in electoral politics and presidential ambitions, cannot maintain bipartisan unity on the issue. Can anyone even imagine a century-long commitment to Iraq? But short of that investment, Iraq will always have problems. In turn, Iraq's plight will translate into problems for U.S. policy, which, as we've seen, cannot be sustained on a long-term basis.

A-historicism

It is often said that the United States has little historical memory. As a relatively new country (compared to China, Iran, or France, for example), the United States does not have much history (no feudalism, for instance), and we do not study much history. From the time of its discovery, America always represented something new: new frontiers, wide open spaces, new possibilities. We are not much past oriented, instead focusing on the present and future. We have not absorbed the great lessons of history concerning the balance of power; moralism and realism in foreign policy; the costs as well as benefits of being a global power; and the limits of our ability to change the culture and behavior of other nations.

Our a-historicism makes us both endearing and frustrating to other nations. On the one hand, others find endearing America's sense of boundless optimism, which other nations lack; its powerful idealism for democracy and human rights; and its sense of the future without the encumbrances of the past. On the other hand, they also find it frustrating on many different levels. No other country fundamentally changes its foreign policy with every new administration, much to the annoyance of our allies who practice continuity. No other country rushes off to bring democracy to countries (Haiti, Somalia, Afghanistan, Iraq) where there is almost no chance of it succeeding. Few other countries have a national program of service like the Peace Corps and send volunteers abroad to assist in third world development, or champion human rights in abusive regimes, or seek to eliminate land mines in war-torn countries. It is good for America to have this missionary-like idealism, but we also need to rein it in a little, to be realistic about what we can and cannot accomplish, and to be more consistent in our execution of policy. Otherwise, as in Iraq, history will come back to snap at us.

Peace Is Normal, Conflict Abnormal

U.S. history has been marked by the relative absence of violence, revolution, and upheaval. We've had our wars, our crime and murder rates are high compared to Europe's and Japan's, and we continue to have domestic political demonstrations. But we do not really experience much political violence. Since the Revolution in 1776, we've had no government overthrown by unconstitutional means. All this stability makes the United States unique in the world compared with other nations.

The relative absence of political violence in our own society has bred in Americans the sense that such violence is not just abhorrent but also abnormal. Instead, Americans believe that peace is normal and war and violence abnormal. But in many countries of the world, widespread violence is a normal, everyday, routine part of the political process. As in Iraq or Afghanistan, a leader or group demonstrates its power by the display and use of violence. We may succeed in getting the leaders to hold elections, but in the years between elections and sometimes in the elections themselves, the police, army, parties, militias, tribes, clans, labor unions, students, and others utilize violence as a way of demonstrating both actual and potential political power.

We Americans and our foreign policy are ill equipped to deal with this scenario. Ours is such a (relatively, again) peaceful society that we think that is normal, but for many other countries and cultures, the opposite is true: peace is abnormal, and violence is the normal state of things. Hence, when we do peacekeeping, nation-building, or democracy-enhancing work in the world, we need to be realistic. In societies where violence is the norm, our peacekeeping role will not always or necessarily be appreciated. We may have to settle for less than peaceful outcomes or the establishment of regular elections freed from violence and intimidations. We can try to change these societies, but we need to recognize the limits on what we can accomplish.

SUPERIORITY AND ETHNOCENTRISM

The peace-violence issue is related to another, even larger issue in American foreign policy: our inability to see and understand the world other than through our own rose-colored lenses. We suffer from ethnocentrism: we view the world through our own norms and values rather than attempting to understand other people and cultures in their own terms and often in their own languages.

There are two sub-aspects of this issue. The first is a strong sense of American superiority. We really believe that our economic and political institutions are the best ever derived by humankind. Hence, through our foreign aid program, the Center for International Private Enterprise (CIPE), and our foreign investment and trade policies, we have sought to export the American economic model to less fortunate lands. Similarly through the National Endowment for Democracy (NED), the National Democratic Institute (NDI), the International Republican Institute (IRI), and other agencies, we have tried to bring the American model of democracy to other countries.

Now it may be that the American economic and political models are superior. For a long time they were. With the government's response to Hurricane Katrina, the flawed elections of 2000 and 2004, the desperate state of our economy in 2009, and the inability of Congress or the federal bureaucracy to respond and get things done, we are not so sure. Arguably, both Japan and Western Europe have surpassed the United States in quality of life issues. In any case, even if we are superior or just think we are, some greater modesty in imposing our solutions on other peoples' countries would be useful.

The second aspect is American knowledge, or lack thereof, about other countries. Americans are appallingly ignorant about other cultures, other societies, other countries, and their political systems. But the facts are, for any American foreign assistance or social, economic, or political policy to work abroad, it must be adapted to local conditions. If we don't know or understand the local conditions (as in Iraq), how can our policies possibly work there? The answer is, they can't. Again, it stems from our ethnocentrism problem, or our inability, either because of our superior, patronizing attitudes or because of our lack of understanding, to deal with countries on their own terms and in their own circumstances.

America Unraveling?

The characteristics listed above are all part of an older, more traditional America. The question now is, are they still relevant in twenty-first-century America?

Up until the 1960s there was widespread consensus on what it meant to be an American. That societal and cultural consensus undergirded the largely bipartisan foreign policy ("policy stops at the water's edge") that we were able to implement.

The Vietnam War, as we will see more clearly in chapter 4, destroyed the consensus that had previously existed on American foreign policy. Meanwhile, the United States was also going through immense, internal, social and political changes. The common basis of consensus no longer exists. The result is that, since the Vietnam conflict, no American president—Ford, Carter, Reagan, Bush I, Clinton, and Bush II—has been able to fashion a foreign policy that enjoys consistent majority support. Perhaps that task, given our incredible diversity and pluralism as a nation, is no longer possible.

CENSUS RETURNS

The 2000 census revealed that Hispanics, Asians, Africans, Middle Easterners, and African Americans were the fastest-growing sectors of the American population. America is no longer a predominantly white, Anglo-Saxon, Protestant (WASP) country. In addition to these ethnic and racial changes, the census revealed that more families are headed by single parents than ever before and that there are now more single-person households in the United States than there are married ones. Without drawing any moral conclusions from these changes, we may reach a political one: given these incredible social-ethnic-racial changes in America, it is simply much more difficult than before to fashion a consensus and policy on which all groups can agree.

RELIGION

As discussed previously, America was once known as a Christian country, but determining whether it still is, is difficult. Trickier is the question of whether Americans want to live in a Christian country and what that means. More than 80 percent of Americans say they believe in God (mostly still the Christian God), and 45 percent attend religious services regularly. Clearly, however, Americans do not want religion or the government to interfere with their private behavior or morality; are suspicious of others, including religious leaders, telling them what they may or may not do; prefer strict separation of church and state; and are generally more secular than they were in the 1960s. Our views on religion have foreign policy implications. For instance, do we really want a foreign policy that would favor Christians over Muslims in Indonesia, the Sudan, or Nigeria, where civil wars are being fought between these groups? Do we want a global "clash of civilizations" or of religions between the Christian and the Islamic worlds?

INSTITUTIONS

America used to pride itself on its can-do spirit and ability to get things done. But is that true anymore? Circumstances such as 9/11, Hurricane Katrina, and the Iraq War have shown us that such huge Washington bureaucracies as the Federal Emergency Management Agency (FEMA), the CIA, the FBI, Homeland Security, the State and Defense departments, the Departments of Energy and Treasury, and so on are not only unresponsive but can't even protect us from outside attack. And Congress appears to have only two interests: reelection calculations and the income from lobbying that ensures reelection. Serving the public interest is secondary to these other core concerns. If our basic public institutions are failing us in these ways, how can we have a functioning foreign policy?

THE NEW TRIBALISM

Since the 1970s the United States has become much more diverse and multicultural than it was before. Identity politics, meaning loyalty to one's own group, race, or ethnicity, is now "in." A commitment to diversity and multiculturalism is good for us—up to a point—teaching and exposing us to other cultures, races, and peoples. But are we now so diverse and multicultural that we lack any commitment to a central core of beliefs? Who are we as a country? Are we on the way to becoming another Lebanon or like the former Yugoslavia, where our ethnic, cultural, racial, and political divisions are so deep and pervasive that the country starts to come apart at the seams? How can we have a serious foreign policy in that context?

THE ECONOMY

Underlying present limitations on American foreign and defense policy is the shaky American economy. Our economic growth rate is anemic; our industries have declined; the housing market has tanked; we are deeply in debt, which we have passed on to future generations; and our main creditors—China and

Saudi Arabia—are both unreliable as well as not necessarily our friends. We are living on borrowed money, we have paid for the Iraq War basically on credit and without calling for any financial sacrifice on the American public's part, and future entitlement obligations, including Social Security, Medicare and Medicaid, and health care, may strip us of the capacity to afford a serious foreign policy. A weakened economy does not provide a sure footing for a global foreign policy.

A PESSIMISTIC MOOD

The polls tell us Americans are worried about the future. Not necessarily frightened of an imminent terrorist attack but anxious about the future in general. Both the presidency and Congress are in bad repute, with Congress ranking even lower (less than 20 percent approval rating) than the president. The public has little confidence—the legacy of Katrina—in any American institutions, with the exception of the armed forces, to get things done. Moreover, Americans are worried and even pessimistic about the future, health care, their jobs, their pensions, competition from abroad, the economy in general, and future terrorist attacks. Most Americans do not believe they will be targeted, but they do think it is likely the country will be attacked again as in 9/11. And, tellingly, they have little faith in the capacity of most American institutions to respond adequately. Furthermore, eight in ten Americans believe the country is headed in the wrong direction. None of these are good signs for future American policy.

AN "ORDINARY COUNTRY"

With the end of the Cold War in the early 1990s, America seems to have lost its primary mission. There is no longer widespread consensus on what we should stand for as a nation. Post–Cold War, we lacked an enemy to focus on, and we were unsure what to do with our power. Both former presidents Clinton and George W. Bush tried to elevate the growth of democracy abroad into a new basis for American foreign policy; and while there have been gains, the democracy agenda has not worked well in countries such as Bosnia, Haiti, Somalia, and most notably Iraq and Afghanistan. Bush also sought to use the 9/11 attacks on the World Trade Center and the Pentagon as a way to rouse Americans to a global war against terrorism and to present himself as a "wartime president." Although that tactic probably got him reelected in 2004, he also foundered on the disastrous war in Iraq. In the wake of these failings, Americans are no longer certain what our global role is or what it should be. Yes, we are still in favor of promoting democracy and human rights but not as enthusiastically as in the past, and now we are not sure how many resources—money and troops—we should commit to pursuing that policy.

SHRINKING COMMON GROUND

What is it that binds America together at this point? On what do we agree? What are our commonalities? Most of us would still give the classic answers to these questions—democracy, freedom, economic opportunity, and the rule of law— but these replies are all vague and general. When we get to specifics, such as how many resources we're willing to expend on laudatory but frustrating campaigns for human rights and democracy, there is far less agreement. Yes, we stand for democracy and human rights but in important yet difficult countries like Russia, Egypt, China, Saudi Arabia, Iraq, or Afghanistan are we really succeeding in those quests? How much money and resources, including American lives in Afghanistan, Pakistan, or Iraq are we willing to put into these noble but also frustrating campaigns? Americans are no longer certain about the answers to these questions. And if the public is unsure, our leaders, who in a democracy ultimately reflect public sentiment, are no more certain on these hard questions than the rest of us are.

A "CAN'T-DO" COUNTRY?

America is in deep trouble. In addition to the factors listed above, we also know that, compared to other countries, our math scores are down, we know little about geography, and our lead in various technical fields is eroding. As a country we are overweight, are indulgent, and have a tendency to blame others for our own missteps. Pessimism about the future is at an all-time high; faith in our institutions has plummeted. Increasingly we see ourselves as a can't-do country, and as other nations pass us by, they see us Americans as lazy and unable to compete anymore. The implications of all these negative changes for American foreign policy are immense. Can they be reversed?

Conclusions

The American historical experience is unique. Largely self-sufficient in resources, protected on all sides by (relatively) safe borders, and avoiding for much of our history Europe's destructive wars, America largely emerged in peace and isolation—and with isolationism as a part of our foreign policy values. Founded on a particular religious, ethical, and cultural basis, America has long stood for democracy, freedom, opportunity, and constitutionalism. We are distinct in the world in putting high moral principle at the forefront of our foreign policy. But now, with the end of the Cold War, the vast failures in Iraq, and immense changes in American culture and society, we are no longer certain what we stand for and how vigorously we want to pursue any of those goals.

Political culture affects foreign policy in many ways. It helps shape public attitudes and perceptions about the issues, it affects how the media cover foreign affairs, and it influences the views held by special interest groups. It also affects the mind-set of leaders and foreign policy decision makers, for political culture indicates what is important, what to pay attention to and why, what will and will not work with the electorate. Political culture establishes the context and perimeters of the American foreign policy debate and sets limits on policy options. Because political culture relates to our fundamental beliefs and values and our prejudices, it shapes our views about ourselves as well as how we see the rest of the world. Thus it is an important influence on how we view foreign countries, their leaders, and appropriate U.S. policy toward them. Political culture not only helps define what our leaders can decide but also whether the public will support the policies.

Political culture changes slowly, often over a generation or two, but it *does* change. New interpretations may arise, and new facts require us to alter our views as the world changes. For example, China and India, two large and important countries that we once thought were too poor and backward to be taken seriously, have now emerged as major global powers that require us to modify our strategies toward them. These types of facts on the ground force us to adjust our attitudes or political culture.

But political culture, for all its usefulness as a concept, is still a quite vague and general term that is open to different interpretations. It is often impressionistic, not as sharp or sophisticated a foreign policy tool as we would like, and thus it exists at a rather low level of foreign policy theory. As seen in figures 3.1 and 3.2, it operates at the broadest and most general level of our foreign policy funnel of causation and in the farthest circle of our concentric rings of explanation. So let us now sharpen the focus and go to the next and narrower level in our funnel or to the next layer in the circle's rings of foreign policy influences. Chapter 4 concentrates specifically on public opinion and foreign policy, where our data and facts are more specific and more precise.

Suggested Reading

Almond, Gabriel A. *The American People and Foreign Policy*. New York: Praeger, 1967.

Almond, Gabriel A., and Sidney Verba. *The Civic Culture: Political Attitudes and Democracy in Five Nations*. Newbury Park, CA: Sage Publications, 1989.

Goldstein, Martin E. *America's Foreign Policy: Drift or Decision*. Wilmington, DE: Scholarly Resources, 1984.

Hartmann, Frederick H., and Robert L. Wendzel. *America's Foreign Policy in a Changing World*. New York: HarperCollins College Publishers, 1994.

Hartz, Louis. *The Liberal Tradition in America: An Interpretation of American Political Thought since the Revolution*. 2nd Harvest/HBJ ed. San Diego: Harcourt Brace Jovanovich, 1991.

Hermann, M. G. "Effects of Personal Characteristics of Political Leaders on Foreign Policy." In *Why Nations Act: Theoretical Perspectives for Comparative Foreign Policy Studies,* edited by Maurice East, Stephen A. Salmore, and Charles F. Hermann, 49–68. Beverly Hills, CA: Sage, 1978.

Holsti, O. R., and J. N. Rosenau. "A Leadership Divided: The Foreign Policy Beliefs of American Leaders, 1976–1980." In *Perspectives on American Foreign Policy: Selected Readings*, edited by Charles E. Kegley Jr. and Eugene R. Wittkopf. New York: St. Martin's Press, 1983.

Hunt, Michael H. *Ideology and U.S. Foreign Policy*. New Haven, CT: Yale University Press, 1987.

Kolko, Gabriel. *The Roots of American Foreign Policy: An Analysis of Power and Purpose*. Boston: Beacon Press, 1969.

Lind, Michael. *The American Way of Strategy: U.S. Foreign Policy and the American Way of Life*. New York: Oxford University Press, 2006.

Mead, Walter Russell. *Special Providence: American Foreign Policy and How It Changed the World*. New York: Knopf, 2001.

Melanson, Richard A. *American Foreign Policy since the Vietnam War: The Search for Consensus from Nixon to Clinton*. 2nd ed. Armonk, NY: M. E. Sharpe, 1996.

Nathan, James A., and James K. Oliver. *Foreign Policy Making and the American Political System*. 3rd ed. Baltimore, MD: John Hopkins University Press, 1994.

Perkins, Dexter. *The American Approach to Foreign Policy*. Rev. ed. Cambridge, MA: Harvard University Press, 1962.

Potter, David Morris. *People of Plenty: Economic Abundance and the American Character*. Chicago: University of Chicago Press, 1973.

Ruggie, John Gerard. "The Past as Prologue? Interests, Identity, and American Foreign Policy." *International Security* 21, no. 4 (1997): 89–125.

Spanier, John W., and Steven W. Hook. *American Foreign Policy since World War II*. 16th ed. Washington, DC: CQ Press, 2004.

Tocqueville, Alexis de. *Democracy in America*. Translated by Arthur Goldhammer. New York: Library of America, 2004.

Verba, Sidney. "Conclusion: Comparative Political Culture." In *Political Culture and Political Development*, edited by Lucian W. Pye and Sidney Verba, 512–60. Princeton, NJ: Princeton University Press, 1965.

Wiarda, Howard J. *Ethnocentrism in Foreign Policy: Can We Understand the Third World?* Washington, DC: American Enterprise Institute for Public Policy Research, 1984.

4

Public Opinion
and Foreign Policy

Political culture, discussed in chapter 3, remains a rather vague concept. American political culture is always changing. Moreover, at this stage, it would be difficult for any of us to say precisely what American political culture is, and even then we may disagree strongly over whether we are a pragmatic or an idealistic people, religious or increasingly nonreligious. Political culture, it is said, is like Jell-O: it looks substantial, but if you try to nail it to the wall, it gets squishy and goes all over the place.

Public opinion, by contrast, is much more precise and accurate. It incorporates the views of Americans as expressed in systematic public opinion surveys. Public opinion surveys are more specific and concrete than are interpretations of political culture. In addition, when well done, such surveys give us real numbers and percentages about people's preferences. They force us to choose among alternative policies, and they provide nuanced interpretations of the data. Public opinion may be defined as the organized, expressed, systematic, and quantifiable voice of American political attitudes. And it takes us one step closer to the core of American foreign policy decision making.

Public opinion has a profound effect on how foreign policy leaders make decisions. All politicians deny, of course, that they are swayed by the polls or public opinion, but in fact public opinion influences decision making in a number of ways. It often determines a president's approach to an issue, setting limits on and ruling out certain options and indicating when to change course. Thus it often directly influences the actual policy decision. Since the Reagan administration, all presidents have had full-time pollsters in the White House.

Public opinion may also be conveyed to the president through the media, interest groups, parties, or members of Congress. We should have no doubt that public opinion is a major influence on U.S. foreign policy.

Public opinion changes, but on the big issues it usually changes slowly. It is estimated that a major presidential speech can change public opinion only by about 5 percent, a full-scale White House campaign even by a persuasive president may be able to change it by only 10 percent. Beyond those efforts, it is difficult to change public opinion to a larger degree because basic cultural values, such as the love of freedom and respect for the Constitution, are involved, and those change gradually.

Since World War II there have been few large shifts in American public opinion on foreign policy, but those that have occurred are crucial in understanding today's political dilemmas. First, in the course of the war and its aftermath, American public opinion went from being two-thirds isolationist to two-thirds internationalist. America had become a permanent player in world politics. Second, during the early decades of the Cold War (1946–66), the public strongly agreed, that same two-thirds, on U.S. strategy: a formidable defense, a tough foreign policy, and containment of the Soviet Union. A third period was ushered in with the Vietnam War. Isolationist sentiment remained constant, reflecting about one-third of the public's opinion, but internationalist sentiment was then split evenly between the pro-war, pro-defense elements (Cold War internationalism) and the antiwar, pro-change (liberal internationalism) elements. This three-way split in public opinion made it increasingly difficult to forge consensus or even a working majority on foreign policy.

This division persisted after the end of the Cold War, but the absence of any serious threat or enemy after 1991 made it easier, under Bill Clinton, to carry out a policy of liberal internationalism. Then, when the 9/11 attacks occurred, for a short while George W. Bush was able to rally public opinion in the cause of antiterrorism. As the wars in Iraq and Afghanistan began to go badly, however, the familiar—and largely unmanageable—divisions reasserted themselves: one-third isolationist (remain uninvolved), one-third liberal internationalist (democracy, human rights, global warming), and one-third conservative internationalist (strong military defense, defeat the terrorists). When the factions are so evenly split, yet so far apart, so that no one commands a majority, how can anyone conduct an effective foreign policy? Answer: only with great difficulty.

Public opinion is not only divided but it is also often uninformed, inchoate, and uncertain. Public opinion may also be confused and contradictory. Americans show an appalling lack of knowledge of history, geography, and international affairs. They often cannot locate different countries on a map, let alone identify their leaders or capital cities; one-third of the public cannot even identify the oceans on both sides of the United States. Regarding the Middle East, they do not know the differences between Shia and Sunni. Nor do they speak the languages of this area. How, one may ask, can we wage war, bring peace, or have a sensible foreign policy in this critical area if we do not speak its language(s) or even minimally understand its culture? We shall have more to say on the issue of knowledge, or the lack thereof, and foreign policy later in this chapter.

Polls and Polling

When using public opinion surveys, commonly known as polling, we need to be very careful. Many polls are inaccurate and strongly biased. The questions asked may be loaded, the pollsters are often untrained and unprofessional, and the number of persons interviewed too small to provide a representative sample. Other problems with polling include respondents who lie or tell pollsters what they think the pollsters want to hear, pollsters or questions that guide the respondents to a preferred answer, or samples that are biased because only those with an ax to grind participate.

Foreign policy analysts or practitioners therefore need to be careful about using polls and skeptical of their results. There are good and bad polls, and we need to be able to tell the difference. Among the most inaccurate are phone-in or e-mail surveys run by radio and television studios since only those with a strong vested interest will take the time to respond. Much the same applies to person-in-the-street interviews conducted by television reporters; they are almost never representative of public opinion.

Polls conducted by candidates, parties, or interest groups are seldom reliable because they are designed to show that person, party, or group in a favorable light. Because polls are expensive, local newspapers or television stations might limit the number of people polled; therefore, their respondent pool may be too small to be representative and produce suspect results. Even national polls where the television anchor solemnly opines that the margins of error are plus or minus 5 percent may be suspect because we don't know how many people were questioned, how the questions were phrased, or how representative was the sample. For example, most surveys underrepresent people in rural areas because polling in those areas is more difficult and expensive.

The best public opinion surveys are those conducted by large, reputable, professional, nationwide polling agencies like Gallup; Harris; the National Opinion Research Center; Penn, Schoen, and Berland Associates; Princeton Survey Research Associates; Quinnipiac University Polling Institute; Roper Center; Survey Research Center at the University of Michigan; and Zogby International. These surveys are professionally designed to avoid bias and professionally conducted by trained pollsters. The Council on Foreign Relations, the Pew Research Center for the People and the Press, and sometimes such major newspapers as the *New York Times* or the *Washington Post* conduct themselves or commission good public opinion surveys. In these polls the questions are carefully worded to avoid bias, a representative sample is used, and the results are carefully tabulated. When surveys are done correctly, they can be very revealing in foreign policy practice and analysis.

What, then, should you look for in a good poll?

1. The heterogeneity of the sample, or whether it reflects an accurate cross section of the entire nation.
2. The sample's size, which in such a large, complex nation as the United States, should be at least two thousand respondents to be representative.
3. The pollster's neutrality, that is, whether the pollster is unbiased and not paid by any group with a vested interest in the poll's outcome.
4. Fair, unbiased questions that are carefully phrased so they are not misleading or bias the outcome.

With these criteria firmly established, a good public opinion survey can be extremely useful. It can give us a sense of the pulse of the nation, which issues and countries are considered important, the balance between domestic and foreign issues, how well the president and Congress are doing their jobs, and the boundaries beyond which policy ought not go.

Public Opinion and Democratic Theory

American democracy is based on the assumption of a literate, educated, reasonably knowledgeable and informed public capable of making rational decisions about matters that concern them. The political theory that underlies American democracy is rooted in the Pilgrims' Mayflower compact, James Madison, Thomas Jefferson, and the Constitution. Our entire educational philosophy, to say nothing of the notion of one person, one vote, is based on the assumption of yeoman citizens doing their duty, becoming well informed, and voting their conscience. Democracy cannot function effectively without these features.

But we all know it doesn't work that way. Voters are not well informed, especially on issues of foreign affairs. Our election campaigns are often limited to sound bites and bumper stickers, with candidates advised to "stay on message" rather than discuss the issues in depth. Not surprisingly, therefore, only 15–20 percent of those eligible actually vote in local elections, and at the national level the turnout may be only 40–45 percent.

As public opinion surveys tell us Americans are poorly informed about international affairs, these results do not give us great confidence in the public's ability to understand and decide about foreign policy issues. They indicate the public cannot locate most of the countries where we are engaged or even identify whose side we are on in most disputes. These same opinion polls show roughly 30 percent of the public lack even rudimentary information about foreign policy issues: who is fighting, where, and what the disputes are. Another 40 percent has at least rudimentary knowledge for they read newspaper headlines, watch the evening news occasionally, and minimally comprehend the issues. Together, these two groups represent two-thirds to three-quarters of the public. That leaves about 25–30 percent who are considered "informed"; that is, they read a newspaper regularly, watch the news at least three times a week, and subscribe to a weekly newsmagazine. We can argue about whether this is enough to be "informed." Only about 1–2 percent may be called "well informed." In addition to the above criteria, the well-informed group watches an evening discussion show (*The NewsHour with Jim Lehrer* or others), votes regularly, pays attention to the issues, and has almost always graduated from college or university. As a student of foreign policy, you too are among this small elite.

Portents for the future are getting worse. The first two groups, the uninformed and minimally informed, are growing as the informed and well-informed groups shrink. Moreover, the latter groups are older and fading while the uninformed and minimally informed are younger. This situation is not a good sign for the future. The problem of a poorly informed electorate is likely to get worse before it gets better, for as many pundits decry the crisis in our education system, we see the long-term results of poor schools—a foreign policy too often based on ignorance.

These comments have major implications for democracy and democratic theory. If Americans are as poorly informed as the surveys indicate, then how can they make sound judgments about policy issues? How can our democracy be participatory if a majority of the electorate does not participate? How then can informed policy decisions on Iraq, China, Iran, Afghanistan, Palestine, etc. be made if the basis of knowledge is so weak? These troubling questions suggest that not only does the United States have a weak basis for enlightened foreign policy but that one of the basic prerequisites of a healthy democracy—an informed electorate—is also lacking. Indeed, the entire idea of representative democracy is challenged.

Implications of a Divided Public Opinion

At this stage there seems to be little consensus on American foreign policy—not just on Iraq but on almost all major issues. With public opinion left deeply divided since the Vietnam War, it has been very hard for our elected leaders to know what to do. The deep rifts in Congress and among foreign policy elites and think tanks often result in bitter rancor. Earlier the divisions in the electorate were labeled as isolationists, liberal internationalists, and conservative internationalists. Now it is time to spell out what these fundamental divisions, which are as deep as our partisan, red state–blue state divide, mean for our foreign policy.

The first group, the isolationists, is left over from the pre–World War II period but now has new life from the libertarian movement and intellectual respectability from the Washington-based Cato Institute. The old isolationists wanted little to do with the outside world. They favored protectionist barriers to keep out foreign products, wanted the United States to stay out of the world wars, and were opposed to the founding of the United Nations. The newer isolationists are more sophisticated and have a stronger argument. They favor a strong, unilateral, American defense; are worried about America's loss of jobs to overseas competition as well as unchecked and often illegal immigration diluting American culture; and are opposed to the United States ceding its sovereignty to unaccountable international organizations. Thus they see the United Nations as not doing much good, they view NATO as useless now that the Cold War is over, and they believe the United States should not get involved in peacekeeping or democracy building in such messy and maybe hopeless places as Afghanistan,

Bosnia, Haiti, Iraq, or Somalia. These positions are not at all "nutty"; indeed, many mainstream foreign policy experts are moving in Cato's direction.

Internationalist opinion, once so strong and unified in support of the Cold War, has now split into two equal factions. Its big division occurred in the 1970s over the Vietnam War, and it is being repeated, with almost the exact same lineup of forces, over Iraq. One group, the liberal internationalists, favors: following a strong democracy–human rights program, getting the United States involved in nation building, sponsoring humanitarian interventions in Darfur and elsewhere, using the United Nations and other multilateral organizations as the means for solving disputes, signing the Kyoto Protocol to the UN Framework Convention on Climate Change on global warming, abolishing nuclear weapons, and upholding the law-of-the-sea treaty as well as the anti–land mines accord. It is generally antimilitary and would greatly reduce the Defense Department's budget. Politically, the liberal-internationalist position is associated with the Democratic Party; with idealism; with Presidents Jimmy Carter, Bill Clinton, and Barack Obama.

Conservative internationalists take up a diametrically opposed position. They favor a strong defense and virtually unlimited spending for the Defense Department. They have little use for the United Nations or other international organizations—except maybe a defense alliance like NATO—because they want the United States to be able to act unilaterally in the world, especially in the war on terrorism, without being hindered by what they see as "worthless" multilateral agencies. They favor democracy and human rights but, except for the neoconservative faction within this group, do not believe the United States should impose democracy in countries that are ill prepared for it. Conservative internationalists tend to think that the anti–land mines treaty, global warming, humanitarian interventions, or nation building should not be high U.S. priorities. The conservative internationalist position can be summed up in the phrase "peace through strength." Politically, that position is associated with the Republican Party; with Presidents Dwight Eisenhower, Richard Nixon, Ronald Reagan, George H. W. Bush, and, in not very competent hands, George W. Bush; and with presidential candidate and senator John McCain, who is almost the personification of this position.

Obviously the three positions outlined above are far apart. But the problem in foreign policymaking runs even deeper than that. For instance, since two-thirds of the country are internationalists, an isolationist candidate cannot win the presidency. Further, look what happens when any one of these three factions pushes new legislation. On the one hand, suppose a liberal internationalist wants to push a strong democracy/human rights/peace/nation-building/humanitarian intervention agenda. That program or its separate parts will be strongly opposed by both the isolationist and the conservative internationalist factions, or two-thirds of the public and their congressmen; that resistance is enough to block any legislation. On the opposite side of the political fence, suppose a conservative internationalist president wants to give more resources to NATO, send more troops into Iraq, and do more nation building in Afghanistan. These policies will again face blockage, or the opposition of both isolationists and the liberal internationalists.

The result is that almost every policy is going to face a more or less automatic two-thirds majority against it. In an emergency, such as the 9/11 attacks, a president is able to garner sufficient support to overcome these blockages; otherwise, about the only policy that two of these factions can agree on is approving more money for defense purposes, which both isolationists and conservative internationalists support. No wonder the Pentagon seems to always come out ahead in these budget battles! Meanwhile, one can see how likely is the other outcome—division, fragmentation, gridlock, and paralysis—on virtually every issue.

Attitudes on the Issues

Part of the problem of U.S. foreign policy derives from the fact that few Americans are interested in the subject. They are not much interested in other countries unless those countries have a direct impact on the United States. When Americans are queried about their interest in news concerning other countries, only about a third say they pay attention (see figure 4.1).

Several things are worth noting in this figure. Note that interest in local community, state, and national news far surpasses interest in news about other countries, which helps explain why television gives so little attention to the subject and why media outlets are closing many of their foreign bureaus. Note too that while interest in other countries is low, that interest perks up when the focus is on U.S. relations with that country. Thus U.S. foreign affairs reporters, to get their stories on TV, always try to give them a U.S.-oriented angle. Third, these figures concerning the U.S. public's interest in other countries are far lower than the levels of interest exhibited by the public in other developed countries, including

Figure 4.1 U.S. Public's Attentiveness to the News

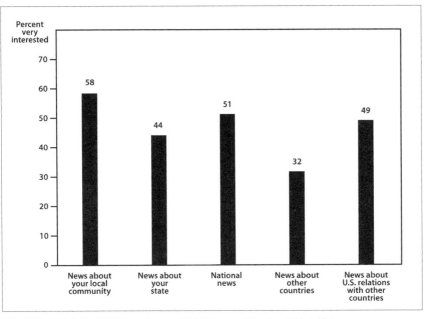

Source: John E. Reilly, periodic (5-year) surveys for the Chicago Council on Global Affairs.

Great Britain, France, and Germany. The latter's greater curiosity probably relates to the countries' close proximity, shared history, and longtime interest in foreign affairs versus America's history of isolationism. Finally we should note that developments after 9/11—fear of terrorism, the Iraq and Afghanistan wars, and the war on terrorism—have coaxed Americans, especially young people, to pay greater attention to international affairs.

A second way of measuring the U.S. public's interest in foreign policy is to ask people if they think it's best for the country's future if it takes an active part in world affairs. Figure 4.2 provides an interesting answer. Note how consistently over sixty years the response has stayed between 60 and 70 percent. It went over 70 percent briefly in the mid-1950s during the height of the Cold War and dipped below 60 percent in 1979–80 while tensions between the United States and the Soviet Union relaxed. The main point is that the public's opinion regarding America's active role in world affairs has remained steady. Since Vietnam, however, two-thirds of public opinion is evenly split between favoring either liberal or conservative internationalist approaches. While close to 70 percent

Figure 4.2 Approval of United States Taking Active Part in World Affairs

Percentage who think it will be best for the future
of the country if we take an active part in world affairs.

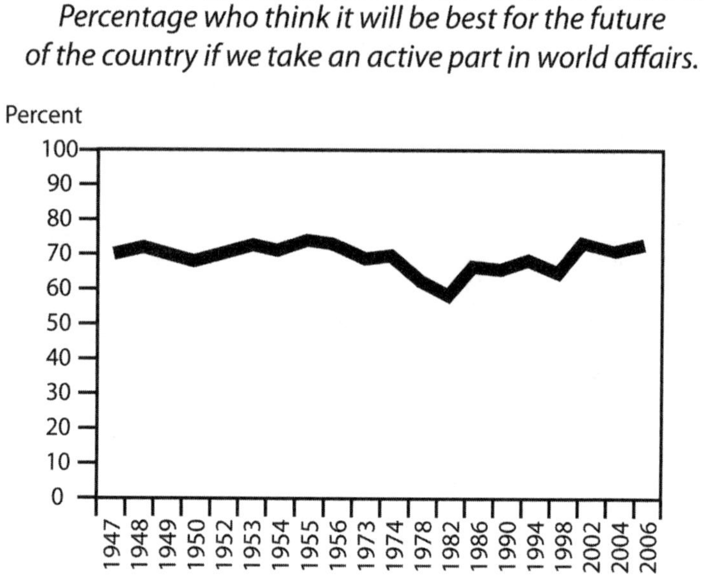

Note: Trend data from 1947 through 1973 come from national surveys conducted by NORC in Chicago. The 1974 survey was conducted by Louis Harris and Associates, Inc. Data from1947 to 1998 were collected using face-to-face surveys; 2002 data were collected using telephone surveys; and 2004 and 2006 data were collected using Internet surveys.

Source: The Chicago Council on Global Affairs, *Global Views* (2006).

favor the United States playing an active internationalist role, another third does not. The public is equally skeptical of nation-building activities.

Next, figure 4.3 covers the issue of threats to U.S. vital interests. When asked what they think will be the biggest critical threats to vital U.S. interests over the next ten years, as might be expected, 74 percent of Americans list international terrorism first, and the possibility of unfriendly countries becoming nuclear powers comes in second with 69 percent. Especially interesting given spiraling energy costs, disruption to the nation's energy supply now comes in third, though when the previous survey was taken in 2004 that threat was not even on the list. The possibility of a China-Taiwan or India-Pakistan clash is low on the list, reflecting the publics' beliefs that being far away, these countries' conflicts are less problematic and that the United States should not get directly or militarily involved in such confrontations.

Figure 4.3 Critical Threats to U.S. Vital Interests

Percentage who see each of the following as a crucial threat to U.S. vital interests in the next ten years.

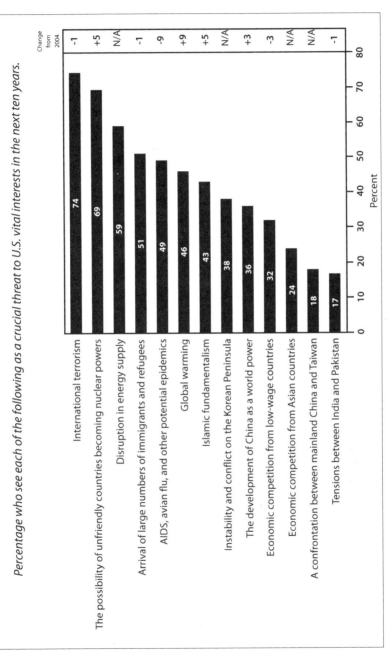

	Change from 2004
International terrorism	74	−1
The possibility of unfriendly countries becoming nuclear powers	69	+5
Disruption in energy supply	59	N/A
Arrival of large numbers of immigrants and refugees	51	−1
AIDS, avian flu, and other potential epidemics	49	−9
Global warming	46	+9
Islamic fundamentalism	43	+5
Instability and conflict on the Korean Peninsula	38	N/A
The development of China as a world power	36	+3
Economic competition from low-wage countries	32	−3
Economic competition from Asian countries	24	N/A
A confrontation between mainland China and Taiwan	18	N/A
Tensions between India and Pakistan	17	−1

Percent

Source: Chicago Council on Global Affairs, *Global Views* (2006).

Figure 4.4 U.S. Foreign Policy Goals

Percentage who think the following should be very important foreign policy goals of United States.

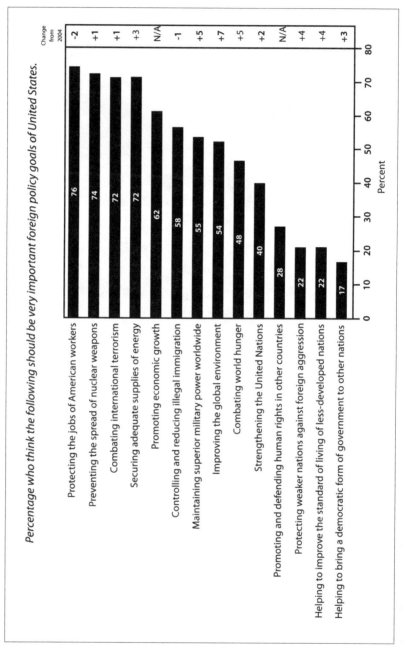

	Percent	Change from 2004
Protecting the jobs of American workers	76	-2
Preventing the spread of nuclear weapons	74	+1
Combating international terrorism	72	+1
Securing adequate supplies of energy	72	+3
Promoting economic growth	62	N/A
Controlling and reducing illegal immigration	58	-1
Maintaining superior military power worldwide	55	+5
Improving the global environment	54	+7
Combating world hunger	48	+5
Strengthening the United Nations	40	+2
Promoting and defending human rights in other countries	28	N/A
Protecting weaker nations against foreign aggression	22	+4
Helping to improve the standard of living of less-developed nations	22	+4
Helping to bring a democratic form of government to other nations	17	+3

Source: Chicago Council on Global Affairs, *Global Views* (2006).

Figure 4.4 reports on the goals of U.S. foreign policy. This graph overlaps in interesting ways with figure 4.3. Note that preventing the spread of nuclear weapons, combating terrorism, and securing adequate supplies of energy are all, again, high on the list. But topping everything else, with the support of 76 percent of the public, is the goal of protecting the jobs of American workers. In short, even in our foreign policy, the top goal, jobs, is a domestic consideration. That emphasis explains why our presidential candidates talk about this issue more than any other and are often opposed publicly to those trade pacts with other nations that the public sees as harming U.S. jobs. This priority also reminds us of the aphorism that you can lose an election if you lack foreign policy expertise, but to win you have to have a solid, domestic economic plan. The bad news for idealists in the liberal internationalist position in this figure is how low on the list are strengthening the United Nations, promoting human rights and democracy, and offering foreign aid to less-developed nations.

An important foreign policy issue is which countries and organizations the U.S. public sees as friendly, helpful, and supportive of U.S. goals and priorities. These findings are presented in figures 4.5 and 4.6 in the form of thermometer readings, or how warm or cold (less than 50 percent) the public feels about certain countries and institutions, respectively.

Note that all the countries toward which Americans have the warmest feelings—Canada, Great Britain, Australia—are English-speaking nations that are products of the same legal and political tradition as we are. Once enemies but now allies, Japan and Germany come next, followed by Israel, Mexico, France, and India. Other European, Latin American, and East Asian countries are farther down the list, in the "cooler" category. Saudi Arabia falls below these but is the highest-ranking Arab country. At the bottom, at "ice-cold rank," are what George W. Bush termed the "axis of evil"—Iraq, Iran, and North Korea—along with Cuba.

The thermometer readings for international organizations do not tell us very much. Topping the list, but still not very high, are the World Health Organization and international human rights groups—probably because their names make it sound as if they do good work. The United Nations registers at 55 degrees, which is tepid. The International Monetary Fund (IMF) gets bad publicity as do, frequently, multinational corporations. I suspect what this figure mainly shows is that most Americans know little about any of these organizations and therefore are mostly lukewarm or indifferent to them.

Figure 4.5 Thermometer of Nations

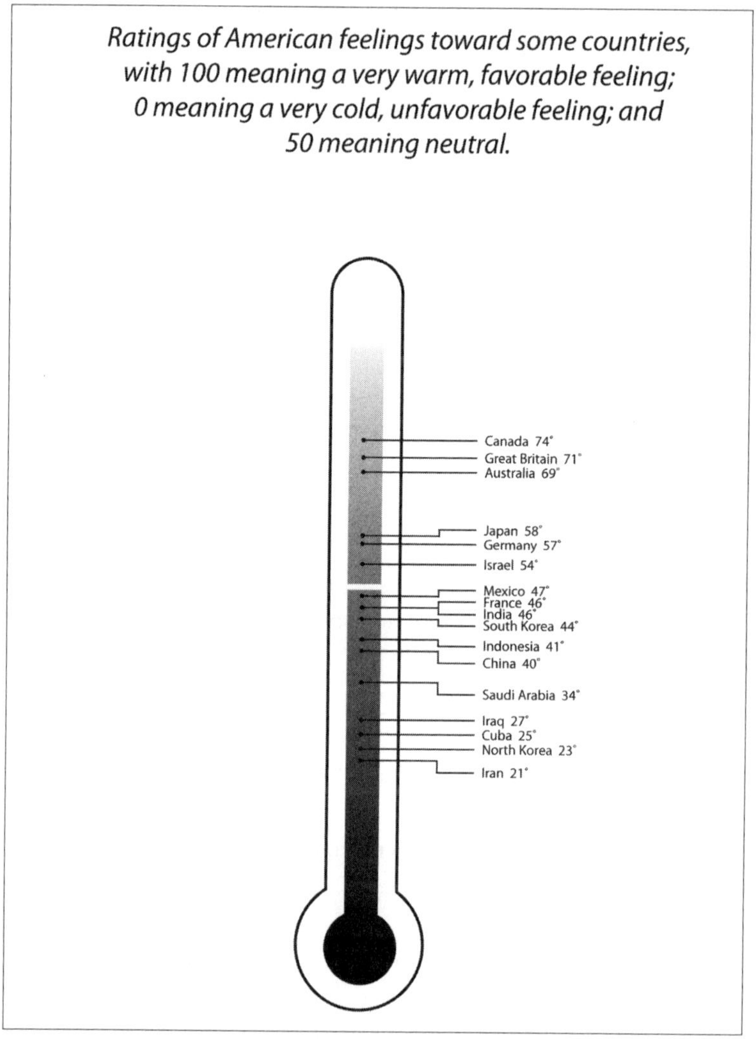

*Ratings of American feelings toward some countries,
with 100 meaning a very warm, favorable feeling;
0 meaning a very cold, unfavorable feeling; and
50 meaning neutral.*

Canada 74°
Great Britain 71°
Australia 69°

Japan 58°
Germany 57°
Israel 54°

Mexico 47°
France 46°
India 46°
South Korea 44°
Indonesia 41°
China 40°

Saudi Arabia 34°

Iraq 27°
Cuba 25°
North Korea 23°

Iran 21°

Source: Chicago Council on Global Affairs, *Global Views* (2006).

Figure 4.7 presents some contradictions and paradoxes, but it is a crucial table, indicating where and under what circumstances the public might be willing to send in U.S. troops. What is surprising is that the top three categories all concern humanitarian issues: stopping genocide, dealing with a humanitarian crisis, and intervening to stop the killing in Darfur. On the one hand, this

Figure 4.6 Thermometer of Organizations

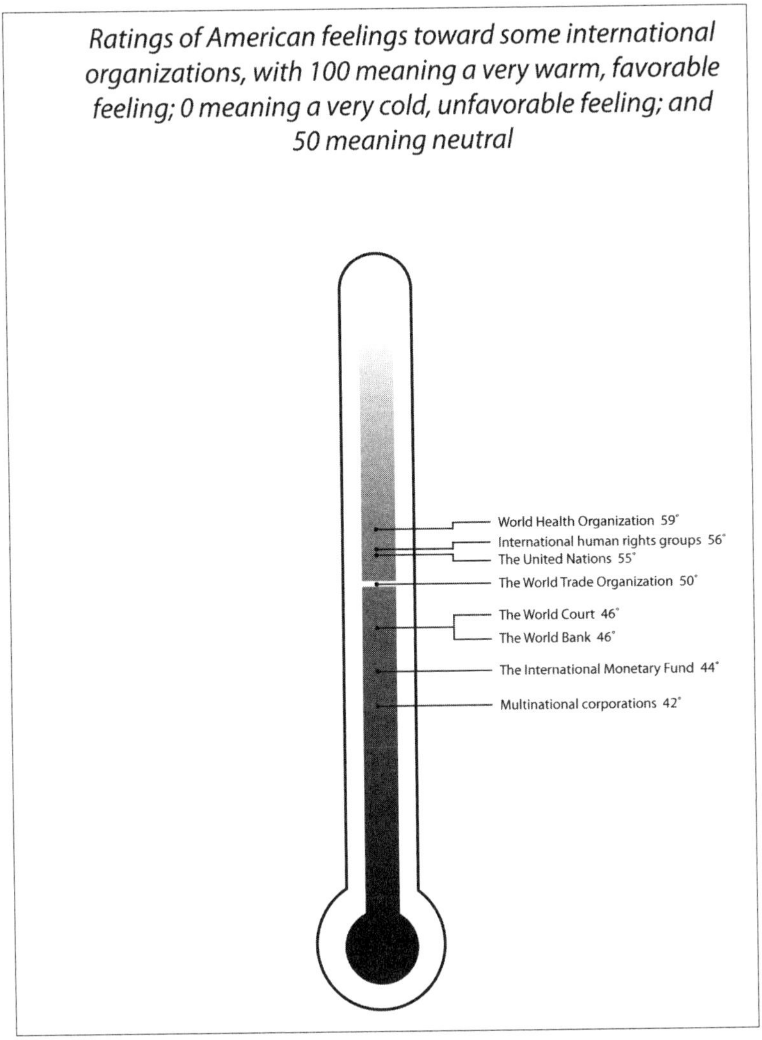

Ratings of American feelings toward some international organizations, with 100 meaning a very warm, favorable feeling; 0 meaning a very cold, unfavorable feeling; and 50 meaning neutral

World Health Organization 59°
International human rights groups 56°
The United Nations 55°

The World Trade Organization 50°

The World Court 46°
The World Bank 46°

The International Monetary Fund 44°

Multinational corporations 42°

Source: Chicago Council on Global Affairs, *Global Views* (2006).

table shows the American public to support humanitarian efforts; but on the other hand, it seems to contradict other data presented that two-thirds of the public does *not* want the United States to be the world's fireman and policeman, responding to every international 911 call. Equally surprising is how low on the list (45 percent) is the public's willingness to use U.S. troops to ensure our

Figure 4.7 Public Support for Sending U.S. Troops Overseas

Regarding circumstances that might justify using U.S. troops in other parts of the world.
Percentage who favor or oppose the use of U.S. troops overseas in the following situations.

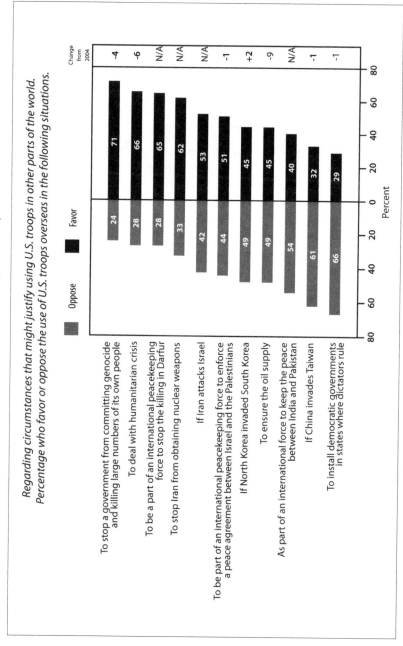

Source: Chicago Council on Global Affairs, *Global Views* (2006).

nation's oil supplies, especially given the finding in figure 4.3 that 59 percent thought protecting the U.S. energy supply was vital. But note in both this figure and figure 4.4 that building democracy in other countries is lowest on the list of priorities.

On international trade (figure 4.8), the public appears to have gotten it just about right. Most respondents believe international trade benefits consumers like themselves (70 percent) and is good for their own standard of living (64 percent); but only 37 percent believe trade creates jobs in the United States while an even lower number, 30 percent, believe trade provides job security for U.S.

Figure 4.8 Impact of International Trade on Selected Variables

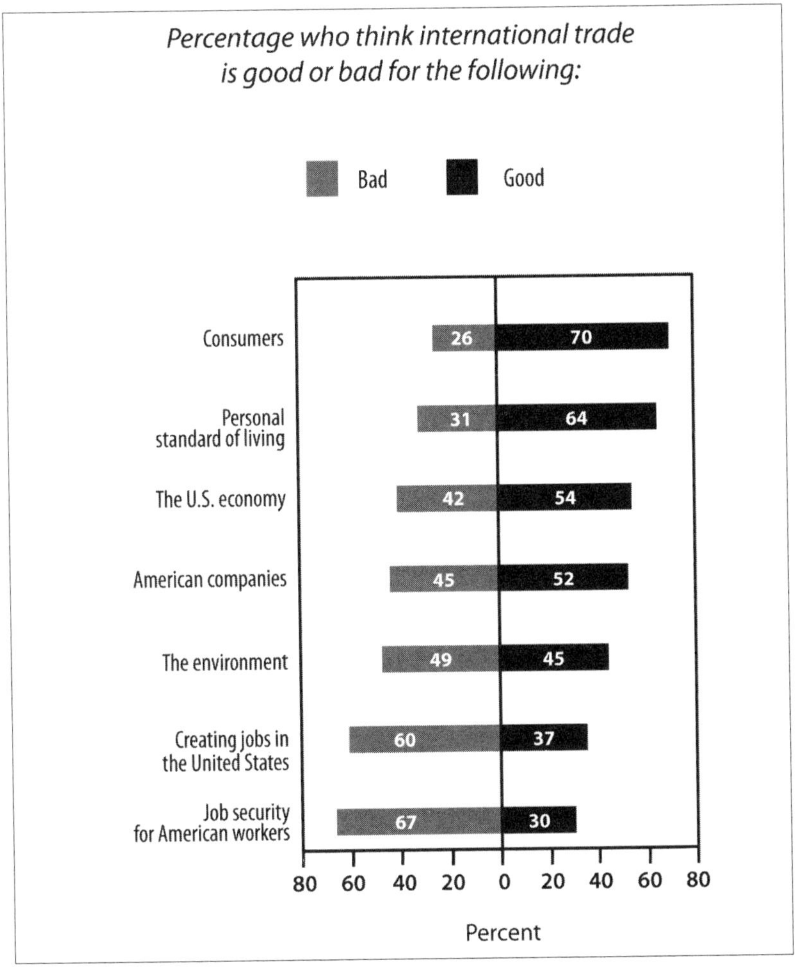

Percentage who think international trade is good or bad for the following:

	Bad	Good
Consumers	26	70
Personal standard of living	31	64
The U.S. economy	42	54
American companies	45	52
The environment	49	45
Creating jobs in the United States	60	37
Job security for American workers	67	30

Percent

Source: Chicago Council on Global Affairs, *Global Views* (2006).

workers. That sounds about right: we all benefit from international trade in the form of lower prices, but some sectors of the U.S. economy, unable to compete with China and other low-wage countries, will lose jobs.

The data provided on another hot issue, immigration (figure 4.9), is also clear and quite consistent. First, the number of people who believe legal immigration should be increased is a small but often vocal minority, hovering between 2002 and 2006 at around 8–12 percent. Second, the number of people who believe legal immigration should be kept the same has increased from 30 to 40 percent over this four-year period. Finally and most politically controversial, the percentage of people who think legal (not to mention illegal) immigration should be decreased has gone down from 60 to about 46 percent. These and other surveys indicate three things: the public is against illegal immigration, it favors legal immigration, and it wants the U.S. government to regain control of its borders.

Another hot issue these days is global warming. The problem with using survey data on this issue is that, with a particularly cold winter or hot summer, with great variations in these seasons, and depending on the region in which

Figure 4.9 Views on Legal Immigration Levels

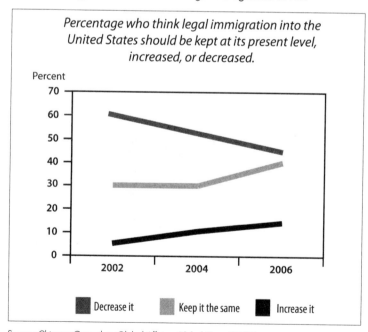

Source: Chicago Council on Global Affairs, *Global Views* (2006).

Figure 4.10 Views on Global Warming

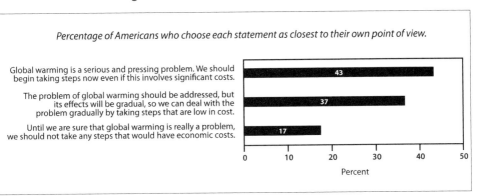

Percentage of Americans who choose each statement as closest to their own point of view.

Global warming is a serious and pressing problem. We should begin taking steps now even if this involves significant costs. — 43

The problem of global warming should be addressed, but its effects will be gradual, so we can deal with the problem gradually by taking steps that are low in cost. — 37

Until we are sure that global warming is really a problem, we should not take any steps that would have economic costs. — 17

Percent

Source: Chicago Council on Global Affairs, *Global Views* (2006).

respondents live, the numbers can vary greatly. After a cold winter, the number of those fearing global warming goes way down, whereas hot, steamy summer days make that same number go up significantly. The best statistics available at present (see figure 4.10) show that 17 percent of the public are unconvinced that global warming is really a problem, 37 percent believe it is a problem that should be addressed in the long term, and 43 percent (but still a minority) see it as a serious and pressing problem. Depending on the seasons, however, these numbers can change quickly.

Now let us get down to some really nitty-gritty issues, the public's attitudes about when to use force in international affairs. First, we need to recognize that among all American institutions, the one that respondents trust most is the armed forces. During Bush's last years, the president's popularity was low (25 percent) and that of Congress even lower (14 percent). By contrast, among various institutions, as shown in figure 4.11, the armed forces receive nearly 70 percent approval ratings and are believed to be efficient, honest, dedicated, and capable of getting the job done. Perhaps that is why Americans often favor a military solution over a diplomatic one and the Defense Department over the State Department, the CIA, or Homeland Security. The rest of the government may be "broken," but the public believes that, virtually alone, the armed services are well run and capable of accomplishing almost any mission. Any vote in Congress that seems to shortchange our troops in the field cannot be supported. Thus Congress was consistently unable to muster the votes necessary to force a withdrawal from Iraq.

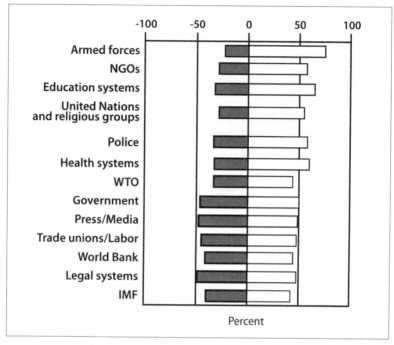

Figure 4.11 Public's Trust in Institutions

Source: WEF/Gallop/Environics Polls

Table 4.1 shows how many Americans still believe in the old adage of peace through strength. The historic basis of U.S. deterrence strategy dictates that the United States should be so strong that no enemy would dare to attack us. Note that as of 2007, 72 percent of Republicans accept this logic, but only 46 percent of independents and 40 percent of Democrats do. Does this signal that Americans are less willing to accept classic deterrence theory and that they are unwilling to spend the necessary funds to sustain the military's strength? Increasingly, Democrats seem to be saying that the United States should rely on international agencies like the United Nations to maintain peace, but that strategy also has major problems and is not popular with the electorate.

Figure 4.12 provides an interesting trend line that shows Americans' desire to "get even" with any country that tries to take advantage of the United States. Note how the line indicating the U.S. public's support of a retaliatory response peaked in 2002 right after the September 11, 2001, terrorist attacks, when the U.S. public's desire to get even with Muslim countries was high. Since then

Table 4.1 Ensuring Peace through Military Strength

| | Agree (Percent) | | | | |
	1997	1999	2002	2003	2007
Total	57	55	62	53	49
Republican	65	70	72	69	72
Democrat	56	53	55	44	40
Independent	54	50	62	51	46
Conservative	—	—	71	61	67
Moderate	—	—	61	55	43
Liberal	—	—	49	33	31

Source: Pew Research Center, "Trends in Political Values and Core Attitudes: 1987–2007" (2007).

tempers have cooled, and the number is now down to 40 percent. What do you think a new terrorist attack would do to this number?

Table 4.2 tells us how many Americans are willing to fight for their country whether it is right or wrong. Note that the percentage of whites who are willing is far higher than that of blacks, but is that difference because blacks recognize that they are more likely to be the ones doing the fighting and dying? College-educated people are less willing to fight than are those who did not attend college, but veterans are more willing to do so than nonveterans are. Almost two-thirds of the polled Republicans said they are willing to fight, but less than half of the Democrats are. That gap explains American attitudes toward the Iraq War: Democrats believe it is the wrong war at the wrong time and therefore want to pull out, and Republicans, while uncertain about the war, were nonetheless willing to stay the course.

A related issue, shown in table 4.3, has to do with Americans' patriotism. The table measures the changes in their patriotism over an eight-year period, 1999–2007. First note the total figures: the percentage of Americans who self-identify as "very patriotic" stays rather consistent, hovering around 50 percent. Note too that the figures for Republicans are considerably higher than they are for Democrats and independents. These figures reached their highest overall

Figure 4.12 Public's Support for Retaliatory Responses after Any Attack

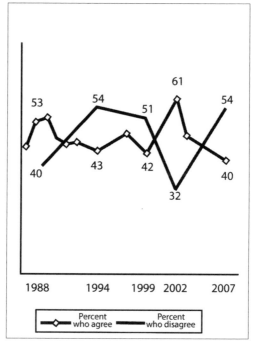

Source: Pew Research Center, "Trends in Political Values and Core Attitudes: 1987–2007" (2007).

level—56 percent—in 2003, after the 9/11 attacks and when the Iraq War began. Since then, however, the numbers have declined, considerably for Republicans and modestly for Democrats.

Tables 4.4 and 4.5 concern the use of torture. The survey data in table 4.4 reflects whether respondents agreed that torture could be justified against suspected terrorists in order to gain key information. Only between 12 and 18 percent believe torture can be used "often." However, 28–31 percent think it can be used "sometimes," and 19–25 percent believe it can be used "rarely." Combining the three categories, a majority believes torture can be justified. About 30 percent of the population, meanwhile, say torture should never be used.

Table 4.5 focuses on the current 29 percent who believe torture should *never* be used. Note that blacks are somewhat more opposed to using torture than are whites; this is perhaps a reflection of the black history of slavery. Women are more opposed to employing torture than men but not by much, and older people

Table 4.2 Willingness to Fight for Our Country, Right or Wrong

	Agree %	Disagree %	Don't Know %
Total	50	45	5
White	53	42	5
Black	31	64	5
College grad	44	49	7
Some college	50	44	6
High school/less	53	43	4
Republican	63	32	5
Democrat	44	52	4
Independent	50	46	4
Veteran household	60	34	6
Nonveteran	48	47	5

Source: Pew Research Center, "Trends in Political Values and Core Attitudes: 1987–2007" (2007).

Table 4.3 Percent Who Claim to Be Very Patriotic

	Agree				Change
	1999	2002	2003	2007	2003–7
Total	49	54	56	49	-7
Republican	64	63	71	61	-10
Democrat	49	50	48	45	-3
Independent	40	50	54	47	-7

Source: Pew Research Center, "Trends in Political Values and Core Attitudes: 1987–2007" (2007).

are more opposed to its use than younger folks are. On a political scale there is a vast margin, with far fewer conservative Republicans opposing torture's use than liberal Democrats. When we test for religion, the differences are slim: white evangelicals are slightly less opposed than white mainline churches, and both Catholics and secularists are less opposed than either of the Protestant groups.

Table 4.4 Views on Whether Torture Can Be Justified against
Suspected Terrorists to Gain Key Information

Response	July 2004 %	March 2005 %	Oct. 2005 %	Oct. 2006 %	Jan. 2007 %
Often	15	15	15	18	12
Sometimes	28	30	31	28	31
Rarely	21	24	17	19	25
Never	32	27	32	32	29
Don't Know	4	4	5	3	3

Source: Pew Research Center, "Trends in Political Values and Core Attitudes: 1987–2007"
(2007).

Table 4.5 Those Opposed to Torture

	Percent
Total	29
White	28
Black	37
Men	28
Women	31
18-29	25
30-49	27
50-64	34
65+	36
Conservative Republican	19
Moderate-liberal Republican	24
Independent	28
Conservative-moderate Democrat	31
Liberal Democrat	45
White evangelical churchgoers	28
White mainline churchgoers	31
Catholics	26
Secularlists	25

Source: Pew Research Center, "Trends in Political Values and Core Attitudes:
1987–2007" (2007).

Figure 4.13 reflects attitudes regarding an interesting but abstract question about going to war. It does not ask specifically about the United States (although that is implied); rather, it asks when countries (any country), on their own, can decide if they will go to war. Ninety percent say countries are justified in going to war if another country attacks them first. Seventy-nine percent say war is justified if they have strong evidence they are in imminent danger of being attacked by another country. President George W. Bush used this explanation in preparing his preemption doctrine. We will call the third bar in the graph the "Iran or North Korea option": 60 percent of the public believes we can go to war if we have strong evidence that another country—Iran or North Korea—is acquiring weapons of mass destruction that could be used against us. Fifty-eight percent believe we can go to war to preserve our territorial integrity while fewer—50 percent—maintain war is justified to prevent another country from supporting an insurgency within their own country. Less than a majority, or 47 percent, support going to war to preserve access to vital reserves such as oil.

Now let us explore the acid test: when and over what issues are Americans, specifically, willing to go to war and not simply engage in peacekeeping or police actions. Those questions are explored in figure 4.14. The answer is, there are not many circumstances in which Americans are willing to go to war. Fifty-eight percent say war is justified if Russia invades Western Europe, but with the Cold War over and Russia's threat greatly reduced, an invasion of Western Europe is highly unlikely anytime soon. If Iran invades Saudi Arabia and therefore threatens our oil supplies, jobs, and lifestyles, 52 percent say they are willing to go to war. But if the government of our neighbor Mexico is threatened by revolution or civil war, less than half, or 48 percent, are in favor of intervening militarily. For the next five possibilities, less than half would agree to use force if Russia tries to overthrow a democratic government in Eastern Europe, if North Korea invades the South, if Arab forces invade Israel, if Japan is invaded, and if Taiwan is attacked by China. The lowest-ranking option on the list—if the Philippines is threatened by revolution or civil war—confirms the findings in figure 4.4: the public is unwilling to get involved in police actions in the third world or to engage in democracy or nation-building campaigns there.

Overall, this table shows that Americans, perhaps weary with the wars in Iraq and Afghanistan, are reluctant to use American forces in war. They now concur that there are few circumstances in which war can be justified.

Figure 4.13 Determining Other Countries' Rights to Go to War

Percentage who think countries, on their own, should or should not have the right to go to war with another country they believe may pose a threat to them.

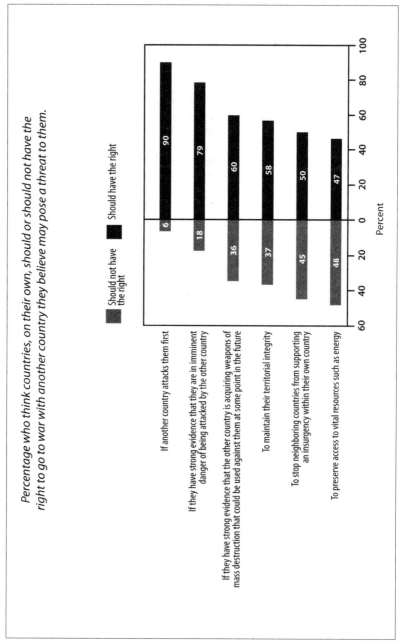

Source: Chicago Council on Global Affairs, *Global Views* (2006).

Figure 4.14 Issues that Call for Using U.S. Troops

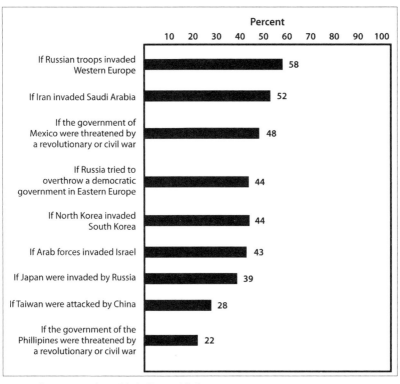

Source: Chicago Council on Global Affairs, *Global Views* (2006).

Influence on Policymakers

The influence of public opinion on policymaking is often hard to measure accurately. For one thing, public opinion is volatile and can change easily. Second, television and its coverage of dramatic, bloody, and even revolting events in Haiti, Somalia, or Darfur can change the public's view. Third, a president who is a skillful communicator, such as Reagan, Clinton, or Obama, can influence public opinion somewhat by how he frames the issues, forcing the public to see them in a new light. Nevertheless, there are limits imposed by public opinion that even a strong president cannot much alter, although it would be interesting to speculate if a forceful president could elevate some of the issues presented in figure 4.14 to a level where a majority would be willing to go to war over them.

How then does public opinion have an impact on foreign policymaking?

1. Public opinion directly affects the actions a president takes. All presidents follow the polls closely, and, despite their protests that they do only what's good for the country, they tend to do what the polls tell them is most popular and helps them get reelected.

2. Public opinion narrows the range of options available to a president. For example, reading figure 4.14, a president would be severely hard-pressed to use U.S. military forces in any but the direst circumstances. Public opinion helps define the confines, or the acceptable range, within which a president may operate.

3. Public opinion may force a president to do something about an issue he prefers to ignore, even if his actions are mainly symbolic and he prefers other options. In response to public opinion, a president may set up a task force to study an issue, give a speech, or establish a commission. All of these steps are designed to give the appearance of doing something tangible without really making significant changes. In taking these symbolic actions, a president may be playing for time, exploring other possibilities, or waiting until the issue goes away, all the while seeking to sway public opinion toward his own preferred action.

4. A skillful president can change or redirect public opinion, but even the best communicator as president can nudge public opinion only by 5 to 10 percent. It's much better for a president to change the question or reframe the debate. For example, instead of saying we're in Iraq for oil or strategic reasons, he can call it a part of the "worldwide struggle for freedom and democracy."

5. Presidents and members of Congress in tight reelection races pay closer attention to public opinion than candidates in safe races. The closer the election, the more the candidate is likely to pay attention to the polls and to tell the voters what they want to hear.

Democracy, Division, and Public Opinion

The discussion in this chapter leads to a mixed view of the role of public opinion and foreign policy in a democracy. On the one hand, the general public is woefully ill informed on most foreign policy issues and even on the geographic location, main actors, and the stakes involved in the key regions, issues, and countries where the United States is involved. How can we make informed decisions—the democratic ideal—if so many of our citizens are poorly informed?

On the other hand, public opinion is also deeply divided. Vietnam was the turning point and also the source of the fundamental rift in foreign policy approaches among isolationism, liberal internationalism, and conservative internationalism. This three-way divide means it is easy to get a 60–70 percent majority against most issues but almost impossible to get a majority for anything. The end of the Cold War compounded the problem by depriving us of the enemy, the now-defunct Soviet Union, against whom public opinion could be mobilized. Who or what now fills that role: Iraq, Iran, China, international terrorism, or Islamic fundamentalism? The answer is, we don't know. Until we do or until we discover a new foreign policy role or a new adversary, public opinion about foreign policy—and hence its impact on our political leaders—is likely to remain confused and divided.

Suggested Reading

Almond, Gabriel A. *The American People and Foreign Policy*. New York: Praeger, 1967.

Baum, Matthew A. "Going Private: Public Opinion, Presidential Rhetoric, and the Domestic Politics of Audience Costs in U.S. Foreign Policy Crises." *Journal of Conflict Resolution* 48, no. 5 (2004): 603–31.

Cohen, Bernard Cecil. *The Public's Impact on Foreign Policy*. Boston: Little, Brown, 1972.

Dallek, Robert. *The American Style of Foreign Policy: Cultural Politics and Foreign Affairs*. New York: Knopf, 1983.

Deibel, Terry L. *Presidents, Public Opinion, and Power: The Nixon, Carter, and Reagan Years*. New York: Foreign Policy Association, 1987.

Entman, Robert M. *Projections of Power: Framing News, Public Opinion, and U.S. Foreign Policy*. Chicago: University of Chicago Press, 2004.

Gergen, David. "The Hardening Mood toward Foreign Policy." *Public Opinion* (February/March 1980): 12–13.

Holsti, Ole R. *Public Opinion and American Foreign Policy*. Rev. ed. Ann Arbor: University of Michigan Press, 2004.

Jentleson, Bruce W., and Rebecca L. Britton. "Still Pretty Prudent: Post–Cold War American Public Opinion on the Use of Military Force." *Journal of Conflict Resolution* 42, no. 4 (1998): 395–417.

Maggiotto, Michael A., and Eugene R. Wittkopf. "American Public Attitudes toward Foreign Policy." *International Studies Quarterly* 25, no. 4 (1981): 601–31.

Martin, William. "The Christian Right and American Foreign Policy." *Foreign Policy* 114 (1999): 66–80.

Oldendick, Robert W., and Barbara Ann Bardes. "Mass and Elite Foreign Policy Opinions." *Public Opinion Quarterly* 46, no. 3 (1982): 368–82.

Rielly, John E. "The American Mood: A Foreign Policy of Self-Interest." *Foreign Policy* 34 (1979): 74–86.

———. "American Opinion: Continuity, Not Reaganism." *Foreign Policy* 50 (1983): 86–104.

———. "Americans and the World: A Survey at Century's End." *Foreign Policy* 114 (1999): 97–114.

———. "America's State of Mind." *Foreign Policy* 66 (1987): 39–56.

———. "The Public Mood at Mid-Decade." *Foreign Policy* 98 (1995): 76–93.

Rogers, W. C., B. Stubler, and D. Koenig. "A Comparison of Informed and General Public Opinion in U.S. Foreign Policy." *Public Opinion Quarterly* (Summer 1967): 242–52.

Rosenau, James N. *The Attentive Public and Foreign Policy: A Theory of Growth and Some New Evidence.* Princeton, NJ: Center of International Studies, Princeton University, 1968.

Schneider, W. "Elite and Public Opinion: The Alliance's New Fissure?" *Public Opinion* 6 (1983): 5–8.

Simon, Jeffrey D. "Social Position and American Foreign Policy Attitudes: 1952–1972." *Journal of Peace Research* 17, no. 1 (1980): 9–28.

Sobel, Richard. *The Impact of Public Opinion on U.S. Foreign Policy since Vietnam: Constraining the Colossus.* New York: Oxford University Press, 2001.

Verba, Sidney, and others. "Public Opinion and the War in Vietnam." *American Political Science Review* 61, no. 2 (1967): 317–33.

Wittkopf, Eugene R. "Elites and Masses: Another Look at Attitudes toward America's World Role." *International Studies Quarterly* 31, no. 2 (1987): 131–59.

Wittkopf, Eugene R., and Michael A. Maggiotto. "Elites and Masses: A Comparative Analysis of Attitudes toward America's World Role." *Journal of Politics* 45, no. 2 (1983): 303–34.

5

The Media
and Foreign Policy

The United States, as we saw in chapter 3, has a distinctive political culture that affects foreign policy in many important ways, and in Chapter 4 we examined public opinion's impact on foreign policy. We are now ready to analyze how this special American political culture and the public opinions of Americans get translated into actual foreign policy.

The process occurs by a variety of means. Perhaps now the main one is the media. Other means of translating values and opinions into policy are elections, interest groups, political parties, and now the Internet and the Worldwide Web. But of all the groups and institutions performing these "transmission belt" functions—that is, conveying the values and thoughts of ordinary Americans to decision makers as well as transmitting policy pronouncements back to the public—the media have emerged as the most important. Americans now receive nearly all their news about foreign policy and other matters from the media. And within the media, television has replaced radio and newspapers as the primary source.

The media are not just the conveyors of news; they have also become participants in the news. As distinct from simply reporting the news in a neutral fashion, the media now interpret the news and have themselves become regular participants in the drama. For example, Christiane Amanpour regularly interjects herself into her stories on Iran, Iraq, Darfur, or Bosnia. When Lou Dobbs sounds off on illegal immigration, he is not reporting the news but editorializing it. In these and other ways, the media help set the agenda and parameters of foreign policy, shape and influence opinion as well as report on it, and often interject their own views and biases into the reporting of the news, thus making themselves players in the process and not just neutral reporters of it.

The new power, pervasiveness, and participatory roles of the media in foreign policy lead to numerous questions. How biased are the media and in what ways? What is the structure of the media that allows them to play such an important role, and what are the problems that are built into that structure? Do the media have the background and sufficient experience and understanding to play such an important foreign policy role? To what extent do the media, rather than the political leadership of the country, set the agenda and define foreign policy issues? What is the relationship among the press, the government, and the public, and how is it changing? How and how well do the media cover foreign policy news? These intriguing and difficult questions form the bulk of this chapter, and their answers carry us a considerable way toward understanding contemporary foreign policy.

The Structure of the Media

The media play a special and an increasingly important role in American foreign policy. But the media are not just conveyors of news and opinion; the media, as a big business, occupy a powerful place in American society. Hence, we begin with a discussion of the structure of the media to appreciate their role in foreign policy.

BASIC FREEDOM BRINGS POWER

First, the media are among the few institutions in the United States that are protected by their own constitutional amendment. Freedom of the press is one of the most hallowed of America's constitutional freedoms. The First Amendment guarantees that the press will be free, open, crusading, and independent from government control. The press has thereby been given a special and privileged place in the American constitutional system, and most Americans favor—up to a point—a strong, free, independent, and even critical press.

Freedom of the press is not an absolute right, however; it sometimes bumps uncomfortably up against other fundamental rights. Does freedom of the press include the right to be, as some reporters are, snarling, offensive, and nasty at presidential news conferences? Does it include the right to examine the garbage of the secretary of state (as happened with Henry Kissinger) or to hide in the bushes to spy on congressmen who may be carrying on extramarital affairs (as happened with senator and presidential candidate Gary Hart [D-CO])? Does it include the right to purloin the hospital or psychiatric records of public officials, the right to see their yearly income tax returns, and the right to tail them like paparazzi, endangering pedestrians and other drivers? Does it include the right to camp on the sidewalk in front of the homes of public officials who may be in trouble, disrupting their personal and family lives for days and weeks while waiting to see if they get fired? When and how do we draw the line between freedom of the press and the right to privacy?

Other difficult questions emerge from watching television news. Does freedom of the press include the right to play loose with the facts and to misrepresent an issue—most often inadvertently because the reporter is not well informed, but sometimes purposely—so as to convey a message that is closer to the reporter's private political views? Does it include the right to broadcast secret, classified information, thereby jeopardizing a diplomatic or military mission and possibly putting people's lives in danger? During photo opportunities at the White House involving the president and visiting heads of state or foreign ministers, do reporters have the right to shout (often rude) questions at the president that have nothing to do with the visitors or their countries and that leave visitors both mystified and insulted? These tough questions have no easy answers. They raise serious issues about where freedom of the press begins and ends and about where it shades off into conflict with other rights and freedoms. They also hint at another issue that is clearly troubling Americans: has the press—especially television—become too powerful while lacking the accountability, responsibility, and checks and balances that should accompany that power so it will not be abused?

THE MEDIA AS A BUSINESS

The second important structural factor of the media is that they are big business, among the biggest in America. Excluding public broadcasting, the main priority of the media as a business is to keep their stockholders happy by showing a profit. The main priority is not necessarily to report the news in a straightforward and objective manner, although corporate management and the news bureaus often conflict and frequently have to bargain and compromise over this issue. The key to this business is advertising, which brings in profits. To the corporation, the news segments (which often lose money) are only one facet of a larger commercial enterprise, but even the news programs must be structured in ways that are oriented toward making profits.

Television as well as newspapers provide information and entertainment to the public in order to give the advertiser a large body of potential customers and to attract advertising fees. Hence, there is intense competition among the major networks—ABC, CBS, and NBC—and CNN, FOX News, MSNBC, and other cable channels as well for audiences and advertising revenues. The networks' news divisions are an integral part of the calculations concerning profits. In assessing the media's role in informing Americans about foreign affairs, therefore, it must always be remembered that the networks are motivated not only by considerations of disseminating the best and most complete information but also by the desire for attracting advertising and making a profit. Larger audiences mean better advertising rates and greater company revenues. Hence, even the news segments and programs are influenced by "showbiz," and their presentation is meant to entertain and attract greater numbers of viewers.

The showbiz orientation helps explain why television news, especially, does a poor job of informing the American public, why its coverage is so superficial, and why it so often focuses on dramatic events ("blood and guts": terrorism, crime, genocide, and natural disasters) instead of on more in-depth analysis. Serious public affairs programs are seldom aired because the majority of the public does not watch them and hence advertising revenues suffer. Morning news shows are developing more entertainment features with less emphasis on hard news. For these programs, directors often hire attractive models and glib announcers who have little background or experience as journalists. Even on the main networks' evening, half-hour news programs, once the advertising time is subtracted, only twenty minutes are left for reporting the news. The news itself increasingly comprises brief sound bites rather than serious coverage or "persons of the week" and other features that are dramatic and eye catching but not very newsworthy. We may lament this low and declining coverage of the news, but the realities of commercial television are such that no other kinds of coverage seem possible.

Balance Shifts to the Visual

A third major structural factor is the media's dramatic shift away from the written word and toward television as the main source of information for the public. Various surveys show that Americans, even those with college degrees, are reading fewer books and are reading at lower levels, preferring *USA Today* or *People Magazine* to serious books on international affairs. Between 1960 and 1970 newspaper readership declined, and television supplanted newspapers as the medium on which the public relies primarily for news. Over the past four decades, the trend has become even more pronounced, with more than 80 percent of the public now relying "primarily if not entirely" on TV for their news digest and with many newspapers cutting back or facing bankruptcy and closure. With many Americans relying on weak and superficial television news coverage for virtually all of its information, however, it is not surprising that many Americans are so poorly informed about foreign policy issues and lack an in-depth knowledge about other countries, as described in chapter 4.

CONSOLIDATION OF THE MEDIA

The fourth factor to consider in evaluating the media's role in foreign policy, in addition to the facts that the media are big business and that television dominates, is that the media have become an increasingly concentrated business. More and more media outlets are concentrated in fewer hands. Large chains have bought up previously independent local newspapers as well as local radio and television stations. What Wall Street calls "acquisitions mania" is as prevalent in this industry as it is in others. Even the large television networks and newspaper chains are being swallowed up by even larger conglomerates that often regard the media as only one source of income among many in their stable of holdings. The corporate owners of the major media outlets always vow initially that they will maintain the integrity and budgets of their news bureaus (which lose money for the networks) for reasons of prestige. When financial reality sets in, budget axes fall on the news bureaus, the pressure for more entertainment-oriented programming sets in, and news coverage declines. The question raised here, however, is not just how concentration and growling oligopoly in the ownership of the media affects their mission but how the growing control over the editorial content of the news does as well.

While cable news outlets, such as CNN, FOX, and MSNBC, have grown and cut into the major mainline networks' profits, an even greater threat is posed by the rise of the Internet and the Worldwide Web. People now have a far larger set of options available from which they can obtain information. You can not only book hotels, plane reservations, and auto rentals on the Web; you can now search for almost every conceivable interest group's website, political platform, and propaganda outlet as well. Computer bloggers now give you instant feedback on political advertising and messages; and have become such a large force that political parties and candidates must pay them serious attention. Those on the conservative right can get their information from such sources as the *Drudge Report* while those on the liberal left tune in to people like Arianna Huffington and her *Huffington Post,* which she calls an "Internet newspaper." The possibilities available in all these new technologies for spreading diverse information are almost boundless. They do have problems, though: they leave the traditional news outlets with fewer readers and viewers than ever, and with little regulation or accountability, there is no way for participants to assess the accuracy of the information they receive.

News Reporting

Turning from the large structural problems in today's media, it is important to understand the organization and system of news reporting, the biases they give rise to, and how technology impacts the nature of the media's coverage for good and for ill. While much could be said on this subject, this discussion will concentrate on a few issues that are relevant to foreign policy.

Recent Trends

The media is moving increasingly away from "hard news" and toward "soft news"—that is, features, sports, entertainment, talk shows, and reports on outrageous acts and behavior. Most Americans like these features; therefore, as profit-making enterprises, the media give the public what it wants to hear. In the process, serious news coverage inevitably gets sacrificed. The problem is especially acute for foreign policy coverage, which is expensive, is difficult, attracts few viewers anyway (unless it is blood and guts, as in Iraq), and therefore receives little attention from the networks.

Another problem is the media's focus on the "star" quality of the news. Anchors, whose job it is essentially just to read news from a teleprompter, are usually chosen now because of their good looks and not necessarily for their journalism skills or their substantive backgrounds. Similarly, network reporters are often selected on the basis of their looks as much as for their journalism experience. Moreover when they identify themselves by name after their reports (Diane Sawyer, Lara Logan, Megyn Kelly, Leslie Stahl), the news and their reporting of it become personalized, the reporters take on a star quality, and their coverage again inevitably suffers. The emphasis is on glamour—showbiz—and not so much on the straightforward reporting of the news.

The heavy reliance of television news on the wire services poses yet another problem. Most of the news broadcast on television (70–80 percent) is not based on its own reporters' research and work but instead is read from reports posted to a share service online. The networks do especially little reporting of international news, and their extensive use of the wire services results in broadcasting secondhand news that is also subject to the additional whims and biases of the wire services.

Changes in Bureaus

Because they are expensive to operate, the number of foreign bureaus that even the major newspapers or television networks maintain has been decreasing. Of course, the best way to cover an international story is to have someone in the field who knows the area or country involved well. The *New York Times* and *Washington Post*, which provide more foreign coverage than any other American newspapers, have between twenty and thirty at least part-time news bureaus worldwide, but that number is declining. Most newspapers and newsmagazines have few or no overseas bureaus. As of early 2009, the *Washington Post* had eighteen located in

1. Baghdad	10. Johannesburg
2. Beijing	11. Saudi Arabia
3. Beirut	12. Paris
4. Berlin	13. New Delhi
5. Rio de Janeiro	14. Nairobi
6. Bogotá	15. Moscow
7. Cairo	16. Mexico City
8. Islamabad	17. London
9. Tokyo	18. Jerusalem

In most of these bureaus the *Post* or *Times* has only one reporter, or the paper may rely on a "stringer," that is, a part-timer who simultaneously works for other news organizations. Note that the *Post* covers the main European capitals but few capitals in Asia, the Middle East, or Latin America. Since some countries have faded in importance, the *Post* has closed its bureaus in Central America, the Balkans, Manila, and Warsaw. The foreign bureau locations of the major newsmagazines *Time* and *Newsweek* roughly parallel those of the *Post*, and often they employ the same stringer. Recently the newsmagazines have also significantly downsized their international coverage, closing many bureaus in the process. The result is that large areas of the world, particularly the third world, are rarely, if ever, covered while Europe still garners relatively more attention.

The problem is compounded when considering television news. Even the largest television networks have far fewer foreign bureaus than do the major print media because their associated costs are deemed too high. A television story requires a crew of three persons at a minimum (the reporter and the sound and camera crewpersons) versus only one for a newspaper story. It is simply too expensive for the networks to send all these people abroad, pay their living costs as well as salaries, maintain a studio and equipment, and so forth. Hence, the television networks usually have only five or six foreign bureaus: London, Paris (or one for all of Europe), Jerusalem, Moscow, Tokyo, and perhaps one for all of Latin America. The single reporter in each of these bureaus is expected to cover the entire respective continent—realistically, impossible to do—which helps account for much of the resulting coverage's superficiality. Sometimes, the network will hire a reporter from the foreign country in which a story is breaking, but it will do so only on a short-term basis. So as networks trim coverage, often owing to budget considerations, the results for their viewers are that many foreign stories are covered insufficiently or not at all. Without being exposed to the necessary background of a possible festering problem, American viewers—often including policymakers—are frequently caught by surprise by developments abroad because they hear about them only after they explode as major stories.

Having too few bureaus and locating them in only a handful of countries lead to a decided media bias in determining which countries and areas get covered and *how* they get covered. For example, during the height of the Cold War, the Soviet Union, as would be expected, received more coverage than any other foreign country. As Russia has continued to experience turmoil and decline since 1989, the media's coverage of that country has also declined. Israel, a small country, nevertheless gets extensive attention because many Americans are interested in it. As important U.S. allies, Great Britain, France, and Germany also receive considerable coverage while China is attracting more notice. Iraq, Iran, and Afghanistan currently receive extensive coverage because of the U.S. military and strategic involvement there. While many stories are happening in other countries and areas every day, these events are not covered on television, so Americans are seldom informed about them. Moreover, when these countries occasionally do make the news, the occurrences usually reinforce our stereotypes about them: terrorism associated with the Middle East, starvation and AIDS with Africa, and drugs and revolution with Latin America. In reality, one would never know all that is happening in the world if one's only source of information was television.

THE U.S. HOOK

Another feature or bias of television news coverage is the tendency to give it a local or American angle. The sad fact is that few Americans are interested in the internal politics of, for example, Colombia or Egypt for their own sakes. Rather, they become interested in these countries only for their American connections, such as combating drugs in Colombia or the killing of American tourists in Egypt. Israel ranks so high on the list of countries the media cover because it is a U.S. ally, it is critical to the U.S.-sponsored Middle East peace process, and being the Holy Land, it is of interest to many Americans. With regard to Iran, Iraq, Pakistan, and Afghanistan, as long as the United States is involved with those countries, they will garner considerable television coverage; but when there is no longer a hook for the U.S. audience, the media scrutiny of these countries will decline. Again, it is not the case that nothing happens in these places after the United States leaves, only that without a direct and immediate connection to the U.S. public's concerns, television viewers lose interest and the coverage declines.

Television distorts as well as informs. It provides misinformation as well as good information, which therefore affects public opinion and, ultimately, foreign policy. For example, much television coverage of the Middle East clearly conveys the impression that all Arabs and certainly all Palestinians are implacably hostile to Israel, which is not in fact the case. The distorted television coverage of the Middle East also would lead one to believe that all Arabs are terrorists; the coverage reinforces our stereotypical beliefs about the area and its people. The media cover another important country, Mexico, and focus almost exclusively on the immigration issue—because that is the angle for attracting U.S. audiences—while ignoring the tremendous social, economic, and political changes taking place in that country. Stories such as these not only provide a distorted picture, often prejudice our attitudes about foreign nations, and sometimes reinforce racial, ethnic, and cultural stereotypes, they frequently undermine our understanding of these countries and American efforts to carry out a sensible and balanced foreign policy.

IMPACT OF TECHNOLOGY

Technological advances are also changing foreign news coverage and not always for the better. In the 1991 Gulf War against Iraq—obviously a major news story—TV network reporters in the field had the use of portable ground stations, satellite phones, truckloads of advanced equipment, and batteries of technicians enabling them to get on the air live via satellite even from the most distant locations. In this situation reporters often had no time to go out and actually report on the story; instead, they were tied to the transmission point, preoccupied with editing and then broadcasting the film that their camera crews had shot. In this case and others, the technological tail begins to wag the news coverage dog, that is, the technological work involved dictated what was broadcast. In the more recent Iraq War the reporters were embedded with U.S. military units and often used the Pentagon's communications resources, which was wonderful for the Defense Department but not conducive for objective news coverage. With continuing technological advances in satellite coverage and cable services, future news programs may be designed for specialized ethnic or sectoral audiences, thus fragmenting the news base even further.

PROLIFERATION OF REPORTERS

Another structural feature deserves mention—the enormous proliferation of reporters. In the 1950s the White House was covered by a few dozen reporters; now hundreds are accredited to the White House alone, with thousands more covering the State Department, DOD, Congress, various interest groups, the think tanks, and so on. This upsurge is not just at the national level; at state and local levels the number of reporters has swollen as well. The profusion of reporters involved has enormously complicated the logistics and process of reporting the news and has obliged virtually all Washington agencies to have public affairs offices to deal with the press. So many reporters—coupled with the copy machine, fax machines, cell phones, and the Internet—look into so many issues that it is virtually impossible in Washington to keep a secret anymore or certainly not for very long. In addition, when reporters go abroad to cover a major story, they may be competing with thousands more journalists who come from other countries. These large numbers mean that journalism is a quite different profession than it was just a generation ago, when a far smaller number of reporters had more personable relations with public officials. Sometimes in pursuing the big stories now, there are so many reporters that a "pack mentality" takes over and leads to aggressive tactics.

Another discouraging feature of television news coverage is the increasing tendency of reporters to interview each other or their own news bureau chiefs during broadcasts. That tactic only compounds a number of the problems referred to earlier. For one, that puts good "face men" (handsome but vapid) and cover-girl women (ditto) on the screen but usually adds nothing to the coverage. For another, when reporters interview each other, their banter may fill a time gap, but they usually impart little knowledge. Only people with expertise can provide the facts, and, increasingly, the newsrooms have access to few of those knowledgeable people.

But let us give credit where credit is due. Even with all its problems, American news coverage is by far the best in the world. In addition, a wide variety of programs—*The NewsHour with Jim Lehrer*, *Nightline*, *The Beltway Boys*, *Think Tank*, and others—do provide solid, informed, in-depth news and information. Many hardworking foreign affairs reporters are constantly struggling and sometimes succeeding in getting their analyses in print or on the air—even if to do that they have to compromise by emphasizing a U.S. angle in their reports. Finally, all-news channels like CNN, FOX, C-SPAN, and others have introduced a revolution in news coverage, and even foreign policy professionals and practitioners increasingly rely on their reports. In foreign policymaking circles in Washington, CNN has probably become just as important in shaping policymakers' views about immediate and fast-changing foreign events as the usual intelligence and diplomatic channels. The nonstop coverage that CNN provides enables almost all Americans to become virtually their own secretary of state—the implications of which are explored in chapter 6.

Political and Ideological Biases in the Media

In addition to the biases that are built into the very organization and structure of the media, reporters and their news organizations also hold political and ideological perceptions that sometimes bias or distort the news that the public receives. This is a tricky issue and a sensitive one among reporters since it relates to the very professionalism, objectivity, and trustworthiness of their work. Nevertheless, when biases fall into predictable patterns; can be measured by media observers, who regularly chart them; and become institutionalized, then plainly the media are not doing their work properly.

The line between objectivity and bias is not always as clear-cut as we might like. In the 1950s it was simply assumed that the reportage would be straightforward, unvarnished, clear, and objective, and that reporting went into the news pages while opinion was reserved for the editorial page. This separation was not consistently maintained, but the goal was clear and, by and large, the rules were followed. But by the 1960s and later, the idea began to spread in journalism schools that reporters should not only report the news but also "interpret" it. When you interpret the news, however, you put your own gloss, or "spin," on it. That process can and did open reporting to a variety of biases. At the same time, such interpretation—most often from a liberal viewpoint—was justified as a means of offsetting the supposedly conservative views of the media owners and editors. Nevertheless, it is a very short step from reporters interpreting the news to introducing their own biases into it.

Since the 1960s the dominant orientation within the media has tended to be more liberal than conservative, more left wing than right wing. In part this is a reflection of a generational shift to a new group of reporters weaned on Vietnam and Watergate; in part it is owing to the kind of education received by reporters in American universities and journalism schools during this period; in part it is owing to the widespread acceptance and enthusiasm among reporters for the more exciting task of "interpreting" the news; in part it comes from the even greater popularity recently of aggressive, hard-nosed, take-no-prisoners, investigative journalism. Whatever the exact causes, the attitude of many of these younger reporters is that government and its officials cannot be trusted, that all institutions are venal and self-serving, that the CIA and the U.S. military are evil, that capitalism is corrupt, and that it is up to them, the reporters, to expose the evils of "the system" and to point the public in a new and reformist direction. Such attitudes are often associated with the "Berkeley generation," or the counterculture of the 1960s and 1970s, and with a radical political agenda. The coverage has become overwhelmingly cynical and negative.

The problem is that such views on the part of some reporters are not representative of the nation as a whole and not even of the journalism profession. They represent a minority view among the public, and that discrepancy helps explain why the public no longer trusts journalists. Moreover, the public interest that the counterculture reporters seek to champion is often not that at all, but the reporters' personal biases being set forth as for the public good. When the biases that come with interpreting the news or with reporters having their own private agendas become too heavy-handed, it is plain that the public simply tunes them out and becomes resentful. This disparity between the values of some reporters and those of the public and the hostility toward reporters to which this gives rise helps explain why, in various press freedom issues in recent years, the public was found to be on the side of the government or the U.S. military and against what are often seen as snooping, prying, rude, overly aggressive, and partisan reporters. It also explains why viewers have deserted the mainline media in droves and now either look to other sources for news or have tuned out altogether.

The young radicals within the journalistic profession not only write or broadcast for their own outlets, but they have also secured positions within the mainstream newspapers, network television, National Public Radio (NPR), the Public Broadcasting System (PBS), and other influential media. They work not just as reporters but also as directors and producers. For quotes, information, guests, and speakers, they tend usually to bring in ideological sympathizers from private groups, the academic community, and their own politically oriented networks. But the overall result is mixed: on the one hand, the presence of these now-entrenched and politically committed persons tends to bias the news broadcast, how and which stories are covered, and the editorial positions taken. But on the other hand, the public has tuned out and become hostile to the press, thereby limiting its influences.

The radicals are an important but minority voice within the media; far more influential is the liberal orientation. On this subject, there is a great deal of information based on interviews with journalists as well as a careful monitoring of news broadcasts conducted by media watchdog groups and journalism schools across the country. These studies have provided some fascinating data on what are called the "elite media," or journalists and broadcasters who work at the most influential media outlets, including *Time, Newsweek*, the *New York Times*, the *Washington Post*, United Press International, Reuters, and the news departments of CNN, CBS, NBC, MSNBC, and PBS. The profile of the elite media looks like this: white (95 percent), male (79 percent), from the East Coast (68 percent), and of the upper middle class or wealthy (75 percent).

Fifty-four percent of the media elite identify themselves as liberal, while only 19 percent call themselves conservative, and the rest say they are independent or neutral. When asked about their colleagues, the differences are even more pronounced. Fifty-six percent say the people they work with are left of center while only 8 percent identify their colleagues as being right of center. As for the media elite's voting record, 94 percent favored the Democrat Lyndon Johnson over the Republican Barry Goldwater in 1964, 87 percent favored Democrat Hubert Humphrey over Republican Richard Nixon in 1968, 81 percent favored Democrat George McGovern over Nixon in 1972, and 81 percent favored Democrat Jimmy Carter over Republican Gerald Ford in 1976. Only one in ten favored Republican Ronald Reagan over Democratic candidates Jimmy Carter and Walter Mondale, respectively, in 1980 and 1984. In 1988 the support for Democrat Michael Dukakis dipped to only two to one over Republican George H. W. Bush. But in 1992, after sometimes giving Democratic candidate Bill Clinton a difficult time in the campaign, the elite media nevertheless voted overwhelmingly for him over Bush by, once again, a ratio of four to one. In 1996, against Bob Dole, the majority was "only" three to one. In 2000 the elite media again heavily favored Democrat Al Gore over Republican George W. Bush, and in 2004 they supported Democrat John Kerry over Bush. In 2008 the elite media favored Barack Obama over Hillary Clinton in the primaries and over John McCain in the general election.

The elite media is uncomfortable with these studies and figures—and not just, as is often said, because they can dish the heat out to others but can't take it themselves. Rather, it is because such studies implicitly attack the media's objectivity and professionalism. The media claim that they can separate their private political views from their professional reporting of the news. But things are seldom that simple. In fact, it is inevitable and unavoidable that the media elite's political views ultimately affect which stories they choose to follow, the way they cover stories, the slant or perspective they give to the stories, and their written or spoken interpretations of the stories. One can never (except for a small handful of absolutely unbiased journalists) strictly segregate one's private moral and political views from how one thinks and does one's job; such biases inevitably enter into the work.

The evidence for media bias on foreign policy may be found in the coverage of numerous issues over the years: The media turned against the war in Vietnam. It was against Ronald Reagan's policy in Central America and against the Soviet Union. It opposed President George W. Bush's interventions in Panama and the Persian Gulf, and it soured on the Iraq War and the war on terrorism. But it supported U.S. humanitarian interventions in Bosnia and Darfur. The detailed and specific examples of bias in the media's coverage are numerous, so the issue is not to try to deny that the media engage in biased reporting when quite plainly they do. Instead, the question is, can this long-term bias be evened out with proper representation of other points of view?

The conservative press expanded in the 1980s, largely in response to the liberal bias. Conservatives have their own newsmagazines and journals—such as *National Review, American Spectator, Policy Review,* and on some issues *Commentary* and *The New Republic*—and in Washington a conservative daily newspaper, the *Washington Times,* counters the liberal *Washington Post.* The conservatives also have their own think tanks (see chapter 8), conservative student newspapers on some college campuses, conservative panelists on talk shows, and a watchdog group, Accuracy in Media, that points out the biases in the liberal media. Conservative talk radio with such hosts as Rush Limbaugh, Sean Hannity, Neal Boortz, Laura Ingraham has also grown up over the last ten years as a powerful counter to the liberal media. However, the numbers given earlier (four to one, liberal over conservative) indicate that the liberal voice is still more prevalent in the media than the conservative one; moreover, conservative opinions have not really permeated the views of educated opinion-leaders in the United States in the way that liberal views have. Furthermore, the ideologically committed conservative voices in the media—for example, Limbaugh, Hannity, Boortz, and Pat Buchanan—often tend to be just as biased and as extreme as their radical left counterparts are.

Since the late-1980s there has been a considerable movement on foreign policy issues—including by journalists—away from the ideological extremes and toward the pragmatic center and more balanced views. Yesterday's radicals and movement conservatives have gotten older and adopted more middle-of-the-road views. The country grew tired of the ideological confrontations of the Carter and Reagan years, and the George H. W. Bush administration returned foreign policy to the center. In addition, many in the media themselves were stung by the charges of bias against them, by the careful and systematic charting of their biases in journalism schools and media studies centers, and by the undisguised resentment of the media shown by the public as well as by government officials. Hence, many media personnel backed away somewhat from their earlier editorializing and sought to make their reporting more objective. There were still many abuses and too many instances of flagrant, one-sided reporting, but often this was mainly owing to naive or inexperienced reporters who sometimes got taken in by a group feeding them biased information. Overall, the media seemed more careful, chastened, and evenhanded than in the past. Then, under Clinton's and especially George W. Bush's administrations, the ideological wars heated up; and all the biases within the media came out again, maybe worse than ever.

Problems of bias in media coverage of foreign affairs still exist. First, the media's coverage is often so oversimplified and superficial that it does not provide an adequate basis for informing the public and allowing it to make discerning judgments about U.S. policy. Second, too many news stories still interpret, or editorialize, and present the issues in a one-sided manner, as if they involved good guys versus bad guys. Third, because reporters are often inexperienced in the areas or countries they cover, they tend to fall back on clichés, into the trap of ethnocentrism (seeing things only through one's own rose-colored lenses rather than from the point of view of the countries and peoples affected), or on simplistic categories learned in some undergraduate course on the history of Western Civilization. Finally, it is clear that various countries in Asia, the Middle East, and the developing world, which are becoming increasingly important to U.S. policy (for example, Iraq, Mexico, India, Iran, Brazil, North and South Korea, China, Pakistan, and Indonesia), are woefully underrepresented in the news. Moreover, the journalists who are sent to report on them are usually not trained in these countries' languages or cultures.

What, then, is a foreign policy analyst to do when reviewing news reports? Herewith are some commonsense suggestions:

1. Be skeptical of what you read and see on television, reserve judgment, and avoid hasty, knee-jerk reactions.
2. Read (or view) widely to get different points of view, and balance them out.
3. Beware of media bias and of incomplete, oversimplified analyses.
4. Sort out which writers, newspapers, TV programs, blogs, and analysts are least biased, know what they are talking about, and are balanced and levelheaded.
5. Develop your own independent basis for judgment. This work may require taking more courses, gaining specialized knowledge, engaging in careful and thorough study, living abroad, attending graduate school, and seeking Washington experience. It is a tall order, but it is the best way to be well informed on foreign policy.

How the Media Cover Foreign Affairs

After determining the structural problems in how the media deal with foreign affairs and the media's inherent biases in reporting the issues, there are also problems related to how the media cover foreign affairs. Let us review these problems and how they impact our understanding of foreign policy issues.

Most reporters at the major news organizations try to cover stories fairly and well. They are often limited, however, by the structural impediments already discussed and by their own prejudices or lack of experience or knowledge.

Part of the problem lies with the new style of reporting in investigative journalism. Investigative journalism requires reporters to be aggressive, uncompromising, and sometimes pushy. That posture frequently enables reporters to attack established institutions, to ferret out sensitive information, and to get to the bottom of the issue. But it also means reporters who use such tactics will not be trusted again with sensitive information, will find their sources drying up, and will be unable to return to the same institutions or persons for future stories. For reporters covering the State Department, the Defense Department, or the White House, a fine line between maintaining their independence, on the one hand, and taking the risk of being coopted, on the other hand, comes with needing to get along with the very people and institutions on which they are reporting.

Another common problem is that some reporters lack experience and knowledge about the countries on which they are reporting. When newspapers were still the public's major source of news, their foreign affairs reporters were often stationed abroad for many years; therefore, they got to know a country or area well by actually living there and were frequently able to write sensitive and well-informed articles that led to major books. The *New York Times*, almost alone among U.S. newspapers, still sends reporters abroad on that basis. Hendrick Smith's *The Russians*, Alan Riding's *Distant Neighbors: A Portrait of the Mexicans*, and Thomas L. Friedman's *The World Is Flat: A Brief History of the Twenty-first Century* (about globalization) are three of the fine books that came out of their experiences as the newspaper's foreign affairs reporters. For most newspapers, though, keeping a stable of reporters stationed abroad became too expensive, and the advent of television and its requirements of three-person crews (now stations usually hire local sound and camera crews) meant even more prohibitive costs. The result is that most foreign affairs reporters now work from a U.S. city, or perhaps from London, and fly abroad only for a few days when there is a major story to tell. Consequently, they usually have little background in the countries they cover; they stay in fancy hotels, which do not allow them to get to know a country; and they operate essentially as short-lived tourist-reporters.

Jokes and stories abound about how such reporters get their information. It is said that their first day's story is based on what they hear from the taxi driver (a notoriously biased source) who takes them from the airport to the hotel, the second day's story is based on the gossip of the fellow reporters who were interviewed that night in the hotel bar, and the third day's story comes from a source at the U.S. embassy. This surely exaggerated portrait does contain a kernel of truth: it is difficult for a reporter who flies in for a brief visit and does not know the country or its language well to get good, solid, independent information.

A third problem, frequently, is that reporters lack previous knowledge of or experience in many of the issues and countries they are obliged to cover. Reporters coming out of America's journalism schools seldom have the language training, the area studies, and the history, political science, and economics background to really understand a country or area well. Far too often the resulting superficial coverage shows their ethnocentrism or their deficient understanding or empathy for the country studied. That, of course, biases the coverage. Even worse than incomplete or inadequate coverage, however, is purposely biased coverage. For example, some reporters rely on the word of guerrilla leaders or rebels because they are assumed to be more trustworthy than the government or U.S. embassy officials. Good reporters should always observe certain rules of thumb: because all sources are self-serving, don't fully trust anyone to give you complete and unbiased information. If you hear out all sides present in the dispute, you eventually learn how to tell who you can trust, or who has fewer axes to grind than others, and how to sift through the conflicting information to arrive at a balanced view.

Another problem is that reporters frequently have too much territory to cover. Suppose you are a foreign affairs correspondent stationed in New York, Washington, or Miami and have several *continents* that you are responsible for. How can you possibly be well prepared in terms of your knowledge and depth to cover them all? The answer is, you cannot—with the result that you may be forced to fall back on biases, ethnocentrism, or simplistic categories learned in an undergraduate classroom. Suppose you are a reporter actually stationed abroad in Rio de Janeiro, Nairobi, or Singapore but responsible for covering, respectively, *all* of Latin America, Africa, or Asia. Although you have a tremendous advantage in covering your area, you also have a larger beat than you had at home, and at least twice a year you have to visit the neighboring countries. The neighboring countries, however, anticipate your visit and know your prejudices, which means they may plan elaborate campaigns to feed you the information they think you need and to keep you from hearing other, contrary sources. When your story, presumably favorable to the group trying to influence you, does appear, the same group will reprint it in its own newspaper as "proof" that an "objective" foreign reporter also advocates its point of view. At that level, foreign reporting becomes a tricky business because the reportage is also being used for other, often private or partisan advantage. Reporters walk a fine line between relying on their sources and knowing that those sources are trying to use them for their own purposes.

The difficulties are compounded when large numbers of reporters from various countries arrive in a country that has suddenly become a hot news story. Often a herd mentality sets in, and the problems of getting accurate coverage are multiplied. The reporters monopolize the hotel space, take all rental cars, monopolize guides and interpreters, and vie with each other to interview the key actors. The key actors may have scores of interviews each day in which they deliver the same message, or they may start charging the media for their time, or the media may compete with payoffs to get the best material. Events such as the Iraq War, the search for Osama bin Laden, or the Middle East peace process become media circuses that sometimes appear bigger than the actual events being covered. There are now so many reporters and so many news organizations worldwide that the profession of journalism and the way stories are being covered have fundamentally changed.

In any discussion of the role of the media in foreign policy, three additional themes require some attention. The first is the increasing ability of the media to set the agenda of American foreign policy. By its coverage of events in Iran, North Korea, Darfur, or Iraq, the media help decide which issues are important, who the principal actors are, what the range of the debate is, and what the alternative solutions may be.

But we need to ask ourselves, if the coverage of foreign events is so often biased, uninformed, and inadequate as suggested here, is it really appropriate for the media to play this agenda-setting role? Are the right questions being asked, is the debate being fairly presented, and are there other options besides those presented in the media?

While the media have considerable influence, they do not have the final decision-making power. On the one hand, they can shape and mold public opinion or set the agenda of the debate, to be sure, but elected or appointed officials make the final, crucial decisions on foreign policy. Similarly, the media can amplify the voices of the individuals and the special interests they choose to highlight, but they do not determine what the national mood on a given issue is. On the other hand, with presidents like Clinton, Bush, or Obama, who are not well informed on foreign policy issues and who are driven for reelection purposes by the desire not to antagonize any group, then the media do have a stronger hand in setting the foreign policy agenda than they would have under a better-informed president.

The second theme has to do with the media's tendency to hype the news, or build up the drama of a news story by focusing on personalities, highlighting controversy, and polarizing the issues. This type of story, of course, makes television more exciting and helps increase viewer ratings and revenues. But are these portrayals accurate? The news shows will often feature an official spokesperson (the secretary of state, for example) but will then cut away to a person with a dissenting view (a member of Congress or interest group spokesperson). Even on such generally fair talk shows as *Nightline* and *The NewsHour with Jim Lehrer*, the preference is for a debate format. The problem is that the media can always find a dissenting legislator, academic, or lobbyist to take the other point of view, but that format disguises the fact that on most foreign policy issues there usually is a dominant consensus among knowledgeable experts. Should a dissenting congressperson's often uninformed or partisan views get the same length of airtime as does a secretary of state, who has immense command of the information and facts? Should a lobbyist or a person with an ax to grind be given the same attention as those who represent the 80 percent or so consensus on the issue? These questions are troubling. The problem is that while debate, conflict, and hype make good television, they overlook the fact that informed opinion is frequently in major agreement on the issues, and good policy may be lost in the process.

The third theme is the media's actual involvement in policymaking. For example, former CBS anchor Walter Cronkite decided after the Tet Offensive that the Vietnam War was unwinnable, and his change of opinion had a powerful impact on the American decision to end the war. Vietnam was the first war carried on live television, and its bloody scenes undoubtedly also helped sway American opinion against the war. On another occasion, CBS got the Israeli and Egyptian prime ministers live on two consoles facing each other with the anchor in the middle, whereupon the anchor tried futilely to negotiate a Middle East peace accord right on national television. Or, when President Reagan went to Moscow in 1988 to sign the historic Intermediate Nuclear Forces (INF) treaty with Mikhail Gorbachev, the television coverage was so obtrusive that it became a participant in the event and not just a recorder of it.

About the U.S. involvement with Somalia in 1992, it was said that "television got us in and television got us out." Tom Brokaw's NBC report on the mass starvation, disease, and death in Somalia helped prompt the initial U.S. humanitarian intervention. In 1993 the killing of many American servicemen in the Black Hawk Down incident and the ensuing televised coverage of their bodies being dragged through the streets proved so repulsive to Americans that the Clinton administration felt it had no choice but to pull out the remaining troops. By the same token, the fear of having more American servicemen killed and seeing it portrayed on television kept the United States from intervening in Bosnia and Haiti for a long time. On the other hand, in the Iraq War, the Bush administration effectively kept the bloody carnage in Baghdad off American television screens and restricted coverage of U.S. service personnel's body bags arriving at the Dover Air Force Base in Delaware.

Television also played a strong role in deciding the outcome of the "friendly tyrants" issue. These rulers, including Mohammed Reza Pahlavi, the shah of Iran; Chilean dictator Augusto Pinochet; Ferdinand Marcos of the Philippines; the apartheid regime in South Africa; and Gen. Pervez Musharraf in Pakistan, had long posed a dilemma for the United States: support these authoritarian regimes because they protect U.S. security interests or abandon them on human rights grounds. It is often a tough call; television helped force the issue. U.S. security concerns—represented by pictures of oil tankers in the Persian Gulf, U.S. planes and ships at the American bases in the Philippines, the strategic minerals of South Africa, or bin Laden on the Afghan-Pakistan border—are "good television" for only one night. But bloody battles in the streets, the Ayatollah Ruhollah Khomeini's revolution, black South Africans struggling for their rights, and protestors being killed in Pakistan make compelling, dramatic television night after night. Hence, in the conflict between strategic and human rights considerations in this television age, the latter will almost always win. Television and its command of the dramatic overshadow more prosaic strategic concerns.

No analysis of television's role in foreign policy would be complete without emphasizing CNN's role. Although other cable news channels have also entered the competition, CNN, with its focus largely on international news, is a twenty-four-hour, all-news television network with worldwide reach. Many Washington think tanks and congressional offices, to say nothing of the White House and Defense Department, tune into CNN all day long—and sometimes all night too. CNN often covers coups, revolutions, and other fast-breaking news live, on the spot, and in color. Often its coverage is better and certainly more immediate than what foreign policy officials get from State Department cables, CIA reports, or DOD analyses—which is why government agencies may keep their TVs on all day. While problems (bias, the incompleteness of the coverage, and so on) also arise from basing foreign policy on cable news, nevertheless, this network and others have instituted major changes in television's coverage of foreign news and therefore of foreign policy. It may be but a first step in an even larger television-cable-Internet-communications revolution.

Conclusion

The media in the United States now play a far more important role in foreign policy than they did previously. Some analysts have begun referring to the media as the "imperial press" because they have arrogated to themselves both greater importance and a larger role. With the protection afforded by the First Amendment, the media have become almost a fourth branch of government. No longer content to just report the news, the media also seek to interpret it; more than that, they often seek to shape the agenda, to hype the news, and to insert themselves into the process. Reporters now routinely interview other reporters, who may or may not have much expertise on the issues.

The rudeness, arrogance, and presumptuousness of many in the press have produced a backlash among the public. Hence, when reporters are roughed up, put in their place, or, as in the Gulf War of 1991, kept away from the front lines by the Defense Department and only fed official handouts, the public now cheers the perpetrators and blames the media. Alternatively, in the more recent Iraq War, the country became so violent and dangerous that reporters could seldom venture out of the Green Zone and then only under military escort. This constraint raises some difficult First Amendment issues, on the one hand, and questions about how well and objectively the war was being covered, on the other. Unfortunately, because of its arrogance and inadequate coverage, the press itself is partly responsible for the public's lack of trust in it.

We have also seen in this chapter that the media tend to be biased. While there is bias, we have to be very careful in determining how and where this interferes with the media's objective reporting of the news and where it does not. In addition, while the bias in the media is tipped mainly toward the liberal side, it is also the case that the media like to attack all established institutions: Congress as well as the White House, Jimmy Carter as well as Ronald Reagan, and Bill Clinton as well as "W." Most of the elite media favored Clinton in 1992 and gave him an easy, even admiring ride in the first months of his presidency; but that did not stop the press by 1994 from savagely attacking the president over a variety of issues. The press also subjected George W. Bush to ugly, mean attacks later in his presidency.

The media have become to a considerable degree the arbiters of our tastes in foreign policy, as well as in other areas, but without always having the knowledge or expertise to justify their playing such a leading role. The media have also taken on a greater importance in influencing foreign policy but not necessarily with a greater sense of responsibility or accountability. The media (like the rest of us) want it both ways: great power but no responsibility. In a democracy, however, that position is not only dangerous and arrogant, but in the long run it is probably unsustainable. Hence, in recent years some of the media have striven harder for objectivity, have not shown their biases so blatantly, and have rediscovered the middle of the road.

In the last forty years the media have been a further fragmenting and polarizing force in foreign policy. They have not just reflected the main rifts over American foreign policy, but they have also been an agent of those divisions and exacerbated them. The press has often contributed to our distrust of public officials, has been critical to the point of hostility, and has helped sow distrust and skepticism about America's purpose and institutions—not without good reason in quite a number of instances. America today is a deeply divided nation, and not content to just report on the phenomenon, the press has been instrumental in helping to polarize the country.

Now let us look back on the positive side. The number of journalists who specialize in foreign affairs has become more numerous and their expertise often more impressive. Their understanding, at least in some cases, of foreign languages and of other societies has improved. Numerous seminars and special training programs in Washington and elsewhere are helping to educate reporters about the countries and issues they are covering. On some areas and issues, the amount and depth of media coverage are significantly better than before. Yet many of the problems identified here, structural and otherwise, remain.

While this chapter has often been quite critical of the press—with ample reason—in closing we should look at its side of the argument. The press is sometimes abusive, but government officials and special interests also often lie to, mislead, and manipulate the media. These sources plant and leak stories, give out false and misleading information, try to manipulate the press for private or particular reasons, or seek to put a favorable spin on press coverage of events. The result oftentimes is a kind of cynical "dance" in which the press tries, but not always by appropriate means, to ferret out the news while public officials try to hide it, control it, or give it a slant favorable to their policies.

Such conflict between the government and the media is not only natural in a democracy based on a system of checks and balances and with a certain level of adversarial relations between the two, but it is also healthy. The question— and a recurrent thread in the analysis—is whether the adversarial nature of this relationship may sometimes get out of hand, resulting not in a healthy system of checks and balances but in conflict, polarization, and the danger of a tearing apart of America's political and foreign policy fabric. Have we now reached that stage in the United States?

Whatever our final answers on these issues, clearly the media are now playing a stronger role in foreign policy, and foreign policymakers must act with that influence in mind. The relationship is symbiotic: the press needs government (and other) spokespersons and public affairs officers as sources of information while the government needs the media to get its message across to carry out a successful foreign policy. The relations between the two are not always easy, but it is now widely accepted that neither can get along without the other. Practitioners of foreign policy in the future will always have to be mindful of the media's strong role in the process.

Suggested Reading

Arno, Andrew, and Wimal Dissanayake. *The News Media in National and International Conflict.* Boulder, CO: Westview Press, 1984.

Bray, Charles W. "Opinion: The Media and Foreign Policy." *Foreign Policy* 16 (1974): 109–25.

Bray, Howard. *The Pillars of the* Post: *The Making of a News Empire in Washington.* New York: Norton, 1980.

Cohen, Bernard Cecil. *The Press and Foreign Policy*. Princeton, NJ: Princeton University Press, 1963.

Drezner, Daniel W., and Henry Farrell. "Web of Influence." *Foreign Policy* 145 (2004): 32–41.

Emery, Michael C., and Ted Curtis Smythe. *Readings in Mass Communication: Concepts and Issues in the Mass Media*. 7th ed. Dubuque, IA: W. C. Brown, 1989.

Entman, Robert M. *Projections of Power: Framing News, Public Opinion, and U.S. Foreign Policy*. Chicago: University of Chicago Press, 2004.

Epstein, Edward Jay. *Between Fact and Fiction: The Problem of Journalism*. New York: Vintage Books, 1975.

Graber, Doris A. *Mass Media and American Politics*. 5th ed. Washington, DC: CQ Press, 1997.

Graber, Doris A., Denis McQuail, and Pippa Norris. *The Politics of News: The News of Politics*. Washington, DC: CQ Press, 1998.

Hallin, Daniel C. *The "Uncensored War": The Media and Vietnam*. New York: Oxford University Press, 1986.

Joyce, Ed. *Prime Times, Bad Times*. New York: Doubleday, 1988.

Larson, James F. *Global Television and Foreign Policy*. New York: Foreign Policy Association, 1988.

———. *Television's Window on the World: International Affairs Coverage on the U.S. Networks*. Norwood, NJ: Ablex Pub. Corp., 1984.

Lashner, Marilyn A. *The Chilling Effect in T.V. News: Intimidation by the Nixon White House*. New York: Praeger, 1984.

Lichter, S. Robert, Stanley Rothman, and Linda S. Lichter. *The Media Elite*. Bethesda, MD: Adler & Adler, 1986.

Mollenhoff, Clark R. *Investigative Reporting: From Courthouse to White House*. New York: Macmillan, 1981.

Nimmo, Dan D. *Political Communication and Public Opinion in America*. Santa Monica, CA: Goodyear Pub. Co., 1978.

O'Neill, Michael J. *The Roar of the Crowd: How Television and People Power Are Changing the World*. New York: Time Books, 1993.

Paletz, David L., and Robert M. Entman. *Media Power Politics*. New York: Free Press, 1981.

Postman, Neil, and Steve Powers. *How to Watch TV News*. New York: Penguin Books, 1992.

Powe, L. A. Scot. *The Fourth Estate and the Constitution: Freedom of the Press in America*. Berkeley: University of California Press, 1991.

Reel, A. Frank. *The Networks: How They Stole the Show*. New York: Scribner, 1979.

Reston, James. *The Artillery of the Press: Its Influence on American Foreign Policy*. New York: Harper & Row, 1967.

Rice, Michael, and James A. Cooney. *Reporting U.S.-European Relations: Four Nations, Four Newspapers*. New York: Pergamon Press, 1982.

Robinson, Piers. *The CNN Effect: The Myth of News, Foreign Policy, and Intervention*. New York: Routledge, 2002.

Rosefielde, Steven, and Daniel Quinn Mills. *Masters of Illusion: American Leadership in the Media Age*. New York: Cambridge University Press, 2007.

Rosenblum, Mort. *Who Stole the News? Why We Can't Keep Up with What Happens in the World and What We Can Do about It*. New York: J. Wiley, 1993.

Rusher, William A. *The Coming Battle for the Media*. New York: Morrow, 1988.

Senter, Richard, Jr., Larry T. Reynolds, and David Gruenenfelder. "The Presidency and the Print Media: Who Controls the News?" *Sociological Quarterly* 27, no. 1 (1986): 91–105.

Serfaty, Simon. *The Media and Foreign Policy*. New York: St. Martin's Press, 1990.

Shaw, Donald Lewis, and Maxwell E. McCombs. *The Emergence of American Political Issues: The Agenda-Setting Function of the Press*. St. Paul, MN: West Pub. Co., 1977.

Smith, Aaron, and Lee Raine. "The Internet and the 2008 Election." In Pew Internet and American Life Project, June 15, 2008 (www.pewinternet.org).

Stevenson, Robert L., and Donald Lewis Shaw. *Foreign News and the New World Information Order*. Ames: Iowa State University Press, 1984.

6

Interest Groups
and Foreign Policy

Political participation through organized interest groups has a long and controversial history in the United States. While James Madison in *The Federalist* portrayed the interplay of pluralistic, counterbalancing interest groups as supportive of democracy, George Washington warned against factions that sapped governmental decision-making authority. The issue thus goes back to the very founding of the nation more than two hundred years ago, and the controversy over the role of interest groups in policymaking continues.

Most of the classic textbooks on American politics portray interest groups as beneficial for democracy. Interest groups, it is said, reflect the diversity of America, help preserve pluralism, present information to Congress and the public, and help disseminate technical data that are useful in writing legislation. But recently interest groups have grown bigger and more powerful, have amassed enormous amounts of money to spend on lobbyists and members of Congress, and have almost literally captured the legislative process. It is now said in Washington that serving in Congress is no longer an end in itself; it is merely a stepping stone en route to an even more lucrative career as a lobbyist. Entire areas of domestic and foreign policy have become the private preserve of big interest groups.

In recent years the number of American interest groups, their concentration in Washington, and their power and financial resources have risen dramatically. Their increased numbers reflect the diversity of American society and politics, but they also reflect the heightened concentration of power in Washington as well as the growing privatization of American policymaking. Some of these groups are so powerful that they have taken over and almost literally run whole areas of American foreign policy. Moreover, as international trade, commerce, and globalization have become more important to the American economy (foreign trade now accounts for about one-third of the gross national product), the role of these interest groups has become even more significant. In essence, Congress has abdicated much of its responsibility for public policy while private interests have moved in and taken control.

These changes have caused a problem in foreign policy circles: the private interest groups have become so powerful and the competition for political advantage so intense that a national, coherent foreign policy in defense of the national interest becomes almost impossible to implement. The executive branch has become so big and bureaucratized that it is all but dysfunctional, and Congress provides almost no accountability and allows private interests to dominate policy. Little pieces of policy are doled out to, or become the special preserve of, private interests while the larger national interest is ignored or abandoned. As various economic, religious, ethnic, and partisan groups have gotten more involved in policymaking since the early 1980s, foreign policymaking—with the exception of the Iraq War, for a time—has undoubtedly become more democratic; but that move has not improved the policy and may have made it worse. With the rise of these powerful, vociferous, well-financed, and manipulative interest groups, U.S. foreign policy runs the risk of—and may have already succumbed to—becoming fragmented, paralyzed, and subordinated to private interest lobbies.

Provocative Questions about Interest Groups and Foreign Policy

The United States is unquestionably in a new era of interest group influence and power. The older Madisonian concept presented in Political Science 101 of competitive interest groups being healthy for American pluralist democracy has been superseded, if not repudiated. Of course, we're all in favor of pluralist democracy; the question is now whether American democracy actually functions that way. Alternatively, we are left with George Washington's worries that the power of factions makes the country ungovernable or, worse, that the factions have captured the government, or parts thereof, for themselves. In short, America's public institutions are in decline while the ascendant private sector is hiving off entire areas of policy for itself and rendering foreign policy incoherent and ineffective.

Here, then, are eight sets of provocative, key questions that raise the essential, controversial issues involved. First, it is sometimes said that powerful interest groups—for instance, big business, big labor, farm groups, ethnic lobbies, and NGOs—have taken over and now literally run whole areas of foreign policy by and for themselves. Is that assessment accurate, and if so, to what extent? What are the relationships of these groups to official or U.S. government policy? Are these private groups in any way accountable, and who, if anyone, holds responsibility? What are the implications for our foreign policy of these private groups holding sway in so many areas?

Next, we have to determine whether these groups' sheer numbers, power, money, and influence are paralyzing the U.S. government and leading to ungovernability. Do they, in effect, have veto power over policy initiatives? Alternatively, is this development so corrupting the U.S. government that it has lost control of policymaking? To what extent has U.S. policy toward China, the Middle East, Africa, and Latin America been captured or corrupted by these powerful interests? And to what extent do they rather than the State Department or other groups that are supposedly in charge control policy?

The third concern covers the potential biases that such powerful interest groups interject into the system. To what extent does policy reflect these groups' private interests rather than U.S. national interests? For example, in policymaking circles concerning southeastern Europe policy, the Greek lobby is more influential than is the Turkish lobby; in the Middle East, the Israeli lobby is far stronger than is the Palestinian or Arab lobby; and in Latin America, the Cuban lobby in the key swing state of Florida dominates not only U.S. policy toward Cuba but virtually all U.S. policy in Latin America. How can we have an enlightened, evenhanded policy in these areas if so much of the policy is dominated, or even run, by groups that support only one side of the issue?

A fourth problem arising from interest groups' involvement is their tendency to have tunnel vision regarding U.S. foreign policy: they go all out, naturally, for their position without keeping in mind the broader conception of U.S. interests. For instance, the U.S. human rights and democracy lobbies have become so vociferous and influential over the last three decades that they have drowned out other—economic, strategic, diplomatic—considerations. Saudi Arabia's regime, we know, abuses its subjects' human rights, but that policy should not blind us to the kingdom's other reasons—oil and strategic location—

for being important to us. Should we allow human rights to become the only foreign policy consideration and excessively pressure the oil-producing states or big, powerful trading partners on these issues and run the risk of destabilizing them, which would be disastrous both for human rights and for all the world's industrial economies?

A fifth concern is the extent of these groups' hold over foreign policy. The influence of private interest lobbies varies over time and by issue. During the Cold War, these groups' influence was held somewhat in check by obvious security considerations, but afterward, lacking a clear threat, the interest groups vastly increased their power over foreign policy. For a time, the 9/11 attacks forced the government to refocus on security issues and conduct the war on terrorism, but as the government apparently perceived that threat as fading, the private interest lobbies again began wielding enormous influence. Some analysts say that now, even if there was another terrorist attack on the United States, the private interests are so powerful that they could no longer be pushed aside. Are these groups indeed so powerful that they would refuse to relinquish their position?

Other questions arise about how lobbyists balance the nation's interests with those of their clients. At one time interest group lobbying was limited to domestic interests, but now foreign-based or foreign-funded lobbies are also powerful. Foreign governments hire their own lobbying or public relations (PR) firms, law firms, and even former members of Congress to represent their interests. Should former U.S. congresspersons, military officers, or State Department personnel be allowed to represent foreign interests against the national interest of the United States?

Another question involves transferring responsibility for government functions to the private sector. Since the beginning of the Iraq War, much of U.S. foreign and security policy has been privatized. For example, we now have in Iraq almost 200,000 private contractors and security personnel; they outnumber the U.S. troops stationed there. Such essential functions as war, diplomacy, and security are now being farmed out to private groups. But who are these groups (we know little about them), are they doing a good job (doubtful), and to whom are they accountable or responsible? The answer to the last question is, effectively, no one. How can a government have an effective foreign or defense policy run by private groups without any accountability?

Finally, we have to face the definitive question: Is this system reformable or even still salvageable? If so, should it be saved? Instituting any reforms would be difficult at best given the various elements involved: huge amounts of money, so many powerful lobbying groups, and so many vested interests, including Congress, the State and Defense departments, and all the big bureaucracies and the interest groups. Plus there is the problem of getting Congress to change its own behavior, which is always a bad bet.

The Growth of Lobbying Activity

The preceding questions provide an orientation and a set of provocative issues for discussion. First, let us look at the recent growth and changes in lobbying activity.

Lobbying in Washington, D.C., has become a growth industry, maybe one of the capital's biggest and one of its most lucrative. Between 2000 and 2005 the number of registered lobbyists more than doubled while the amount that lobbyists charge their clients has increased by as much as 100 percent. The total number of Washington-based lobbyists is now more than fifty thousand people, or an average of nearly a hundred lobbyists for every member of Congress. Of course, the more influential congresspersons, committee and subcommittee chairs, House and Senate leaders, and congressionally based presidential candidates attract far more lobbyists than the average politician.

Three main factors have led to the increase in lobbying: the rapid growth in government under both Democratic and Republican administrations, many companies and interest groups that are awash in money, and wide acceptance among all groups that they need to hire professional lobbyists to get their share of federal funds. Lobbying, of course, also takes place at state and local levels, but because the big bucks are mostly in Washington, that is where almost all lobbying on foreign policy issues takes place.

Revenues at Washington's top public relations firms are now more than $100 million per year. At Washington's leading law firms, which are often just lobbying agencies in disguise, revenues are even higher. Lobbying agencies can't hire people fast enough: for a former member of Congress or a congressional aide who often has inside knowledge about legislation as well as the legislative process, starting salaries have risen to about $300,000. That number is double what that person made as a congressperson or top aide. If, as often happens, the former member becomes the head of a trade association, the starting salary may be in the millions of dollars. So few members return to their hometowns after their defeat or retirement because serving in Congress or as a top staffer is a stepping-stone to a more lucrative position as a Washington lobbyist. As Robert Livingston, a Republican former chairman of the important House Appropriations Committee and now head of his own thriving lobbying firm, put it, "There's unlimited business out there for us."

As late as the 1960s there were still relatively few lobbyists or interest groups in Washington, and only a couple dozen members of Congress held powerful positions and needed to be persuaded to support particular legislation. Now that almost every congressperson is a subcommittee chair, lobbying has become a big, global business. Clients may include foreign governments and business groups as well as domestic corporations. Most of the lobbying groups are themselves now big businesses with a decidedly corporate look. They offer a full menu of client services, including public relations, lobbying, research, polling, direct mail, advertising, television commercials, and reelection fund-raising and political advice. Some specialized lobbying firms offer what they call "boutique services"—that is, an array of activities specially designed for a single congressman, client, or issue.

What oils the machinery of government is, of course, money. One of the key problems with present-day interest group lobbying, which has now gone far beyond Madisonian, competitive pluralism, is that so much money is available and already in the system. It completely skews the legislative process in the following ways. First, members of Congress worry all day, every day about money for their campaigns. Members of Congress are absolutely dependent on special interest groups for their reelection campaign funds. Even for reelection in a relatively safe district, it takes millions of dollars.

Once they accept the groups' funds, they are beholden to the special interests. That money buys the members' favors, special access, and even legislation. The wall of separation between lobbying and governance thus breaks down. Next, lobbyists provide not just campaign funds but also polling, consulting, media, and even campaign managers to the candidates.

Then the lobbyists routinely write the legislation that is supposed to regulate them, include articles in the laws passed that directly benefit their clients, and draft "earmarks" that give special federal funds or tax advantages to their individual clients. That leaves the public, which cannot hire teams of lawyers, lobbyists, tax specialists, and PR firms, out of the process. What happens to democracy when its citizens and voters are effectively removed from the process?

Traditional Interest Groups: Big Business,
Big Agriculture, Big Labor

Symbiosis is a term used in biology to describe a relationship in which two organisms live in intimate association, often feeding off each other and mutually serving each other's needs. That term precisely describes the relationship of business, agriculture, labor, and other interest groups to American foreign policy. These interest groups and the U.S. government work closely together, they support each other's interests, and sometimes entire government agencies are in large measure turned over to the interest groups, becoming almost the private grazing fields of these groups.

Such a relationship goes considerably beyond what we think of as interest group lobbying. Lobbying still goes on, but we are now talking about more than that: the incorporation of interest groups directly into government decision making, the takeover of certain departments or bureaus (the Commerce and Treasury departments by business, Agriculture by farm groups, Labor by the union movement), and the hiving off of whole areas of foreign policy by private groups for themselves—i.e., the human rights offices by the human rights lobbies. In political science and comparative politics, this development is called "corporatism": the incorporation of private groups into decision making and the granting of virtual monopoly power over certain areas of public policy to these groups. Thus, we revisit the question, what happens to public accountability and democratic oversight when significant areas of foreign policy are turned over to private groups? The answer is, accountability and public oversight are sacrificed.

Big Business

The role of business in U.S. policymaking is larger than most of us suspect. Among major interest groups, big business is especially important in a free market system like ours because the health and vitality of the entire economy depend on private businesses delivering the jobs, goods, and prosperity that Americans expect. Here's where the symbiosis comes in: the United States needs business to help maintain a prosperous economy of full employment while business needs the government to provide a regulatory and tax system conducive to making profits.

Fully 40 percent of the profits of the nation's three hundred largest companies are now earned abroad, and international trade generates about 35 percent of our GNP. The foreign or international side of business, therefore, is quite large. Moreover, with the Cold War over and the war in Iraq winding down, more and more of our resources will be devoted to developing and maintaining international economic relations. Two conclusions follow: the international divisions of both big business and the U.S. government agencies dealing with trade will be expanded, and business will play an even larger role in U.S. foreign policy.

The influence of big business over foreign policy extends far beyond traditional lobbying efforts. Business is by far the largest influence on U.S. foreign economic policy; in fact, it dominates or may even control large areas of international economic and foreign policy. Entire areas of the U.S. government— the Commerce and Treasury departments, the Office of the Trade Representative, the Export-Import Bank of the United States, and so on—have all but been turned over to, or are largely working for, the business sector.

At the same time, even with all that power, business does not control U.S. foreign policy. The Marxian approach, which sees the U.S. government operating simply at the behest of big business, is not accurate and is far too simplistic. It ignores several factors: the role of government input and regulation altogether, the capacity of the countries where business invests to also shape the process, and the symbiotic relationship between business and government, where each gets something out of the relationship. Also, it is no longer the case, as happened sometimes in the past (for example, the United Fruit Company in Guatemala), that U.S. companies can seat and unseat the governments of small, weak countries almost at will. The world doesn't work that way anymore, and most companies nowadays try to be good citizens in the countries where they invest.

That said, business influence on foreign, especially economic, policy is immense and not limited anymore to such large interest groups as the Chamber of Commerce or the National Association of Manufactures (NAM). Rather, every trade association (dentists, lawyers, pharmaceutical manufacturers, and so on) and every individual Fortune 500 company has its own Washington lobbying operation. The process is both more pervasive and subtler than the sometimes heavy-handed interference of the past. Business is now so well integrated into government economic policy that it is part of the government. Some say it *is* the government for it has been incorporated into almost all government decision making. Its members occupy cabinet positions, are part of the decision apparatus in many agencies, and effectively dominate the personnel choices and government policy decisions in areas of interest to U.S. business. In many economic policy areas the business groups have more experience and more expertise than the entire U.S. government; therefore, when decisions are made, their expertise prevails, or else their own personnel or persons in government sympathetic to their point of view are already in place to make the decisions favorable to business interests.

Following are specific ways big business influences American foreign policy:

Lobbying

It is important to emphasize that lobbying no longer consists of just visiting members of Congress in their offices. It also involves providing Congress with information, influencing the staffing of committees, and sticking articles in legislation that benefit one or a group of companies or actually writing key parts of the legislation.

Campaign Finance

Business is by far the largest contributor to election campaigns, and politicians are desperate for money to finance those campaigns. Hence, symbiosis again: congressmen need big business and business needs Congress. Not only do such contributions guarantee business access, as in the past, they also guarantee legislation favorable to the group. Despite their protestations to the contrary, congressmen can be "bought," and it happens all the time. Usually subtle smoke screens disguise from the voters the extent of the bribery; in fact, we call it "campaign contributions" instead.

Interchange of Personnel

Thousands of former U.S. military officers now work for private companies and parlay their past connections to garner lucrative contracts for their companies. Similarly, former State, Treasury, Commerce, or Trade Representative officials work in the private sector and use their connections and expertise for their companies' benefit. Perhaps the biggest offenders are former members of Congress and their staffs who later work for lobbying firms and take their inside knowledge and connections to secure legislation favorable to the companies that hire their firm. Almost all the lines between the private and public spheres are breaking down. Efforts to reform these practices meet with strenuous objections from members of Congress themselves.

Advising

Private companies have branches that regularly serve as advisers or consultants to the government. For example, the National Petroleum Institute, a private lobby group, advises both the Energy and Interior departments. The Halliburton Corporation and KBR "advise" the U.S. government on Iraq War strategy. Defense contractors, such as Lockheed Martin, Northrop Grumman, and Raytheon, have subsidiaries that make recommendations to the government on military products. Does it surprise anyone that they counsel the government to buy their own products?

Personal Contacts

At the highest levels in Washington, D.C., everyone knows everyone else. Former members of Congress, think tank personnel, journalists, government officials, and interest group representatives all attend the same receptions, are on a first-name basis, and know each other's politics and job backgrounds. Hence, when they need something done politically, they know whom to call. It used to be that Washington movers and shakers were known by the size of their Rolodexes; now all this information is computerized.

Revolving Doors

When the Democrats are in charge of Congress or the White House, all their friends, cronies, and political allies from the think tanks, law firms, and lobbying agencies receive appointments to high government positions, where they often offer favors to their former private sector allies. When the Republicans are in power, the Democrats retreat to their former think tanks, law firms, and lobbying agencies while the Republicans take over the cushy government jobs and extend favors to their friends and allies. This incestuous, insider, revolving-door system may or may not serve the public interest.

Government Programs

The U.S. government lacks expertise on business and commerce. So when it needs to run a program abroad that encourages investment, or free markets, it often turns to private business to run it. The private sector can do things that the U.S. government cannot do, such as management, connections, marketing, and finance, but it also tends to favor its own or allied firms to get the job done. Conflict of interest runs rampant in these arrangements.

U.S. Embassies Abroad

U.S. embassies used to pride themselves on the quality of their reporting on the political or economic conditions in the country where they were located. Now that most of that information is available over the Internet, those reporting skills are less valued. Today, therefore, U.S. embassies serve as lobbying agencies for U.S. businesses abroad, helping them get contracts, advising on investment opportunities, and helping pave the way for them to get started. Again the emphasis on serving big business shows how the line between private and public concerns are blurred and the immense importance and extended influence of U.S. business.

Power and Influence Abroad

Many of these big companies have even bigger budgets and can mobilize more lawyers, more Wall Street connections, and more international influence than can most third world countries. In addition, in this era of globalization, when economic issues are so important and all countries desperately need investment, the power of international business is further enhanced. A foreign country would be foolhardy these days to nationalize a U.S. firm (unless, like Venezuela, it has unlimited oil wealth) or to stray from orthodox economic policy. If it does, it will be cut off by that company and from global capital and investment. Such a move can quickly be your ruin.

In all these ways, big business, more than any other large interest group, is woven into the fabric and policymaking machinery of the U.S. government. A former cabinet secretary said that "the business of America is business," for without private business the U.S. economy, jobs, and standard of living would all go downhill. Thus business and the government enjoy a close, symbiotic, and mutually beneficial partnership; moreover, in many areas of foreign policy, private business *is* the government. In this way, no matter which party is in power, private business is a part of the decision making; without it the United States would fail economically. This certainty gives private business enormous power, not only over the economy, but over government programs and policy as well. Business is simply indispensable to a strong American economy, which, in turn, is essential to a successful foreign policy.

BIG AGRICULTURE

The United States is no longer a rural or agricultural country. Farmers make up less than 2 percent of the population; therefore, farm groups—the Grange, National Farmers Union, and American Farm Bureau—often lack clout on the national stage, although they may have influence locally and in farm states. Many of the same trends we saw affecting business and the media also affect agriculture: greater concentration of ownership into large agri-industrial concerns, the incorporation of farm lobbies into governmental decision making (in this case, through the Agriculture Department), the near-complete takeover of that department by agricultural interests, and the privatization of some areas of ostensibly government responsibility by farm groups.

While farmers are small in numbers, their agricultural products account for about 15 percent of U.S. exports and earn about $400 billion yearly. That makes agriculture a big business and gives big agriculture considerable influence at the national and international levels. U.S. agriculture is the most productive in the world, is the world's largest supplier of wheat and corn, and is one of the few economic sectors in which the United States still registers a trade surplus.

Agriculture policy was frequently used as a weapon in the Cold War and is still frequently employed for international political purposes. President Carter cut off grain exports to the Soviet Union in retaliation for the Soviets' invasion of Afghanistan in the 1970s, but with agriculture-rich Argentina filling the grain gap, only U.S. farmers, not the Soviets, were hurt by the embargo. In the 1990s, after the Soviet Union had collapsed, the United States reversed course and sought to supply Russia grain to avoid food shortages; but by then Russia was so poor it could not pay, and the U.S. government had to subsidize the grain sales. The government has also used food aid to try to leverage better policies in such failed states as Haiti, Somalia, Iraq, or Ethiopia, only to discover these countries' governments were hoarding it to jack up prices, selling it instead of giving it to their starving populations, or channeling it only to favorite ethnic and political groups that supported the regime in power. Hopefully, we've learned over the years that food aid is a blunt and often ineffective instrument to use to bludgeon other countries.

One of this book's main themes is the degree to which domestic politics often overwhelms foreign policy, and certainly U.S. agricultural policy offers abundant examples of that. To cite one case, the United States has long maintained an embargo on sales of agricultural products, among others, to communist Cuba. One can argue about the policy merits of the embargo, but they are becoming less relevant than the politics of the issue. On the one side stands the powerful

Cuban community in Florida, a swing state in every presidential election, that wants to keep the embargo at all costs as punishment against Fidel Castro. On the other side are farm groups and their representatives in Congress who want to sell surplus grain to Cuba. This debate has little to do with the foreign policy merits of keeping or abolishing the embargo; instead, it has become mainly an issue of domestic politics.

Another issue is ethanol and U.S. efforts to achieve both greater self-sufficiency in energy production and a cleaner environment. The largest producer of ethanol in the world, Brazil also has the most advanced ethanol technology. Brazil has ethanol to export, and the United States has a crying need for it. Plus Brazil's sugarcane-based ethanol is much more efficient than the ethanol made from U.S. corn. But the compelling logic of purchasing ethanol from Brazil is blocked by Florida sugar producers who want to protect their domestic market (even though they don't produce enough for U.S. needs), understand very well the importance of Florida in U.S. national politics, and have made major contributions to both U.S. political parties. They have been joined by Midwestern farmers (and their members of Congress), who are seeing corn prices skyrocket as the United States has invested in ethanol production as a fuel. Again, domestic politics overcomes all rational calculations of U.S. national interests.

The Target Export Assistance Program (TEA), later renamed the Market Access Program (MAP), illustrates the themes discussed here. The Agriculture Department established the TEA with the laudable goal of increasing U.S. agricultural exports; however, it came to be staffed and was literally taken over by big agricultural firms' personnel, who ran it for their own private advantage. The program was supposed to assist small farmers and export basic foodstuffs like wheat and corn; instead, it focused on luxury agricultural products like almonds and mink that came from the large agri-industries, which had contributed heavily to the parties. With virtually no accountability, these giant firms abused the system. For example, they used it to sell their own brand names—McDonald's or Sunkist—instead of generic products. The General Accounting Office, now the Government Accountability Office, found extensive corruption, political favoritism, inadequate administration, and no responsibility. One could cite dozens of government programs like it.

These and other developments in agricultural exports point toward many of the same conclusions reached regarding big business:

- There has been increased concentration in large agri-industrial companies.
- More and more agricultural products are being exported.
- The Department of Agriculture had become a major player in U.S. foreign policy.
- A close, symbiotic relationship exists between the Department of Agriculture and agri-business in which the Department of Agriculture is no longer an independent agency but has been "captured" by the big firms.
- The public interest has been subordinated to the interests of large agricultural business interests.

BIG LABOR

Along with big business and big agriculture, big labor also has an important foreign policy role. Although these three groups are usually far apart on domestic policy, on foreign policy they often work together.

Big business, big agriculture, and big labor are no longer just private lobbying groups as described in classic interest group theory. Rather, they are entwined with government in such close and symbiotic ways that they have become quasi-official, or part of the governmental system. These groups are regularly consulted on pending legislation; they sit on the numerous boards, task forces, and commissions from which policy recommendations derive; and they have insinuated themselves into the very fabric of government decision making. Sometimes entire offices, agencies, or departments are handed over to these groups as a reward for political support. They have hived off whole areas of public policy for themselves with little accountability or responsibility. The incorporation of these groups into semiofficial roles, supported and often financed by the government, is part of the larger corporatization (private groups incorporated into official functions) of American political life. While this trend is problematic enough, of additional concern is how all these groups perform the public functions accorded to them.

Big labor, like big agriculture, is a declining group numerically but still a powerful voice in Washington policymaking. Since the late 1980s the percentage of unionized workers in the United States has declined from 15 percent to about 9 percent of the workforce. The percentage will continue to fall as manufacturing jobs in the United States decline and globalization continues. Despite the falling numbers, no politician—in Congress or the White House—wants to cross organized labor. That move would cost votes, campaign contributions, and, most importantly, campaign workers on election day. Organized labor, in addition, can often exercise veto power over appointments, new programs, and, especially nowadays, trade agreements. Politicians, therefore, treat labor with kid gloves and rarely scrutinize its activities, especially in the foreign affairs arena. Successive administrations have learned that big labor, just as big business and big agriculture, can be useful in carrying out foreign policy.

Why does organized labor play a major role in foreign policy? Industrial and labor relations are one of the main anvils on which the structure of the modern state and society are hammered out. As countries industrialize, particularly in the third world, labor unions play an increasingly important role. These unions can be communist, socialist, or more conservative in character. During the Cold War especially, but continuing today, the United States much preferred conservative unions over socialist and communist ones and, if there were no conservative ones available, socialist unions over the communist kind. To advance this agenda, the U.S. government enlisted big labor, the American Federation of Labor and Congress of Industrial Organizations (AFL-CIO), in the program. The labor organizers came from the AFL-CIO (they knew how to do it), but the money came from the U.S. government, specifically the clandestine CIA budget.

The program began in Europe after World War II. By aiding noncommunist and anticommunist trade unions in Greece, France, and Italy, it sought to prevent the communist unions from seizing power and turning their countries into satellites of the Soviet Union. The program in Europe can be judged a success, helping develop those countries into the modern, stable democracies they are today.

But as the Cold War in the late 1950s shifted focus away from Europe and toward the third world (Cuba, Korea, Vietnam, China, Indonesia, the Philippines, Latin America), the program of aiding non- or anticommunist unions shifted with it. In these areas, however, the program was far less successful. Basically the AFL-CIO (and the U.S. government) had little experience in the third world; the program would necessarily have to involve creating new unions—much more difficult—instead of, as in Europe, aiding established ones; the union people we sent abroad were not very good at their jobs; and then finally the funding (covert, from the CIA) was all wrong. The result was that in quite a number of countries the U.S. programs aided radicalization rather than curbing it and ruined the trade union movements rather than assisting them.

During the early 1980s, recognizing the previous failures, the program and its funding changed. Labor's foreign policy activities (along with those of business) were then organized under the National Endowment for Democracy, a quasi-private, quasi-public agency that promoted U.S. foreign policy positions abroad by championing democracy. The funding also came directly and publicly from Congress rather than the CIA. The program of assisting democratic, noncommunist trade unions was concentrated on Central America and the former satellites of the Soviet Union in Eastern Europe. Now, with the Cold War over and during the war on terrorism, it mainly concentrates on the Arab countries of the Middle East.

Labor's other big issue these days is international trade and U.S. trade policy. Organized labor wishes to erect protectionist trade barriers to keep out foreign products and thus save well-paying U.S. jobs. For the same reason, it opposes trade agreements with foreign countries because their products often undercut the price of U.S.-produced goods. Organized labor's policies are good for its members in the short term in protecting their jobs, but they force everyone to pay more for most products. Labor has put pressure on Congress, especially on Democrats, to kill these trade agreements, but most members of Congress do not want to be seen as against free trade and for high prices. A working (so far) compromise is to include labor and environmental requirements in the trade bills that Congress passes.

Big labor is nowhere near as powerful as big business in influencing foreign policy. Labor does have veto power over some issues and appointments, and it remains a powerful influence in Congress and at election time. But in terms of having a large and powerful effect on the economy, business interests are far more influential than labor is on an everyday basis. Nevertheless, many of the problems identified with business and agriculture also apply to labor: an ostensibly private interest group, it dominates a major area of foreign policy (labor relations abroad); it hives off of an entire area of public policy (the Labor Department); it lacks public accountability and responsibility; and again it blends and blurs the line between its functions as a private interest group and its impact on public policy.

The Proliferation of New Interest Groups

We are used to dealing with big business, agriculture, and labor when we consider the influence of interest groups. Less well known are the myriad, new, often single-cause and specialized groups that have been established, including religious groups, environmental groups, human rights lobbies, ethnic groups, ideological factions, foreign interests, and nongovernmental organizations. The exponential growth of these groups and their ability to mobilize through the Internet have made American foreign policy much more complex and difficult. These groups can literally flood Congress, or the world for that matter, with messages on short notice. The involvement of all these new groups has made American foreign policy more democratic and participatory than before; whether it has led to better foreign policy, however, is questionable.

Three events or developments help explain the rise, proliferation, and influence of these new interest groups. First, the Vietnam War of the 1960s and 1970s brought millions of people, mainly as protesters of U.S. foreign policy, into the political arena for the first time and gave rise to hundreds of new antiwar, pro-human rights, activist interest groups. The second was the proliferation in the 1970s and 1980s of new media and cable news outlets, which bring foreign policy news and issues dramatically and instantaneously into everyone's homes and offices. It happens so rapidly, in fact, that the public is often as informed on foreign policy issues as our diplomats, who themselves get their information from these sources. And the third is expansion of the Worldwide Web. Internet access enables everyone to become a foreign policy blogger and gives rise to the phenomenon of individuals, operating out of their own homes, organizing successful, global campaigns to ban debilitating land mines, for instance.

These changes have not only brought thousands more organized interest groups into the foreign policy process, they have also made foreign policy more partisan and ideologically oriented. Almost anyone can be her or his own secretary of state on behalf of almost any issue, and the range of options has now also broadened, sometimes to include some truly nutty ideas. People have strong, if not always well-informed, views, and Congress and the executive branch, if they wish to be reelected, must pay attention to even the most disparate views. To garner more exposure, many of the new groups, both progressive and right wing, ally with other groups, bundle their energies, and gain even greater influence.

We cannot detail the activities of all these myriad groups here. Instead, we will provide an outline of their variety and scope.

RELIGIOUS LOBBIES

Among the newer, activist religious lobbies are the U.S. Conference of Catholic Bishops, the National Council of Churches, the Lutheran Council, the Methodist

Board, the historic "peace churches" (Quakers and Unitarian Universalists), the Assemblies of God, the Moral Majority, and Focus on the Family. These groups have been mainly interested in interjecting a moral or religious voice (their own) into foreign policy on such issues as abortion and family planning, immigration rights, disarmament, or human rights. Often these groups begin rather naively as single-interest lobbies but then acquire skills and staff and branch out to address a wider range of issues. From a Washington foreign policy point of view, these groups are difficult to deal with because they are very pious, are dedicated true believers in their own narrow viewpoints, and often wear their clerical collars or habits when testifying or visiting Capitol Hill. They are influential because politicians do not want to get on the wrong side of major denominations or religious groups. For a member of Congress it is considered bad form to kick a nun, a pastor, a rabbi, or a priest out of the office. Also, the national offices of these religious groups in Washington, D.C., are usually much more radical—and even rabid, left or right—on the issues than are their own congregations out in the various states.

HUMAN RIGHTS GROUPS

The main human rights advocacy groups are Amnesty International; Asia, Africa, and Americas Watch, under the auspices of Human Rights Watch; the Public Interest Law Institute; Freedom House; and the Washington Office on Latin America (WOLA). Most of these are secular, nondenominational groups, but they often overlap with the religious groups discussed in the preceding paragraph. Since the 1970s as human rights have gained importance in U.S. policy, these groups have also grown, often serving as watchdogs of human rights abuses in foreign countries. On most human rights issues these groups agree with U.S. government policies, but in some spectacular instances they vigorously disagree. The human rights lobbies are single-interest groups while the government must be concerned with all aspects of policy. For example, these groups accuse China, the Hosni Mubarak regime in Egypt, Saudi Arabia, and the government in Colombia of major human rights abuses, but the U.S. government has to weigh other salient issues when determining its stance with these countries. China is an emerging world power, the Mubarak regime protects Israel and U.S. Middle East policy, Saudi Arabia has vast oil reserves that we need, and the government of Colombia is also a leader in the fight against drugs and terrorism. The question in all these cases then becomes, how much attention should the government pay to standing up for human rights, which the human rights lobbies want, versus pursuing a broader, multi-issue concept of U.S. interests?

ETHNIC GROUPS

The best known of the ethnic lobbies are the American Israel Political Action Committee (AIPAC), the Cuban American National Foundation (CANF), and the Irish-American Defense Fund (IADF). Other influential ethnic lobbies are the Armenians, Greeks, and Italians. Within Congress are the black and Hispanic caucuses. TransAfrica Forum lobbies, especially among African Americans, on African and Caribbean issues; and Arab, Turkish, and Palestinian lobbies are just beginning to act as effective interest groups. Almost all the foreign embassies in Washington hire law firms, public relations agencies, and professional lobbying agencies to present their point of view. Taking their lessons from AIPAC, CANF, and other successful ethnic lobbies, these embassies try to mobilize their constituencies in the United States—Czechs and Slovaks in Chicago and Cleveland, the Portuguese in southeastern Massachusetts, Dominicans in New York, Poles in Pennsylvania and elsewhere—on behalf of issues of interest to their old countries.

All these ethnic lobbies try to present the case that what's good for their countries is also good for the United States, but is it, always or necessarily? Some groups have a virtual stranglehold on U.S. policy in their region: the Cubans on Latin America, AIPAC on Middle East policy, the Greeks on Cyprus and southeastern Europe. The United States sides with Israel in the Middle East, but that choice has come at the cost of immense hostility on the part of Arab and Palestinian people and is one factor stimulating Islamic fundamentalism and terrorism. The Cubans, because of Florida, are able to dominate U.S. Latin America policy in ways that skew our approach to the region. The Greek lobby is the strongest voice on Greek-Turkish relations in Cyprus while the Armenian lobby (mainly from another important swing state, California) is a strong voice on American-Turkish relations. The danger here is that, for the purposes of garnering electoral votes and campaign money, the politicians will accept one side's view in a disputed area, or almost literally turn our foreign policy over to that group, instead of being evenhanded and pursuing genuine, U.S. national interests.

IDEOLOGICAL GROUPS

These groups include Lawyers Concerned; Physicians Concerned; Committees in Solidarity with the People of various countries (Central American countries in the 1980s, South Africa in the 1990s, Iraq and Afghanistan today), MoveOn, and other specially organized, usually ad hoc associations oriented toward specific issues. Many were organized during or in the aftermath of the Vietnam War; they tend to be strong on college campuses and among radicalized groups but have little influence on Washington policymaking. They tend to be too radical for most Washington mainstream politicians, they have little money to donate to political campaigns, they usually lack a Washington office to better influence policy, and their ad hoc nature means they are usually temporary and not well organized.

Among recent presidents, Bill Clinton and George W. Bush were both polarizing figures. For a decade (1991–2001) without intensely divisive foreign policy issues, these two presidents often provoked deep, personal, and ideological passions. The intense divisions in the country were also present in the two main parties (see chapter 7). Meanwhile, the wars in Iraq and Afghanistan have emerged as controversial issues and, as during Vietnam, have provoked radical groups to demonstrate and march on Washington.

ENVIRONMENTAL GROUPS

Most of these groups, including the National Wildlife Federation, Sierra Club, Nature Conservancy, Environmental Action, and Natural Resources Defense Council, have been oriented historically toward domestic environmental issues. But now, with a new agenda of global issues—pollution, acid rain, famine, global warming, oxygen and resources depletion—these groups and others are taking up foreign policy issues and have become active at the international level as well. The environmental groups have been active in lobbying for the inclusion of environmental standards in recent U.S. trade agreements, pressuring Mexico on pollution in border areas and urging Brazil to discontinue burning of the ozone-rich Amazon jungle.

Now with the focus on climate change and global warming, the environmental groups are very active at the international level. Even the Defense Department has an office that assesses the environmental impact of military bases, munitions storages, nuclear waste, and war fighting. In part because they knew Congress was opposed to it, neither Clinton nor Bush was committed to the Kyoto Protocol, for which domestic and international environmental groups severely criticized the United States. Now that the evidence for long-term climate change is more conclusive, the United States appears ready to support environmental agreements that do not include Kyoto's objectionable antigrowth features.

Nongovernmental Organizations

In recent decades there has been a tremendous increase in the number and influence of NGOs, both in the United States and internationally. As the name implies, NGOs are mainly private or nongovernmental groups, but many receive funding from the government, political parties, and other private interest groups. Thus, they are not always so "private" or disinterested as they appear, and they are often as tied into Washington policymaking as are big business, agriculture, and labor.

These groups often advise the government on policy matters within their sphere of special interest. Often, like other interest groups, they provide personnel and policy recommendations to the government agency or department that deals with their issue of interest. They may also receive grants or contracts from the government or private interest groups to pursue their special interests. Thus, the line between private and public is blurred again: instead of these being nongovernmental groups, some of them may be referred to as "GONGOS" (government-nongovernmental organizations, a name that is a contradiction in terms) or "PONGOS" (private-nongovernmental organizations, which are in the pay of other interest groups). We therefore need to carefully sort out those groups that are really independent and those that are fronts for other organizations.

Foreign Lobbies

Almost every country represented in Washington has now hired a law firm, a lobbying organization, and a PR firm to get its message across. These contracts and retainers can be very expensive, which puts poor third world countries at a considerable disadvantage. The larger, richer countries also have the advantage that they have bigger staffs; know how to go about influencing Congress, trade agencies, and regulatory bureaus; and, in general, know how to operate in Washington with the media, think tanks, NGOs, interest groups, and their own ethnic communities. Smaller, poorer countries, by contrast, lack staff, lack money, and don't know how to influence the process. Moreover, non-Western countries' embassies often have conflicts with the PR or lobbying organization they hire over language, culture, and how best to present the countries' images.

CELEBRITIES

We now have this phenomenon in Washington where Hollywood, music, or sports celebrities drop in to plead for their favorite causes. Likewise, Washington politicians travel to Hollywood and raise money among the glitterati for their campaigns. It is part of the celebrity-ization of American politics, including foreign policy, where many of these Hollywood types have strong views but little knowledge. Angelina Jolie can attract attention (and make congressmen drool) and gain publicity for the cause of poor third world children; but neither she nor many others of the Hollywood stripe have even a college education. So why should we value their opinions on the issues any more than we do the man-in-the-street? Answer: politicians should not, except for the momentary publicity and special interest money they may be able to bring and for the pictures with celebrities that they crave.

DISCUSSION AND CONTROVERSY

All these new groups have added enormously to the number and variety of interest groups involved in foreign policy. Herewith is some commentary on these groups that is designed to stimulate discussion and debate.

When many of these groups, growing out of the Vietnam antiwar movement, were first organized in the 1970s, most were associated with liberal, radical, or new left causes. During Jimmy Carter's presidency (1976–80), many of their representatives found places within the government where they could put their ideas into practice. Then during the Reagan years (1980–88), conservative NGOs sprouted, including the Conservative Caucus, the National Conservative Political Action Committee, Focus on the Family, and others. Thereafter, our government has alternated not just between administration and parties but also between the lineups of interest groups. When the Democrats (Bill Clinton) regained power, all the old left-wing groups followed him into office and positions of influence; when the Republicans (both Bush administrations) were in office, all the conservative groups inherited those same jobs. Moral of the story: your vote in November elects not just a president and Congress but also a panoply of interest groups that will accompany these elected representatives into office.

Many of these groups are thin organizationally. Their names may sound powerful and their stationery may boast an impressive list of board members, but often these so-called interest groups consist of a single person, a computer, a mailing list, and a handful of interns. Their "offices" may consist of a post office box number, their boards may never meet, and their group might not have any organization or mass membership. So we need to be very careful when we weigh the influence of these groups on policy: some have real influence while others are mainly paper organizations.

Many of these groups' publicly stated agendas do not always reflect their real agendas. During the 1980s, for example, some of the groups organized ostensibly on behalf of human rights or Central America had as their real goal to embarrass and thus defeat the Reagan administration. Similarly, in the 1990s conservative groups took positions on the key issues of the day—U.S. involvement in Haiti, Bosnia, or Somalia—not just because they believed in them but also to damage Bill Clinton's standing and derail his reelection. Much the same applies today. Some groups opposed to the Iraq War were more interested in defeating the Republicans than they were in presenting a sound war strategy. Moral of the story: many interest groups are purely partisan organizations for whom politics is more important than policy.

Many of the interest groups discussed here are single-issue groups or have tunnel vision regarding policy. Their *only* interest is human rights, arms control, the environment or, alternatively, NATO, a bigger DOD budget, or the war on terrorism. They tend to go all out for their particular issue and to be absolutist and moralistic in their approach. But the policymaker, while listening to this cacophony of interest group voices, has to weigh many, often conflicting factors and decide when to use diplomacy and when to use military force, how to balance human rights versus strategic interests, and when to use "soft power" (Joseph Nye's term for persuasion, cultural exchanges, public diplomacy) and when to employ "hard power" (a show of naval or air force might).

All these groups presume to speak for their membership, but do they really? Frequently, while the central headquarters supports one position, its far more numerous membership, now reached via targeted direct mail or the Internet, supports another. The U.S. Conference of Catholic Bishops, for example, is strongly pro-immigration, favoring amnesty and a path to citizenship for those already in the United States, but their membership in the churches is 70 to 80 percent against it. The central Methodist lobbying group in Washington is antimilitary and antiwar, but 70 to 80 percent of their membership voted for George W. Bush twice. The pattern holds for almost all groups: their central offices are far more activist and radical than is the membership. In a democracy this disparity becomes a problem for if the leadership strays too far from the mainstream, their members will desert them. And for policymakers, the dilemma is, do they court the groups' leadership or its members?

Another feature of these groups that adds to their political clout is networking. That is, while one group concentrates on human rights policy, another related group deals with immigration issues, and a third mobilizes antiwar sentiment, but all three groups may be part of the same political network, share the same overall agenda, and may operate out of the same office space, answering each other's phones and so forth. For example, in Washington's Dupont Circle neighborhood or on Capitol Hill, there are office buildings occupied by a variety of these groups that are known as "liberal buildings" or "conservative buildings." Such networking within the same building among like-minded groups helps them to bundle their influence, save costs, and make the group appear bigger and more influential than it is.

There are now NGOs for virtually every area of foreign policy: immigration, human rights, refugees, peace, democracy, population control, pollution, global warming, nuclear nonproliferation, the environment, and so on. Their literature suggests that these groups put pressure on the government but are not a part of it; however, that perspective is outmoded. In many instances, these groups *are* the government; that is, they have captured whole agencies or areas of policy for themselves. The human rights groups may thus control the human rights office in the State Department; environmental groups control the environmental impact office in the Defense Department; the family planning office is run by population control advocates; and so on. Some whole areas of policy have been ceded over to these groups. In other words, private groups have been placed in charge of entire areas of supposedly public foreign policy, with precious little accountability or responsibility to the electorate. Of course, the policies that emerge from these arrangements always seem to reflect, as well as benefit, the particular groups involved. It is often hard to see where the public interest begins and ends and where private interests take over.

The Privatization of Foreign Policy

From private groups hiving off and controlling entire areas of foreign policy for themselves, it is only a short step to the actual privatization of foreign policy. In fact by this time, whole functions of foreign and security policy have been privatized, usually to the detriment of good foreign policy. The most obvious and visible example is the private security police, replacing the city police, that now guard virtually all public buildings in Washington, D.C., and elsewhere in the country. But that is only the tip of the iceberg. In fact, the privatization of foreign and security policy is occurring at many levels of government. It is a trend that carries immense and ominous consequences.

The privatization of public services began in the 1970s at the local government level. Strapped for funds, many local governments determined that they could save money by employing private contractors to perform public functions —tax collection, trash collection, and even fire fighting—than they could by taking on more public employees. Then in the 1980s, with conservative Ronald Reagan in the White House, the urge for state downsizing, deregulation, and privatization spread to the national level. The Reagan administration deregulated such areas as airlines, trucking, and pharmaceuticals and privatized or partially privatized such government functions as the post office, the government retirement system, previously government-run health care, and even some schools. However, when Reagan sought to bypass congressional restrictions and privately fund an anticommunist war in Central America, he ran into trouble with Democrats, Congress, and the public.

Nevertheless, the idea was so popular that it persisted and was expanded under both Clinton and Bush. It appeared to be a way to hold runaway government spending in check. Through privatization, the government could either save money or pretend that it was, by taking whole areas of public functions off the books and placing them in private hands. That way the government could also disguise its budget shortfalls. And sometimes it even resulted in cheaper, better, more efficient services!

The State Department, the CIA, and the FBI have been less affected by this trend toward privatization than has the Defense Department. In strife-torn and drug-infested Colombia, the State Department has hired approximately 750 private contractors to snuff out drugs and work with the Colombian police, military, and government in battling guerrillas and narco traffickers. The CIA also uses private airlines and private contractors for its covert activities.

But it is in the Iraq War effort where privatization is especially notable. Back in the Pentagon, what used to be military functions, such as procuring shoes, body armor, and weapons for our troops, have been removed from military officers and given to civilian contractors who often have little understanding of military functions or the needs of troops in the field. In Iraq itself, private contractors do everything from driving trucks to cooking for the troops to providing security services.

Many of these private security forces hire former military personnel. More than seventy thousand of them are armed and thus make up a private army. About thirteen hundred private contractors in Iraq have died, or about one-quarter the number of U.S. military casualties. Blackwater Security as well as Halliburton provided most of this private army, but other companies are involved as well, and Blackwater's contract was later cancelled and the company abolished. The work these private companies do is essential to the war effort. Among other things, the presence of so many private contractors frees up the regular, uniformed U.S. armed forces to do the actual war fighting. It also makes it appear that the United States has committed fewer forces than it actually has and that the costs, since many of these private activities are off the books, are less than they are.

But the problems with this strategy are immense and the long-term consequences enormous. First, almost no U.S. laws, civilian or military, apply to these contractors, so in Iraq, they often behave as if it is the Wild West. Second, there is very little U.S. oversight of their activities—by Congress, the Government Accountability Office, or anyone else. Third, the usual military rules regarding the careful use of force do not apply to private contractors; consequently, there have been numerous cases of contractors shooting innocent Iraqi civilians or even fighting with rival contractors. Next, the contractors are obliged only to their client, the Defense Department, and may not have any loyalty to the U.S. national interest. Fifth, without an effective government in Iraq, there are only weak Iraqi laws that cover the contractors' behavior, including in some notorious cases the killing of Iraqis. Finally, and perhaps most importantly, without laws, rules, or oversight, there is no real system of accountability or responsibility for these private contractors.

Iraq is the most dramatic case, but such privatization of what used to be public or governmental functions is going on all over the world. In this closed system, the private contractors themselves neither reveal much about their activities, nor, because they are private, are they obliged to do so. And in this system, the main contractors then subcontract the work out, layer after layer, to other, smaller operators. Thus it becomes almost impossible to ferret out information about their activities. Even DOD doesn't know fully what its own subcontractors are doing out in the field.

Basically, the government has outsourced large parts of our foreign and strategic policy. Just as big business outsources jobs, we are similarly outsourcing foreign policy. While there are obvious advantages to this strategy, the disadvant-ages may well outweigh them all. The American public must decide.

Conclusion

Let us return to the series of questions with which we began this chapter. The answers we have gleaned to these questions not only shed light on what is new in U.S. foreign policy but also on why the policymaking process is so complex and difficult, sometimes gets out of hand, or produces unintended consequences.

First, it is the case that some major interest groups have partially taken over, hived off, and quasi-privatized whole areas of foreign policy. Not just big business, agriculture, and labor, but some major NGOs and ethnic lobbies are so powerful that they largely control policy regarding their country or issue. Often these groups have influence, not because of some power grab, but because they know the issues and the stakes better than do U.S. government personnel. Most often the groups work in conjunction with the State and other departments, but using their political influence they may go directly to the president and get him to change a policy made at lower levels. Thus, the line between private interest group and public policymaking is lost and so, often, is accountability and responsibility.

Second, these groups' sheer power, numbers, and influence sometimes para-lyze our ability to respond sensibly on foreign policy. Often their countervailing power leads to gridlock and paralysis, or the competition among them becomes so intense that the government itself is unable to act. Is the United States becom-ing ungovernable? Look at FEMA's response after Hurricane Katrina, and now apply the same critical standards to foreign policy. Sometimes the U.S. govern-ment is so paralyzed by internal group conflict that it is unable to carry out *any* sensible policy.

Third, the uneven influence of these groups introduces all kinds of biases into the policy process. It used to be that left-wing groups were better organized than conservative ones, but since the 1980s that has changed. However, big business is still more powerful than labor, the Israelis wield more influence than the Palestinians, and so on. These imbalances not only bias our policy, but the shouting matches that often accompany these debates make devising a middle-of-the-road policy much harder.

Related, fourth, is the problem of tunnel vision. These private groups tend to go all out for their particular point of view. They do not consider other points of view and are often unwilling to compromise. Policy responses become polarized, again making it more difficult to arrive at some middle ground.

Fifth, the power of these groups may wax and wane depending on the global situation. After the Cold War, the power of these groups grew enormously, but after 9/11, President Bush gathered enormous power in his own hands and largely ignored the interplay of interest groups. We can argue, of course, depending on your support of the ensuing war or Bush's policies, whether greater interest group input might have prevented some of the mistakes made in Iraq. In any case, with the war in Iraq apparently winding down, the interest group struggle over policy seems to be revving up again, at least on those issues that do not directly involve the terrorism threat, such as trade and immigration.

Sixth is the issue of privatization. Not only is foreign policy subject nowadays to intense private interest group pressure, but a considerable share of policy has now been privatized. We have turned over whole areas of foreign policy, mainly support services but not just those, to private contractors. One understands the logic of these steps—the private sector can often do it better and cheaply—but the government has not adequately dealt with the negatives. It has allowed private groups, without accountability and little oversight, in Iraq and elsewhere to hire personnel who may be out of control, are carrying guns, and sometimes engage in armed conflict with local militias. They serve as representatives of U.S. foreign policy, but their only real obligation is to their immediate employer.

Finally, can the American foreign policymaking system be saved? Is it still reformable? The answer is, only with great effort and only in the long term. Because the problems are so great, current practices are so ingrained, and the divisions in the country are so deep, reform will take Herculean effort and a long time. I see the problems as so deeply entrenched that they may not be reformable, even in the long term. What then do we do?

Suggested Reading

Bauer, Raymond Augustine, Ithiel de Sola Pool, and Lewis Anthony Dexter. *American Business and Public Policy: The Politics of Foreign Trade.* 2nd ed. Chicago: Aldine-Atherton, 1972.

Bergsten, C. Fred, Thomas Horst, and Theodore H. Moran. *American Multinationals and American Interests.* Washington, DC: Brookings Institution, 1978.

Cohen, Benjamin J. *In Whose Interest? International Banking and American Foreign Policy*. New Haven, CT: Yale University Press, 1986.

Cohen, Richard. "Getting Religion." *National Journal* (September 14, 1985): 1080–84.

Edel, Wilbur. *Defenders of the Faith: Religion and Politics from the Pilgrim Fathers to Ronald Reagan*. New York: Praeger, 1987.

Holloway, H. "Interest Groups in the Postpartisan Era: The Political Machine of the AFL-CIO." *Political Science Quarterly* 4 (Spring 1979): 117–33.

Hula, Kevin W. *Lobbying Together: Interest Group Coalitions in Legislative Politics, American Governance, and Public Policy*. Washington, DC: Georgetown University Press, 1999.

Huntington, Samuel P. "The Governability of Democracy: USA." In *The Crisis of Democracy: Report on the Governability of Democracies to the Trilateral Commission*, edited by Michael Crozier, Samuel P. Huntington, and Joji Watanuki. New York: New York University Press, 1975.

Mathias, C. M. C. "Ethnic Groups and Foreign Policy." *Foreign Affairs* 59 (1980): 975.

Mearsheimer, John J., and Stephen M. Walt. *The Israel Lobby and U.S. Foreign Policy*. New York: Farrar, Straus, Giroux, 2007.

Milbrath, L. W. "Interest Groups and Foreign Policy." *Domestic Sources of Foreign Policy* (1967): 231–51.

Nathan, James A., and James K. Oliver. *Foreign Policy Making and the American Political System*. 3rd ed. Baltimore, MD: John Hopkins University Press, 1994.

Ornstein, Norman J., and Shirley Elder. *Interest Groups, Lobbying, and Policymaking*. Washington, DC: CQ Press, 1978.

Russett, Bruce M., and Elizabeth C. Hanson. *Interest and Ideology: The Foreign Policy Beliefs of American Businessmen*. San Francisco: W. H. Freeman, 1975.

Said, Abdul Aziz. *Ethnicity and U.S. Foreign Policy*. Rev. ed. New York: Praeger, 1981.

Smith, Tony. *Foreign Attachments: The Power of Ethnic Groups in the Making of American Foreign Policy*. Cambridge, MA: Harvard University Press, 2000.

Terry, Janice J. *U.S. Foreign Policy in the Middle East: The Role of Lobbies and Special Interest Groups*. Ann Arbor, MI: Pluto Press, 2005.

7

Parties, Politics, and Foreign Policy

Political parties in the United States have not historically been thought of as major actors in foreign policy. In part, this notion originates in the strong currents of isolationism and exceptionalism, or the idea that America is different from other nations, that have long been present in American history. In part, it stems from the notion that the United States is so big and powerful that we don't need to pay serious attention to other nations. And, in part, it is also related to the absence of major threats historically to the American homeland. Of course, the parties, as agencies of electoral mobilization, have reflected these popular sentiments. The question now is, have the attacks of 9/11, the war on terrorism, the war in Iraq, as well as changes in America itself, changed all that by bringing the parties into a larger foreign policy role?

Most American elections are decided not on foreign policy issues but on such domestic bread-and-butter issues as jobs, taxes, health care, inflation, interest rates, and the overall performance of the economy. The conventional wisdom of professional politicians is that a candidate can lose on the basis of lack of knowledge of foreign policy but cannot win on the basis of foreign policy expertise alone. In the 1992 election, with the Cold War over, Bill Clinton and his political guru, James Carville, downplayed George H. W. Bush's foreign policy expertise and concentrated on domestic issues ("It's the economy, stupid"). George W. Bush in 2000 continued the focus on domestic peace and prosperity but, after the terrorist attacks on the Pentagon and World Trade Center in 2001, reinvented himself as a "war president." That position carried him through the 2004 election, but as the war in Iraq went badly virtually all the presidential candidates in 2008 distanced themselves from Bush and "his" unpopular war and sought to redirect the electorate's focus on domestic issues: health care, gas prices, immigration, and the overall economy.

The mix between domestic policy issues and foreign affairs remains complicated, however, and it is still volatile and full of uncertainty for presidents and presidential candidates. Republicans in 2008 were torn between their desire to support President Bush or, as the war in Iraq turned sour, to distance themselves from him. Democratic candidates favored ending the war, but they could not be seen as abandoning the troops or leaving them ill equipped in that far-off desert war zone. Although the polls and the results of the 2006 election, in which the Democrats gained control of both houses of Congress, showed Americans were tired of the war and wanted out, they could not be interpreted to mean the voters favored a precipitous withdrawal that would endanger our troops, leave Iraq in chaos, or result in American disgrace. Barack Obama learned only the first part of this lesson—withdraw the troops—from the 2008 election; he may still have to learn the second part—leave Iraq stable and don't endanger or discredit the troops.

Foreign policy thus remains a major concern for American voters. During the long Cold War with the Soviet Union, foreign policy issues were consistently a top priority with American voters. After the Soviet Union collapsed in 1991, economic issues came to the fore. Now with 9/11, Iraq, and the war on terrorism, foreign policy concerns are in the forefront again but usually in combination with economic issues. The issue is actually more complicated than that: increasingly, American voters are seeing that the health of the domestic economy is closely related to what happens in the wider world. Think of the following's impact on the country: skyrocketing oil prices, the huge loss of American jobs to foreign countries, chaos in Pakistan, America's dependence on immigrant labor, global climate change, and the fear and disruption sown by international terrorism.

In this modern, globalized, interdependent world, we can no longer separate domestic policy from the international environment. The distinction between the domestic economy and the foreign policy agenda has been blurred because domestic prosperity is intrinsically linked to the international economy and politics. Scholars refer to issues, such as climate change or immigration, that are both international and domestic as "intermestic." Voters increasingly recognize these linkages as well; consequently, the political parties and their candidates must do so also if they want to win. Hence, while the two major

American political parties have not paid much attention to foreign policy in the past, except sporadically and usually in time of war, now they must do so if for no other reason than that jobs and prosperity at home are closely related to events abroad.

American Political Parties, Past and Present

It used to be said that American political parties were very different from European parties. European parties, more so than their American counterparts, tended to be national parties, that is, more centralized, more ideological, and with broader functions, clear program differences, and a stronger interest in foreign policy. They also had the institutional basis—party foundations, branches devoted to foreign affairs, and links with like-minded parties abroad—that enabled them to play more of a foreign policy role than the U.S. parties did. But many of these aspects are now changing: while the U.S. parties are still more pragmatic, less ideological, and more state or locally based than the European parties are, the American parties, too, are becoming more divided, more ideological, and more national and international. Once again the divide between domestic politics and international affairs is breaking down as the world becomes more interconnected.

American political parties, first of all, still tend to be more locally, county, state, and regionally oriented than are European parties. Except at election time, the parties' national organizations located in Washington tend to be the weakest link in the chain. In between elections, the national parties have few staff and are all but moribund. They lack a strong central administration, program, and platform. Moreover, the parties stand for different things depending on their locale: they are more liberal in the North and on the West Coast and more conservative in the South and West. Hence, politicians must take different stands depending on what part of the country they're in. The parties' weak national organization and their corresponding focus at the local, county, state, and regional levels also explain why they are not much concerned with foreign affairs. Foreign policy requires a single, consistent, national organization and position that, historically at least, the decentralized American parties did not provide.[1]

1. There is now a growing literature of what is called "local foreign policy." It involves the increasing inclinations of local or state governments to stake out their own positions on foreign policy or even to conduct their own foreign policy without bothering to tell federal officials in Washington. The Supreme Court has ruled that only the federal government may conduct foreign policy; nevertheless, states and localities continue to act unilaterally on issues of concern to them.

Now the parties have evolved. America has divided clearly into red states and blue states as the ideological differences between the parties have become sharper and more polarized. Candidates for office at local and state levels are being forced to toe the national party line on the issues. Because of television coverage, it is no longer possible to say one thing in one part of the country and say something different in another. These changes have made the American parties more ideologically consistent but less flexible and pragmatic. Now with positions on the issues as well as all-important campaign funds controlled by the expanding national organizations and their staffs, candidates must conform to central party directions or they are cut off from party support. Even families' party preferences are influencing where they decide to live, with conservatives more likely to settle in the South and West and liberals on either coast or in the North.

A second feature of the two main American parties is that they have long represented multiple class and social interests, whereas European parties mainly stood for the working class versus the bourgeoisie. The American parties tended to be pluralistic and, for electoral purposes, sought to be all things to all people. Such pluralistic and nonclass-based politics were probably healthy for American democracy, but those same features made it hard for the parties to speak with one voice or to project a clear image on foreign policy. Because so many groups and interests had to fit within the tent, party platforms were typically vague on the issues. The parties did not want to lose the support of any of their constituent groups by staking out too strong a position. They usually settled for moderate positions that sounded good and had uplifting rhetoric but generally represented the lowest common denominator.

Third and related, the American parties were not very ideological. The contrast with their European counterparts is again pronounced. The United States has no communist or socialist parties on the Left and no monarchist or fascist parties on the Right. In their quest to occupy the broad center of the political spectrum and thereby capture the most voters, American parties avoided adherence to any one single ideology. Consequently, the American parties did not have much contact with parties abroad, which were more ideological. As catchall parties seeking to draw in diverse voters, the American parties did not have a clear-cut stance on foreign policy; instead, the picture was one of diversity, ideological variation, and various and crosscutting loyalties.

Now all these features are changing as well. The parties are becoming more ideological and polarized, making compromise increasingly difficult. The American party system is becoming like Italy's, with two ideological "families" vying for control of the federal purse strings for themselves, their clients, and their constituencies. On one side, we have the family of order, with folks who are richer, more conservative, more religious, Republican, living in the South and West; and on the other, we have the family of change—poorer, less religious, discontented minorities, Democratic, living in the North or on the East and West coasts. The differences between the two parties are cultural, social, racial, geographic, and religious as well as political and economic; the gaps have become so wide as to be almost unbridgeable. These sharp contrasts account for the often nasty, mean-spirited, take-no-prisoners character of our political and partisan debate.

A fourth feature of American political parties in the past is that they were fluid and flexible. American parties would stand for one thing one day and another thing the next; there was no clear ideology. Different factions within the parties spoke with different voices, and there were distinct regional points of view. These features made the parties flexible and able to compromise.

It is hard to find that flexibility nowadays. Party positions have hardened. Politicians have to toe the party line. For instance, a Republican in Congress had to support President Bush's positions on the Iraq War or lose a choice committee assignment and have the Republican National Committee cut off reelection campaign funds. Likewise, Democrats had to oppose the war or the party leadership would similarly punish them. Such rigidities leave little room for compromise or for a nuanced, middle-of-the-road position.

American political parties, other than presenting candidates at election time, serve few important functions. This fifth feature has not changed very much; indeed, most political scientists see political parties in decline all over the world: North America, Europe, Asia, and even the developing world. The United States is not unique in this regard.

The theoretical literature on political parties suggests that they are important "articulators" and "aggregators" of interests; that is, the parties articulate political platforms and bring together (aggregate) various groups to support it. But we already know that the parties are usually quite vague when presenting party programs, function merely as skeleton organizations in the intervals between elections, and—as compared with the European parties that do job training, run education programs, and perform a variety of other functions—do little more than help manage primary and general election campaigns. As for formulating programs, that function more and more has been taken over by interest groups, political action committees (PACs), think tanks, and the media. These groups usually channel their ideas and interests directly into the political system rather than through the parties as intermediaries. American parties do not do much and even the functions they do perform are declining in importance.

It also used to be said, in keeping with the comments above about the fluidity of American parties, that our parties shared another feature: they lacked discipline. Individual members of Congress could largely vote as they pleased, say what they wished, and not pay too close attention to either the party platform or the wishes of the leadership. But this aspect is also changing. Again, members of Congress are expected to conform to the party's ideals or face the consequences. It is harder to be a "lone ranger" or to vote one's conscience. The parties are now more disciplined than before; however, whether that control is beneficial for the American political system or for foreign policy remains to be seen.

The last feature of American political parties that requires commentary is the disconnect between voting on domestic and foreign affairs. On domestic issues members of Congress, Democrat or Republican, tend to vote in accord with the public opinion in their districts. They vote that way on foreign affairs too but pay less attention to their constituents' opinions. If a congressperson brings home the goods (jobs, pork, patronage) on domestic issues, then the constituents, especially since few Americans pay close attention to foreign affairs, are inclined to give that member a free hand on international issues. Republican senator Richard Lugar is conservative on domestic issues but fairly liberal on foreign affairs, whereas Independent senator Joe Lieberman is liberal on domestic matters but close to the Republicans on international issues. With parties becoming more ideological and disciplined, it is becoming harder to maintain such a bifurcated (or "two-faced") position.

Many of the traits that we have ascribed to the American political parties are historic characteristics. Some of them remain continuous; others are changing. The historically flexible and nonideological character of the parties is giving way to more rigid, partisan, and ideological politics. The partisan battles in Congress and between political candidates have gotten nastier as well. Regional differences are in decline for it has also become harder, because of media scrutiny, for a presidential candidate to say one thing in one part of the country and something else in another. At the same time, as the parties become more ideological, the right wing of the Republican Party pushes the party further to the right while the left wing of the Democratic Party similarly drives that party in more progressive directions. In the process, moderates, liberal Republicans, and conservative Democrats are all losing influence or, as in the South, are switching parties. The center gives way.

These changes make it easier to identify the parties on ideological grounds. But lost in this trend toward greater ideological purity are flexibility, pragmatism, and middle-of-the-road positions as well as the ability to compromise and get things done. More ideological and more disciplined parties result in a hardening of political positions, greater anger and nastiness between the parties, and gridlock. While the United States seems to be moving toward a more European style of greater ideological and class-based politics, it seems unlikely that change will produce better policy. Instead, it appears to lead to only more paralysis and anger.

The Parties and Foreign Affairs: About Face?

With some exceptions, the Republican Party, strongly rooted in the Midwest where international events seldom intruded, was generally isolationist before World War II. The Democratic Party of Woodrow Wilson and Franklin D. Roosevelt was more internationalist, but it also led us into World Wars I and II.

In the 1970s and 1980s these positions began to reverse themselves, with the Republicans standing for a strong foreign and security policy and the Democrats, after Vietnam, reluctant to get involved abroad. By the 1990s the positions of the two parties changed again, with the Democrats wanting to do peacekeeping and nation building ("liberal internationalism") and the Republicans, while standing for a strong defense ("conservative internationalism," or "realism"), were reluctant to get involved in third world conflicts. Under George W. Bush, the Republicans fused a strong defense with peacekeeping and democracy promotion in Iraq and Afghanistan but in ways that were enormously costly and not very successful. After Bush, the country is unlikely to want to engage in such expensive—in terms of lives and resources—interventions any time soon, even while preserving the policy of keeping a strong defense and advancing, where feasible, the cause of democracy abroad.

Let us sort out all these changes in detail and the conflicts and positions that arose for they still inform the parties today.

Although Theodore Roosevelt had been a strongly internationalist president and Herbert Hoover had traveled and had a strong interest in international affairs, the main orientation in the Republican Party prior to World War II was toward isolationism. The Republican-controlled Senate refused to ratify Democratic president Woodrow Wilson's League of Nations; as the clouds of another world war loomed in the 1930s, the Republicans sought to keep America out of it. They were not against America's involvement in world events; rather, the Republicans believed in a strong America, a fortress America, and that we should not get involved in other countries' or regions' affairs. The Republicans heeded first President George Washington's warnings that we should avoid "entangling alliances."

The Democratic Party points with pride to President Wilson and his internationalist orientation but, similarly reflecting the views of the isolationist electorate, sought almost at the onset of hostilities to keep the United States out of World War II. President Franklin Roosevelt successfully guided us through the war and became more internationalist in his thinking. His successor, Harry Truman, similarly responded to the early Soviet moves in the Cold War, launched the Marshall Plan's program of aid for European reconstruction, organized the NATO alliance, and began the Point Four Program of assistance for developing countries. The Republicans were also becoming more internationalist during this period: Republican senator Arthur Vandenberg led the pro-internationalist turnabout in Congress, and President Dwight D. Eisenhower was certainly internationalist in his thinking as he led the United States during a crucial period of the Cold War.

Indeed, the period from World War II until the early 1970s may be characterized as an unprecedented era of internationalist consensus in U.S. foreign policy. Both Democratic (Kennedy and Johnson) and Republican (Nixon and Ford) presidents supported a strong, anti-Soviet, Cold War position. There were, of course, still differences between their two parties. In the constant trade-off between "guns" and "butter," the Republicans placed more emphasis on a strong defense (guns) while the Democrats wanted more Great Society–like social programs (butter). But these were matters more of degree than in kind: in actuality, both parties supported a strong defense and a firm foreign policy.

As we have seen, a big change came with the Vietnam War in the late 1960s and early 1970s. The Republicans under President Nixon, with Henry Kissinger as, first, his national security adviser and then his secretary of state, remained committed to a hardheaded, realist policy. In Vietnam that meant hitting the enemy hard with bombing raids and softening them up, even while continuing to negotiate an end to the war. For Democrats, appalled at the war and seeking to capitalize on the electorate's rising antiwar sentiment, Vietnam turned them into the antimilitary "Peace Party." In supporting McGovern's failed presidential bid of 1972 and then Carter's presidency, the Democratic Party became the party of détente (an easing of tensions with the Soviets), human rights, and democracy building. Capitalizing on these stances, the Republicans quickly labeled them "peaceniks," the "party of unilateral disarmament," and "soft on communism."

That split, with some changes, remains present today and is at the heart of the Democrats' foreign policy dilemma. The party is seen as "soft" on defense issues, if not as outright antimilitary. The public does not always trust the Democrats on foreign or strategic policy. Thus after Carter's presidency, we had three successive Republican administrations—two under Reagan, who was seen as tough on defense and Soviet relations, and one under George H. W. Bush, who had a strong foreign policy background. Only after the Cold War did the public see fit to elect Clinton, another Democrat, who wisely ran on a domestic policy platform. George W. Bush was also elected on a domestic policy basis—namely, "compassionate conservatism." After the terrorist attacks in 2001, Bush treated the terrorist threat as a war issue—the "war on terrorism"—and not a law enforcement issue. The "war president" garnered support from the public that secured his reelection in 2004. Unlike his father, however, he had little foreign or defense policy experience, and the ill-conceived and incompetently planned war in Iraq went badly.

Meanwhile, the Democrats, who supported the Iraq War early on, began to change their position as the war became a quagmire. But the Democrats faced a terrible quandary. On one hand, if they opposed the war or its funding, the Republicans immediately accused them of failing to support the troops and of aiding and abetting the enemy. On the other hand, they could not support a war to which they were opposed. The Democrats then compounded their problems by interpreting their congressional gains in the 2006 midterm election as a referendum of opposition to the war. Although the public had clearly turned against the war, no one wanted a precipitous and dishonorable withdrawal that disgraced the United States. Withdrawal, yes, but with our honor intact—that is the foreign policy high wire that Barack Obama must walk.

So that is where we stand. With his ruinous (in terms of costs, prestige, and lives lost) and poorly managed war, Bush squandered much of the advantage Republicans had enjoyed on national security issues since Vietnam. However, given the policies the Democratic Party has espoused over the last forty years, the public does not quite trust the Democrats with leadership on foreign policy either. How can we carry out a successful foreign policy in this country if neither political party has sufficient public trust to manage the complex, dangerous issues involved?

Ideology of the Parties

American political parties have not, historically, been very ideological. Instead, the two main parties were known as catchall parties, home to diverse group and regional orientations and to a great variety of interest groups and individual views. Over the last forty years, however, the parties have become more partisan and ideological, serving further to break down the bipartisan foreign policy consensus that reigned through the mid-1960s and adding to American fragmentation, division, and current ungovernability. The end of the Cold War and the war on terrorism further entrenched these partisan ideological differences.

The 1968 election was the last time the United States had a presidential election not dominated by major ideological differences over foreign policy. In 1960 the two candidates, Nixon and Kennedy, were fierce rivals, but they were also realists and did not differ very much on foreign policy issues. In 1964 Democrat Lyndon Johnson and Republican Barry Goldwater were poles apart ideologically, but that election was mainly about domestic issues, not foreign affairs. In 1968 the Democrats were internally divided over the Vietnam War, with liberal senator Eugene McCarthy taking a strong antiwar stand in the primaries; but in the November election both Humphrey and Nixon took essentially realist positions, promising to negotiate an end to the war but with American dignity and honor intact.

By 1972, however, the situation had dramatically changed. Within the Democratic Party the more radical, antiwar faction had captured the party machinery and the majority of the delegates. This group nominated George McGovern, a former history professor and an antiwar senator from North Dakota. McGovern was swamped in the presidential election, losing all but two states, but his candidacy permanently changed the Democratic Party. It became known as the Peace Party, which supported an antiwar position, favored a nuclear freeze, and sought détente with the Soviet Union.

By 1976 the McGovernites were firmly in control of the Democratic Party. The Vietnam War had ended, but the Democrats' idealistic agenda of peace, détente, weapons control, and human rights was still dominant. In Jimmy Carter they found a candidate who would champion those causes but also, as a Southerner and Naval Academy graduate, seemed unthreatening. The Republicans stuck to their realist positions as exemplified in the candidacy of Gerald Ford.

By 1980 the country had had enough of Carter's idealism, which seemed to have produced only major gains for the Soviet Union, the humiliating capture of the U.S. embassy hostages in Iran, and more Marxist regimes in the third world. In a time of global tension, the Republicans nominated Ronald Reagan, who promised to be tough on the Soviets and follow a realist strategy. At this time many realist Democrats like Jeane Kirkpatrick and the Committee on the Present Danger (which promoted "peace through strength") deserted the Democratic Party and became Republicans or "neoconservatives."

Meanwhile, Reagan himself, while continuing as a realist, stole much of the Democrats' agenda by championing the cause of democracy abroad. However, Reagan pursued this policy not just for idealistic reasons à la Carter but because he viewed it as an extension of realism. His pro-democracy stand was a way to win allies abroad while also undermining the Soviet Union.

The Reagan policies—a strong defense, standing up to the Soviet Union, but also a pro-democracy stance—were followed by his successor, George H. W. Bush. Bush and his team were realists and carried out one of America's more effective foreign policies, presiding peacefully over the collapse of the Soviet Union, the reunification of Germany, and the democratization of Eastern Europe. By this time both parties agreed on the democracy–human rights agenda, although the Democrats were somewhat more idealistic about it and the Republicans more realistic.

For the 1992, 1996, and 2000 elections, foreign policy almost disappeared as an issue of contention between the parties. In the relatively peaceful interim between the Cold War and the war on terrorism, the United States was overwhelmingly powerful on the global stage and seemed to have no major enemies. Hence, in the 1990s Democrat Bill Clinton won two elections largely because of his domestic policy (on the economy, social programs, and reform), and in

2000 Republican George W. Bush beat Democrat Al Gore in a contested election that likewise had few foreign policy issues.

After 9/11 Bush turned his main attention to foreign policy issues, even though he was woefully inexperienced on foreign policy. Proclaiming a war on terrorism, he attacked the Taliban in Afghanistan, targeted Saddam Hussein in Iraq and militarily occupied the country, and labeled North Korea, Iran, and Iraq as "terrorist states" and part of the axis of evil. Bush also advanced the doctrine of "preemption" under which the United States reserved the right to attack any terrorist group or state before it attacked us.

Although Bush had criticized Clinton's nation-building policies in Haiti and Somalia as wasteful and wishy-washy, he now championed nation building in Iraq, Afghanistan, Lebanon, Pakistan, and other unstable countries. And while he had been skeptical of Clinton's idealistic democracy initiatives in the third world, post 9/11 Bush himself launched a truly breathtaking global campaign to bring democracy to the Middle East and other areas as a way to bring stability to these regions and advance U.S. interests. But whether countries like Iraq, Afghanistan, Pakistan, Egypt, Syria, Iran, and others are much more democratic now or can be made democratic through U.S. guns and pressure remains an open question.

Where, then, do the two parties stand ideologically now in terms of foreign policy? The Democrats, as a legacy of Vietnam, are still more reluctant to use force in international affairs and harbor a certain disdain for the U.S. military. They are much more inclined toward soft power, including diplomacy, the use of international organizations like the United Nations, or humanitarian interventions (Haiti, Darfur). At the same time, they favor the policies of liberal internationalism and support these preferences: the Kyoto Protocol on the environment, the UN Convention on the Law of the Sea, human rights, and global action on climate change.

The Republicans, in contrast, tend to be realists in foreign policy. They are more willing to use military force and stand for a hardheaded defense of the national interest. But these differences have been fudged first by Reagan and then by George W. Bush, both of whom favored global campaigns to promote democracy and soft-power nation building in Iraq and Afghanistan. And they pursued all these policies at enormous, budget-busting costs and with the support of a party that once prided itself on fiscal responsibility.

Neither party has yet resolved the fundamental contradictions in its own platform. The Democrats need to come to grips with the use of force in international affairs and to recognize that the military instrument, along with diplomacy, covert action, and soft-power humanitarianism, provides a useful tool in America's foreign policy that should be used sparingly but sometimes and appropriately. Republican "realists" need to recognize that the world has changed, that force alone is insufficient, and that democracy, nation building, and other seemingly soft policies can also be instruments in advancing U.S. interests. At the same time, both parties need to acknowledge: (1) the limits of U.S. military power to effect change—witness Iraq or Afghanistan; (2) the need to be selective in promoting democracy and nation building for the same strategies will not be universally applicable; and (3) the necessity of conducting a careful cost-benefit analysis before embarking on any large project, be it waging a war in Iraq or Afghanistan, engaging in democracy or nation building, or offering humanitarian assistance.

Campaigns, Primaries, and General Elections

The question for us to mull over here is why, since the 1960s, the Democrats have generally fielded candidates who are so weak on foreign policy. Since the Vietnam War, Republicans have won seven of eleven presidential elections. Only Jimmy Carter in 1976, Bill Clinton in 1992 and 1996—both Southerners—and now Barack Obama have managed to win the White House for the Democrats, and their electoral wins were decided mainly on domestic issues, not foreign policy. By the same token we also need to ask, while the voters have perceived the Republicans as stronger and more solid on foreign policy, did George W. Bush squander that advantage with his mistake-prone war in Iraq?

The answer to the question regarding Democratic presidential candidates being weak on foreign policy lies in the American system of primaries, which in both parties give disproportional influence to party ideologues and radicals. These factions are especially vocal and influential during the primary season. Often the strength of the extreme factions in the first primary states of Iowa and New Hampshire is such that they can secure the nomination for one of their own or, failing that, can exercise veto power over other, more moderate candidates and programs.

Republicans have what is called the "Goldwater," "Reagan," or "far right" wing of the party. This wing is often seen as conservative or even ultraconservative and as associated with evangelical religious groups, now referred to popularly as the "Religious Right." Its leaders include former presidential candidate Pat

Buchanan, religious leaders Pat Robertson and James Dobbins, George W. Bush, and some neoconservatives like William Kristol or Charles Krauthammer, who give this position intellectual firepower. This group stands in contrast to the more moderate wing of the party—with Condoleezza Rice, Colin Powell, and Richard Lugar—which favors a less ideological, more centrist, and more national interest–driven policy.

For a long time—until Ronald Reagan's ascendancy—it was thought that, if the conservative candidate won the Republican Party's nomination, he would lose disastrously in the general election, as did Barry Goldwater. But Reagan proved that a candidate who came from the right wing, by standing for a strong defense and a foreign policy of global leadership, could not only win the nomination but also win the presidency. George W. Bush continued in this tradition: he was elected in 2000 as an affable, nonthreatening candidate who espoused compassionate conservatism and would continue the Clinton economic boom (domestic policy). After 9/11 he became a foreign policy (war) candidate and won again in 2004 on the basis of the public's perception of him as a strong leader.

In the last thirty years, the Republican Party has moved considerably to the right while centrist Republicans have been sidelined. When Republicans move to the right, however, it plays to their strengths: strong defense, established foreign policy, and a national interest–driven agenda. Sometimes Republicans go too far and nominate a person whom the public thinks is extremist (Goldwater in 1964) or who is seen as squandering American strength in a too costly war (Bush in Iraq). Bush was not up for reelection in 2008, but his mistakes may have cost Republican John McCain the presidency. But the main point is a hard-line conservative candidate plays to Republican strengths, not weaknesses.

The Democrats have a worse problem to overcome. Their radical wing also tends to dominate in the early primaries, but this wing is often seen as comprised of peaceniks who are antiwar and antimilitary; favor the soft power issues of human rights, the environment, and democracy over hard power; and want U.S. might to be restrained through multilateral institutions. This wing of the Democratic Party came to prominence during the Vietnam War, seems to resurface every time the United States engages in or threatens military action, and is particularly exorcised over Iraq. It has never seen a defense policy that it liked and was almost viscerally opposed to Bush and "his" war in Iraq.

The problem for the Democrats is that these antiwar, antimilitary, peace-at-any-cost voters have a near lock on the early primaries, as Hillary Clinton found out. Winning the Democratic nomination without these elements' support is difficult. These groups are not representative of the nation as a whole; moreover, their influence plays to the general public's perception of the Democrats as weak on foreign and defense policy. To the extent that a candidate must play to the wishes of these groups to win the nomination, he or she runs the risk of alienating centrist voters and losing the general election. Bill Clinton was able to overcome this problem because, when he ran, the country was at relative peace, and he could run on a domestic policy platform rather than a foreign policy one.

Witness the dilemma candidate Hillary Clinton faced in the 2007–8 primaries, when foreign policy issues (Iraq and the war on terrorism) were again front and center. Her early statements on foreign policy were quite moderate and reasonable, designed to appeal to centrists and independents in the general election. But then two things happened: she was outflanked on the antiwar left by both Barack Obama and John Edwards, and her pollsters told her that to win in the primaries she'd have to take a stronger antiwar stand. Pragmatically, she moved progres-sively to the left on the Iraq War and foreign policy, but it was still not sufficient for her to get the nomination from the strong antiwar wing in the Democratic Party.

Both parties, therefore, have problems they have to overcome. The Republicans have moved to the right and, in so doing, have sacrificed the moderate, centrist, and sensible wing of the party—that is, the party of George H. W. Bush. Also, with George W. Bush's seemingly reckless policies in Iraq and elsewhere, the Republicans may have squandered the advantages they had long enjoyed with the public on foreign and defense policy. Meanwhile, beholden to their peacenik, antimilitary factions, the Democrats have a hard time convincing the public that they can be trusted on foreign policy, unless, of course, the Republicans carry out such a disastrous policy that they hand power to the Democrats.

The Party Institutes of International Affairs

Most American election campaigns are decided on the basis of domestic issues, such as the economy, immigration, health care, and so on. Unless there is an existing or looming crisis or the public feels threatened, foreign policy issues tend to occupy a lower-order priority. For example, right after 9/11 and during the midterm elections of 2006, foreign policy loomed large, but then the war on terrorism began to fade in importance. Similarly with the Iraq War: when it was going badly and American troops were being killed on a daily basis, the public was very much concerned; but when the war started to go better ("the surge"), the issue faded from the front pages and domestic policy issues again gained prominence. Hence the two main American parties have largely concentrated on domestic concerns.

Unlike the political parties of Europe, the American parties have never seen themselves as part of some overriding international party bloc. As catchall parties that are diverse and ideologically pluralistic, the U.S. political parties neither fit into some nice, neat ideological category nor want to subordinate themselves to some larger international movement. In addition, again unlike their European counterparts, the American parties have not created large-scale mass movements for youth, women, businessmen, and other groups that associate with like-minded groups abroad. One final difference with the Europeans is the American parties had never, until recently, created permanent, institutionalized "foundations," or branches of the parties, to advance the party's foreign policy ties and positions, whether the party is in power or in opposition. By tradition, history, organization, functions, and interests, American parties *as parties* have not in the past been equipped for or oriented toward a strong international role.

Only recently, during the last twenty-five years, have the two major American parties begun to take on a larger and more institutionalized international role. In 1983–84 legislation authorized the creation of the National Endowment for Democracy, a congressionally funded but semiprivate agency established to assist in the creation and nurturing of democracy in Russia, Eastern Europe, Africa, Latin America, Asia, and now increasingly the Middle East. As a result, both parties have each created an international affairs institute: the National Democratic Institute (NDI) and the International Republican Institute (IRI). They both operate with small staffs (fifty to seventy persons) and on modest budgets that they receive from Congress and from the private sector. Both are engaged in democracy promotion, an important undertaking if it is done correctly.

But both institutes are still groping to find a proper role, and their range of functions is not entirely clear. Is their mission to advance democracy or to serve U.S. foreign policy goals, which as in Egypt, Pakistan, China, or Saudi Arabia may not exactly be the same in the various countries where they operate? Should they concentrate on the Middle East and Arab democracy (or the lack thereof), which is the current preoccupation, or spread their resources among all developing areas? Should they focus on building democracy from scratch in such "failed states" as Haiti, Somalia, or East Timor or on consolidating democracy in more important Eastern Europe and Latin America? These and other hard questions have not yet been resolved.

Then, there is the organizational structure of these institutes to consider. Only a country dominated by partisan politics would structure them in such a complicated way. First, the two institutes are creatures of the political parties, so they are often dominated by patronage, partisan considerations, and political favoritism. Second, both institutes must apply to NED as an umbrella organization and to the U.S. Agency for International Development (USAID) for funding for their projects, adding layers of inefficiencies to their operations. Third and again for political reasons, when Congress created NED, it funded two additional institutions: the Center for International Private Enterprise to advance the American model of laissez-faire capitalism abroad and the American Institute for Free Labor Development (AIFLD) to advance the model of U.S.-style labor unions and collective bargaining. All these institutes, created purely to satisfy domestic political constituencies, overlap in confused ways, compete and clash with each other, and often respond to political initiatives that conflict with their avowed purpose of democracy promotion.

The NDI and the IRI organizations have distinct differences, some of which reflect their partisan ties. For example, while the IRI is close to and supports moderate Christian-Democratic parties in Latin America and elsewhere, the NDI tends to support parties affiliated with Socialist International. While the IRI does a great deal of polling and party organization work, the NDI concentrates more, just as they would in the United States, on mass mobilization and voter registration drives. The NDI also has an easier time raising money from their sponsors, the NED and USAID, because Democrats dominate these parent organizations and favor their own party institute. Both institutes maintain offices abroad in the countries where they are working and send election observers overseas to scrutinize other countries' elections. Both also serve as recruiting and training grounds for young American party activists who want to participate in politics and foreign policy at high national levels.

The National Endowment for Democracy as well as NDI and IRI were created at a time when both Marxism-Leninism and right wing authoritarianism were beginning to fade in the world and democracy was already on the rise.

This development was what Harvard political scientist Samuel P. Huntington famously called the "Third Wave" of world democratization, which began in the late 1970s. Because democracy was already on the rise, it is hard to say how much of democracy's success in recent decades was owed to the efforts of the NED, the NDI, and the IRI and how much to the people and global forces in the countries and areas undergoing democratization. Three things are certain, however: world opinion has now shifted in favor of democracy, those mostly responsible for democracy's success are the people and organizations in the countries affected, and the NED, the IRI, and the NDI have helped contribute to the success of these democratization programs.

An interesting fact is that almost all of these democracy-advancing agencies are still headed by the same persons who were present at their creation in the 1980s. But the politicized and inefficient structure under which they were organized initially is wasteful, is dysfunctional, and does not well serve the cause of advancing democracy abroad. In addition, none of these agencies has yet come to grips with the facts that democracy is not the same everywhere and that democracy in the Arab and other third world areas must be adapted to the cultures in which it is operating. It is likely that, once the present generation of leaders of these U.S. democracy organizations leaves, Congress will take a good, hard look at changing the system of how the United States assists democracy abroad.

Advising Candidates—and Going to Washington

For many students of foreign policy and international affairs, their teachers, and the legions of analysts in the Washington think tanks, it is the height of ambition to serve as an adviser to a candidate and then accompany him or her to Washington if that candidate wins and they are offered a high policy job. Academics, though they may be quite knowledgeable, are not always themselves the best political candidates: they are often too aloof, indecisive, or intellectual. But professors and think tank analysts do often advise the candidates, and if their candidates emerge victorious, they may be asked to go to Washington and occupy a slot at the State or Defense departments, the CIA, or the National Security Council. Unless their ambition is to be president, that appointment may be as high as a student of foreign policy can aspire to achieve.

Where do these advisers come from? How are they chosen? How do they attach themselves to a candidate? There is no single answer to these questions or single route to high-level foreign policy influence, but there are patterns.

Presidential candidates who come from the House or the Senate already have office and committee staff, aides, and volunteers from which to build an election campaign. Governors usually have their teams of advisers from their home states: political cronies, former college or law school buddies, and often some academics from the state university who may have taught the candidate or worked with him or her on various programs.

The main recruiting grounds for high-level foreign policy advisers, however, are the Washington think tanks (see chapter 8). There, the launching of a presidential campaign (now often three or more years in advance of the election) sets off a frantic flurry of activity to land positions as foreign policy advisers to candidate X or Y. Most think tank analysts have served in government before, they know how campaigns are run, and they know the policy process. They have the advantage over most university-based academics of being in Washington, knowing the candidates over the years, being close to the television studios, and knowing not just the issues but also the politics and insider information about the issues. Hence, along with staffers, aides, interns, and cronies, aspiring candidates turn to the think tanks like AEI, the Brookings Institution, CSIS, or the Heritage Foundation, which often provide dozens of advisers to the various campaigns.

There is often considerable competition among individual analysts to get close to and work on a budding candidate's staff. To capture the candidate's attention, you can engage in the following activities: One tactic is to send the candidate or candidates with whom you agree on the issues some of your recent articles or op-eds on foreign policy issues. Another is to try and meet with the candidate or his close advisers when he visits your city or think tank. Next, scour the newspapers when campaigns are first being formed, see if you know anyone on the list of advisers, and try to use that connection to advance your own possibility as a policy adviser. Modesty is not necessarily an advantage when you're trying to advance your policy career this way.

You may then be asked to help the campaign prepare answers to possible questions the candidate may be asked in the TV debates, to prepare brief position papers on the issues, to help fashion the foreign policy planks in the party platform, or even to write a speech for the candidate. You need to be prepared to do this work without compensation and even to dip into your private savings to fly around the country advising the campaign. All the while, remember that the odds of your candidate emerging victorious are pretty slim. But if you want a high-level (or even low-level) policy position, you have to be prepared to make these sacrifices.

If a candidate wins the party's presidential nomination and begins the fall election campaign, the circle of foreign policy advisers may swell to fifty or seventy-five people. Typically, these advisers will be experts on various geographic areas or on such global issues as the environment, democratization, and human rights. For the candidate, they will fashion positions on the issues, help prepare for the presidential debates, and write speeches. Very often there are strong rivalries between the advisers who were with the candidate from the beginning, when he or she was a "nobody" and the money was scarce, and those Johnny-come-latelies who joined the campaign only after the nomination was decided. If the candidate wins, all these advisers will expect top positions, but since not everyone can be secretary of state or national security adviser, the president-elect risks more tensions, usually carried over into the administration, when he has to choose among them.

In national elections, advisers from the top Ivy League universities tend to play a prominent role. They are very smart people, and the candidates like to have people from Harvard or Yale around them. The candidates do not always want their advice; instead, they may just want the prestige with the voters that having these Ivy Leaguers around provides. Sometimes the advisers' scramble to gain the candidates' ear (and thus become secretary of state) is comic opera. They may shower them with their academic writings, which they'll never read; they use friends and even distant acquaintances to try to get access to the candidates' inner circles; and they try to corner them out on the campaign trail during the primaries to demonstrate how smart they are. Much of the process by which one becomes a presidential adviser is unseemly, but if that is your lifelong ambition, it may be worthwhile.

Several conclusions emerge from this discussion of how academics, think tankers, and specialists on foreign policy become advisers to the president. First, the competition is intense. Like the candidates themselves, you have to campaign for these positions. Second, if you're from the Ivy League, you often have the inside track. Third, the candidates themselves are cynical. They may not want you for your policy advice but only because your think tank or Ivy League affiliation lends luster to their campaign. Finally, you need to recognize that your efforts to get close to the candidate can be demeaning, like bootlicking. If engaging in that behavior is worthwhile to you for the sake of the expected payoff—a policy job in Washington—then, by all means, go for it. Keep in mind also that loyalties are fickle. If your candidate loses out in the primaries, switch your loyalty quickly to one of the other guys.

Divided, Fragmented, and Partisan Government

Divided government refers to a situation in which Congress (or at least one branch of it) is in the hands of one party and the White House is in the hands of the other. It is part of the system of checks and balances Madison and the Founding Fathers devised to prevent the abuse of power by any one branch or the government as a whole. But divided government also increases the possibilities for gridlock, paralysis, and ineffective government. Checks and balances are all well and good in non-crisis times, but in urgent situations, when the country needs to make major decisions quickly and carry out policy effectively, checks and balances can be a severe liability. For instance, in the Iraq War, the parties find each other's position untenable: leading Democrats wish to withdraw quickly, and the Republicans want to put in enough forces to win decisively. The impasse will result in more bloodshed, enormous expense, and a prolonged conflict with no end in sight.

In the United States we have been in a situation of prolonged, even "permanent," divided government, and the public, interestingly, seems to prefer it that way—up to a point. Between 1968 and 1992 the United States had a system of almost continuously divided government, with the main exception being the Carter years (1976–80). Polls and voting returns have shown that the public did not think that divided government was a bad arrangement. Voters preferred a Republican in the White House governing on the basis of the twin issues of fiscal restraint and a strong defense, but they wanted Democrats in Congress on the basis of "caring" and "fairness" issues. Voters split their tickets even if it produced gridlock, voting for Republican presidents and Democratic Congresses.

Clinton's victory in 1992 changed that dynamic. For the first time since the 1976 election, voters had elected both a Democratic president and a Democratic Congress. The pattern quickly reasserted itself in 1994, when the Democrats lost control of the Congress for the first time in fifty years. President George W. Bush likewise had a Republican Congress to work with when he was first elected in 2000 and, because of 9/11 and the terrorist threat, that continued through the next two congressional elections; but in 2006 the Democrats won control of Congress again. Gridlock continued and, if anything, got worse. The

Democrats were entirely unsuccessful in putting budgetary or other restraints on the president's Iraq policy, and both the president and Congress fell to all-time lows in the public's ratings of how effectively they were doing their jobs. In 2009 Barack Obama entered the White House with substantial Democratic majorities in both houses of Congress.

There is undoubtedly a trade-off, as the founders intended, between the checks and balances of divided government and the presumed efficiency and effectiveness when Congress and the White House are of the same party. Those who favor a clear and consistent foreign policy tend to be disappointed in how the American system works; in European parliamentary systems, for example, neither divided government nor such inconsistent foreign policy as America has would be possible. Yet that's how checks and balances work and, apparently, what the voters have often preferred.

The problem with the current U.S. system is not just divided government but also fragmented government. At one level, the State, Defense, and Homeland Security departments, the CIA, and the FBI are all at odds with each other, with each often pursuing separate policies. At another, powerful interest groups—big business, agriculture, labor, and others—have taken over whole areas of foreign policy for themselves. At a third level, groups within Congress—the Black Caucus, Hispanic Caucus, Women's Caucus, regional groups, and so on—have their own interests to advance, which they often pursue irrespective of the American national interest. When the internal differences within the parties and factional, personal, and ideological differences between the parties and within Congress are added to the mix, we can see why the system has become so divided and dysfunctional. Members now joke that each congressperson has his or her own foreign policy. Forging a consistent working majority out of such a fractious, egocentric, partisan body has become almost impossible.

Not only are Congress and legislative-executive relations more partisan, but the interpersonal relations among the members of both branches are nastier, uglier, and meaner as well. Goodwill and bipartisanship have declined almost to the vanishing point while backstabbing, coldness, and personal vindictiveness are all on the rise. Members of Congress do not like each other very much anymore, and their relations with the White House are equally poisonous. The sense of comity, mutual respect, and give-and-take that once characterized Congress is gone. In its place are mean-spiritedness, intense dislike of the opposition, and confrontational politics. When the issues are posed in such partisan, personal, downright nasty, and ideological ways, compromise and the finding of a middle ground become almost impossible. In this atmosphere, where politicians no longer want to work together, how can you have a good, sensible foreign policy?

So what has happened to this great country of ours? Why has the richest country in the world become so discontented with itself? Why, amidst such high living standards, are we so partisan and so mean and ugly to each other? Most important for our purposes here, how can we carry out an effective foreign policy in this context of such deep partisan differences?

In political Washington, serious people are now raising these issues for the first time. Can we still salvage the American system of government? How can it be changed, if at all? Or must we scrap the entire system and start over again?

Suggested Reading

Blechman, Barry M. *The Politics of National Security: Congress and U.S. Defense Policy.* New York: Oxford University Press, 1990.

Clausen, Aage R. *How Congressmen Decide: A Policy Focus.* New York: St. Martin's Press, 1973.

Herrnson, Paul S. *Party Campaigning in the 1980s.* Cambridge, MA: Harvard University Press, 1988.

Hinckley, Barbara. *Stability and Change in Congress.* 4th ed. New York: Harper & Row, 1987.

Lindsay, James M. "Congress and Foreign Policy: Why the Hill Matters." *Political Science Quarterly* 107, no. 4 (1992): 607–28.

———. "Congress, Foreign Policy, and the New Institutionalism." *International Studies Quarterly* 38, no. 2 (1994): 281–304.

Lindsay, James M., and Randall B. Ripley. "How Congress Influences Foreign and Defense Policy." *Bulletin of the American Academy of Arts and Sciences* 47, no. 6 (1994): 7–32.

Mayhew, David R., and R. Douglas Arnold. *Congress: The Electoral Connection.* 2nd ed. New Haven, CT: Yale University Press, 2005.

McCormick, James M. *American Foreign Policy and Process.* 5th ed. Itasca, IL: F. E. Peacock Publishers, 1998.

Pomper, Gerald M., and Susan S. Lederman. *Elections in America: Control and Influence in Democratic Politics.* 2nd ed. New York: Longman's, 1980.

Purvis, Hoyt H., and Steven J. Baker. *Legislating Foreign Policy.* Boulder, CO: Westview Press, 1984.

Sorauf, Frank J., and Paul Allen Beck. *Party Politics in America*. 6th ed. Glenview, IL: Scott, Foresman, 1988.

Wittkopf, Eugene R., and James M. McCormick, eds. *The Domestic Sources of American Foreign Policy: Insights and Evidence*. 4th ed. Lanham, MD: Rowman & Littlefield, 2004.

8

The New Powerhouses: Think Tanks and Foreign Policy

Think tanks are major new actors on the foreign policy scene, and they have become increasingly influential. The phenomenon of the think tank and its role in international affairs is a new one; therefore, so far it has not been adequately treated in the literature on American politics and foreign policy. Yet it can be argued that the major U.S. think tanks are every bit as influential in shaping American foreign policy as the political parties, interest groups, and other institutions surveyed in this book. The think tanks have taken their place among the most important foreign policy actors in Washington, D.C. Plus, they are fun, fascinating places to work.

What Are Think Tanks?

Think tanks are different from other institutions with which we are more familiar. Think tanks are centers of research and learning, but unlike colleges or universities, they do not have any students, do not offer any courses, and do not try to offer a smattering of expertise on all subjects. Instead, they have student research interns, they hold seminars and forums, and they concentrate preeminently on key public policy issues. Think tanks contain no departments of English, art, or chemistry, although one of the more prominent "tanks" has a division of religion, philosophy, and public policy. Think tanks are not like foundations because they do not give money away; instead, they try to raise money for their studies from foundations and other sources. They are not corporations because, while they have a product—namely, research—think tanks are not profit-making organizations. Finally, they are not like interest groups because although some do engage in lobbying, their primary purpose is policy influence.

Think tanks are research organizations whose primary purpose is public policy research and whose location is in or has close connections with (at least the more important ones do) Washington, D.C., where they can more effectively influence the public policy debate. Think tanks focus chiefly on economic, social, and political policy issues and recently have concentrated on defense, security, and foreign policy issues as well. They seek not just to do research and write about these issues, however, but to influence the policy debate toward their point of view and to put forth their solutions to public policy problems.

What members of think tanks do is *think* (and write, publish, and disseminate their products) about public policy issues and serve as advocates for their public positions. More and more, it is the think tanks—not so much the parties, the interest groups, Congress, the White House, or even the media—that have begun to set the public policy agenda and define the issues. It may sound ludicrous at first, but the fact is that these days members of Congress, presidents, and their secretaries of state do not have the time or the specialized knowledge necessary to think about, to research, and to fashion the recommendations on major public policy issues. So the think tanks often do it for them. It is the members of the think tanks who have the ideas and expertise, can do the necessary background work and research, and are able to put their ideas into attractive forms that are then translatable into public policy proposals.

Think tanks have essentially begun to do the government's thinking for it. The persons who work at the think tanks are experts in various areas of public policy analysis: housing, health care, education, the economy, or foreign policy. Their scholars either come up with the new ideas based on their own research, or they rationalize and put into articulate, public policy form the ideas and conclusions that other academics, politicians, and government officials had already arrived at but were unable for various reasons to put in writing or into a framework that policymakers could use. The think tanks tend also to perform an integrating role when the national bureaucracy is divided or when too many groups are involved in a policy issue and no coherence among them is possible. Then the think tanks may step forward and provide the policy perspective that is necessary.

The think tanks provide an essential service. In an era when many books, statements, and speeches are ghostwritten by persons other than their purported authors; when the budgets of various government agencies are prepared not by the agencies themselves but by private contractors; and when even the testimonies of cabinet secretaries are often written not by the secretaries or their staff but by outside consultants, we should not be surprised to find the think tanks performing public policy work and not necessarily the government agency we would assume to be responsible for such work. The activities that the think tanks perform are part of what we will call the "privatization" of the American public policy process. Such privatization is widespread in the government and is a result in part of its overwhelming size and inefficiency and the sheer lack of time to do long-range planning in the public bureaucracies. The work the think tanks do is essential, and if the government cannot or will not do it, then these private agencies will have to fill the void.

Implied in the preceding discussion is the suggestion that such privatization involves risks and dangers as well as advantages. There is almost no public accountability or oversight of the think tanks' activities, resulting in a particularly risky situation when the think tanks start to perform quasi–public policy roles. Moreover, with the proliferation of think tanks in recent years—there are now eight or nine big ones but literally hundreds of more specialized ones—each think tank wants its point of view to be the dominant one. These myriad think tanks, with their strong political positions all along the political spectrum from extreme left to extreme right, reflect the nation's politics: the think tanks are often as partisan, as ideological, and as divisive as is the nation as a whole. One of the main theses of this chapter is that the think tanks both reflect and add to the politicization, fragmentation, and creeping paralysis that we have repeatedly seen as among the main—and dangerous—characteristics of contemporary American foreign policy.

Why Think Tanks Have So Much Influence (In Contrast to Most Academic Scholars)

Many of us who teach foreign policy courses are frustrated policymakers. Here we are, knowing quite a bit about foreign policy issues and having written extensively about our areas of expertise, and no one calls on us for our advice. Many foreign policy instructors believe that, if only given a chance, they could do an infinitely better job at foreign policy than the present administration, whatever the administration. Many would much rather be making American foreign policy than teaching it, but no one has ever tapped them for a position.

Hence, many teachers are often caustic, and sometimes bitter, in their criticism of American foreign policy, especially recognizing that they are frequently better informed than the responsible U.S. government officials and that their knowledge could be put to use.

This observation is not meant to disparage our teachers in foreign policy courses. The fact is there are often good reasons why policymakers do not tap scholars and intellectuals, and their expertise on foreign policy issues, from our colleges and universities. They mainly have to do with the contrast between how foreign policy issues are discussed on campus and how they are dealt with in Washington, D.C. Anyone who wishes to plug into this debate, or become a policymaker, should understand and realistically come to grips with these differences.

First, for policymakers, the writings of academics tend to be too abstract and theoretical. Such writing is usually too far from political realities to be of much use to them. Hence, they don't pay much attention to academic foreign policy writings.

Academics and policymakers also differ in their approaches to an issue. Academics tend to be concerned with developing models and discovering general laws of behavior, whereas policymakers tend to emphasize the concrete and the particular and to be suspicious of "grand theories." Policymakers don't have the time, or the inclination, to wrestle with grand theories like dependency analysis or state-society relations. Instead, they need to know how to vote or decide *today* on military aid to Pakistan.

A third difference between academics and policymakers is in their ideology. Academic writing nowadays is often too far on the left for policymakers to feel comfortable with it. Policymaking and policymakers, almost of necessity in a democracy, must stick close to the center of the political spectrum, or to the mainstream. Otherwise, they will lose public support and votes, and their policies will fail. By contrast, academics, who do not have to face the task of explaining and gaining support for their recommendations among a skeptical public or of having to face the voters every two years, tend to write in an ideological vein that is not always supported by domestic public opinion.

Next, academics are not usually aware of the bureaucratic limits that face policymakers. The policymakers' range of choices is typically quite constrained, and they must operate within a bureaucratic matrix of diverse interests and responsibilities. Their options and freedom to chart new paths are very limited. Hence, the advice the policymakers receive from the academics, who are not ordinarily aware of these bureaucratic pressures and constraints, is not often very useful to them.

Neither is the academic analyst always aware of the everyday political crosscurrents in Washington—that is, who's up and who's down, who has whose ear and when, what the different factions in the administration are and their current jockeying for power, and the rivalries between the different foreign affairs bureaucracies. Without such knowledge, the academic's "rational actor" advice is likely to be of only limited utility.

It is precisely these flaws that the Washington-based think tanks, and the academics who serve on their staffs, can avoid. It also explains why the think tanks have such influence and most college- and university-based academics do not. The think tank scholars tend to produce concrete analyses and recommendations, not abstract ones; they are seldom preoccupied with general models; they know the bureaucratic ins and outs; and they keep current on the everyday political and bureaucratic changes that their academic counterparts outside of Washington cannot possibly track. Hence, the think tanks know how to plug into the system in ways that academic scholars generally do not.

Let us provide three brief illustrations of these points to make them more concrete:

First, at a conference on defense strategy that brought together academics, military officials, and foreign policy planners, a navy admiral said what academics have long known but are often reluctant to admit: "You academics should have no illusions that you have any influence on policy. The Navy *knows* what it wants; the policy papers you prepare have not one iota of influence on policy." He continued, "However, if we can use your papers in our fights with the Army or the Defense Secretary or with the Congress over the appropriation for the Defense Department, then we will use your arguments. But don't think you have any influence on real policy because we have already decided which way we want to go."

The moral of this story is that academic writings may be used as rationalizations for decisions already arrived at, or in internal bureaucratic battles, but they are seldom used to present a series of options to policymakers. This knowledge will shape the kinds of policy papers that academics, or in this case denizens of the think tanks, will send to policymakers.

Next, during a revolution in Portugal some time ago, the U.S. ambassador to Portugal and the U.S. secretary of state strongly disagreed about the nature of the revolution and what should be done about it. The secretary was convinced that Portugal was lost to communism and that the American response should be to mobilize the CIA or send in NATO forces. The ambassador, by contrast, did not believe the revolution was hopelessly lost to the Communists and wanted to give the Portuguese a chance to work out a democratic solution to their own problems. An academic who knew Portugal and who was also acquainted with the bureaucratic struggle between the two men helped influence the outcome by feeding information about Portugal and its institutions to the ambassador, enabling him to more strongly argue his case. In an unusual turn of events, because an ambassador does not usually take on his boss, the secretary, in this way, the ambassador prevailed. Furthermore, the outcome was also favorable: Portugal is today a flourishing democracy and faces little if any communist threat.

The moral of this story, again, is that academics can influence policy, but only if they know (1) the details of the bureaucratic struggle taking place within the foreign policymaking system and (2) how and in what format to channel useful information into the system.

Finally, two academic colleagues, friends as well as specialists on Africa, sought to influence the policy debate on that troubled region. The one stayed on campus, gave flaming speeches, issued ideological diatribes, and fulminated against the administration. He gained some student following, but his shrillness and ideological attacks had no influence on policy whatsoever. The other scholar also favored a more enlightened approach toward Africa. He went to Washington, joined a leading think tank, studied the administration's statements to understand its concerns, wrote reasoned and sensible articles about the region, and eventually was recruited as a consultant into the State Department, where he helped work on African issues.

Here the moral is obvious: shrill criticism does not work (except maybe on campus) and among the general population may produce the opposite effects of those intended, but the person who takes the time to learn the system and to understand what motivates policymakers can effect change.

This discussion of how scholars can and do influence policy is also relevant to our understanding of think tanks and what they do. Think tanks are largely staffed by public policy–oriented scholars who are often Washington insiders and know how to influence the debate. In contrast to their academic colleagues in the universities, they know where the pressure points are, who's in and who's out, when the appropriate moment to air their viewpoints is, and how to go about doing so.

The think tanks play an especially important role in linking research to policy. In addition to their own independent research, the think tanks serve as a broker between academic work and policymaking. The think tanks thus perform liaison functions. They sift and filter the academic research for ideas that are useful and will fly in a policy sense. At the numerous conferences they hold, the think tanks often invite the best academic minds on the subject to Washington. Then the think tank scholars' job is to translate the academics' generally abstract prose into terms that a policymaker can manage. They must cut out the theory, the conceptual framework, and the models and turn the knowledge and information contained in the scholarly papers into concrete, practical language and recommendations.

Think tank scholars make the academic research realistic and down to earth. They know the bureaucratic infighting, the political constraints, which ideas have a chance and which do not, and how, where, and when to feed these ideas into the system. In this way the think tanks can help make academic research look useful, reasonable, and workable to the policymakers. They define the options, give their arguments depth and sophistication, and provide rationales for policy or help steer it in new directions. The think tanks can thus define the parameters of the debate, educate the public and Congress, show what will work and what will not, and demonstrate how to get from point *A* to point *B*. Such work may not always be in accord with pure academic research, but it is infinitely more practical and certainly has a far stronger effect on policy.

In the analysis so far, we have drawn the lines rather sharply between campus-based academic research and the public policy research and dissemination done by the think tanks. While these general points still hold, the argument needs to be qualified in certain ways. First, some academic scholars—primarily at Ivy League universities and often those with specialized knowledge at other universities as well—do have an influence on policymaking. Second, at some institutions (Harvard's Weatherhead Center for International Affairs is the best example), specialized foreign policy research centers exist that represent hybrids between the university world of pure research and the think tank world of policy-oriented research. They not only serve to bridge the gap between these two arenas but are also influential policy centers in their own right. Third, the case can be made that, while university-based academics usually have little influence on everyday policy, through their students as well as their writings they may have influence in longer-range terms. Finally, many of the new recruits to top-level posts in the Defense or State departments and the CIA are former academics— that is, often frustrated ones who want to make policy rather than just write or lecture about it. It is another way in which the line between academic work and actual policymaking is being increasingly blurred.

The Council on Foreign Relations and the Think Tanks: From an Old Elite to a New Elite in Foreign Policy

For a long time after World War II, the Council on Foreign Relations was the dominant private organization in the foreign policy field. The council had actually been formed right after World War I to help generate public support for Woodrow Wilson's Fourteen Points, which became the basis of the armistice with Germany. Centered in New York, the council attracted elite, establishment figures. It was not so much a think tank (although the council now does have its own research staff) as a gathering place for wealthy, well-placed New Yorkers who had an interest in foreign policy. During the period before and right after World War II, when the United States still had strong isolationist tendencies, the council was a center of internationalist sentiment. It put on programs, listened to speakers talk about various parts of the world, and published the leading journal in the field, *Foreign Affairs*.

The council's membership is by election only. Membership was thus kept select and limited. It consisted mainly of prominent Wall Street bankers and lawyers as well as diplomats. During the 1940s and 1950s a large portion of the foreign policy leadership was recruited out of the council: Dean Acheson and John Foster Dulles, David Rockefeller and Douglas Dillon, Averell Harriman and John McCloy, and a large number of ambassadors and assistant secretaries. Although there were partisan differences, most council members thought of themselves as moderates and centrists. They were the backbone of the consensual, bipartisan foreign policy that prevailed up to the Vietnam War.

By the 1960s criticism of the council began to be widespread. The economist John Kenneth Galbraith denounced it as irrelevant and resigned. It was said to be too Waspish, to be too old fashioned, and to have too few women, minority, and younger members. Conservatives criticized the New York–centered organization as a part of the "Eastern liberal establishment." And leftist critics held it responsible, as a bulwark of post–World War II foreign policy, for the assumptions that led to American intervention in Vietnam.

Since the 1980s the council has vigorously moved to refurbish its image and its position. It recruited new members among women, minorities, and younger people. It opened a branch in Washington and sought to recruit members from other parts of the country besides the East Coast. The council has a more vigorous research program, and its activities have expanded.

In the meantime, however, a fundamental transformation in foreign policy-making influence has been taking place. The center of foreign policy influence has shifted from the New York–based Council on Foreign Relations to the Washington-based think tanks. The council has lost its place as the dominant or virtually only private influence on foreign policy. The think tanks have now filled that role, with a major impact on U.S. foreign policy.

Let us sum up the changes that this shift from the council to the think tanks implies.

1. Power in foreign policy has definitely shifted from New York, which once was dominant not only in banking but also in foreign affairs, to Washington.
2. It has shifted from Wall Street bankers and lawyers to the scholars and public policy specialists who inhabit the think tanks.
3. It has shifted from an older generation whose assumptions were based on the experiences of the 1930s, World War II, and the emerging Cold War to a new generation shaped by the 1960s, Vietnam, and the war on terrorism.
4. It has shifted from the middle-of-the-road and bipartisan elements that were predominant in the council to the much more partisan, ideological, and political elements that are in the think tanks.

Regarding the main theme of this book, this last change is particularly worrisome. With American foreign policy already split, fragmented, and often in disarray, the think tanks, with the divisions among them and their more partisan and ideological approaches, may well be instruments to further this discord. That hypothesis is where we begin.

The World of the Think Tanks

The world of the think tanks is fascinating and ever changing. Think tanks come in a variety of forms and locations. Some are located on or near university campuses; others are independent. Some serve basically as research centers for the U.S. government; others do not accept government contracts at all. Some are large and some are small. Some have a single focus or issue for which they are known; others work on a variety of subjects. Here we will be concerned chiefly with the large and influential Washington-based think tanks, since that is where considerable power lies.

First, however, let us look at what may be termed the "minor leagues" of think tanks. They are sometimes referred to as the "feeder system" because they often feed ideas and budding personnel into the larger think tanks. This league includes the Mershon Center for International Security Studies at the Ohio State University, the Foreign Policy Research Institute in Philadelphia, and the Institute for Foreign Policy Analysis in Cambridge, Massachusetts. Specializing in foreign policy and national security issues, these small "tanks" have staffs of maybe ten to twenty people and budgets usually in the neighborhood of $1 million to $2 million. They specialize in foreign policy and national security issues. Because they are outside of Washington and, therefore, can neither know about nor directly influence the everyday workings of policymaking in the nation's capital, these think tanks tend to concentrate their efforts on publishing scholarly books and articles on longer-range policy analysis in order to influence the scholars, editorialists, and others who do have a direct influence on policy.

Deserving special recognition in this category is the National Committee on American Foreign Policy (NCAFP). Founded by leading realist thinker Hans J. Morgenthau, the NCAFP has a small budget and staff, just as the others mentioned above, but has influence disproportionate to its modest size. Located in New York, the committee publishes its own journal, *American Foreign Policy Interests*; has an elite Board of Trustees and Board of Advisers that enable it to tap into high policy circles; and employs high-level round tables, task forces, and conferences to issue reports that go directly to top policymakers. In this way and on a relatively small budget, the NCAFP is able to leverage its foreign policy influence. It does not have a large stable of scholars on its payroll as the big Washington-based think tanks do, but by tapping its expertise and good connections of its boards and associated experts, it can channel its reports directly into the policy discussion. In an era of tight budgets for most think tanks, the NCAFP model is increasingly seen as an economical but effective formula for other policy advocacy groups.

A second category is the think tank that does most of its work for the government. Examples include the RAND Corporation, which used to be an Air Force think tank and now is more independent; the Center for Naval Analysis (CNA), which does research for the Navy; or the BDM Corporation, a multimillion-dollar private firm whose business is chiefly with the Defense Department and which has recently been bought out by the even larger Ford Aerospace Corporation. But because these think tanks do chiefly contract research for the government and are not independent, general foreign policy think tanks, they are not our chief focus here.

A third category is major think tanks that have influence but are nonetheless (and almost a contradiction in terms) outside of Washington, D.C. The Hudson Institute was located in Croton-on-Hudson, New York, and headed by Herman Kahn, a visionary thinker who specialized in futuristic studies. Kahn became famous for "thinking about the unthinkable"—that is, taking a rational, calculating approach to nuclear war strategy rather than a purely emotional one. He was practically a one-man think tank, although he did vastly increase Hudson's staff and budget. He died some time ago, and the institute moved to Indianapolis. Now its operation is situated in Washington and has an office in New York. It takes mainly neoconservative positions on the issues and is in the midsize range of think tanks with a budget of approximately $10 million.

Another one of the larger think tanks outside of Washington is the Hoover Institution on War, Revolution, and Peace. Centered in three beautiful buildings on the lush Stanford University campus in Palo Alto, California, Hoover is one of the most influential and well funded of the think tanks. It has a marvelous library (begun by President Hoover, after whom the institute was named), wonderful facilities, a first-rate research staff, and aggressive, top-flight leadership. Although Hoover is known as a conservative think tank, its scholars are about equally divided between Republicans and Democrats and include many centrists, but its relations with the more liberal and often left-leaning Stanford faculty are often tense. Many of its personnel went into the Reagan and George W. Bush administrations, and the institution is most famous for its research on economic and social policy as well as foreign affairs. Like the Hudson Institute, it has a Washington office; its California staff keeps in touch by often twice-monthly long plane rides (the red-eye) between the West Coast and the East.

Think tanks in Washington present an ever-changing panorama. Sometimes a think tank's message may be in; at other times it may be out. The budgets of the various think tanks may also rise and fall, depending on the times, the administration in power, or the generosity of the tank's main funders. Ideology is another factor: a political position that works in one period may not be popular in another. Finally, since think tanks are less well institutionalized than political parties or government institutions, they tend to rise and fall more easily, becoming influential at one time but fading in impact at others.

Over the last thirty years the number of think tanks in Washington and, by now, at the state and local levels has grown tremendously. In the 1970s only a couple dozen think tanks existed in the entire country; now there are hundreds of them. Most of these are small and specialized, with budgets usually less than $1 million and concentrating on only one specialized, or pet, issue. They may have a director, an office manager, one or two scholars or activists, and a handful of student interns, or their "office" may consist mainly of a mailbox. For the policy in which they specialize, they may be able to carve out a small niche, but their influence is usually limited. These small think tanks may lead a precarious existence, waxing and waning with their particular issues.

Our main concern here, however, is with the major, independent, better-institutionalized, Washington-based think tanks that concentrate on foreign policy. There are eight or nine of these (depending on which ones we count), varying considerably in size and influence. These are, going from left to right on the political spectrum, the Institute for Policy Studies (IPS), the Center for American Progress, the Carnegie Endowment for International Peace, the Brookings Institution, the Council on Foreign Relations, the Center for Strategic and International Studies, the American Enterprise Institute for Public Policy Research, the Cato Institute, and the Heritage Foundation.

INSTITUTE FOR POLICY STUDIES

The Institute for Policy Studies is the most left wing of the think tanks. It was founded in the early 1960s by dissident government employees Marcus Raskin and Richard Barnet, who advocated a radical critique of American foreign policy and a dismantling of the capitalist system. It has an office in Washington, D.C., several affiliates abroad, and a staff of fewer than fifty people. IPS was funded chiefly by the Samuel Rubin Foundation. Founder of the Fabergé cosmetics firm, Rubin at one time was a registered member of the American Communist Party.

IPS represents the "hard" Left in American politics. It is not just liberal but often Marxist, with some of its associates veering into full-fledged Marxism-

Leninism. IPS pictures the United States as "the most evil society in history" and blames the United States and capitalism for virtually all of the world's ills. It sees its mission as liberating people from their "colonial" status and reconstructing society along socialist lines. It is against all defense measures and has consistently sided with countries hostile to the United States. Because of its activities and the suspicion that it was supported by the Soviet Union, IPS was the object of repeated FBI and Internal Revenue Service probes. In turn, IPS is suspicious of and hostile toward outsiders who make inquiries about its funding and internal affairs.

IPS reached the height of its influence during the Vietnam War protest years, and some of its stalwarts even found their way into the Carter and Clinton administrations. During the administrations of Presidents Reagan, George H. W. Bush, and George W. Bush, and the more conservative turn of the country, IPS became the think tank that time forgot—at least in Washington, although not on some college campuses. IPS was especially effective in getting its personnel invited to speak at many American colleges and universities; and while its influence on Washington policymaking is small, it does have some support among radical students and faculty.

CENTER FOR AMERICAN PROGRESS

The Center for American Progress was founded in 2003 and is already an influential voice in politics. CAP has pioneered using the Internet to reach its supporters, and its scholars and policy analysts do instant briefs on the policy issues of the day.

CAP was founded by John Podesta, Clinton's former chief of staff, and is staffed almost entirely by veterans of the Clinton administration. Although the center is trying to diversify its funding, most of its money comes from George Soros, the billionaire financier who has recently turned his attention to politics and was dedicated to removing George W. Bush and the Republicans from power. Soros was also the founder of the New York–based Open Society Institute, which in the 1990s was influential in building democracy and free markets in Russia and Eastern Europe.

CAP represents the left wing of the Democratic Party. It saw a niche between the Marxist IPS and the center-left position of the Carnegie Endowment, the Brookings Institution, and the Council on Foreign Relations. As the Democratic Party and its candidates moved to the left after two successive defeats by George

W. Bush, CAP cleverly positioned itself to take advantage of this trend. Its scholars and officials tend to come from the party's strongly antiwar and progressive wing.

This position is both an opportunity and a trap for the center. If a left wing Democrat wins the presidency, it will be rewarded with positions in the administration. But if a conservative Democrat or a Republican wins, it will, because of its ideological and leftist positions, be left out in the cold. So dependent on the funding of one man, CAP could find itself in bad financial trouble very quickly if Soros gives up on the organization. Hence, its position is precarious. It could fade away as rapidly as it arose. Many CAP members were tapped for government service in the Obama administration.

THE CARNEGIE ENDOWMENT

The Carnegie Endowment for International Peace was established in 1910. Its name and money came from Andrew Carnegie, the Pittsburgh magnate who not only was one of the pioneering founders of the U.S. steel industry but also was determined to dedicate a large share of his huge fortune to the prevention of future wars. Centered for many years in New York, the Carnegie Endowment was a major supporter of the pre–World War II League of Nations and the postwar United Nations. It was irreverently known as a "peace shop."

The great advantage that the Carnegie Endowment enjoys is money. It has a huge endowment from the Carnegies and can carry out its vigorous agenda largely paid for by the income from the endowment. Thus, unlike at other think tanks, its directors and scholars do not have to spend much of their time raising money for their projects.

Some three decades ago the Carnegie Endowment's main offices moved to Washington, D.C. No longer interested in just peace studies, the endowment launched a broader foreign policy program that included third world development, weapons of mass destruction, human rights, Europe and NATO, Africa, democratization, civil society, and Latin America. Under President Jessica Tuchman Mathews, daughter of noted historian Barbara Tuchman, the endowment invigorated its agenda and brought in new and younger policy analysts. In addition to its Moscow office, it recently opened branch offices in Beijing, Beirut, and Brussels and now calls itself the world's "only globalized think tank." Carnegie does not have the same size staff as do the Brookings Institution or Center for Strategic and International Studies, but nonetheless it has emerged as a significant voice among the Washington think tanks.

BROOKINGS INSTITUTION

On the moderate and eminently respectable left is the Brookings Institution. Although its roots may be traced back to as early as 1916, the Brookings Institution was founded in 1927 when three groups, two of which were backed by a St. Louis businessman, Robert Brookings, merged. The institution occupies a splendid building on Massachusetts Avenue (right next to the Carnegie Endowment) in the heart of Washington, D.C. Its budget is between $30 million and $40 million (more than ten times greater than IPS's budget), which places it right up there with the largest Washington think tanks.

Brookings became famous largely on the strength of its economics "faculty," who were champions of Keynesian economics as early as the 1950s and whose viewpoints triumphed during the Kennedy administration. Only later did Brookings begin to expand its foreign policy activities, focusing on nuclear strategy, the Middle East, and general foreign policy issues.

Over the years Brookings has moved toward the center politically, where the big money to support its research and the bulk of public opinion lie. A short time ago Brookings chose Republicans as its president and vice president, recruited more centrist scholars, and began to raise the bulk of its money from the same corporate sources as do the more conservative think tanks. Its current president is former journalist and Clinton administration official Strobe Talbott. Brookings has moved away from a strong ideological posture, and its foreign policy activities and publications are also serious, scholarly, and middle of the road. Most observers, in fact, have not seen very many ideological differences in recent years between the Brookings Institution's foreign policy positions and those of the Council on Foreign Relations or CSIS. But as Brookings moved to the center-left, that created a hole on the liberal left that was filled by the Center for American Progress.

COUNCIL ON FOREIGN RELATIONS

The Council on Foreign Relations appeared earlier in this chapter as a New York–based, establishment organization whose members met periodically to discuss foreign affairs. Like Brookings and the Carnegie Endowment, the council was organized after World War I and developed over the decades as a rather staid and not very dynamic organization that was roundly criticized by many of its own members. It was more a discussion group than a modern think tank.

But that began to change in the 1980s when the council, like the Carnegie Endowment during the same period, opened a Washington office and moved beyond its role as a forum for discussion and began hiring its own staff of scholars and policy analysts. These changes served to convert the council into a real think tank that also had an impact on Washington policymaking.

The council still holds to its forum and discussion format, but its analysts and study groups now also produce their own op-eds, books, and reports. It houses specialists on Asia, Europe, Latin America, the Middle East, and Africa as well as such crosscutting issues as democratization, arms control, and trade policy. Ideologically, the council's publications run across the political spectrum but are usually either nonpartisan or close to the slightly left-of-center position of the State Department and the Washington foreign policy establishment. In terms of personnel, the council's Washington staff is not as large as that of the think tank biggies like Brookings or CSIS, but the fact that it devotes all its resources to foreign policy and does respectable work makes it an influential voice.

CENTER FOR STRATEGIC AND INTERNATIONAL STUDIES

The Center for Strategic and International Studies was founded in 1962 as a foreign policy offshoot of the American Enterprise Institute, which at that time still focused on domestic economic policy. It was founded by two of AEI's former associates—Richard Allen, who became President Reagan's first national security adviser, and David Abshire, who later became an ambassador and presidential troubleshooter—plus former admiral and chief of naval operations Arleigh Burke. CSIS was different from the other Washington think tanks (and more like the Mershon Center or Hoover Institution) in that from the beginning it was associated with one of Washington's leading universities, Georgetown. But the relations between Georgetown and CSIS steadily worsened (the more liberal Georgetown faculty members were seldom brought in on the more lucrative research opportunities available at CSIS) until in 1987 they formally separated, a divorce that was probably detrimental in the long term to both institutions.

In the 1960s and 1970s CSIS had only a limited staff and resources, but through the 1990s, it steadily grew until its budget reached almost $30 million. The affiliated staff includes a number of highly visible foreign policy specialists of cabinet-level rank: former secretary of state Henry Kissinger, former secretaries of defense Harold Brown and James Schlesinger, and former Carter NSC adviser Zbigniew Brzezinski. Unlike the Carnegie Endowment or the Brookings Institution, CSIS has a limited endowment; therefore, it must raise virtually all of its operating funds every year, with the staff often spending upward of 40–50 percent of its time raising money for its various projects. Despite this time spent in fund-raising, CSIS still manages to produce an impressive amount of research and publications.

CSIS has been aggressively courting larger donors and expanding its seminar, publication, and outreach activities. It stands generally for a realist position in foreign policy, which defines it as centrist and middle of the road. Its leadership historically has been Republican, albeit liberal Republican, but more recently it has served as an out-of-office haven for many Clinton administration officials. Its research product is mainly centrist and nonpartisan.

THE AMERICAN ENTERPRISE INSTITUTE

The American Enterprise Institute for Public Policy Research was founded in 1943 as an advocacy agency for free enterprise; it later emerged as a full-fledged but still conservative think tank. During the 1950s, when Brookings took up the Keynesian cudgels, AEI remained committed to a free market approach. It is largely because of its orientation toward the role of government in the economy (broad for Brookings, limited for AEI) that Brookings was baptized the liberal think tank and AEI the conservative one. For a long time, in fact, AEI and Brookings were the two major (and virtually only) think tanks in Washington; both had large budgets approaching $30 million by 2007.

In the 1970s and 1980s AEI began building up its foreign policy staff to match its already stellar economics staff. It concentrated on defense policy, NATO, general foreign policy, Latin America, and the Middle East. The foreign policy staff largely comprised centrists, liberal Republicans, moderates, and serious scholars. Although there continued to be differences between AEI and Brookings in their economic policy recommendations, in the foreign policy field, AEI's research products were hardly distinguishable from those of Brookings and CSIS.

Not having its own voice turned into a problem for AEI. By the mid-1980s AEI was deeply in debt and plagued by major management problems. Some donors complained that, with its increasingly centrist and pluralist foreign policy orientation, AEI had lost its mission and sense of purpose. In addition, AEI was outflanked on the right by the aggressive Heritage Foundation, which began to draw the conservative money that used to go to AEI. Its budget shrank to $8 million, and its president was fired.

In a series of purges in the 1980s and 1990s, AEI let go or pensioned off almost its entire foreign policy staff. In their place it hired a number of neoconservatives. Some analysts feel that AEI's foreign policy team is now even more conservative than that of the Heritage Foundation, which has long been thought of as the major think tank on the political right. AEI's research productivity and publications, and its reputation as a major center for foreign policy research and influence, had plummeted as well; but the organization regained influence under President George W. Bush.

HERITAGE FOUNDATION

The Heritage Foundation is a relative newcomer among the leading Washington think tanks. It is also the most conservative.

Founded in 1973 by two former congressional aides, Edward Feulner and Paul Weyrich, the Heritage Foundation represented the far right, or most conservative, wing of the Republican Party. A number of its early leaders and associates had been a part of Barry Goldwater's losing presidential campaign in 1964, and they sought to keep the conservative flame alive. By the mid-1970s they had become followers of Ronald Reagan. Later they would champion George W. Bush.

The Heritage Foundation's initial funding came from wealthy sponsors like Joseph Coors, the beer manufacturer, and parking garage mogul Richard Scaife. It also tapped into what is called "the movement," or the large number of ideologically committed conservatives in the United States. Alone among the think tanks, it used direct mailings to raise funds among small donors, reaching 150,000 persons who gave perhaps ten or twenty-five dollars per year.

The think tank grew slowly in the 1970s but expanded meteorically in the 1980s when its man, Reagan, was elected president. It vastly expanded its staff to about 120 people, bought its own building on Capitol Hill, and began a vigorous program of seminars and publications. Its *Mandate for Leadership* volume provided a blueprint of policy proposals for the Reagan and Bush administrations, and, like the Hoover Institution and AEI, twenty to thirty of its personnel went into each of these administrations. As a kind of clearinghouse for young committed conservatives of the movement, the Heritage Foundation found jobs for many others who were hot off the college campuses and eager to serve.

The Heritage Foundation also benefitted from the AEI's decline during this period. The foundation had staked out a frankly conservative position to the right of AEI and began to attract more and more of the conservative financial support that had previously gone to AEI. Moreover, it was noticeable that after the mid-1980s, when foreign ministers, heads of state, and other visiting dignitaries came to town, they often went to the Heritage Foundation to visit or hold a seminar. It was a measure of the fact that their embassies in Washington had adjudged the think tank to be a rising and influential power in the Reagan and Bush administrations.

Other think tanks still view the Heritage Foundation as often superficial and a Johnny-come-lately, however. It is seen as more a lobbying organization committed to advancing its own policy agenda than as a serious research institution. Unlike the other think tanks, the Heritage Foundation has hired few academic stars but many ambitious young people whose scholarly credentials are not yet established and whom it, therefore, does not have to pay well. They are worked very hard, producing what the other think tanks refer to derisively as "instant analyses," that is, hastily prepared reports culled from newspaper files that the Heritage Foundation can then place on the desks of members of Congress within twenty-four hours. Many of these reports are heavily loaded ideologically and politically. For that reason, the Heritage Foundation's research products in the past have had a dubious reputation among scholars. It should be recalled, however, that its main purpose has not been to produce original research; rather, it wants to shape and influence the policy debate. By that measure it has been phenomenally successful.

Sad to say, most members of Congress and their aides, as well as journalists, White House officials, and policymakers in the executive agencies, do not have the time to read the weighty, scholarly tomes that independent researchers or Brookings or AEI prepare. Although scholars have not yet faced up to this reality, the Heritage Foundation successfully produces short, pithy papers on short notice that tell these busy congresspeople and their aides how they should vote. Members of Congress and other policymakers cannot be informed on all the complex details of every issue that comes their way, so the brief, direct, and straightforward Heritage papers and recommendations are often a godsend to them. Over the years the Heritage research products have also improved.

CATO INSTITUTE

While AEI and the Heritage Foundation have long dominated the conservative side of the political spectrum, the Cato Institute has recently emerged as a major influence as well. Cato is the libertarian think tank, and for a long time, as the "anarchist" think tank, its policy pronouncements were not taken seriously. But now that the country is more libertarian, Cato's research reports have also improved greatly. On foreign policy it is against most U.S. alliances like NATO, against foreign interventions such as that in Iraq, and in favor of free markets and free trade. Washington policymakers now take Cato's foreign and defense policy analyses seriously.

How Think Tanks Exercise Influence

How do think tanks go about exerting their influence? Why do their books and studies have an influence on policy while so many of the studies produced by academic scholars do not?

Considering the second question first, the fact is that countless books and studies are produced on so many foreign policy subjects these days that even scholars cannot keep up with the writings on their country, area, or issue of expertise. Busy government officials, who usually do not have the same academic background in a field that scholars have, are far less able to stay current, so they pick and choose carefully what they read.

Also, there is a pecking order, or a set of presumptions about who or what is worth reading. Whether it is a mistaken presumption or not, policymakers assume that the scholars who inhabit the Washington think tanks, especially the larger ones, are at the top of their fields or higher even than their counterparts in the Ivy League institutions. In actuality such a rank order is probably exaggerated, and a good university department is as strong in terms of its research as the contingent of scholars at any of the leading Washington think tanks. But in Washington and in the rest of the country, where people's reputations are often as important as what they really do, if busy government officials have only limited time to read and get informed, where do they turn first? The answer is, to the think tanks, because that's where they believe the real expertise lies. It also helps that they often know personally the people involved.

Now, how do the think tanks actually go about influencing policy? They employ several methods and have become very adept and clever at getting their research products and messages out there.

Lunches, Seminars, Dinners

Virtually every day the think tanks host programs on one subject or another. Members of Congress and their aides, White House and State Department officials, journalists, and other opinion leaders are invited to these meetings. Not only are the food and drinks free, but if a policymaker doesn't attend, he or she might miss something and then others will have an advantage. Usually these forums offer an opportunity for scholars from the think tanks to showcase their ideas or a new study that they have just produced. For example, at AEI, lunches and seminars on the Middle East were de rigueur for persons wanting to have a say or influence policy on that area.

TELEVISION AND THE MEDIA

Think tank scholars regularly appear on such programs as *Nightline, The NewsHour with Jim Lehrer*, and the evening news. They are not necessarily better informed than university scholars, but they do have several advantages over these academics. The think tank personnel are known to the media programmers, their offices in Washington are practically next door to the television studios, and it does not cost the networks anything to bring them in compared with flying their own crews out to some college campus. For many of these same reasons, think tank scholars are often quoted in the press.

PUBLIC APPEARANCES

Think tank scholars have virtually daily opportunities (if they wish) to speak before college and university audiences, seminars and forums, professional associations, State Department or other training programs, foreign exchange groups, or the audiences of other think tanks. This exposure makes them well known nationally and even internationally. At some future time, when policymakers are looking for someone to give advice, they will most likely call on the speakers they heard at one of these forums.

ACCESS TO POLICYMAKERS

Think tank scholars have direct access to policymakers. They are in the White House, the State and Defense departments, and other government agencies for meetings virtually every day. Because of people's presumption that they represent the top ranks of the country's scholars, think tank personnel are able to get through doors and have appointments with people whom others cannot see.

CONGRESSIONAL TESTIMONY

Think tank scholars often know personally the congressional staffers who schedule hearings, or those staffers know who they are. Hence, when a committee or subcommittee is looking for testimony on a particular subject, it will usually call on persons from the think tanks. Also, since Congress is itself a partisan institution, its members know that by calling on representatives of several like-minded think tanks, they can get testimony that supports the conclusions they have already reached. This certainty is always comforting to members of Congress.

ADVISORY PANELS

Think tanks have high-level advisory panels for virtually all their programs. These boards consist of outside persons, usually prominent in the worlds of business, banking, and industry. By making these appointments, the think tanks can list many more important persons of wealth and influence on their letterheads and in their annual reports. These same persons also help them raise funds and get their studies into the right hands.

PERSONAL CONTACTS

Think tank scholars, because of their presence in Washington, ordinarily have a vast range of personal contacts. These colleagues include not only fellow scholars from other think tanks and the universities but also journalists, government officials, business executives (who often sit on think tanks' boards of directors), labor officials, foundation heads, representatives of foreign governments, and so forth. The range of people with whom think tank scholars come in personal contact is far broader and at a much higher level than is true of most university-based academics. Think tank scholars are able to take advantage of these relationships to get their message across to a wider audience.

GOVERNMENT EXPERIENCE

The think tanks are prime recruiting grounds for new government talent. Many longtime think tankers have gone in and out of government service several times. They go in when their preferred party comes to power and back to the think tanks when the other party is in power. There are few things headier for think tank scholars than a chance to work in the government and put the ideas they have been writing about and nurturing for so long into actual practice. Of course, because they are already in Washington, are well connected, and have probably signed up to be on one or another of a presidential candidate's advisory teams far in advance, their chances of getting an interesting position at the State Department, the National Security Council, or another agency are far greater than those of a university scholar who may be just as knowledgeable on the issues.

STUDIES AND PUBLICATIONS

The think tanks are adept at getting their products out to where they will be read and paid serious attention. They maintain vast and highly specialized computer mailing lists that are constantly updated and that enable them to reach quickly virtually every well-known person in the country on any particular issue. They have publications and public relations offices that prepare press releases about the study, organize press conferences for a new book, do summaries that then appear on the op-ed pages in leading newspapers, get their authors on the talk shows, and send out endless free copies to garner publicity. After all, no study will have influence unless important people read it. The think tanks also have facilities for bringing their scholars' work to the attention of opinion leaders and decision makers. On Central America policy, for instance, the writings of CSIS and AEI scholars were important in returning the Reagan administration to a more moderate and centrist position. Quite a number of these scholars even have their own syndicated newspaper columns and newsletters.

An informal but useful way to measure the influence of the think tanks (or of other scholarship) is to follow the dissemination of their reports and memos. The government runs, in part, on the basis of memos. If a State Department or DOD official or an analyst at the CIA or the NSC has your study in front of him and open at the time he is writing his own memo to the secretary or the director or perhaps the president himself—if, in short, he is using your ideas and analysis at the time he writes his own memo—then you have influence. If your study is not open in front of him or, worse, you do not even know who the responsible official is, you do not have influence. It is that simple.

Think Tank Dynamics

If you are a scholar, think tanks can be very nice places to work. On the one hand, they are like universities in their dynamism and intellectual excitement. On the other hand, they have no students so no teaching obligations, call very few of those endless committee meetings that plague university faculties, and have no heavy layers of bureaucracy. As we know, most professors love their students, but as think tank scholars often ask, what could be better than no teaching commitments, no committees, and no bureaucracies?

The staff salaries at the think tanks also tend to be far higher than those offered in colleges or universities. There is an almost unlimited photocopy, postage, and long-distance telephone budget. Think tank scholars have (often several) research assistants as well as secretarial help. The larger think tanks have their own staffs for the dining facilities, kitchen, editorial and publications office, conferences and travel, administration, and fund-raising office. It is far easier to be a productive scholar when all these facilities are at your disposal and when a friendly editor is right down the hall. Think tanks are nice places for student interns and research assistants to gain experience too.

Although on balance the benefits seem to greatly outnumber the disadvantages, there are some drawbacks to working at think tanks. Foreign policy issues in Washington are fickle, rising and falling with the headlines, and there is no permanent tenure at the think tanks. For example, one of the think tank presidents justified the expansion of Latin America programs at his institute by referring to Central America as a "growth industry." Crudities aside, this assessment was great for the scholars in that program as long as Central America was seen as a critical policy arena, but once the attention had passed on to other areas—Iraq, Iran, Afghanistan—the Central America program and the scholars associated with it could expect to be cancelled.

Some scholars will also feel uncomfortable doing public policy research (as distinct from value-free research), since public policy research is almost inevitably partisan, political, and somewhat one sided. In addition, there is a growing tendency within the think tanks for management, not the individual scholars, to decide what topics will be researched. The scholars may also be required to do fund-raising, an activity that makes some of them feel uncomfortable, and the management system in most think tanks tends to be top-down, not the grassroots and participatory variety seen in most universities. Further, as in most Washington agencies, the public relations officials tend to have more say than their talents or abilities would seem to indicate; that is, they sometimes have more power in their think tanks than do the scholars.

Now let us turn to the issue of think tank influence in different administrations. If we position the main think tanks on a political spectrum, the picture will resemble table 8.1.

If we next consider which of the think tanks have influence—measured in terms of receptivity to their ideas or the number of scholars who enter government—in a liberal-Democratic administration (Carter, Clinton, and

Table 8.1 Ideological Spectrum of Washington Think Tanks

Left	Moderate Left	Center	Moderate Right	Right
IPS	Carnegie Endowment	CSIS	AEI	Heritage Foundation
Center for American Progress	Brookings Institution			CATO Institute
	Council on Foreign Relations			

Obama), the loop would look something like that in table 8.2. Thus, within a liberal-Democratic administration, the Carnegie Endowment, the Brookings Institution, and the Council on Foreign Relations will occupy the center; CSIS will take positions on the right; and the Center for American Progress and IPS will be given a few positions on the far left. AEI, the Cato Institute, and the Heritage Foundation will be excluded. AEI will be thought of as the "responsible opposition," however, and the Heritage Foundation and Cato as "far out," or too far to have any influence at all.

Table 8.2 Think Tank Influence in Liberal Administrations

Left	Moderate Left	Center	Moderate Right	Right
IPS	Carnegie Endowment	CSIS	AEI	Heritage Foundation
Center for American Progress	Brookings Institution			CATO Institute
	Council on Foreign Relations			

In a conservative-Republican administration (Reagan, George W. Bush), the loop of influence will look like that in table 8.3. Note that here AEI is in the center, CSIS the left, and the Heritage Foundation and Cato the right. Brookings is now thought of as the responsible opposition, and IPS and Center for American Progress are thought of as the far left.

Table 8.3 Think Tank Influence in Conservative Administrations

Left	Moderate Left	Center	Moderate Right	Right
IPS	Carnegie Endowment	CSIS	AEI	Heritage Foundation
Center for American Progress	Brookings Institution			CATO Institute
	Council on Foreign Relations			

In a centrist administration (Ford, George H. W. Bush, Johnson), the loop would look like table 8.4. Thus, CSIS becomes the center, AEI the right, and the Carnegie Endowment, Brookings, and the Council on Foreign Relations the left. IPS, CAP, Cato, and the Heritage Foundation are excluded from influence in such an administration.

Now, finally, if we superimpose these three loops, we also see some interesting patterns (see table 8.5). Note that, as in a multiparty political system, the "party" of the center, CSIS, has influence in all administrations simply because it is in the center. AEI, the Carnegie Foundation, the Council on Foreign Relations, and Brookings have power in two-thirds of the cases. They are still considered influential even when their affiliated parties are out of power. On opposite sides of the political spectrum, the situations of CAP and IPS, on the one hand, and Cato and the Heritage Foundation, on the other, are also analogous: two-thirds of the time they are out of the loop and not taken seriously. It takes special circumstances for either of these more radical think tanks to exercise power: a sharp swing to the left of the Democratic Party to bring the Center for American Progress and IPS into influence, and a sharp swing to the right of the Republican Party to bring the Heritage Foundation or Cato to power.

Table 8.5 illustrates a political science maxim: the center groups have power all of the time (usually out of proportion to their actual vote or strength), the moderately partisan or ideological groups have influence most of the time, and the radical elements are chiefly left out in the cold. Democratic politics and pluralism, of necessity, mean centrist politics.

This configuration and these loops of influence should not be thought of as immutable, however. The power and influence of these think tanks rise and fall. For a long time Brookings and AEI, the two great liberal and conservative

Table 8.4 Think Tank Influence in Centrist Administrations

Left	Moderate Left	Center	Moderate Right	Right
IPS	Carnegie Endowment	CSIS	AEI	Heritage Foundation
Center for American Progress	Brookings Institution			CATO Institute
	Council on Foreign Relations			

Table 8.5 Think Tank Influence in All Administrations

Left	Moderate Left	Center	Moderate Right	Right
IPS	Carnegie Endowment	CSIS	AEI	Heritage Foundation
Center for American Progress	Brookings Institution			CATO Institute
	Council on Foreign Relations			

antagonists (the "thinking man's think tanks," as they were sometimes called) had the field almost to themselves. Then along came IPS and CSIS in the 1960s, the Heritage Foundation and Cato in the 1970s, and the Center for American Progress in 2003. All of the major think tanks seemed for a time to be booming ahead in terms of larger staffs, more activities, and ever-larger budgets. Then IPS suffered a precipitous decline, AEI went into a downward slide from which it has since recovered, and CSIS also endured intermittent budget difficulties. Some think tanks emerge with greater influence depending on the times, issues, and political winds; others decline; and still other, smaller, more specialized think tanks may also have influence on particular issues.

Think Tank Funding

The question we raise in this section is, to what degree do the sources of think tank funding bias the research work and the resulting products?

Few think tanks raise much money "democratically"—that is, from the general public. Among the big think tanks, only the Heritage Foundation has been able to develop and effectively use the device of direct mail solicitations. But, of course, the think tank appeals to a special ideological clientele, or persons who have strong conservative views and support the foundation with small donations. The Council on Foreign Relations gets its money mainly from membership dues, and other think tanks are starting to raise money by charging for admission to their events and seminars.

Contract research is another touchy matter. Brookings and CSIS accept a limited amount (about 15 percent of their budgets) of contract work from the government. AEI, meanwhile, has consistently turned down all contract work because it wants to maintain complete independence in deciding what topics to research and to keep its research from being tainted.

Among the major think tanks, only the Carnegie Endowment and Brookings have large endowments—that is, money donated to the institution with the understanding that it will be invested and only the earned interest will be used to fund current projects. Their large endowments give Carnegie and Brookings a cushion during the ups and downs in other forms of giving. All the other think tanks are trying similarly to build up sizable endowments, but this work requires time and the careful cultivation of large donors.

At the same time, it's dangerous for a think tank to be dependent on just one or a handful of donors. For instance, George Soros, the one big donor to the Center for American Progress, is a mercurial figure. What if he changes his giving plans? Or with CAP so tied to the outcome of the election campaigns, what happens if its favored candidates fail to win? In either case, the center could be in bad trouble quickly.

Support from major foundations is also important for the think tanks and account for about 20 percent of their budgets. The think tanks tend to draw support from like-minded foundations, according to ideological criteria: the more liberal Ford, Rockefeller, Mellon, and MacArthur foundations give mostly to Brookings and sometimes to IPS and CSIS while the more conservative Scaife, Pew, Olin, Bradley, and Smith Richardson foundations give chiefly to AEI and Heritage. This pattern of ideologically based giving is clear, even though by their charters—to say nothing of the tax laws—the foundations are supposed to be nonpolitical.

The biggest source of support for the think tanks is private business and business foundations. Such gifts are, of course, tax exempt. Upward of 60 to 70 percent of the several conservative think tanks' support comes from the largesse of big business because those think tanks are most in accord with its point of view. But now even the liberal Brookings is raising more and more of its money from the business sector, which is also having the effect of drawing the institution's ideology more toward the center. IPS is antibusiness and anticapitalism, so it does not attract much support from big business, but it does get funds from some offspring of the earlier scions of industry who, although very rich, are often committed to capitalism's demise.

The relationship between the think tanks and big business is changing, however. First, business firms and foundations are increasingly designating their gifts for specific research projects rather than for general budgetary support as they had done in the past, thus muddying the distinction between contract and noncontract research. Second, the tax laws have changed, making it less attractive for companies to give money to the think tanks. And third, business firms are tending to give more money to local charities (the opera, the orchestra, parks, playgrounds, educational opportunities) and thus get back immediate credit for their generosity in their own neighborhoods rather than giving it to the think tanks, where the returns are not so immediate or so obvious.

Above and beyond these issues of funding is the question of bias. If so many of the think tanks are so heavily dependent on big business for such a large share of their support, doesn't that necessarily bias their research products? Money does talk here, as well as in the political party arena, after all. And so the answer is yes but not in blatant and obvious ways. That is, none of the larger think tanks is really a lobbyist for big business, nor can business really "buy" a research result that it desires. At the same time, all the major think tanks—IPS is the exception, and it has little influence—tend to champion open, free market, capitalist economies and to be suspicious of, if not in some cases hostile to, statism and central planning. All of these positions serve the interests of big business. While they do not lobby for specific business interests, the main think tanks both refrain from criticizing big business or their lobbying activities and provide an overall intellectual climate in which business can flourish. Indeed, one can explain the Brookings Institution's move toward the ideological center as a reflection of its efforts to attract business financial support.

Conclusion

The analysis presented in this chapter tends to confirm the hypotheses with which we began:

1.   Power in foreign policy has shifted from New York to Washington.
2.   It has shifted from the Wall Street bankers and lawyers who were in the old, New York–based Council on Foreign Relations to the scholars and academic professionals who inhabit the think tanks (including now the scholars at the council's Washington office).
3.   It has shifted from an older to a newer generation.
4.   It has shifted from middle-of-the-roaders to much more ideological and politicized analysis in the think tanks.

This last point especially deserves elaboration because it relates to a more general theme raised in this book. The Council on Foreign Relations was an agency of bipartisan consensus in an earlier time, but the think tanks now tend to be partisan and fragmented. They range up and down the political spectrum, from extreme left to extreme right; hence, the think tanks have become still one more set of agencies contributing to our foreign policy fragmentation and divisiveness. The point should not be exaggerated, since the several major think tanks often work together on various projects, their scholars tend to be personal as well as professional friends who attend each other's conferences, and at least among the more centrist tanks—AEI, Brookings, the Carnegie Endowment, the Council on Foreign Relations, and CSIS—there has long been a considerable degree of consensus, especially in the foreign policy area. But at present even this state of affairs may be changing.

Now we are left with a situation in which, instead of the single, bipartisan, consensual voice on foreign policy that we once had, eight or nine major think tanks and hundreds of minor ones are competing for attention and trying to get their viewpoints across. This situation has often led to a more contentious, more partisan and ideological, and more fragmented and polarized foreign policy debate. The older unity has broken down and in its place has come myriad rival, often squabbling, voices. The think tanks have been both a reflection and a further agency of this greater divisiveness and disarray. This divisiveness will undoubtedly continue, just as the country and the political parties are intensely divided.

The think tanks represent a whole new range of voices on foreign policy. In recent years they have also become very influential, providing ideas and publications as well as feeding their people directly into important government positions. At the same time their influence, while considerable, should not be exaggerated. The think tanks are only one of a great variety of sources—interest groups, political parties, and many others—that feed options, information, policy positions, and people into the U.S. government. Nevertheless, the think tanks have the power in some cases to alter perspectives, affect policy decisions, and exercise direct influence. They help define the boundaries of public policy debate and offer agendas and options. They confirm changes already afoot in some areas and lead them in others, catalyzing and popularizing new ideas. As they help bridge the policy gaps between the executive and legislative branches and among a variety of agencies, they also bring together academic and Washington-based policy-relevant research, formulate the transition position papers between administrations, and educate the media, congressional staffers, policymakers, and the general public on the issues. These are all important functions, and, in the shifting kaleidoscope of influences that is our foreign policy, the think tanks have assumed a major role.

Suggested Reading

Abelson, Donald E. *American Think-Tanks and Their Role in U.S. Foreign Policy.* New York: St. Martin's Press, 1996.

———. *A Capitol Idea: Think Tanks and U.S. Foreign Policy.* Montreal: McGill-Queen's University Press, 2006.

———. *Do Think Tanks Matter? Assessing the Impact of Public Policy Institutes.* Montreal: McGill-Queen's University Press, 2002.

Destler, I. M., Leslie H. Gelb, and Anthony Lake. *Our Own Worst Enemy: The Unmaking of American Foreign Policy.* Rev. ed. New York: Simon & Schuster, 1985.

Dickson, Paul. *Think Tanks.* New York: Atheneum, 1971.

Easterbrook, G. "Ideas Move Nations: How Conservative Think Tanks Have Helped to Transform the Terms of Political Debate." *Atlantic Monthly* (January 1986): 66.

Feulner, Edwin J. *Ideas, Think-Tanks and Governments: Away from the Power Elite, Back to the People.* Washington, DC: Heritage Foundation, 1985.

Herspring, D. R. "Practitioners and Political Scientists." *PS: Political Science and Politics* 25, no. 3 (September 1992): 554–58.

Hicks, Sallie M., Theodore A. Couloumbis, and Eloise M. Forgette. "Influencing the Prince: A Role for Academicians?" *Polity* 15, no. 2 (1982): 279–94.

Kuklick, Bruce. *Blind Oracles: Intellectuals and War from Kennan to Kissinger.* Princeton, NJ: Princeton University Press, 2006.

Linden, P. "Powerhouses of Policy." *Town and Country*, January 1987.

Powell, S. Steven. *Covert Cadre: Inside the Institute for Policy Studies.* Ottawa, IL: Green Hill Publishers, 1987.

Reed, Julia. "The New American Establishment." *U.S. News and World Report*, February 8, 1988.

Smith, James Allen. *The Idea Brokers: Think Tanks and the Rise of the New Policy Elite.* New York: Free Press, 1993.

Stone, Diane, and Andrew Denham. *Think Tank Traditions: Policy Research and the Politics of Ideas.* New York: Palgrave, 2004.

Sundquist, J. L. *Research Brokerage: The Weak Link.* Washington, DC: Brookings Institution, 1978.

Watson, Cynthia Ann. *U.S. National Security Policy Groups: Institutional Profiles.* New York: Greenwood Press, 1990.

Weiss, Carol H. *Organizations for Policy Analysis: Helping Government Think.* Newbury Park, CA: Sage, 1992.

Wiarda, Howard J. *Conservative Brain Trust: The Rise, Fall, and Rise Again of the American Enterprise Institute.* Lanham, MD: Lexington, 2009.

9

Washington Social Life and Foreign Policy

Not all of Washington policymaking takes place within or through formal institutions. Political parties, Congress, and the executive branch are all important actors in the policy process; we are familiar with the roles they play because they are inscribed in our laws, constitution, and textbooks. But the process also works through more informal ways, including luncheons, dinners, informal get-togethers, telephone calls, personal connections, friendships, alumni networks, patronage connections, sorority or fraternity ties, political deals, informal understandings, family relations, schmoozing over drinks with colleagues at the end of the day, and even a subtle gesture or the wink of an eye. These informal connections that we know little about are just as important as the formal processes outlined in books. Most analysts and Washington insiders understand that to be effective in foreign policy they need to know how both the formal institutions and these informal channels of influence operate.

This chapter explores some of these informal channels of influence. Relying mostly on institutional analysis (the powers of the president, Congress, foreign affairs bureaucracies, and so on), most foreign policy textbooks, probably because their authors have never lived in Washington, ignore these informal dynamics. But most Washington insiders know that the informal channels of influence are as important, or more so, than the formal, institutional ones. Hence, this chapter contains some information about living and working in Washington, how the city and its many receptions and informal gatherings work, how the real insiders operate, and the various levels of Washington social life.

This focus is not on Washington foreign policy made according to the gossip columns, although they do figure into it too. One can learn plenty about

Washington policymaking, however, from reading both the news and the style (or social) sections of the city's paper, the *Washington Post,* and from attending all those parties and receptions that go on virtually nonstop in Washington. The argument here is that (1) a great deal of serious foreign policymaking does take place at informal social levels; (2) a good part of Washington political life, including foreign policy, does revolve around gossip, informal connections, and interpersonal, behind-the-scenes maneuvering; and (3) those who wish to understand and influence the process need to appreciate how these informal channels operate. Washington social life, in short, is a fit subject for discussion in a foreign policy book precisely because it is the level at which a great deal of winnowing (of people and policies), negotiating, and maneuvering on foreign policy issues takes place.

Washington, D.C.—the City

Until the 1960s Washington, D.C., was widely considered to be a slow, staid, rather provincial, quite boring, relatively unimportant, Southern or maybe border-state town. It was not a great place to live. The country's real centers of influence were Boston, New York, Philadelphia, Chicago, Detroit, and eventually Los Angeles. Washington was a small town by comparison and with little to recommend it: no industry, little commerce, no stock market, little banking, no great fortunes, little culture, no first-rate universities, few decent restaurants, little social life, only political (as distinct from economic and financial) power. Moreover, with its summertime heat and humidity, Washington was virtually unlivable for four or so months per year, which helps explain even now why the Supreme Court ends its term in June and Congress is seldom in session in the summer months. As capitals go, Washington suffered badly in comparison with London or Paris.

Members of Congress and other officials also saw Washington as the political capital but not much else, a place of temporary but not permanent residence. Most congressmen maintained their families back in their districts, where their real homes were and where they lived, and they took up temporary residence in the Willard or Mayflower hotels when they worked in Washington. Like the Supreme Court, congressional sessions ended in June and resumed again in mid-September. The notion of public service was mainly that of temporary public stewardship of a position and not of a full-time and permanent political career. Congressmen thought of public service as temporary, a public obligation and sacrifice for the sake of the country. Most had lives, careers, families, businesses, and law practices back in their districts to which they intended to return—and usually did—after their years of service. In addition, at that time, the pace of a legislator's life was more leisurely and much less frenetic and nonstop than it is now ("the permanent campaign," as Clinton adviser James Carville called it). The real business of the country—raising a family, running a business, practicing law, building friendships and connections, having a life (as we now say)—took place back in the hometowns from which the congressmen came.

All this has changed in the last fifty years. Washington is now a cosmopolitan city. It has fine museums, restaurants, universities, and cultural centers. It is not only the center of the nation's political life, but it has also become a major business, banking, and commercial center. Salaries are high by national standards, and every year Washington attracts a new crop of America's best and brightest recent college graduates, lured by idealism, politics, power, and the desire to affect American policy. Its Virginia and Maryland suburbs have become attractive places to live, and central air-conditioning now makes the city livable all year round. With its many sidewalk restaurants and cafés, lively nightlife, nonstop politics, diversity and pluralism, and yearly infusions of smart, enthusiastic young people, Washington has become one of the most attractive places—if not *the* most attractive place—in the country to live. As a capital, its beauty, attractions, and aura of power and purpose make it the equal of London and Paris.

An aura of power and doing important work in Washington makes it especially appealing for people, young and old, who want to participate in and improve public policy. Washingtonians like to say that it is *the* most important city in the most important nation in the world. It is the seat of national government authority, the center of domestic politics, and the focus of global foreign policy. All the main issues run through Washington; without Washington's participation, no policy can be successful. Living in Washington and working on foreign policy give you a sense of power and importance, for everything that happens in the world passes across your doorstep. For these reasons, Washington is a vibrant, dynamic city, which, as the center of the nation's and really the globe's political life, provides endless fascination as well as the opportunity for change, renewal, and new faces every two or four years, depending on the election results.

These changes in the city's stature have altered the sociology of the city as well. For almost all members of Congress and government workers, Washington has now become a permanent home and no longer just a temporary residence. Their families will live and grow up in Washington and not back home in their congressional districts. In fact, Washington is such an attractive place to live—not just for the politics and policy but also for the other high-income opportunities—that even if politicians are defeated in an election or give up their policy positions, most do not return to their hometowns or districts. They stay because their friends and families are here and the best opportunities, as a lobbyist or think tanker, are here. Who would want to go back to their local county seat after they've tasted high power and politics in Washington? In addition, below the policy level, Washington provides hundreds of thousands of construction, clinical, and service jobs to recent immigrants, minorities, and those lacking higher education.

But Washington has other, less attractive features. Housing and other prices are extremely high, and the traffic jams and commuting can be horrendous. Washington is an attractive and seductive city, but the power and wealth there can also be ruinous of morality, lives, and careers. In addition, the sense of self-importance that pervades Washington can easily degenerate into arrogance and a condescending attitude toward the rest of the country, as we see in more detail below. Washington also has one of the country's highest crime rates (watch where you walk, jog, or park at night), sometimes tense race relations, terrible public schools, some awful urban slums, rising social problems in the inner city, and a local government in the District of Columbia that is often seen as inept and corrupt.

Even with all these problems, Washington remains a beautiful, vibrant, and exciting city for those interested in public policy or, specifically, foreign policy. It is also a Southern city in many ways: its occupants play political hardball but with a gentility and politeness that seem almost uniquely Southern. Family and political connections, clique and clan rivalries, and deep interpersonal relations— the main focus of this chapter—play a strong role in Washington as they do in a Southern or maybe any small town. The *Post*'s style section often captures the area's strenuous social life, as well as the frequent foibles of its inhabitants, and how and why that affects policymaking in ways that many other newspapers miss. To understand Washington, however, knowledge of both the formal and institutional *and* the informal and interpersonal is essential.

Inside and Outside the Beltway

The Beltway is a sixty-three-mile stretch of the interstate highway system that encircles all of Washington, D.C., and its near suburbs. Inside the Beltway are located the White House, Congress, the Supreme Court, the State Department, the Pentagon, the CIA, and virtually all the other federal government agencies, as well as the headquarters of the political parties, almost all the important interest groups, the big think tanks, and almost all other influential political actors. Inside this circular highway, designed originally to divert traffic around instead of into the capital city, is truly where the seat of governmental and political power is located.

But "inside the Beltway" is more than a geographic location. It is also a symbol and metaphor for how Washington thinks, acts, and operates. Unlike any other city in the rest of the country, Washington's main focus, and only industry, is politics. In Washington politics is a passion; at home, work, or socializing, politics and public policy are an all-consuming interest. If you are an English major and think you will talk great literature at Washington dinner parties, or if you are a scientist who thinks current research should be a subject of conversation in Washington, you are mistaken—and it's likely Washington will not be for you.

In Washington, politics and policy are virtually the only topics of conversation. Moreover, numerous, seemingly endless insider political stories, rumors, and gossip are passed around not only to colleagues but also to spouses and children (if you're a spousal scientist or literature major, take note). Washington politicians, lobbyists, think tankers, and journalists have whole storehouses of jokes, stories, understandings, and insider gossip and information—focused solely on politics and policy—that is all their own and that they love to tell to fellow insiders. Thus, really and symbolically, the term "inside the Beltway" means being in on all this news and gossip, reveling in it, and using it to regale friends and allies. Being a Washington insider—someone who works inside the Beltway—is similar to being in a special sorority or fraternity with your own secret passwords, codes, and insider information.

People who live in other parts of the country are seldom aware of all these insider jokes and stories or how the process works; what is more, they do not seem to care all that much. They are preoccupied with their jobs, families, and local and more immediate events, not national or international politics. Polls tell us the general public is more interested in their cars, backyard barbecues, and lawns than with foreign affairs. Moreover, people outside Washington have simplistic views. They believe that foreign policy ought to work the way the Constitution or some long-ago-discarded high school civics text says.

Those who work inside the Beltway know better; that is, they know informal, personal, group, or political connections count and often more so than the formal constitutional process does. Furthermore, those inside the Beltway, the repositories of such insider information, are rarely willing to share their knowledge with outsiders. The insiders prefer to maintain their own monopoly of information not only because that works to their advantage but also because that helps maintain the legitimacy and mythology of the system, which might be repudiated by the electorate if the general public found out just how sleazy, power- and money-hungry, and corrupting the system often is. So while those inside the Beltway treasure their insider status and information, they also have an interest in not letting the rest of the country in on their secrets.

This insiders-versus-outsiders mentality naturally breeds certain resentments. Outsiders resent it when insiders speak their own language, keep them in the dark, or refuse to give them the full information. They may take their revenge at election time, as seen in 1994 and 2006 when control of Congress changed hands. Because of such strong outsider resentments, some politicians (Carter, Reagan, George W. Bush, both Obama and John McCain, and even congressmen who are themselves insiders) choose to run *against* Washington in their campaigns. They rail against the bigness, bureaucracy, and, above all, arrogance and smugness of Washington, knowing they can win votes with this strategy. Jimmy Carter retained his hostility to Washington insiders even after becoming president and refused to learn the ropes of how to function there; it is no wonder that insiders usually consider his tenure a failed presidency. By contrast, Presidents Reagan, George H. W. Bush, and Clinton, regardless of other flaws, all made their accommodation with Washington's ways and power brokers and were more successful presidents. The moral is: as a politician it's OK to run against Washington, but once you're there, you'd better learn to get along with the Washington insiders or your term in office will not be successful.

Why are these considerations so important? First, Washington policymakers do not just operate through formal channels; informal channels are also crucial. To tap them, a president and his administration must rely on Washington insiders to get things done. Second, as president, to get Congress to support your policies, you've got to socialize with its members, invite them over, share a drink and gossip with them at the end of the day, schmooze with them, and take the time to learn their political problems and the pressures on them. Third, a similar approach is required with the government bureaucracy. You have to work with it to implement your program, praise its hard work and dedication, empathize with its problems instead of just being critical, and give it pay raises. Fourth, a successful administration also needs to cultivate the media in order to be well liked by it and to convey a favorable image. Becoming a Washington insider is thus important for the success of your policies, since it is not by merit alone but also by the ability to get along and go along with Washington's mores that administrations succeed or fail.

A fifth and important reason for becoming a Washington insider and participating vigorously in its social life is to learn new and useful information. Perhaps this advice is not as important at the presidential level since the president's public appearances are now highly choreographed events, but certainly presidential aides, National Security Council advisers, and Department of State or Defense personnel need to be out on the social circuit. All those Washington parties and receptions night after night (and now at lunch and breakfast too) are not just for pleasure; rather, these get-togethers are where you gather new information, learn new details, and find out who is rising in power. This information is not that which gets reported on the evening TV news; instead, it is the private, inside-the-Beltway variety. As a policymaker, you need to know as much information as possible and from diverse sources. You have to attend all these social functions, not just to be fed and entertained but because that enables you to do your job better.

The difference between a Washington insider and an outsider can be explained in various ways, but a couple of illustrations will help illuminate the differences. Outside Washington, for example, people tend to say "the Clinton administration did this" or "the Bush administration did that," as if these were monolithic, unified, single-minded administrations that always spoke with one voice. But when Washington insiders hear such blanket statements, their eyes tend to glaze over. They know issues are rarely that simple. They want to know who in the administration, what agency, what faction, the White House or the State Department, the president or his staff, who among the staff, whether it is the secretary of state or the secretary of defense or one of their underlings. Is this person who spoke out rising in power or on her or his way out? Is it an official statement or an off-the-record (and, therefore, often more accurate) one? Is it from someone close to the centers of power or at lower levels? Only a Washington insider can keep current on all these factions and pressure points, who's in and who's out, who knows and who doesn't; and only by being in Washington as a regular on the social circuit can a person have the knowledge to understand all the current pressure points, what they all mean, and how the policy process operates in and through them.

It often takes years for a policymaker to learn all these factions and pressure points, to get acclimated to the Washington social circuit (which can also be harmful over the long term to your beltline, blood pressure, heart, and liver), and to learn how to operate in this matrix. It takes time to learn the actors, all the backstories, and the institutional and personal relationships. But even then you may miss something, and the details change over time as new people arrive. But that's what makes it fun and interesting to longtime Washingtonians: however much you've learned, you've got to keep adjusting your strategies and tactics to take account of new circumstances.

While learning the process is a lifelong experience, the reverse process is much more rapid. When people lose their positions, leave Washington, and return to their hometowns, soon the phone rings less often, fewer invitations arrive, and they're out of the loop. Even worse, within a matter of days, they find they are no longer insiders with access to that vast wealth of information available on the Washington social circuit. If you prided yourself in the past on being the best-informed person in Washington on your particular issue, it's depressing to find yourself so quickly uninformed. That helps explain why so few members of Congress, executive branch personnel, or think tankers ever leave Washington: they crave being fully informed and getting all the inside news. Plus it's lucrative and can be translated into high-paying lobbyist jobs.

These observations have important implications for how we study foreign policy and international relations. While international relations concentrates on the relations of nations, the global balance of power, and the interconnections among countries, most foreign policy texts focus on the main institutional or governmental actors involved, namely, Congress, the president, and so on. Both of these perspectives are useful, of course; but here I am suggesting a whole 'nother realm of politics and policy—that is, Washington's social life and personal connections and how they influence policy and, beyond that, the entire domestic basis of foreign policy—is just as important. It is often our Washington-based domestic politics that drives foreign policy as much as or more than the various international situations in which the United States becomes engaged. In order to understand foreign policy, you must also know the domestic politics underlying the issue and not just at the level of formal government institutions but also through understanding their associated informal networks, which are emphasized here.

Levels of Social Life

Washington social life—and the political gossip and exchange of views that go with it—operates at many different levels. In Washington as elsewhere, there's a pecking order, or what is usually referred to as the A-list of invitees (the president, cabinet members, and other high muckety-mucks), the B-list (undersecretaries and commanding generals), and the C-list and D-list, which cover everyone else. Mainly, you make it on these lists because of your high government position, not necessarily because of your personality, looks, or talents. Consequently, when you lose your high position, you're off the list. Washington insiders often have connections and social relations at several of these levels.[1]

At the highest, A-list levels in terms of prestige are invitations to White House events: formal state dinners, White House–sponsored conferences, small group meetings with the president or his advisers, and even the White House mess (a naval term meaning dining room) for senior staff and their guests. State dinners for a visiting president or prime minister are quite formal and glitzy affairs, but even at these events, lasting impressions may be made (think ex-Russian president Boris Yeltsin's reckless drinking, for example) and key guests can often slip away for some private conversation. The White House also sponsors a seemingly endless round of lunches, meetings, and Lincoln bedroom sleepovers,

---

1. I can't resist telling a funny personal story here. For one period in my career, I taught as a faculty member at the National War College, which trains high-level military and civilian officials in foreign policy and international relations. It is considered a C- or D-list position. Because of my earlier career in one of Washington's main think tanks, however, I know all kinds of people at high levels—former vice president Dick Cheney, former secretary of state Colin Powell, former UN ambassador Jeane Kirkpatrick—who are definitely on the A-list. I am invited to dinners and receptions at that level too. On one of these occasions I ran into my National War College commandant, a status-conscious, two-star general, who was shocked to see me socializing at that level. The next day he called me into his office and accused me of socializing above my rank. Now isn't that ridiculous! In supposedly egalitarian America, there are no rigid ranks. We believe in socializing, if invited, with whomever we want to, and it's nobody else's business. But in the Washington social setting, you're apparently expected to socialize only with those at the your list level. Actually, there's a larger problem here: in terms of Washington's social ranks, no one knows what to do with professors. We don't fit easily into either military or civilian ranks or job categories. So at official dinners, for example, hostesses don't know where to seat us because we don't fit in. My own unbiased view, of course, is that especially prestigious professors and think tankers deserve to be at the highest social levels, the A-list.

with the president usually putting in a brief appearance. These occasions carry enormous prestige. Even though the White House mess, located in the basement, is not known for its food or elegance, an invitation there is still highly valued because it means you're meeting with a presidential adviser.

All the major foreign policy agencies in Washington (the State and Defense departments, the CIA) have private dining rooms for their senior staff and large cafeterias for other employees. These are all organized by rank: a private dining room for the secretary or director on the top floor, another for undersecretaries, a third for assistant secretaries and program or office directors, and the general cafeteria in the basement. Rather like that old and tired joke about what all those government bureaucrats carry in their briefcases (answer: their lunch), these multiple dining rooms are used mainly for eating; but at the high levels they are also, virtually every day, used for policy meetings. Private interest groups may, for a fee, hold conferences or receptions in the State Department's reception rooms in which usually both private individuals and public officials will be present for an exchange of views.

Foreign embassies are also major centers of social life and, with it, policy influence in Washington. The British, German, Japanese, Israeli, and French embassies are usually considered the most effective at getting their message out in Washington, with Canada, Saudi Arabia, and Mexico becoming more effective. These embassies have big budgets, they host many social events that U.S. policymakers often attend, their diplomats are well trained (speaking fluent English and understanding U.S. culture as well as Americans do), and they know how to influence the policy debate. As noted in chapter 6, the embassies and their governments hire law firms, PR agencies, and lobbyists to augment their influence and even reach out to their constituencies in the United States for their help in influencing members of Congress on policy issues. Other embassies from smaller, third world countries try to follow the same tactics, but they usually do not have the resources to communicate their message effectively.

Private dinners and receptions still constitute a major part of Washington social life. These may range from six to ten persons at the dining table held in a middle-class private home to larger groups of forty to fifty in one of the large mansions built around Washington in recent years. Many of the famed Washington hostesses from earlier decades (Pearl Mesta, Anna Chennault) who could entertain virtually the entire foreign policy establishment in their lavish living rooms are passing from the scene. Nowadays hosts favor smaller, more intimate social gatherings and dinner parties. These occasions may take the form of periodic cocktail parties to which one invites friends, colleagues, and political acquaintances or dinners to which close colleagues and political collaborators are invited. The locus has also changed. In Washington novels, the dinner parties are usually held in the wealthy Georgetown neighborhood, but today they're as likely to be in the Maryland or Virginia suburbs of Bethesda, McLean, Chevy Chase, Arlington, Fairfax, Potomac, or Great Falls as they are to be in Georgetown. At such receptions and dinners one can relax, be less formal than in the office, swap stories and insider gossip with friends without fear (hopefully) of what you said becoming a matter of embarrassing media attention the next day, and devise and plan political strategies. Such informal get-togethers among foreign policy influentials are still important in shaping and making policy.

The biggest change in Washington's social scene in the last thirty years has been the growth of institutional entertaining, that is, receptions, lunches, and dinners hosted by institutions rather than private individuals. These institutions include interest groups, think tanks, political action committees, business lobbies, and PR firms. On Capitol Hill, every day dozens of such receptions, hosted by a variety of interest groups, may occur. Members of Congress are always invited, but, unless they have a particular interest in that issue or group, they rarely attend. Instead, they send their staffs. Young staffers and interns quickly learn which of the groups serve the best food. In fact, there are networks on Capitol Hill—whole phone- and computer-based networks organized by staffers—devoted to getting a free dinner at one of these receptions before they go home at night. Once you hear which lobby is holding a reception that day, you call up all your friends who, in turn, call other friends. Or you flit from one reception to the next—what Washington calls "grazing"—to find the best food.

Similarly, every day the think tanks sponsor a lunch, dinner, reception, or program—often eight or ten in the bigger tanks—featuring a speaker or a panel of experts and a question-and-answer period. Such receptions usually bring together members of Congress and their staffs, executive branch policymakers (from the State Department, DOD, the CIA, and the White House), journalists, think tankers, and interest group representatives. What attracts these attendees is not just the food and drink (often quite elegant) but a presentation by a high-level policymaker, the launching of a new book or research project, a seminar or conference, or a visiting prime minister or foreign or defense minister. In this way Washington social life is intimately tied to political and policy discussions, and the good food and drinks help fuel the discussion. Moreover, as the cost of private entertaining has become prohibitive (figure on at least $300 per guest), these institutionally sponsored receptions have become even more important as the place where foreign policy specialists mingle.

Such gatherings are usually organized by regional specialization—Africa, Asia, Europe, Latin America, the Middle East—or by functional issues, such as human rights, climate change, trade policy, and so on. They are important in airing, sorting out, and understanding policy issues and eventually funneling these findings to policymakers. Such meetings also serve as the means by which newcomers, such as interns and young staffers or research assistants, become acquainted with the issues and the more senior movers and shakers on policy. So it's important to get on the mailing lists of all the big Washington think tanks and institutions where these events take place. In addition, such events provide a forum in which a high-policy person tries to convince a knowledgeable audience that his or her preferred policy is the correct one. Hopefully, these forums, which in Washington go on night and day, help sift good ideas from bad ones, good policy and good officials are separated from their opposites, and foreign policy consensus gets built. In short, through all these meetings, forums, and informal get-togethers, the good wheat, in a policy sense, gets separated from the chaff.

What happens at these events? There are no hard-and-fast rules or procedures, but we can provide a general picture. If it's a morning event, there is usually time for coffee, soft drinks, rolls, and bagels, followed by a speaker or a panel discussion involving three or four persons. Lunch meetings observe the same format. The lunch itself is usually informal, a serve-yourself buffet (sandwiches, pasta, salad) because of the prohibitive costs of a catered, sit-down lunch. At evening events there's usually a social hour with drinks and appetizers, beginning at six o'clock; a speech or presentation from six-thirty to seven-thirty; and often a dinner and question-and-answer session until nine o'clock. In addition to your regular job, being active in the policy process you may attend two or three such events per day, three or four days each week. Again, too many of these social events can be hard on the waistline and internal organs, but remember that attendance helps you stay informed on your issue.

Each of these groups with foreign policy expertise in particular subject areas, such as NATO or Latin America, forms a kind of policy community. Policy differences are then fought out—with Republicans versus Democrats or on the basis of other lines of cleavage—within these separate communities. The

Latin Americanists may debate among themselves as to what to do concerning populist president Hugo Chávez in Venezuela, the Asianists may focus on the rise of China, and so on. Each of these communities consists of staffers or would-be staffers, government officials, think tankers, journalists, among others. The best and brightest of them will, hopefully, go on to occupy high policy positions.

It may be surprising to learn how small these communities are. For example, the community of serious policy activists with a primary interest in Latin America may number only fifty to seventy-five people; for NATO and Europe, it may be 125 to 150; for the Middle East and Asia, about the same number; and for Africa, maybe twenty-five to fifty. None of these really forms a closed foreign policy elite; rather, the ranks are informal and always open to newcomers with good ideas. These groups may get together three to four times a week at different think tanks and discuss different countries or hot issues. Also, these groups are not homogenous. Diverse professions and points of view are represented as are both major parties. As the partisan and ideological lines in Washington have hardened, however, these experts may gather both all together and in smaller, more politicized bodies. But they still share an interest in a common geographic area or issue, and it is from these communities that many recruits for policy positions in new administrations often come.

But wait a minute, some will say, how come when I was an intern in Washington I didn't get invited to any such exciting events? How come I didn't have an impact on policy? That's probably because you were too low on the pecking order or only in Washington on a short-term basis, or you needed more seasoning or more education with an advanced degree. But for you there's also a fun Washington social life: wine and cheese at your think tank or lobbying organization, a beer blast on Friday afternoons, and all those endless sidewalk cafés and bars that seem to cover every inch of Connecticut and Wisconsin avenues or in Georgetown or the downtown area. Your opportunity to influence policy at the higher levels described here may have to wait for a return trip to Washington, when you come equipped with more experience and that advanced degree.

Washington "Friendships"

If you want a friend in Washington, an old saying goes, you should get a dog— or maybe a pet rock! Washington is a city of fickle interests, of often fleeting friendships, and of rapidly changing political preoccupations. Iraq is the issue one day, Iran the next, China the third, and so on. Policy attention spans (and often the jobs that go with them) are frequently short lived and follow the headlines on television.

Washington is also a city of recent arrivals. Few Washingtonians were actually born there or have deep roots or family ties. Most residents are newcomers to Washington, drawn there by a job, a cause, or a political campaign. Washington is not usually where you grew up, where your strongest friendships are, where your family is, or where people accept you (warts and all) for who you are. Friendships in Washington tend to be fleeting, and they are often related to the position you hold in the power structure.

This Southern city is filled with friendly people who often extend gracious hospitality, but Washington can also be cruel and uncaring. Friendships in Washington tend to be based on your political position and power more than on your nice personality or sterling character. People are usually friendly to you and may invite you to lunch or dinner because of the power and influence you have, not necessarily because of your intrinsic worth as an individual or because they really like you. On that basis, friendships in Washington are often temporary and superficial. They may dissolve as quickly as they are made.

This type of socializing is disconcerting and even disillusioning to many Washington newcomers who are used to the warmth, serenity, and permanence of real friendships. Newcomers who have been elected or appointed to important positions are lionized and fawned over at first, invited to many dinners and social events, and mentioned often in the press. This treatment is flattering, but such expressions of friendship are often superficial, more political than genuine. People want you as a "friend" because of the important position you hold, the influence you wield, or your ability to do favors in return, and not necessarily out of true friendship.

The acid test of true friendship in Washington comes when you lose your high political appointment or are defeated in an election. Then, count the number of friends you have and the calls or invitations you receive. As soon as you leave your important position, another person will fill the post, and he or she will get all the flattering attention you previously enjoyed. It bears reemphasizing that the position and its influence are all important and not so much—because they come and go—the persons filling it. Think, for example, of former defense secretary Donald Rumsfeld, who was tremendously powerful and on the A-list while in office, but now that he is out of office, he is all but completely forgotten and ignored. In the political arena, you learn to distinguish between true friendships and political friendships. With the former, quite rare, people still call you even when you're down or have fallen from power; with the latter—much more common—people lose interest as soon as you're no longer important.

This system is not altogether bad as long as you understand its givens. But Washington newcomers or those who've risen to high positions quickly and then mistake the attendant flattery for genuine friendship often turn bitter when their former friends no longer call. If you understand the system of political relationships and its conditions, however, you can avoid the disappointment over dissolved friendships and the phone that seldom rings anymore. You simply need to accept that some friendships are real, some are political, and the two should not be confused. Or else, get that dog or pet rock!

Other Channels

In addition to the foreign policy receptions, dinners, and social circles, several other channels of informal influence need to be noted. The facts are that (1) America is a tremendously pluralistic country, with multiple channels of influence, and (2) the entire system is so malleable that, if you're a lobbyist or a foreign diplomat and you find that one avenue of influence is closed off to you, there are always others worth trying. Few of these channels of influence receive the serious study they deserve, but their importance is such that we need to discuss them albeit briefly.

One of the most important of these influences is the large Washington law firm. Many of the bigger firms, such as Arnold and Porter, function more as high-powered (and high-priced) lobbying agencies than as traditional law firms that prepare wills, divorces, and property closings. The bigger firms have several hundred lawyers associated with them and branch offices in other major American cities and abroad. The fees for these Washington firms are quite high, with some billing hundreds of millions of dollars per year. As tax and other kinds of legislation, as well as regulatory law, have become more complex and as American society has become more litigious, the role of these large firms has expanded enormously. Moreover, as American foreign policy has turned increasingly toward complicated commercial and trade issues as well as the war on terrorism, these large law firms have experienced a dramatic rise in their business. They not only interpret U.S. and foreign countries' trade laws for their clients, but they also serve as lobbyists to get the U.S. government to protect American businessmen against unfair foreign trade practices. The big firms perform multiple services as go-betweens with their clients, the U.S. government, and foreign governments. A relatively new phenomenon in this area is the merging of big law firms and big lobbying organizations, oftentimes with big PR firms as well, to form a particularly potent conglomerate of influence.

University alumni associations can also be important influences in Washington and can provide access to key officials. Old school ties continue to count! For example, when Gerald Ford was president, his alma mater, the University of Michigan, and especially its alumni association, was particularly active. Being a Michigan alumnus gained people access that they wouldn't otherwise have had. Usually, the state congressional delegation can be counted on to work closely with the state university's alumni association as well as other state groups.

The ties to the states are important in other ways as well. Representatives and senators are elected from their states or state districts, and their staffs also tend to come mainly from their home states and from the state university. These ties are stronger in the South, Midwest, and West, where the state universities tend to be the most prestigious, than in the East, where private colleges are strong. In the former group of states, a political hopeful's first connections are often made in the state university's student government associations and are continued and expanded in the state university law school. One goes from there directly into local, state, and eventually national politics. At every level, the candidate picks up a coterie of loyal supporters and allies who often accompany him or her to Washington and into Capitol Hill or executive branch positions. There, a social alliance and long ties of loyalty form among persons who hail from the same state, which is important in terms of jobs, access, and political loyalties. Incidentally, because of these patterns, Washington has a unique subculture with sizable communities of persons from every state in the country, and they all form important webs of political connections.

Another category of important power wielders is the individual lobbyist who knows Washington intimately and has a reputation for getting things done. Examples from the past include Robert Strauss, a Texas wheeler-dealer and former ambassador; Joseph Califano, a former Lyndon Johnson aide and Carter administration cabinet member turned lobbyist; former national security adviser Richard Allen; and Tommy Boggs, the son of former legendary Louisiana congressman Hale Boggs. Bill Clinton, George W. Bush, and Barack Obama all have longtime friends outside government whom they listen to on foreign policy issues. These men are all well-connected power brokers. When their clients have a problem that needs solving, they know whom to call, what buttons to press, and how to get the bureaucracy to move and take action. They have the advantage of knowing how the government works from an insider's viewpoint, they maintain good connections in the press and with other influential groups, and they have friends in high places to whom they can turn for assistance. These are only a handful of the most influential wheeler-dealers; at slightly lower levels, thousands of former members of Congress, ambassadors, and government officials who make a handsome living by using their previous job connections and insider knowledge to get things done for their clients.

There are many other informal networks in Washington whose members help each other out with job information and knowledge of the policy process, and thereby they also influence that process. These include women's groups, such as the informal network Women in International Security; ethnic groups of all varieties who aid each other's causes; religious or prayer groups; extended family ties; military officers' clubs and cohorts from academy graduating classes; teacher-student ties that extend from campus to Washington; business deals that involve multiple actors; and patronage relations (you do a favor for me and I'll do the same for you) of all kinds. These and other informal social networks are always in a state of flux. Their influence rises and falls and sometimes lies dormant until someone or some issue (for example, climate change) energizes the base. These groups all reflect the incredible, pluralistic kaleidoscope of diverse interests that is American democracy.

Conclusion: In Front of and Behind the Curtain

Most Americans understand the role of formal institutions, such as what the Constitution says and the roles of the president and Congress, in foreign policy. They also understand the logrolling in which Congress and interest groups engage. Almost completely unknown to outsiders, however, is the role of informal, interpersonal connections and the Washington social circuit as described here. These networks are seldom reported in the media, they are the hardest for people outside the Beltway to fathom, and most Americans are unaware of their significance. All these social gatherings, lunches, receptions, and forums are not just fun and games; they are how things get done and are a fundamental part of the political process. As Max Friedersdorf, who headed the White House legislative affairs office, once said, "You have to go to the parties to stay informed."

The image we should have in mind in trying to understand this aspect of Washington policymaking is that of a stage in a theater production. In front of the curtain is what we all see: the props, the setting, and the actors (Congress, the president, others) carrying out their roles publicly and according to the script (the Constitution). But behind the curtain all kinds of other things are happening backstage: stagehands and the production manager frantically run around, improvisations are devised as some actors blow their lines, desperate last-minute phone calls and shady negotiations are worked out, and behind-the-back deals occur among owners, producers, and reviewers (the public). The bustle of activity behind the curtain is often not at all the same as what the public observes in front of it.

So it is with Washington policymaking. Some parts of it are public, or visible for all the press and the electorate to see. But behind the scenes there may be an even vaster range of activities taking place: internal plotting, favors being called in, clean and sometimes dirty business deals being negotiated, arm-twisting, inside influence being wielded, lots of posturing and bluffing, naked ambition showing, and sometimes money changing hands. In this arena, the Washington social circuit has an important role, for it not only enables policymakers to unwind and socialize, but it also provides spaces where agreements are often reached, deals are struck, and the policy process is moved forward. The president's life is usually too public for him to engage freely in such intense social activities, but his staff and White House aides certainly do. They are out there every day at one reception or another. In these ways the vast webs of Washington social life, which remains both unstudied and largely unknown outside the Beltway, begin to acquire an importance that rivals—and maybe even surpasses—that of the formal institutions with which we are more familiar.

Suggested Reading

Alsop, Stewart Johonnot Oliver. *The Center: People and Power in Political Washington.* New York: Harper & Row, 1968.

Berne, Eric. *Games People Play: The Psychology of Human Relationships.* New York: Ballantine Books, 2004.

Broder, David S. *Behind the Front Page: A Candid Look at How the News Is Made.* New York: Simon & Schuster, 1987.

Brzezinski, Zbigniew. *Power and Principle: Memoirs of the National Security Advisor, 1977–1981.* New York: Farrar, Straus, Giroux, 1983.

Cannon, Lou. *Reagan*. New York: Perigree Books, 1982.

Cater, Douglass. *Power in Washington: A Critical Look at Today's Struggle to Govern in the Nation's Capital*. New York: Random House, 1964.

Clifford, Clark M., and Richard C. Holbrooke. *Counsel to the President: A Memoir*. New York: Random House, 1991.

Fiorina, Morris P. *Congress, Keystone of the Washington Establishment*. 2nd ed. New Haven, CT: Yale University Press, 1989.

Gotlieb, Sondra. *"Wife Of": ... An Irreverent Account of Life in Powertown*. Washington, DC: Acropolis Books, 1985.

Haig, Alexander Meigs. *Caveat: Realism, Reagan, and Foreign Policy*. New York: Macmillan, 1984.

Hess, Stephen. *The Ultimate Insiders: U.S. Senators in the National Media*. Washington, DC: Brookings Institution, 1986.

MacPherson, Myra. *The Power Lovers: An Intimate Look at Politics and Marriage*. New York: Putnam, 1975.

O'Rourke, P. J. *Parliament of Whores: A Lone Humorist Attempts to Explain the Entire U.S. Government*. New York: Atlantic Monthly Press, 1991.

Peters, Charles. *How Washington Really Works*. 3rd ed. Reading, MA: Addison-Wesley Publishing, 1992.

Quinn, Sally. *Regrets Only*. New York: Simon & Schuster, 1986.

Sabato, Larry. *PAC Power: Inside the World of Political Action Committees*. New York: Norton, 1984.

———. *The Rise of Political Consultants: New Ways of Winning Elections*. New York: Basic Books, 1981.

Smith, Hedrick. *The Power Game: How Washington Works*. New York: Random House, 1988.

Stockman, David Alan. *The Triumph of Politics: Why the Reagan Revolution Failed*. New York: Harper & Row, 1986.

Weatherford, J. McIver. *Tribes on the Hill*. New York: Rawson, Wade, 1981.

10

Congress:
The Broken Branch

Of all the institutions of the U.S. government that are "broken"—and there are quite a few—the one that is most fractured, most dysfunctional, and most in need of fundamental overhaul is Congress. With the lowest approval rating of all government institutions, Congress is deeply divided on a host of major policy issues, has all but been completely captured by the big-money lobbyists, and appears incapable of conducting the nation's important business. It is riddled with patronage and corruption, far more oriented toward protecting and enhancing its perks and privileges than in working on legislation, and absolutely dependent on ever-larger infusions of cash to serve its main preoccupation—that is, their own reelection.

In 2006 the leading experts on the institution, Thomas Mann and Norman Ornstein, published a book whose title sums up the argument that Congress is *The Broken Branch*.[1] I would go a step further: I see Congress at this stage as so hopeless and so incapable of reforming itself that it should be abolished. We should try again and institute another kind of system. The trouble is, since Congress itself would have a hand in the change, we would probably get something even worse.

So in discussing Congress, we start from this depressing existential premise: Congress is hopeless but incapable of reforming itself, and starting over again would likely produce something worse. How can we carry out foreign policy if one of the three branches of the U.S. government is dysfunctional?

1. Thomas E. Mann and Norman J. Ornstein, *The Broken Branch: How Congress Is Failing America and How to Get It Back on Track* (New York: Oxford University Press, 2006).

Congress and the Plan of the Book

In this and succeeding chapters, we examine those institutions—Congress, the State and Defense departments, the National Security Council, and the office of the president, among others—that are responsible for making American foreign policy and for ultimately deciding what the policy will be. Heretofore, we have been looking at those groups, interests, and influences that *shape* foreign policy outcomes; now, we begin to look at those who make the decisions.

In terms of the two figures from chapter 3, the funnel of causation and the rings of concentric circles, we are now getting close to the mouth of the funnel or the center of the rings. In treating Congress, we are dealing with only 535 persons—435 in the House, 100 in the Senate—a greatly reduced number when compared with the other groups and institutions discussed thus far. That number is significantly augmented, however, with thousands of support and staff people who work on Capitol Hill, many of whom are well informed on foreign policy issues and some of whom are even more powerful than the members of Congress they serve. Nevertheless, the main point holds: Congress is one of the key institutions responsible for policymaking, and within Congress, the number of persons involved specifically in foreign or defense policy is smaller still. And that makes the point about the dysfunctionality of Congress look downright scary.

Who's in Charge of Foreign Policy?

Over the last forty years—again the watershed was the Vietnam War—Congress has moved aggressively to play a larger role in foreign policy. That trend was interrupted temporarily by the attacks of September 11, 2001, when, as in all crises, Congress deferred to presidential authority; but since then the trend toward congressional assertiveness has continued. During the 1960s Congress grew increasingly uneasy over the conduct of the Vietnam War, in the 1970s it moved to check and curb presidential authority in foreign policy, and during the 1980s it assumed coequal status with the president and even tried to take over some areas of foreign policy for itself. With the end of the Cold War, Congress was generally more restrained in asserting itself on foreign policy, but now with 9/11, the war on terrorism, the war in Iraq, and trouble brewing in Iran, North Korea, and Pakistan (among others), Congress is again playing a leading role or, in thinking of its frustration in dealing with the Iraq War, trying to assert itself.

Congress is the most democratic of our three branches of government, and its assumption of a greater foreign policy role is part of a larger process of the democratization of foreign policy under way since the 1960s. While this process has made American foreign policy more responsive to the popular will, it has not led to a more enlightened or effective foreign policy. Neither is it clear that Congress should constitutionally enhance its power in these ways or seek to micromanage policy.

Here are some of the key questions that arise out of the new congressional assertiveness on foreign policy and that thread through this chapter:

1. Can the United States have a workable foreign policy run by a large committee—Congress—without the central direction and coherence that only the executive branch can provide?
2. Will a foreign policy dominated by Congress produce a situation of 535 "secretaries of state," each with his or her own agenda and reelection calculations in mind?
3. Will a foreign policy run by Congress, the most partisan of the three branches, politicize foreign policy even further?
4. With members of Congress always thinking in short-range terms—until the next congressional election—how will they provide any continuity and long-range planning in foreign policy?
5. How can Congress conduct foreign policy without any embassies abroad, an intelligence arm, diplomats, military forces, and country-by-country expertise?
6. Is Congress's assertiveness on foreign policy unconstitutional? Isn't the president still the commander in chief of the armed forces, the chief diplomat, and the person responsible for foreign policy?

Congress and the President: An Invitation to Struggle

In times of crisis—World Wars I and II, the Cold War period (1947–91), and immediately after the 9/11 attacks—the president dominates foreign policy. Congress will usually defer to the president's leadership. It is assumed that the executive branch has more access to foreign affairs information, including intelligence, than does Congress. In addition, the public wants and expects the president to lead in times of crisis.

Congress usually reasserts itself in periods of relative peace, such as the decade between the Soviet Union's collapse in 1991 and the attacks of 9/11. Perhaps Congress's more forceful position today is because the terrorist threat seems to be receding, many in Congress are convinced that the Iraq War was a mistake and that the president miscalculated, and the public seems to agree with that assessment. Thus, members of Congress felt it was safe to politically oppose George W. Bush's policies.

Again, this issue is tricky, especially for the Democratic majority in Congress. On the one hand, the Democrats want to end the war in Iraq and bring the American soldiers home. On the other hand, they cannot vote to cut off funds or leave Iraq precipitously, for then they are open to the charge, which the Republicans have been good at exploiting, that they are abandoning Iraq and denying the troops the necessary funds and equipment to extract themselves safely. Aware that if U.S. forces leave Iraq and then another terrorist attack occurs, it would be enough to cost the Democrats the entire next election, the congressional leadership has repeatedly backed down. Instead, the members have played politics with the issue, saying rhetorically that they are against the war but then voting for the funds to sustain it.

The origins of this conflict between congressional and executive leadership on foreign policy go back to the Constitution and its system of overlapping power and checks and balances that the Founding Fathers purposely built into it. For example, the president is the commander in chief, but only Congress has the power to declare war. Thus, when the president sends troops abroad, he usually avoids calling for a declaration of war. Is the sending of U.S. military forces to Haiti, Afghanistan, Iraq, and dozens of other countries an act of war requiring congressional authorization, or does it lie within the president's discretion as commander in chief? Who decides this issue? Where do we draw the line? What if the president sends the troops, but Congress refuses to pay for the action? Then what? Herein lie some of the great conflicts and controversies of our day.

Similarly, by the Constitution, the president negotiates treaties, but Congress must ratify them. What if Congress refuses? Or suppose, as often happens, the president negotiates an "executive agreement" that looks every bit like a treaty but the executive has defined it as something else. Executive agreements do not require congressional approval, but they nevertheless acquire the force of law. They are also more flexible than treaties and can be changed or abrogated more easily. You can probably guess that presidents much prefer executive agreements so they can avoid the necessity of gaining congressional approval while Congress much prefers to act on treaties, which they can amend or reject.

Much the same applies to ambassadorial and other high-level foreign affairs appointments. The president nominates, but the Congress must consent. In the past, congressional approval of such appointments, unless the person named had a record of drug use or other egregious behavior, was more or less automatic; but now the partisan divides are so rancorous and the anger between the president and Congress so often so great that even many routine appointments are closely scrutinized. Frequently, a single senator (one of one hundred!) can put a hold on an appointment indefinitely on grounds that may be personal dislike or partisan politics rather than the nominee's qualifications. A president may retaliate by making a recess appointment, which is done when Congress is not in session, and it is good for one year. But Congress can refuse to go into recess, which it did over the Christmas holidays of 2007 when the junior senator from Virginia, who lives just across the Potomac River from Washington, kept Congress open "continuously" (for about a minute per day) so President Bush could not make any recess appointments.

A key area, of course, is money. The president is in overall charge of foreign policy, but Congress alone has the power to pass appropriation bills. The president may lead all he wants in foreign policy, but without money his initiatives will not go far. Without the funding for foreign aid, the State Department, the Defense Department, and the CIA, the United States cannot have an effective foreign policy. Presidents sometimes do find a way around Congress, however. President Theodore Roosevelt once sent the U.S. fleet halfway around the world and then defied Congress not to provide the funding to bring it back. Similarly, President Bush sent U.S. forces into Iraq and then defied Congress not to support "our boys."

The U.S. Constitution's system of checks and balances is so complex and has so many vague passages that it is impossible to say definitely who is in charge of foreign policy. Moreover, the relations between the president and Congress vary over time depending on a large number of imprecise factors: the context of the time, the personalities of the president and congressional leaders, the political situation, the balance of power in Congress and the country, the national mood, and the issue(s) at dispute. Bill Clinton, for example, began his presidency with a Democratic Congress to carry out his mandate, but after 1994 Congress was in Republican hands, the Monica Lewinsky case discredited the president, and he lost much of his effectiveness. Similarly, George W. Bush started his presidency with a Republican Congress, lost it in 2006, and was discredited by his conduct of the Iraq War.

What we can say about the Constitution, therefore, is that it provides an invitation to struggle over foreign policy. There is built-in conflict between the executive and legislative branches. Moreover, the Constitution is sufficiently ambiguous in so many important areas that the issue of presidential versus congressional power in foreign policy cannot ever be resolved completely. Tension and conflict over international affairs should be thought of as the norm and not the exception.

Americans as well as friends and foes alike will just have to live with the fact that U.S. foreign policy will always be less coherent, less unified, less consistent, and more conflict prone than are most European countries' policies. Conflict over foreign policy is built into the American political system because the Founding Fathers designed it that way. The disputes that arise between Congress and the president, therefore, can ultimately be resolved in the political process only through elections, the interest group struggle, negotiations, political deals, and changes in public opinion. Such uncertainty on foreign policy will leave many persons uncomfortable, but that is the nature of the American system. It is what the founders intended, and it is unlikely to change soon, so we will just have to work through the system we have, however inefficient and conflict prone it may be.

Now the issue is complicated by one additional step. Normally, foreign policy requires presidential leadership and congressional oversight, or what former congressman (and chair of the House Foreign Affairs Committee) Lee Hamilton, one of the few congressional experts on foreign policy, called a "creative tension" between Congress and the executive.[2] Under President Bush, however, not only were the president and Congress at loggerheads, but Congress was all but dysfunctional and the president was woefully inexperienced on foreign policy or dealing with other countries. When both the legislative and the executive branches are not working or are incompetent or both, then what do we do? And will President Obama be able to change these fundamental features of the U.S. system?

2. Lee Hamilton, *A Creative Tension: The Foreign Policy Roles of the President and Congress*, with Jordan Tama (Washington, DC: Woodrow Wilson Center Press, 2002).

Congress: Politics and Partisanship

Congress as an institution is in bad repute. Among the main American institutions, Congress ranks the lowest. It falls below the president, private corporations, the armed forces, the Supreme Court, the medical profession, and even the media. Actually, the public's respect for all American institutions has declined over the decades as we have become more skeptical and cynical, but the decline in respect for Congress is the steepest of all. Why? It stems from a combination of factors.

First, the public dislikes the excessive partisanship. Congress, we already know, is the most partisan of the three branches. In Congress, politics and partisanship seem to dominate all decisions, often at the cost of the national interest. While Congress seems to revel in partisanship, the public has become fed up. It wants real solutions to our national problems, not just constant partisan posturing with no solutions in sight.

Second, the public decries the decline in civility among the members of Congress. With all the backbiting, Congress is a nasty place to work these days. Once, congressmen could disagree over policy issues but then go for a drink and remain good friends afterward, even across party lines. Now members of Congress and the leadership rarely mingle socially with each other, let alone members of the other party, any more. Instead, they are at each other's throats, with comity and civility all but completely broken down.

The country has witnessed a third distressing development over the years, the institutional decline of Congress. As an institution, Congress has grown indifferent to reform, exercises almost no oversight of policy, and tolerates unacceptable levels of corruption, especially among its own members. Ethics reform of Congress by Congress is considered a laugh and an oxymoron. Congress cannot police itself, so why should we expect it to be responsible in governing the country?

Voters also deplore the absence of a work ethic exhibited by their representatives. Congressional work schedules are constantly shrinking. At most, Congress works from Tuesday afternoon to Thursday morning, or about a day and a half per week. In addition, it takes very long "breaks," far longer than what the rest of the population enjoys for vacations. Meanwhile, members of Congress enjoy some of the world's best and free perks: health care, air travel, vacations, and interns. Some of the "old lions" seem unable to keep their hands to themselves while around the thousands of interns who swarm Capitol Hill; young staffers learn quickly that many congressmen have a roving eye. As one can imagine, members of Congress love their perks and position, but most do not work very hard.

A fifth reason Congress's reputation has suffered is that today money appears to drive everything in politics. Money, it is said, is the "mother's milk" of politics, which these days depends on huge infusions of money, especially for election campaigns. A congressional campaign can now cost tens of millions of dollars while a Senate race can run to a hundred million dollars or more. With members spending so much time every day fund-raising, they have precious little time for legislating. In addition, the entire process is inherently corrupting. Though members of Congress repeatedly deny it, they do provide special favors to those big lobbying organizations that donate to their campaigns, at the expense of the public. To paraphrase an old aphorism: money corrupts, and the need for ever more money corrupts absolutely.

Sixth, the public finds members' obvious desires to be perpetually reelected offensive. Political science has convincingly demonstrated that, holding all other variables constant—the politician's party affiliation, red or blue states, gender, rural or urban district—the factor that best explains congressional voting be-havior is the desire to be reelected. In other words, they work only for their self-interest or self-aggrandizement. They do not want to suffer electoral defeat and have to return to their home districts and do actual work. Close observers of Congress have known for a long time, and the public is catching on as well, that members of Congress serve their own (reelection) interests first and only secondarily (and often as an afterthought) those of their districts and constituents. The sense is growing stronger that, when politicians say they are working diligently in the public's (as distinct from their own private) interest, the voters should not believe them for a minute.

Finally, the public is tired of the seamy side of politics. Is Congress full of crooks? It often seems that way. One member of Congress was discovered with a hundred thousand dollars in his freezer; in his defense he claimed the FBI violated the separation of powers by searching the freezer. Other members have been caught with their hands in the till or accepting illegal donations. Earmarks (without oversight) to benefit favored groups or projects in the members' districts are a growing problem, and an even bigger one is that lobby groups provide huge pools of cash to politicians and expect favors in return. How is that different from outright bribery? There is a rotten smell about Congress these days, and the voters are increasingly sensing it.

Given the partisanship, the political posturing, the deceptions, the self-interest, and the corrupting role of money and lobbying in Congress and on U.S. politics generally, it is sometimes a wonder that the United States still manages, at times, to carry out a good and sensible foreign policy. But often it does not, and Congress and the executive are both to blame for that. It is hard under the American constitutional system to carry out foreign policy with the advice and consent of an often-dysfunctional Congress, but now that same Congress is seeking to go several steps further toward actual congressional control and dominance of foreign policy.

The New Congressional Assertiveness: Causes

Congress has become both more dysfunctional in recent years and, concurrently, more active and assertive in foreign policy. At the same time that Congress is the most discredited of all major government institutions, it is also claiming a stronger role for itself in managing American policy. Here we look at the main causes of the new congressional assertiveness, and in the next section, we analyze the issues on which Congress is asserting itself.

DECLINE OF THE SENIORITY SYSTEM

Under the old seniority system in Congress, members of the House or Senate who had served the longest—usually conservative Southerners from safe, one-party states where their reelection was assured—used to hold the important leadership positions and wielded the most power as chairs of the Defense, Foreign Affairs, and Ways and Means (appropriations) committees. But in the mid-1970s a group of young, ambitious members of Congress revolted against the old system, changed the rules, and enabled themselves to move up quickly. By coincidence and aiding the change, some of the elderly chairs retired or died around this time, and the growth of a two-party South accelerated the turnover as well.

Seniority remains an important factor in committee chair assignments, but it is no longer the only one. Hence, new, younger, ambitious congresspersons can rise in power faster. These younger members also tend to be more partisan and ideological, eager to garner publicity and make their mark, and less willing to defer to presidential authority on foreign policy or other matters.

PROLIFERATION OF SPECIALIZED SUBCOMMITTEES

Back in the 1960s there was only one Senate Foreign Relations Committee and one House Foreign Affairs Committee. Since then, these committees have sub-divided into a variety of specialized subcommittees, with one for every area of the globe (Africa, Latin America, etc.) and one for every functional issue (arms control, democracy promotion, etc.). Counting the newer intelligence committees and subcommittees, about thirty committees and subcommittees in Congress have foreign affairs responsibilities.

With so many committees and subcommittees that everyone can be a chair, the joke in Congress now is that you don't even need to learn everyone's name any more; instead, just address everyone as "Mr. Chairman." On a serious level, the proliferation of subcommittees means that almost anyone in Congress who wishes to can hold hearings on nearly any subject. On a serious issue like the Iraq War or torture, a dozen or more committees may hold hearings, which result mainly in publicity and television time for their chairs. Policymakers must spend inordinate amounts of time preparing for these hearings, often only to be embarrassed or berated by the congresspersons. Policy by subcommittee hearings is not the best way to run policymaking. Moreover, with so many subcommittees, Congress can now poke into almost any aspect of policy, including many that should be handled quietly and by the executive branch.

Larger, More Politicized Staffs

Over the last several decades, the size of congressional staffs has increased enormously, by seven times overall in the last fifty years. Most of the increase is in the size of personal office staffs, but the size of committee staffs and total legislative branch staff has been enormous as well. Most congressional offices are literally overflowing with staff crammed into closet-sized cubbyholes.

Much of this staff increase is owing to the burgeoning congressional work-load over the years, with more meetings to attend, more letters and e-mail to answer, and so on. Equally important, congressional involvement in myriad issues (in part stemming from the proliferation of subcommittees) also demands more and more staff. Members of Congress may have only twenty-five to thirty persons working on their personal staffs and scores more on their various committees and subcommittees. Many of these staffers have advanced degrees and know as much about the issues as their executive branch counterparts do. An important senator like Ted Kennedy, for instance, may have seventy-five to a hundred staffers whose expertise on foreign affairs is as great as that of the State Department.

Many of these energetic, young staffers are more partisan and ideological than the members of Congress they serve. Their job is to make their bosses and themselves look good; therefore, staff members may be better at promoting their boss's and their own interests than in advancing the national interest. Thus, the staff may push a member into a position that he or she may not want to take but that serves staff interest, and they may also get him or her to sign off on legislation the member hasn't yet read.

The growth of staff and their behind-the-scenes activities have often resulted in a widening chasm between the executive and legislative branches, adding further to the fragmentation and disarray in American foreign policy. Although having Congress and its staff micromanage policy is not a good way to conduct our foreign affairs, sometimes executive branch policy is so badly conceived and executed that Congress has no choice but to get into the act.

DECLINING PARTY DISCIPLINE

In the past, party leaders in Congress could enforce party discipline on younger members and tell them how to vote. Now exerting that control has become much more difficult.

During the 1980s and '90s, Congress came close to being a free-for-all. Members were all over the place in terms of their votes. They voted more as individuals or in blocs, such as the Black Caucus or Hispanic Caucus, than according to party dictates. Many members were known as lone rangers because of their fierce independence. On such crucial issues as trade agreements, Central America, and even defense appropriations, members of Congress often voted their individual self-interest and not necessarily according to what their party leaders said.

More recently, discipline has tightened up again. The main instrument by which the leaders control member votes now is the disbursement of campaign funds. If you go along with the leadership, you get the money to fund your reelection, and if not, you get cut off. Since money is so crucial to successful campaigns, the threat of a cutoff is very effective. It keeps the members in line. But even then, many members still vote their own way and then negotiate over campaign funds later.

TECHNICAL EXPERTISE

In addition to the ever-larger staff and the expertise available there, Congress has access to a range of agencies that work just for Congress and give it levels of specialized knowledge often rivaling the executive branch. These include the Government Accountability Office (GAO), the Congressional Budget Office (CBO), the Congressional Research Service (CRS), and the entire Library of Congress. Using the highly trained staff found in these agencies, Congress can challenge a president on just about any issue, including foreign policy. Because in today's complex world, knowledge is power, these agencies can provide members of Congress with as much in-depth analysis as the NSC, the State Department, and DOD have available.

The GAO has become known for its studies of corruption, not just in the United States but in other countries as well, which Congress can then use to lambaste presidential foreign policy in a particular country. With the CBO, Congress has its own budget arm, enabling it to question the defense or intelligence budgets, to criticize waste in the Iraq War, and to challenge spending on almost all foreign policy issues. The CRS provides Congress with its own research branch and enables any member to request from the service's stable of first-rate scholars a well-informed, twenty- to thirty-page position paper on any subject on one day's notice. And in the Library of Congress, Congress has the best research library in the world and another superb staff capable of doing research, writing speeches, and finding even the most arcane nuggets of information for Congress. These agencies give Congress a level of technical and policy expertise—and, hence, power—that it never had before.

YOUTH AND AMBITION

Two generations of politicians have come to office guided by what I call the "post-Vietnam syndrome of values." These often rebellious and antiauthority types have little respect for the seniority system and are apt to be suspicious of U.S. interventions abroad, of the Defense Department, and of the executive branch. As narcissistic products of the baby boomer generation and later, they tend to be self-centered and crave publicity. As we have seen these members of Congress seldom get along well with their colleagues, are highly partisan, and do not often find value in compromise.

Does this development explain why Congress is such a mean-spirited place to serve or work these days? Is this change why Congress's approval rating has sunk to 14 percent in some polls? No, not entirely, but it provides a good start.

The new members of Congress do not always share the older generation's belief in peace through strength. They are impatient to make their mark quickly so they can move up to the Senate or to even more lucrative pay as a lobbyist. They prefer a greatly reduced U.S. presence abroad and a "peace dividend" so they can devote more funds to the social and economic benefits and entitlements on which their reelection depends. The new members, products of the "me generation," mostly look out for themselves. The former cooperative and bipartisan spirit in Congress has faded as the body has moved toward raw, self-centered ambition.

Concentrating on one's own advancement, of course, leaves little time for defending the national interest. The older appeals to self-sacrifice are ineffective when everyone is pursuing his or her self-interest. Certainly carrying out an effective foreign policy in this context becomes very difficult.

TELEVISION

Television enables all these younger and intensely ambitious politicians to leap to the forefront of national headlines. Television can provide instant "stardom"— think of Barack Obama—even to obscure, first-term representatives and senators. It enables an unknown congressman to go on national television and share equal time with the president or the secretary of state. The media especially like confrontational appearances, which they tout as "good television." Thus, television has become the fastest way to national recognition, stature, and maybe even a presidential bid.

Congress now has the benefits of an elaborate television studio right in its own office buildings on Capitol Hill. Members no longer have to go across town to the major networks; they can appear directly from the Capitol Hill studios or even their own offices. They can even use these same studios to make short clips to send to their home districts. Cameras in the Senate and House chambers can similarly be used to present them in a favorable light on a topic of compelling national security interest, when in reality the chamber is usually empty and the sound bites only sound compelling. Of course, since Congress controls the studio, only coverage that makes its members look good is allowed. Congress has its own makeup artists, hair stylists, and voice coaches—all designed to make its members appear serious and "presidential."

The focus on and preoccupation with television have many downsides. It lowers the level of serious debate to a thirty-second sound bite, stresses appearance rather than substance, and with its emphasis on confrontation, polarizes the debate on issues. It further undermines seniority and the committee system by enabling low-level members to grab TV prime time. It also brings to the fore those who are glib and handsome but devoid of ideas, shallow, and uninformed. Television may literally be dangerous: it is said that you should never get between certain members and a television camera or you're liable to be trampled.

AIR TRAVEL

Another reason for the increased congressional involvement in foreign policy is the ease of modern, international jet travel. Almost no area in the world is more than one day's travel time away. With the short congressional workweek, politicians can be in many areas of the world by Thursday night and in almost all by Friday morning. For a trip to Iraq, for example, they can have dinner with the ambassador that Friday evening, be briefed by the commanding officer and be pictured with the troops the next day, spend Sunday shopping, and return on Monday. The entire trip plus escorts may be provided on military, executive branch, or now even congressional aircraft.

Obviously, these visits are very superficial. One hopes that the junketeering politician can learn something in a two-day visit, but mainly such visits provide opportunities for a photo op, some television coverage, and, usually, reinforcement of the congressperson's foregone conclusions. With a good and informed staff, the congressperson can also use these opportunities to challenge White House policy and appear as knowledgeable on the subject as the president. And with the relaxed congressional workweek, he or she can even return in time to conduct the nation's business. Much of this is charade, but that is how Congress functions. Modern jet travel and instantaneous communications thus enable members of Congress to act as their own secretaries of state, traveling around the world, making their own foreign policy, and even challenging the president for foreign policy dominance.

DISTRUST OF THE PRESIDENT

Because of Vietnam (Lyndon Johnson), Watergate (Richard Nixon), serial philandering and lying (Bill Clinton), and Iraq (George W. Bush), when our presidents misled the public and were discredited for their actions, Congress has come to distrust the presidency. Vietnam led Congress to conclude the executive should not be exclusively in charge of foreign policy. Since then, most presidents (except George H. W. Bush) have given Congress few reasons to be optimistic about presidential foreign policy leadership, and George W. Bush evokes only disdain over foreign policy.

Congress has profound misgivings about the competence and capability of the White House to exercise leadership in foreign policy. Congress usually sees the White House as inept, bumbling, and, above all, not to be trusted with leadership in international affairs. Of course, Congress sees itself as more responsible than the president and believes that the president should share power with it on foreign policy. Instead of an "imperial presidency," they would prefer an imperial Congress. But the public sees Congress as even less competent, less trustworthy, and more despicable than the president. How can we have a good, decent, serious foreign policy if both branches are so thoroughly discredited?

The New Congressional Assertiveness: Effects

The previous discussion highlighted the causes of Congress's new assertiveness in foreign policy. Now we turn to what Congress has actually done to affect foreign policy and give itself a greater role. Legislation in the last thirty years, as well as new practices, has changed the executive-legislative relationship, giving Congress more power. The president still leads in most areas of foreign policy, especially in times of war or crisis, but Congress has become a not-quite-equal partner. This greater congressional assertiveness, however, does not seem to have produced better foreign policy. Instead, we have seen only greater conflict, a mishmash of conflicting responsibilities, ongoing battles between Congress and the White House over the Iraq War and other issues, inconsistent and contradictory policy, and severe governmental gridlock and paralysis.

Keep in mind former congressman Lee Hamilton's admonition that there is and should be a creative tension on foreign policy between Congress and the executive. However, in the present circumstances, there is precious little that is creative in the relationship, and the tension of which Hamilton speaks is more like hatred, disgust, or even "war."

THE WAR POWERS ACT

Many of the legislative acts over the last three decades seeking to limit presidential foreign policy prerogatives grew out of the Vietnam War. More recently, limitations have been sought because of similar frustrations stemming from the Iraq War.

The War Powers Act of 1973 came directly out of Vietnam. Recall that the Constitution requires Congress to declare war, but that stipulation has seldom hindered a president from sending forces abroad without a declaration of war.

For Congress, Vietnam was different because (1) it was not just a small police action but a large war, with five hundred thousand troops committed; (2) it was costly (as in Iraq), draining funds from pet projects that Congress preferred; and (3) it was a losing battle, with Congress feeling the heat to pull out the troops.

The War Powers Act sought to remedy this situation. It provided that any commitment of U.S. military forces to any global hot spot for longer than sixty days must receive the approval of Congress. The president could thus still respond quickly to an emergency and dispatch troops if it was for less than sixty days, but anything longer than that would require legislative approval.

The War Powers Act was passed by a Democratic-controlled Congress aimed at reining in a Republican president (Nixon). It was a highly partisan piece of legislation. But no president since then has wanted to be constrained by its provisions. First, it may be an unconstitutional intrusion on the president's role as commander in chief. Second, it is poorly written and unclear. For example, the president is obliged to consult with Congress, but the act does not specify either beforehand or afterward, whether such consultations involve all members or just a few, or how much information the president must give to Congress. Third, the legislation is difficult to enforce. Suppose when the sixty days are up our troops are in the midst of fighting or only halfway through a peacekeeping or humanitarian mission. Must the president stop the mission while Congress decides if it can continue? These and other uncertainties have kept the War Powers Act from being effective during most of its thirty-five-year existence.

THE LEGISLATIVE VETO

Another means by which Congress tried to expand its power in foreign policy was through the use of the legislative veto. Congress (actually only a handful of members) asserted that it had the power by a simple majority to veto presidential actions. Once again, the goal was to limit the president's discretion in the dispatch and deployment of military forces.

But every schoolchild knows that, while the president has the power to veto acts of Congress, nowhere in the Constitution does it say Congress can veto presidential actions. Congress has the power of the purse and can refuse to support presidential initiatives, but nowhere is it given veto power. Therefore, it did not come as a great surprise when the Supreme Court struck down the would-be congressional veto as unconstitutional.

Extremely frustrated by its powerlessness over foreign policy, Congress continued to try to find ways to exercise a veto by other means. As the Iraq

War turned sour, for example, Congress first sought to persuade Bush into withdrawing and then attempted to cut off funds for the war. When the White House quickly countered that cutting off funds would hurt "our boys," Congress quickly, and repeatedly, wilted under the pressure instead.

INTELLIGENCE OVERSIGHT

Another legacy of the Vietnam War era, when CIA "dirty tricks" involving assassinations of heads of state and support for human rights–abusing regimes were revealed, was greater congressional oversight of U.S. intelligence agencies. Heretofore, intelligence oversight had been largely limited to pro forma reviews in the House and Senate Armed Services committees, and the chairmen usually went along with whatever the CIA wanted to do. But in the 1970s, after several spectacular and well-publicized failures, which were all exposed at great length in hearings Senator Frank Church conducted, Congress determined to clamp down.

New legislation, passed over presidential objections, led to the creation of two new committees in the House and Senate designed specifically to oversee covert operations and to exercise stronger congressional oversight over all intelligence activities. Quite a few of these committee members, and their staffs, were hostile to the CIA; moreover, with all the unfavorable publicity the Church Committee generated, the political climate was less favorable to the CIA. During the late 1970s, the Democratic-controlled Congress greatly reduced the CIA's size, budget, and effectiveness.

Even with the creation of the two new committees, or maybe because of them, relations between Congress and the intelligence community remained prickly. Though CIA officials appeared before the committees behind closed doors, anti-CIA staffers often leaked their testimony to the press within hours. Such publicity had the effect of scuttling the CIA's covert operations, which is what these staffers wanted. Because of the frequent leaks, the CIA became leery of giving secret information to Congress. Congress, in turn, accused the CIA of covering up or hiding the facts. In addition, foreign allies became reluctant to share their intelligence with the U.S. agencies, knowing it was likely to be leaked. The impasse has not been satisfactorily resolved to this day.

HUMAN RIGHTS CERTIFICATION

During the Cold War and under threat from the Soviet Union, the United States maintained alliances with some nasty regimes. These generally military and authoritarian regimes had poor human rights records. The U.S. government faced what was called the "friendly tyrants" dilemma: what to do about regimes that were undemocratic and violated human rights but were also anticommunist and served U.S. interests.

During the 1970s there was rising interest in international human rights, and Jimmy Carter made human rights the centerpiece of his administration. Then Ronald Reagan turned the human rights issue on its head by focusing on abuse under communist regimes and less under rightist governments that were U.S. allies. Even today the issue is highly politicized, with Democratic administrations focusing their criticism on right wing regimes and Republican administrations more inclined to criticize leftists. Both sides agree, fortunately, that terrorist states are bad, but even here there are partisan differences in their approaches, with Republicans inclined to use military force and Democrats favoring soft power.

Everyone by now is in favor of supporting human rights in general terms, but in specific instances the consensus breaks down. Moreover, while we value human rights, we need to balance other important U.S. interests involved as well. Everyone knows that Saudi Arabia, China, and Pakistan abuse human rights, but they are also, respectively, the world's largest oil supplier, an emerging global power, and an ally in the war on terrorism. It's over difficult cases like these that politicians mostly disagree.

During Carter's presidency, Congress passed legislation requiring the State Department to create a new Bureau of Human Rights and Humanitarian Affairs, which was renamed the Bureau of Democracy, Human Rights, and Labor in 1994. One of the bureau's responsibilities was to issue a yearly report on the human rights situation in all the world's countries. Testimony was also required from administration officials on the progress of human rights in all countries to which we give aid. If there was no progress, U.S. assistance to the country was supposed to be terminated. But questions arose: What if there was precious little or no progress and yet the country was vital to U.S. interests, as Egypt is to the Middle East peace process or Pakistan to the war on terrorism? Should we then ignore the human rights abuses for the sake of other, maybe bigger U.S. interests, or should we stress human rights and thus risk destabilizing a friendly ally whose support we need?

The result was a lot of hypocrisy and dissembling. In some cases the government ignored the requirement of human rights reporting or softened the language on specific countries. In other cases, administration officials regularly lied to Congress about human rights progress in vital countries because the government did not want their aid cut off in the midst of a crisis. This ongoing problem frequently leads the government to balance out human rights concerns with other important U.S. interests: economic, political, diplomatic, and strategic.

THE POWER OF THE PURSE STRINGS

Congress must initiate all money bills. The president can set forth his agenda, but unless Congress passes the appropriation, his initiatives will not be implemented.

In the past, this "power over the purse" was usually exercised prudently and with restraint. Especially in foreign policy, the president led and Congress, with some amendments, provided the funding. The national interest was usually served.

But now Congress exercises the power of the purse more tightly and in greater detail. Congress uses its power of appropriation not only to modify executive initiatives but also to change them fundamentally or reverse them. This is especially true in a situation of divided government, with one party in control of Congress and the other holding the White House. Thus, while Congress cannot constitutionally lead in foreign policy, it can exercise great influence through the appropriation process. Congress, for example, may turn down or hold up trade agreements negotiated by the executive, it may discontinue assistance to regimes of which it disapproves, or, as in Iraq, it may try to force a policy change and threaten to cut off funds for the war effort. Congress may also tack on human rights requirements to foreign assistance bills, mandate compliance with certain goals as a condition of funding, or grant or withhold (permanent) normal trade relations status to certain countries to make sure they comply with U.S. requirements.

Members of Congress frequently slip provisions regarding their favorite countries as amendments or earmarks into bills that have nothing to do with foreign affairs. They may also try to micromanage U.S. relations with other nations to such an extent that they tell U.S. embassies or foreign aid missions abroad, who are much closer to the issues involved, what policies to carry out or which groups to assist. Of course, the frequent partisan and poisonous relations between Congress and the White House do not lead to much cooperation or coherence in U.S. policy.

Remember also that Congress, especially the House, is our most partisan branch of government, and representatives, who serve two-year terms, are constantly fund-raising and calculating their reelection possibilities. With vir-tually all legislation and especially trade deals, members of Congress vote on the basis of domestic considerations—that is, their own reelection possibilities and careers—and not necessarily for the national interest.

TREATIES AND EXECUTIVE AGREEMENTS

The United States is a party to about a thousand international treaties, but it has signed nearly eight times that number of executive agreements. Treaties require a two-thirds vote of the Senate for ratification while executive agreements require no congressional action. Thus, the executive branch much prefers executive agreements and Congress the treaty process.

Executive agreements were once seen as useful supplements to larger treaties (on which Congress did vote) or to deal with small matters between countries that did not rise to treaty status. But today, executive agreements can run to several hundred pages. They are treaties in everything but name. The sheer number and details of many executive agreements have led Congress to conclude they are really treaties and only called something else to avoid congressional scrutiny. Congress is, therefore, demanding that it be in on the action and is pressuring the White House to consider executive agreements in the same category as treaties. The White House is resisting this move because it likes the flexibility of the executive agreements and prefers not to have Congress, with its different interests and demands to the other party, involved in the process.

The issue has become another matter of great contention between the two branches. Obviously, in his negotiations with other countries the president needs the flexibility that executive agreements provide. But there are far too many executive agreements, and the White House cannot continue using them to avoid constitutionally mandated congressional reviews. Recently the White House has compromised and frequently brought along and included in the initial treaty negotiations a group of congresspersons from both parties and both houses. That way, Congress is involved but the president still leads.

NOMINATIONS

The appointment of U.S. ambassadors, Department of State personnel, and representatives to the United Nations and other international bodies is another policy area in which Congress has flexed its muscles. According to the Consti-tution, the Senate is charged with approving, or disapproving, all U.S. ambassadors sent abroad, as well as the UN ambassador, and foreign affairs officials down to the assistant secretary level. Approval used to be almost automatic, assuming the nominee was not a thief or a drug pusher.

In Washington's current politically charged atmosphere, all such nominees are now closely scrutinized, not necessarily on merit grounds, but on political or ideological grounds. Because of what's called "senatorial privilege," a single senator can put an indefinite hold on an appointment. Meanwhile, the nominee has probably given up his or her previous job, is without income, and must wait for a "day in court" (the Senate), which may never come. Such holds are grossly unfair to the candidate.

A president may then try to shame the Senate or the individual senator into taking up the case. The nominee, after all, deserves a vote, up or down, one way or another. Alternatively, when the Senate is away on recess, the president may make a recess appointment and enable the candidate to take up his job for up to one year but still without Senate approval. For example, John Bolton, President Bush's conservative nominee for ambassador to the UN, received such a recess appointment, but then he had to relinquish that position when his time ran out and the Senate still refused to hear his case. All this conflict and confrontation, of course, come at the cost of U.S. foreign policy.

BIASED HEARINGS

When Congress holds hearings on foreign policy issues, American citizens have a right to expect those hearings to be unbiased, nonpartisan, and aimed at ferreting out the truth. Out of such presumably balanced and serious hearings, we expect Congress to oversee policy initiatives of the executive branch and arrive at fair, unbiased policy determinations.

In actual fact, nothing could be further from the truth. None of the adjectives used in the previous paragraph—unbiased, nonpartisan, true, balanced, serious—applies. In this more politicized era, even hearings are preeminently political events. They are organized and designed to support the congressional majority's views and to embarrass the president or the opposition. They choose witnesses who support the majority's predetermined position and not for their objective views; therefore, many serious scholars refuse to testify. Few congressmen show up, but many interns do; they use the testimony presented to write their term papers. Hearings are not intended as a careful, judicious presentation of policy alternatives but as a show designed to make the majority look good.

Congressional hearings have become a charade. They are so politicized and members of Congress are so eager to use them for partisan advantage that they are no longer serious or useful forums for foreign policy discussion.

CONGRESSIONAL TAKEOVER OF FOREIGN POLICY

Since the 1970s Congress has been nibbling at the edges of executive dominance in foreign policy, asserting its own prerogatives, and trying to tip the balance toward the legislative branch. Most of these efforts have been piecemeal, but in several notable instances Congress has asserted its own dominance in foreign policy and moved to usurp presidential leadership.

During the 1980s, when Central America was a hot issue, House speaker Jim Wright decided to implement his own foreign policy program there. Fed up with the Reagan administration's policy, Wright, without any authorization or constitutional authority, flew to Central America on a fact-finding mission, met with several presidents, and then launched his own peace initiative, which top Democrats had already agreed on before the trip. The White House fumed, for Wright had not consulted it or the Department of State and his junket undermined the White House's own peace plan. Wright's efforts were widely seen as a congressional attempt to usurp constitutional and presidential authority in foreign affairs.

In May 2008 Speaker Nancy Pelosi, who has no background in foreign affairs, undertook a much-publicized trip to Iraq and Syria as a way of undercutting President Bush's Iraq policy and staking out an opposition position. Meanwhile, in Washington, Democrats in the House sought repeatedly to undermine administration policy by urging a no vote on Iraq War funding, publicizing select atrocities committed during the war, or seeking to close down the Guantánamo prison camp.

Of course, one could argue with the Reagan administration's policy in Central America, and certainly the Iraq War has been badly conceived and managed. But constitutionally the president is in charge of foreign policy, not Congress. In addition, in the cases cited, the administrations were in the midst of delicate but secret negotiations aimed at altering the policy, which the opposition's initiatives and resultant publicity undermined. Nevertheless, precedents have now been established in which Congress not only asserts coequal power with the president on foreign policy but also moves to conduct foreign policy on its own. Some have referred to this as a "congressional coup d'état."

Conclusion

Specialists in foreign policy seldom look on Congress kindly. Congress is generally poorly informed on foreign policy, panders to constituent demands, and introduces dangerous partisanship into foreign affairs. At the White House, State Department, and other executive departments, where there is real foreign policy expertise, members of Congress are usually referred to in unflattering terms: "clowns," "middlemen," and "incompetents."

To be fair to Congress, its members operate under intense pressures. They must be reelected every two years (in the case of the House), and part of their responsibility in a democracy is to explain administration policy to their constituents. But if the policy is wrongheaded and failing, then what do they say? They can't just stand idly by while their constituents go in another direction and they themselves go down in electoral defeat. Plus, Congress itself does have a constitutionally mandated role to play in foreign policy, that is, to exercise oversight, to check and balance, to hold hearings, and to appropriate the funds or not. Members of Congress are often torn by these conflicting pressures, as is the rest of the country.

The significant increase in congressional power and assertiveness since Vietnam, and its resurgence with Iraq, has added to our foreign policy confusion while doing little either to check executive power or to change the policy. The president still leads in almost all areas of policy; Congress is mainly left to throw roadblocks in his way. Members of Congress do enjoy their new foreign policy power, which helps their reelection ambitions; therefore, it is unlikely to change soon. Furthermore, at least in some areas—human rights certification, for example, or treaty making—the White House has by now acquiesced and allowed more congressional involvement. These trends suggest that a return to the older era of absolute presidential dominance is unlikely; instead, Congress has become a partner, albeit still a junior partner, in decision making. Whether this development has improved American foreign policy remains an open question.

Hence, the "invitation to struggle" between legislative and executive branches will continue, and doubtless new permutations of this age-old struggle will evolve. The president still leads in foreign policy, but congressional assertiveness continues to rise. On both ends of Pennsylvania Avenue, politics and partisanship will continue to influence foreign policy but even more so on Capitol Hill, with its short election cycle and its greater partisanship, than in the White House.

Thoughtful members of Congress know that they cannot lead on foreign policy without diplomats, intelligence services, or armed forces—all of which are part of the executive branch. Congress can, therefore, exercise oversight, but it cannot substitute itself for the president. Presidents also recognize that in the present era they must consult and share some responsibility with Congress. That's what Lee Hamilton meant when he used the phrase "creative tension" to describe executive-legislative relations.

Recent debates have moved quite a bit beyond this point. In the last administration, President Bush blamed Congress for undermining his Iraq War effort and felt it was putting the United States at risk in the war on terrorism. Meanwhile, Congress viewed the president as inept, uninformed, and leading the country in wrong direction. Meanwhile, sick of the squabbles and the constant partisanship, the public gave both the president and Congress historically low approval ratings.

This situation reflects a broken government. More than paralysis or gridlock—terms used in the past to describe fractious executive-legislative relations—we are now witnessing an advanced sclerosis of the American system. Undoubtedly, the support for Barack Obama in 2008 reflected the American public's desire for a new leader who could overcome the country's deep divisions of class, race, culture, religion, geography, and partisan politics. But the more sophisticated among the electorate also recognize that the divisions are so deep and the fissures so wide that no one man in one administration can do much to overcome them. Gridlock, paralysis, and broken government are likely, therefore, to continue well into the future.

Suggested Reading

Abshire, David M., and Ralph D. Nurnberger, eds. *The Growing Power of Congress.* Beverly Hills, CA: Sage Publications, 1981.

Crabb, Cecil Van Meter, and Pat M. Holt. *Invitation to Struggle: Congress, the President, and Foreign Policy.* 4th ed. Washington, DC: CQ Press, 1992.

Deibel, Terry L. *Clinton and Congress: The Politics of Foreign Policy.* New York: Foreign Policy Association, 2000.

Destler, I. M., and Eric R. Alterman. "Congress and Reagan's Foreign Power." *Washington Quarterly* 7 (Winter 1984): 91–101.

Dodd, Lawrence C., and Bruce Ian Oppenheimer. *Congress Reconsidered.* 8th ed. Washington, DC: CQ Press, 2005.

Fisher, Louis. *Constitutional Conflicts between Congress and the President.* 5th ed. Lawrence: University Press of Kansas, 2007.

Franck, Thomas M., and Edward Weisband. *Foreign Policy by Congress.* New York: Oxford University Press, 1979.

Hamilton, Lee, and Jordan Tama. *A Creative Tension: The Foreign Policy Roles of the President and Congress.* Baltimore, MD: Johns Hopkins University Press, 2002.

Hersman, Rebecca K. C. *Friends and Foes: How Congress and the President Really Make Foreign Policy.* Washington, DC: Brookings Institution, 2000.

Hinckley, Barbara. *Less Than Meets the Eye: Foreign Policy Making and the Myth of the Assertive Congress.* Chicago: University of Chicago Press, 1994.

Kelley, Donald R. *Divided Power: The Presidency, Congress, and the Formation of American Foreign Policy.* Fayetteville: University of Arkansas Press, 2005.

King, Anthony Stephen. *Both Ends of the Avenue: The Presidency, the Executive Branch, and Congress in the 1980s.* Washington, DC: American Enterprise Institute for Public Policy Research, 1983.

Lindsay, James M. "Congress and Foreign Policy: Why the Hill Matters." *Political Science Quarterly* 107, no. 4 (1992): 607–28.

———. "Congress, Foreign Policy, and the New Institutionalism." *International Studies Quarterly* 38, no. 2 (1994): 281–304.

Lindsay, James M., and Randall B. Ripley. "How Congress Influences Foreign and Defense Policy." *Bulletin of the American Academy of Arts and Sciences* 47, no. 6 (1994): 7–32.

Pastor, Robert A. *Congress and the Politics of U.S. Foreign Economic Policy, 1929–1976.* Berkeley: University of California Press, 1980.

Smyrl, Marc E. *Conflict or Codetermination? Congress, the President, and the Power to Make War.* Cambridge, MA: Ballinger Publishing, 1988.

Spanier, John W., and Joseph L. Nogee. *Congress, the Presidency, and American Foreign Policy.* New York: Pergamon Press, 1981.

Turner, Robert F. *The War Powers Resolution: Its Implementation in Theory and Practice.* Philadelphia, PA: Foreign Policy Research Institute, 1983.

Warburg, Gerald Felix. *Conflict and Consensus: The Struggle between Congress and the President over Foreign Policymaking.* New York: Harper & Row, 1989.

Whalen, Charles W. *The House and Foreign Policy: The Irony of Congressional Reform.* Chapel Hill: University of North Carolina Press, 1982.

11

Bureaucratic Politics:
Turf Battles Among Agencies

Foreign policy, as we saw in chapter 2, is not just a rational process in which we weigh policy options and decide judiciously on what's best for the country. Instead, politics in the broadest sense—logrolling, partisanship, political deals, trade-offs, election-year posturing, the servicing of private interests—is also involved. The succeeding chapters on public opinion, the media, political parties, interest groups, think tanks, and Congress have detailed how intensely partisan and politicized American foreign policy has become.

In addition to the private and political interests involved, we learned that bureaucratic interests within the U.S. government also impact policymaking. The government's foreign policy agencies not only compete with each other, but as their relative power and influence change over time, their different internal styles, political cultures, and standard operating procedures make it difficult for them to work together.

In the Cold War era, the main U.S. agencies (and rivals for budgets and power) involved in foreign policy were the State Department, the Defense Department, and the CIA. Then in the 1990s, when drugs, immigration, and international trade became major issues, the Commerce Department, Treasury Department, Office of the Trade Representative, Drug Enforcement Agency, Justice Department, FBI, and Immigration and Naturalization Service also got into the foreign policy act and became competitors with the older agencies for foreign policy money and influence. After the terrorist attacks of September 11, 2001, the government established the Department of Homeland Security (DHS) and the Transportation Security Administration (TSA) to deal with security threats and an intelligence czar under the auspices of the Office of the Director of National Intelligence (DNI) to coordinate all the many U.S. intelligence services. One of the main discoveries after the 9/11 attacks was that U.S. intelligence agencies failed to share information about the terrorists that they already had in their files with other agencies. We shall see if all these new agencies are any better at protecting us from terrorists, or if the government has just added new "players" to the bureaucratic competition.

There are three main bureaucratic-political issues that are important to this discussion. First, such agencies as the State and Defense departments, the CIA, the Justice Department, DHS, and so on are supposed to perform separate but interrelated foreign policy functions, which are then coordinated through the National Security Council and by the president. But, in fact, these agencies are not well coordinated; instead, they compete rather than cooperate. Further, the NSC is too weak to force them to cooperate, and the president often lacks sufficient knowledge to be an independent arbiter for them.

Next, the relative power of these agencies has changed dramatically over time. In their budget and turf battles, for example, the State Department has been the big loser, with its budget and influence declining since the 1960s, while the Department of Defense has been the big winner. In recent decades this imbalance has resulted in the military playing a far greater role and in what many are calling the "militarization" of foreign policy. Is this direction a good thing?

A third important change is the tremendous proliferation of new agencies involved in foreign policy in addition to all the departments, agencies, and directorates already mentioned. But that is just the beginning. On drug policy, for example, no less than forty-three U.S. government agencies are involved, and on trade and terrorism, there are even more. Further compounding the issue, these agencies are not well coordinated. How can a government have an effective foreign policy with that many agencies involved and almost no coordination between them? Answer: it can't. And its ineffectiveness is a big problem.

Department of State

In the great game of bureaucratic politics over the last five decades, the big loser has been the Department of State. Ostensibly, the main agency for American foreign policy, the department has many problems, both internal and external, and has been losing power over the years relative to other agencies. It has lost so much influence that in recent crises like Iraq or Afghanistan, people ask, "Where is the State Department?"

Every recent American president has felt compelled to give a speech early in his term and state that the State Department is the main instrument of foreign policy and his secretary of state its main voice. But almost as soon as that speech is delivered, the president tires of dealing with the department, makes the NSC his main foreign policy agency, and uses the Defense Department to get things done. The State Department shrinks into oblivion.

Unlike other agencies, the Department of State has never fully modernized its functions or attitudes. In the decades before World War II, it was a small agency, with its recruits coming mainly from the elite Ivy League colleges and its personnel being mostly white males who were not specialists but generalists who ran foreign policy from the proverbial seat of their pants. Part of the department's difficulties today stem from these still persistent elitist attitudes.

The period from World War II until the mid-1960s was the State Department's heyday. Its accomplishments included carrying out the Marshall Plan and the Point Four Program; creating NATO and dealing with the early Cold War; and establishing the Alliance for Progress. The department grew from a few hundred Foreign Service officers (FSOs) to a few thousand and moved from the cramped quarters of the Old Executive Office Building next to the White House to a gigantic new building in Foggy Bottom, a half mile away. But many of its problems persisted: it was still considered too elitist and snooty; it hired too few women, minorities, and specialists; it offered weak analyses; and it was unable to build a domestic constituency to support American foreign policy.

State's decline dates from the mid-1960s. No one single cause is to blame. Instead, it suffered after Vietnam, Iraq, and other foreign policy failures; its persistent arrogance and elitism; its failure to develop specialized knowledge of the difficult countries and areas of the world; its inability to cultivate good relations with Congress and the American public; and, of course, its eclipse by the Defense Department. In recent years, because of the Iraq War and the war on terrorism, the department's budget has increased and it has begun recruiting new personnel; however, its long-term decline will unlikely be reversed unless it makes more fundamental changes.

The secretary of state is responsible for the department's overall direction and management with the assistance of five undersecretaries—all of whom are political appointees. Below that level are the regional bureaus for Latin America,

Europe, Africa, Asia, and the Near East. There are also functional bureaus that deal with global issues, such as terrorism, arms control, human rights, democratization, etc. Each of these bureaus is headed by an assistant secretary and several deputy assistant secretaries. They are usually a mix of professional FSOs and political appointees, similarly requiring congressional approval. Next are the regional offices (in the Latin America bureau, one for Central America or the Andean region, for instance), and then finally are country desks for just about every country and "political entity" (for example, the Palestinian National Authority) in the world. Although their precise relations have not been entirely clear lately, the department also houses the U.S. foreign aid program (USAID), the public affairs and public diplomacy office (formerly the U.S. Information Agency), and the Arms Control and Disarmament Agency (ACDA).

In addition to these jobs and offices in Washington, the State Department also maintains embassies and consulates (for visa matters) in most of the 192 nations that are members of the United Nations. FSOs in embassies abroad report on economic, political, and security issues in the countries or regions to which they are assigned. Some say these activities have become superfluous in an age when most of this information is available on the Internet, but most foreign policy analysts believe there is still no good substitute for firsthand reporting and observation. However, with its nonspecialist orientation and its FSOs' often weak language and cultural training, many question how good the State Department's reporting is.

State has some able and talented people, and its entrance exam is very difficult. But it is also widely thought of as out of touch with the American people. State Department personnel tend to think that they are better informed than the electorate, and that attitude has put it in conflict with all recent American presidents. The State Department subculture is still dominated by an overreliance on Ivy League universities, but at the same time, it tends to be anti-academic, favoring generalists over persons with real area, regional, or issue exper-tise. Women and minorities are still woefully underrepresented, particularly at high levels, and the department does not welcome outside scholars or political appointees. It is still, after all these years and countless efforts at reform, a quite closed community that has not kept pace with modern times. Most recent secretaries of state have given up on their own department, resorting to relying on a handful of key advisers and keeping the rest of the department at arm's length.

The State Department has few friends and allies either in Washington, where congressional support is necessary, especially at budget time, or in the country at large, where its officials are looked on negatively as "striped-pants, cookie-pushing diplomats." A crucial explanation, in this more politicized era, for the department's poor standing and reputation is that it has no political constituency. Unlike the Defense Department, which is good at public relations and has a military base (and the jobs that go with it) in most congressional districts in the country, the State Department has no such foundation of support. Hence, when it gets in trouble or needs budgetary or moral support, no one in Congress or the country at large will come to its aid. Morale in the department is, therefore, extremely low.

Defense Department

The Department of Defense has been the main beneficiary of the State Department's decline. Its budget is about twenty times larger than the State Department's—$600 billion versus $30 billion—and reflects the relative power of the two departments. Defense has everything that the State Department lacks: a large budget, influential friends in Congress, a broad political constituency, and a heroic image among the American public. When Americans are asked which institution they trust the most and think of favorably, the U.S. armed forces come out on top by far—far more than the president, Congress, or the State Department.[1] And that preference translates into foreign policy influence for the Department of Defense.

In recent decades DOD's influence has increased enormously not just in military and security matters but in political and diplomatic areas as well, areas traditionally reserved for the State Department. With its enormous budgets, political credibility, and large constituencies, the Defense Department has gradually taken over whole areas of foreign policy in which the State Department, consequently, has been reduced almost to irrelevance. When U.S. commanders at the four-star level survey their "domains" in Latin America, Europe, the Middle East, Asia and the Pacific, and now Africa as well, they see vast territories, often dozens of countries, that they are responsible for, and they have immense power at their disposal. The regional commanders have huge office staffs, vast ship and air fleets at their command, thousands of soldiers with awesome weapons they

1. The figures (2008) are: armed forces, 69 percent; Supreme Court, 34 percent; the president, 25 percent; Congress, 14 percent; and State Department, 9 percent.

can dispatch, and the power and perks of a potentate. Small countries are likely to be overwhelmed when one of these commanders and his large retinue pay a visit. The State Department and U.S. embassies abroad often wonder why DOD has so much money and resources, and they have so little.

While the U.S. armed forces' strength gives the Defense Department enormous power in our domestic politics, their ostensible purpose is to deter any enemy from ever attacking the United States. At the heart of U.S. deterrence strategy is the notion that we must be so strong that no one would ever dare attack us for fear of the retaliation that would follow. It is a paradox of deterrence that we must be so powerful that those awesome weapons we have should never be used. But a number of questions arise. Why didn't all that deterrence keep the terrorists from attacking us on 9/11? Have our military officials prepared for today's kind of guerrilla-terrorist war, or are they still fighting the Cold War? Is an organization as big (three million persons), as bureaucratic, and as resistant to change as the Defense Department amenable to change at all?

These questions, in turn, raise some even larger ones that are at the heart of this book. Is the United States still a superpower, or have we squandered our opportunities to lead? Does the United States still serve as the undisputed leader in a unipolar world, or with the rise of China and other countries, must we now adjust to a multipolar world with numerous power centers? Does the condition of the U.S. economy or our educational system, and our inability to adequately respond to Hurricane Katrina or wage the war in Iraq, mean that we are in trouble as a country and, hence, as a global power? These issues must remain at the forefront as we survey the U.S. defense posture.

The United States has not had a long history as a superpower. During the nineteenth century our main concerns were domestic tranquility and westward expansion. The Spanish-American War of 1898 and World War I brought the United States into the world arena for the first time among several world powers. After these wars we demobilized our armed forces quickly and went back to normalcy. We were prepared to do the same after World War II, but when the Cold War started immediately afterward we were unable to do so. It is really only from the late 1940s that the United States emerged as a superpower and began the immense military buildup that continues to this day.

That period, specifically since 1947, when the National Security Act was passed, saw a significant reorganization of the American armed forces. Up to that point, the three armed services (Army, Navy, Air Force; the Marine Corps achieved equal status in 1952) had been separate services. The National Security Act brought them together in a single Department of Defense. That same act created the Office of the Secretary of Defense (OSD), the Joint Chiefs of Staff, and the CIA. It was one of the most important and far-reaching pieces of legislation ever in U.S. security policy history.

Over the next sixty years the Defense Department grew into a large, multifaceted agency. DOD does not just implement U.S. military policy but wields powerful influence in the formulation of foreign policy—maybe the most important. With a vast organizational structure centered in his office, the secretary of defense is an especially important figure who, as an adviser to the president on foreign policy, is often more important than the secretary of state and has the command of large forces and lethal power at his fingertips. Directly under the secretary are all the armed services, the offices of the joint chiefs, all the regional commands, and all the military intelligence services. The regional commands are especially important in carrying out foreign policy and have a structure that mirrors the State Department's, with military missions stationed abroad and with their corresponding country desks—again, one for every country and every mission in the world—in the Pentagon. It used to be that the State and Defense departments were about equal in their power abroad and their bureaucratic influence in Washington, but now DOD has surpassed the State Department in terms of power relations both at home and abroad.

Two agencies within the Defense Department are of special importance for foreign policy analysts. The Office of International Security Policy (ISP) does policy planning (like the State Department's Office of Policy Planning but with much more clout), recommends policy on arms control, does counterterrorism planning, and monitors all political and economic trends related to NATO, the war on terrorism, U.S. strategic goals, and so forth. The Office of International Security Affairs (ISA) deals with security assistance, U.S. military missions abroad, international energy and economic issues, and the oversight of treaties and agreements with other nations. In addition, ISA provides a political component to the military assessments done elsewhere in the Pentagon and houses DOD's regional and issues-oriented offices. A close consideration of both ISA's and ISP's functions shows that they carry out virtually every duty the State Department performs. These DOD offices are not limited just to military or strategic affairs but encompass political, economic, and diplomatic functions as well. Everything the State Department can do DOD can do too, often better and undoubtedly bigger. That assessment says a great deal about where power lies in Washington.

The Defense Department's subculture is very different from that of the State Department. State Department personnel have historically come from the elite schools and from the Northeast, and they tend to be liberal on political and moral issues. By contrast, the Defense Department personnel are much more conservative, religious, and Republican (about 90 percent) and hail from small towns or rural, often Southern, America. These contrasts in the two institutions' subcultures add to the political and inside-Washington rivalries that exist between them. You could say, reflecting the party divide, that the State Department is blue while DOD is red. State often disagrees when it has to carry out a conservative-Republican foreign policy, and DOD chafes when it has to serve under a liberal Democrat. The Don't Ask, Don't Tell policy regarding gay people serving in the military, while not fully acceptable to both sides in the controversy, is one of many compromises between the two competing subcultures that exist in Washington.

The military is conservative in another way: it is reluctant to use the force that it has available. In part, it doesn't want to see its soldiers killed or wounded, and in part, it wants to avoid another Vietnam. In that war, not only was the United States defeated, but the military itself also suffered a loss of morale and was discredited. It has taken a long time for the armed forces to recover from Vietnam. For that reason, the Pentagon is leery of nation-building activities (Somalia, Haiti, Iraq, and Afghanistan) for which it is not well trained, and the military services are also opposed to the Iraq War. But these professional soldiers are subordinate to the civilian authorities, so when the president or the secretary of defense gives an order, they salute and obey.

This discussion has focused on the armed forces as if there is a single military culture, and indeed there is one that is conservative and built on order, hierarchy, and the military command structure. But each service—Army, Navy, Air Force, Marines—also has its own subculture, or its own traditions, habits, and ways of doing things. Despite the emphasis on "jointness"—all the services cooperating and working together to save costs and improve effectiveness—of the last twenty years, these rivalries, competitions, and distinct procedures persist. They are reinforced by the powerful alumni associations that all the services have and that serve as strong lobbying groups in Washington. While jointness remains an ideal, and while every young officer on his or her way up must serve in a joint assignment in order to be promoted, the divisions remain and, while often wasteful and expensive, are unlikely to be erased anytime soon.

The military must also address other problems. DOD needs to:

- Replace the dated Cold War concepts with new strategies.
- Revamp its stultifying bureaucracy, which prevents either reform or military effectiveness.
- Narrow the growing gap between the military and the civilian population stemming from the all-volunteer army and the fact that few children of the educated elites go into the armed forces.
- Completely retrain the military in counterinsurgency, antiterrorism, and peacekeeping functions.
- Tackle pressures that come into the military from the broader society, such as racism, special treatment of gay people and women, and poor education.
- Improve the capacity for the armed forces, which are not well equipped by culture or training, for nation-building roles; or let the civilians do it; or abandon the effort.

The Defense Department has exerted a growing influence in American foreign policy since World War II. Increasingly, its roles are economic, political, and diplomatic and not just military. Moreover, in the internal turf wars of Washington, DOD is a powerful voice, maybe the most powerful voice. The Pentagon and the armed services are badly in need of reform, but because they defend America and represent the most popular U.S. institution, it is all but impossible for politicians to criticize the military. Their solution thus far has been to shower it with ever-greater budgets, but whether that option is buying us any greater safety or security is not certain.

The Central Intelligence Agency (CIA)

The Central Intelligence Agency is one of the least known and least understood agencies in the U.S. government. The image most Americans as well as foreigners have of the CIA, largely shaped by bad, one-sided movies, is of a super-secret spy agency full of out-of-control James Bond types, roaming the world, killing people, and undermining governments.

The actual situation is more complex and less dramatic. First, because the CIA is a big, bureaucratic organization like the others considered here, roughly 80 percent of its activities are routine, normal, and administrative—in other words, downright boring. Second, the covert operations on which all those movies and TV shows are based represent only a small part of its activities. Most of the people in the CIA are assigned to the analytic side, researching and writing reports similar to those done by the State Department. Third, the CIA rarely, if ever, initiates an action on its own. Almost everything it does, including torture and water boarding, is authorized by the president or his National Security Council (see chapter 12), although elaborate safeguards are put in place so the president can deny ("plausible deniability") that he authorized an action that later proves to be illegal or a fiasco.

There is an inherent tension in a democracy between the openness of a free society and the secretiveness required of a spy agency. The United States has never handled this dilemma well. While the CIA needs to undertake some operations secretly, the media, as well as private investigators, are constantly trying to unearth those secrets. In the 1950s and 1960s Congress exercised minimum oversight of the CIA, but by the 1970s, after a series of damaging exposés, Congress investigated and put in place a stronger oversight system, with separate intelligence committees in both the House and Senate. Too much oversight, however, hamstrung the agency from carrying out its functions. Then came 9/11 and the war in Iraq. In both instances the CIA's intelligence was faulty, leading to angry recriminations against the agency and a wholesale restructuring of American intelligence.

The United States does not have a long history of intelligence operations; the dominant attitude was that we should not read other people's mail. But during World War II the Office of Strategic Services (OSS) ran spy operations, and in 1947 the CIA was created under the National Security Act, that major security reorganization that also created the Department of Defense. The CIA grew rapidly into a big bureaucracy, which is currently located in the Washington suburbs in Langley, Virginia. It achieved some notable successes in Europe in the 1950s in keeping the Communist Party from coming to power in such key allies as France, Greece, and Italy, but it was much less successful in the third world. During the 1960s and 1970s its main preoccupation was the Cold War struggle against the Soviet Union; to that end, it often supported repressive military regimes in Asia, Africa, Latin America, and the Middle East. But as an inefficient and bloated government agency with thirty thousand employees, it disastrously failed to predict either the collapse of Soviet communism or the rising challenge of international terrorism.

When the Cold War ended in 1991, the agency and its future were unclear. The question was, why do we need a large spy agency if we no longer have any enemies? Some proposed that the CIA go into the business of industrial spying. The Clinton administration's response in the 1990s was to reduce the CIA's size and budget. The CIA argues that these reductions caused it to miss the terrorist threat while others blamed incompetence within the agency.

We usually think of the CIA as *the* secret spy and intelligence-gathering agency of the U.S. government. In fact, the United States has more than twenty intelligence agencies, and since 9/11 the number has continued to grow. It includes the several defense intelligence services; the Secret Service; the FBI; the TSA; the special services within the Justice, Energy, State, and Treasury departments; the Capitol Police; homeland security; and others. In addition, the National Security Agency (NSA)—not to be confused with the president's National Security Council—monitors all the world's telephone connections, and the National Reconnaissance Office (NRO) runs the U.S. spy satellite systems. All these agencies compete for power, budgets, and turf. Under that logic, they often refuse to share intelligence information with the other spy agencies. That obstinacy was, we now know, one of the key failures of 9/11: some of the agencies had information about the planes' hijackers prior to the attacks, but they refused to communicate it with other agencies, and no one saw the big picture of this plot unfolding.

The CIA has a complicated internal structure. First, like all big bureaucracies, the CIA has a large administrative arm that handles everyday operations, or the clerical, travel, and staff functions that have nothing to do with spying. Second, the CIA has a sizable technology division that, overlapping with the NSA and NRO, gathers telephone and satellite intercepts. Third, the CIA has a large analytic arm made up of "tweedy" professorial types who take all the immense data the CIA gathers and analyze it for patterns, trouble spots, and country instability. This branch overlaps with the State Department's Bureau of Intelligence and Research. If you want to work for the CIA, are good at analyzing political trends and writing reports, but don't want to be a spy, this division may be the place for you. Only one of the CIA's directorates does actual spy work and special operations.

The CIA's internal culture is unique and quite different from that found in either the State Department or DOD. First, as a spy agency, there is a large element of secrecy and even paranoia. For a long time employees got on unmarked buses to get to work, there were no pictures on the walls for fear of bugs (*not* the crawling kind), and visitors had to be accompanied even when they went to the bathroom. Second, it used to be a gung ho organization, like the military, convinced that it was engaged in the nation's frontline defense; but now much of that esprit is gone, leaving behind an attitude of largely bureaucratic self-defense. Third, depending on the perceived enemy, the CIA's personnel—and their attitudes and style of behavior—have changed over the years. During the Cold War years the agency recruited many Eastern Europeans; then when the Central American civil wars heated up in the 1980s, it recruited Hispanics. Now, as might be expected, after the failures of 9/11, it is trying desperately to recruit Arabic speakers, officers, and analysts.

A fourth cultural or political-cultural dimension at the CIA reflects the different activities of its directorates. To oversimplify only a little, the technology branch is full of computer nerds, and the administrative directorate consists of civil servants who are just like those found anywhere else. While the analytic branch has mostly professorial types (often failed academics unable to get tenure in their universities), the operations directorate has many "cowboys" who correspond to James Bond types. Frequently within the CIA there is conflict between the tweedy academic types who do the analyses and the gung ho cowboys who are eager to see action.

The attack of 9/11 represented a massive intelligence failure. Why didn't our government see it coming? Although there was plenty of blame to go around—at the FBI and the White House as well as the CIA—someone in particular had to be held responsible. The CIA was subjected to withering criticism; some in Congress even wanted to abolish the agency. But that never happens in Washington; instead, the answer was to make the agency bigger by throwing money at the problem. Because the breakdown was widely perceived to be a coordination failure, it would presumably be solved by creating the position of intelligence czar, or super director, to coordinate all intelligence operations, as well as a new, cabinet-level Department of Homeland Security to bring together some dozen agencies from eight different departments.

But these reorganizations, as should have been foreseen, only triggered more turf wars. First, the CIA, the FBI, and the several defense intelligence agencies argued that their missions were so distinct and so important that they should not be put under the intelligence czar's control. But why have a director of national intelligence specifically for coordination purposes if he cannot control or organize the agencies that most need coordinating? To be fair, the Defense Department argues that its intelligence agencies need to be free to concentrate specifically on military intelligence, which the other agencies often neglect. While true, it is an insufficient reason to think that defense intelligence cannot be coordinated with other agencies through the supposed czar. The result of the reorganization so far is the DNI has succeeded in achieving better coordination among sixteen of the intelligence agencies under his purview, but some agencies remain almost completely outside the czar's control. Further, no one in Congress or elsewhere knows who's in charge of U.S. intelligence—the CIA or the DNI. So are we safer or better off? No one knows, or can know, until the next attack.

The situation with the Department of Homeland Security is far worse. This new cabinet-level department, created almost overnight, brings together twenty-two distinct agencies and more than two hundred thousand employees with different backgrounds and responsibilities. Housed in a ramshackle building that looks like a cut-rate motel, with torn carpeting and modest offices, the new department is still struggling to unify its many disparate parts. The department's agencies include the Federal Emergency Management Agency, which bungled the response to Hurricane Katrina; the TSA, which manages airport security with the maximum possible inconvenience to travelers; the Immigration and Naturalization Service (INS); the U.S. Customs Service; the Coast Guard; the Secret Service; and the Animal and Plant Health Inspection Service. It is a virtually impossible task to integrate all these agencies into one coherent department. DHS is really a collection of separate fiefdoms with widely varied functions rather than a department with a single purpose. Since it was established only in 2002, we should probably be sympathetic to what DHS is trying to do, but meanwhile the department is subject to all kinds of Washington jokes. It is the only government agency that thinks it's a grand accomplishment when nothing bad happens! DHS is still a work in progress.

As a global power with global reach, the United States needs a good intelligence system. It also requires the ability to carry out covert operations. Think of the system as you would an archer with a quiver full of arrows. One arrow is for diplomacy; another, for military operations; a third, for covert operations. There will be many times when the diplomatic arrow is too weak; the military one, too strong; and a third arrow, a covert action, is required. Think of the thousands of lives, the hundreds of billions of dollars in expenditures, and the fracturing of our political system that would have been saved if we had used a covert operation to remove Saddam Hussein in Iraq instead of waging a full-scale war. One can think of hundreds of instances, past, present, and future, where a decision maker would want the covert operation arrow in the quiver.

Currently, however, U.S. intelligence operations face many problems. The locus of power or responsibility is uncertain. Is it with the CIA director, the DNI, or the DHS secretary? Each is vying for increased power and budgets. Meanwhile, within both DNI and DHS, powerful bureaucratic frictions are being worked out as the multiple agencies agglomerated within these two entities try to establish their relationships with each other and with their new bosses. Over at the CIA, at the same time, the self-examination still continues regarding how it was so wrong about 9/11 and Iraq, whether its intelligence-gathering and analytic abilities are sufficient for today's needs, over the use of torture, whether it can recruit enough Arabic-speaking agents to fill current needs, and whether in a big bureaucratic agency, it can improve its crucial analytic assessments. Ultimately, the entire family of U.S. intelligence agencies is in bad trouble on countless fronts. It is doubtful if the many problems will be solved anytime soon.

The Treasury, Commerce, and Justice Departments

In decades past, the State and Defense departments and the CIA were virtually the only three foreign policy actors. But that is no longer the case. Now the world is more complex. New issues have come to the fore. The world has become more globalized and interdependent. Issues like illegal immigration, drugs, climate change, pollution, and so on that used to be considered domestic problems are now international issues as well. They cannot be solved by one country acting unilaterally; rather, multiple countries and multiple interests are involved.

A few years ago, foreign policy experts coined the term "intermestic" to describe issues that had both international and domestic implications. With the rise of these new issues a large number of new agencies—the Treasury, Commerce, and Justice departments; the FBI; the Drug Enforcement Agency; the Immigration and Naturalization Service; the Office of the Trade Representative; and the Department of Homeland Security—joined the foreign policy arena. The number of agencies and big bureaucracies involved in foreign policy has also multiplied.

With numerous new actors engaged in the process and more bureaucratic politics and interests to be sorted out, all this expansion has made our foreign policymaking much more complicated. It was hard enough to carry out American foreign policy when the State Department, DOD, and the CIA were the main actors competing with each other; now, on almost any issue, dozens of U.S. government agencies are involved. The proliferation of agencies has caused two main problems. First all these new issues and agencies have greatly increased the bureaucratic competition for control of U.S. foreign policy, intensifying government gridlock and making it almost impossible to carry out a coherent and sensible U.S. foreign policy. The second is that, since most of these new actors have been principally domestic agencies in the past, they often lack the training, foreign affairs expertise and experience, and language skills to deal with other countries and cultures.

Since the 1980s, as trade has increased, as investment has expanded, and as the world has become more globalized and interdependent, international economic issues have become much more important. Upwards of 35–40 percent of the U.S. economy is now dependent on international trade. Especially after the Cold War ended and during Bill Clinton's presidency, international economic issues became increasingly significant. Recognizing this development, President Clinton created new agencies and task forces to deal with the world's rising economic interdependence. After 9/11 the U.S. government's concern with economic issues took a backseat for a while to the war on terrorism, but global economic interdependence continued apace. Undoubtedly economic issues will continue to rise in importance as evidenced by the debates over jobs (or the loss thereof), trade agreements, the value of the dollar, competition from China, third world debt matters, falling U.S. productivity, hedge funds, market collapse, and so forth. All these areas are first and foremost both domestic and international issues in addition to being both economic and political issues.

Take the subject of trade, for instance. Everyone knows that international trade helps stimulate economic growth. A multiplier effect operates here: for every dollar invested in trade, approximately two dollars come back in growth. But not all groups benefit; the rising tide lifts many but not all boats. Some workers get left behind as manufacturing jobs shift abroad. Thus trade becomes a political issue as well as an economic one.

Or consider the third world debt issue. Many third world countries are neck deep in debt. They have borrowed and borrowed and cannot pay their debt holders. Various schemes have been proposed to give the debtor countries some relief, from outright forgiveness of their debts to letting them pay for their debts through various conservation or carbon-reducing plans. But talk of debt forgiveness or debt-for-conservation trades enters the realm of politics and diplomacy, for if the debtor nations cannot pay, someone else must. Debt then ceases to be an economic issue; it becomes a political one.

Another important problem is drugs and their harmful effects on individual users, their families, or the nation as a whole. The primary agency charged with combating drugs is the DEA, another law enforcement agency of the Justice Department. But as mainly a domestic affairs agency, the DEA is not well equipped by training and background to deal with the international flow of drugs into the United States. And with some 80 percent of the drugs coming from abroad, mainly from Latin America, the State Department, the FBI, the Coast Guard, and even the Navy get into the act of combating drugs. At last count, at least forty-three U.S. government agencies were involved in the war against drugs. Here is a vast bureaucratic politics issue: how do you coordinate the activities of forty-three agencies to achieve an effective policy? Answer: you can't. Several successive administrations have appointed a drug czar (like the intelligence czar) to coordinate the policy, but many government agencies, such as the CIA, the FBI, and the military, remain outside the supposed czar's authority. In addition, without cabinet rank, the drug czar could not knock heads and get the other departments to fall into line. The result is that the czar's authority is limited, the power of the position has declined, and the war on drugs has not been successful.

These and other international economic issues are the responsibility of the Treasury Department, the Commerce Department, the Interior Department, the Environmental Protection Agency, and the Office of the Trade Representative. The rising importance of economic issues has brought these agencies into the forefront of foreign policymaking. Each of these departments has by now created a division specifically devoted to international affairs and have taken their place beside the State Department, DOD, the Homeland Security Department, and the CIA as major foreign policy actors. This new lineup has two main effects. First, these new participants have exacerbated the bureaucratic politics and rivalries of U.S. foreign policymaking by adding more participants, more conflicting jurisdictions, more overlapping responsibilities, and, hence, more turf battles. And second, since most of these are, above all, economic policymaking agencies, they are not often well equipped for foreign policy. They are staffed, naturally enough, mainly by economists who lack the language training, the foreign country and area studies expertise, and the international affairs background to carry out a successful policy. Many of us have been in conferences and policy meetings abroad where these agencies' representatives couldn't speak the national language, didn't know the country or region, had no connections abroad, and hadn't a clue as to how to get country X to comply with U.S. policy.

Many of the same comments apply to the Justice Department, the FBI, the DEA, and the INS. Essentially law enforcement agencies, these agencies are responsible for enforcing U.S. laws and putting lawbreakers in jail. Frequently, in dealing with drug issues, money laundering, or illegal immigration, the law enforcement agents indict and possibly jail high-level cabinet officials, senior military officers, or even the president of the country involved. But that duty often undercuts the mission of the State Department whose job it is to maintain good relations with these countries. Good relations are not enhanced by putting other countries' officials in jail or, worse, as has sometimes happened, kidnapping them from their own countries to stand trial in the United States under U.S. law. The concomitant issues are compounded because all these agencies are new actors on the foreign policy stage, often adding to the confusion, the overlapping jurisdictions, and the competing responsibilities that are at the heart of bureaucratic politics. Moreover, just as with the economic agencies discussed above, these law enforcement agencies are woefully lacking in foreign language speakers, foreign country and area expertise, and knowledge of the big picture of U.S. foreign policy. Their job is law enforcement, a perfectly legitimate responsibility, but in dealing with other countries, they frequently fail to take into account that their work must be subordinated to larger foreign policy concerns.

One of the worst offenders in this regard is the FBI. For a long time legislation had provided for a neat division of labor between the FBI and the CIA: the FBI dealt with domestic crime and surveillance while the CIA did the spying overseas. But these rules have been fudged: the CIA now engages in domestic surveillance too, and the FBI has missions in virtually every U.S. embassy abroad. However, among the agencies most responsible for the failures to anticipate the 9/11 terrorist attacks on the United States, the FBI bears heavy responsibility.

As with the other agencies already considered, the FBI's newfound importance in the international arena has added another complicated feature to the bureaucratic politics of foreign policy. The FBI consists mostly of lawyers, and like the agencies considered earlier, it also lacks agents trained in foreign languages, expertise in foreign countries and cultures, and the empathy needed to operate in today's international world. Being above all a law enforcement agency, the bureau has agents abroad who want only to enforce the law—namely, U.S. law.

Since 9/11 the FBI, under the Patriot Act, has seen its powers vastly expanded on both the domestic and international fronts. The FBI collected information on thousands of Americans and their friends, as well as the activities of Americans living abroad and foreign nationals. It collected this information, often illegally, by means of wiretapping telephones, securing access to bank records and credit reports, and hacking into private computer e-mails. On the one hand, the FBI can justify these activities as part of the war on terrorism. On the other hand, civil liberties issues are involved. It has been revealed that in collecting this information the FBI often went way beyond both its congressional mandate and what the courts would allow. At the same time, to give credit where it is due, the FBI should be commended for resisting the harsh and illegal interrogation techniques the CIA and the military intelligence services used to pry information out of suspected terrorist prisoners during the war on terrorism.

Conclusion

American foreign policy is frequently referred to as a "family" of operations. Nowadays, the term "stakeholders" is used to refer to all those groups and agencies that have an interest, or stake, in a particular policy issue or arena. The stakeholders may include private sector groups as well as the various government agencies involved. When all these groups and agencies come together, as they do frequently at the various Washington think tanks or at the government agencies themselves, anywhere from seventy-five to a couple hundred of these groups may be represented. The issue then is how to get a coordinated and effective policy out of all these interest groups and government agencies.

Formerly only three major agencies were involved in assisting the White House and National Security Council on foreign policy: the State Department, Defense Department, and CIA. These agencies had more or less equal rank and observed and honored a long-standing division of labor: the State Department handled political and diplomatic relations with other countries, DOD did military and security, and the CIA was responsible for intelligence and, occasionally, covert action. Sometimes there were rivalries among these three agencies, and, hence, the term "bureaucratic politics" was coined to describe their competition.

But as the world has become complex and interdependent, new issues like drugs, trade, immigration, terrorism, and globalization have become more important. Therefore, various new agencies have risen to prominence in American foreign policy to deal with these issues. They include, as we've seen, the Treasury and Commerce departments and the OTR on international economic policy, the DEA and the Justice Department on drug policy, the INS on immigration, and the FBI, the TSA, and the Department of Homeland Security on international terrorism. This list, by no means, is complete because, on specific policy issues, other government actors—for example, the Coast Guard on drug interceptions—also get into the act. All these new agencies have enormously complicated U.S. foreign policymaking and made it almost impossible to carry out good, effective policy. And then, if a president and an NSC are weak on foreign policy, the policy coordination function that the White House is expected to perform may be done badly or not at all. That was the case in George W. Bush's administration, which had powerful secretaries of state and defense and an assertive CIA director but a weak and poorly informed president and NSC director.

Some interesting long-term conclusions emerge from this treatment of the different U.S. government agencies involved in foreign policymaking. The first is to map the winners and losers. Since the 1970s in the Washington power game, the State Department has clearly been the big loser in foreign policy influence while the Defense Department is the big winner. DOD has assumed so many areas of foreign policy that recently the secretary felt compelled to issue a plea for the State Department and other civilian agencies to reassert themselves and carry out the diplomatic, political, and nation-building functions that properly belong to them in Iraq, Afghanistan, and elsewhere.

The other big winners have been the economics departments and agencies, such as the Treasury and Commerce departments and the OTR, whose influence has risen as international economic issues have become more important. Similarly, the agencies associated with the war on terrorism—the CIA, the FBI, DHS, the Defense Intelligence Agency, TSA, and the DNI—have also garnered increased budgets and influence. (When looking for a postgraduation policy job, always apply to those agencies whose budgets are increasing.) Other agencies—namely, the DEA and the INS—seem to rise and fall in influence depending on how hot the issues they deal with (drugs and immigration) are.

What makes this issue of bureaucratic politics so interesting as well as so hard to resolve is that each of these competing agencies has a legitimate right to be involved in the issues. The Defense Department is not just usurping the State Department's influence; on issues like Iraq, Afghanistan, and the war on terrorism, DOD has a legitimate and constitutional right to be involved or even to be the lead agency. Likewise on economic policy, the Treasury and Commerce departments and the OTR all have a legitimate right to be involved for it is their jurisdiction. On drug policy, the FBI and the DEA should be involved since law enforcement is their responsibility. The problem here is not of one department or agency taking over another's issues but of these agencies having overlapping, legitimate jurisdictions. In these situations, their rivalries and turf battles intensify. That formulation enables us to understand better the issue of bureaucratic politics, but it does not solve the problems associated with it.

The problems of carrying out foreign policy in a context of bureaucratic politics become clear in this chapter. In every one of the issues considered here—drug policy, dealing with terrorism, international economic policy—the main themes that emerged were remarkably similar. The difficulties the agencies face stem from:

1.   Their inexperience—especially the newer ones—in foreign policy in terms of language skills, country and area expertise, and knowledge of working abroad.

2.   Their policy gaffes, such as the FBI's sometimes too zealous pursuit of druggies.

3.   Their tunnel vision, which results in their pursuing their own narrow goals without regard for the larger picture of U.S. policy.

4.   Their lack of coordination among other agencies that even the associated czars (for drug policy, counterterrorism, and the war in Iraq) cannot solve.

5.   Their many bureaucratic rivalries and turf battles over budgets, personnel, and policy responsibilities.

6.   Their confrontations and the resultant gridlock, which when added to that between the parties or between Congress and the White House, produces true paralysis.

7.   Their overall inability to contribute to an effective, long-term policy for dealing with the complex issues involved.

In theory, it should be possible to solve the problems associated with the bureaucratic politics phenomenon. One way is to appoint a czar to coordinate counternarcotics efforts or to create a Directorate of National Intelligence to oversee and coordinate all the intelligence agencies. Also, a strong president can sometimes force the feuding agencies to cooperate, but a president's term is only four or eight years while these bureaucracies and their skillful bureaucrats have longer tenures and are quite good at frustrating even presidential directorates. A third option, now well institutionalized, is to create interagency task forces and coordinating bodies, meeting regularly, through the National Security Council. But these last two possibilities, which are addressed in chapters 12 and 13, depend on either a president who is knowledgeable in foreign policy and willing to knock heads of his own cabinet members or an NSC sufficiently informed and strong that it can actually get these big departments and agencies to cooperate. We will see to what extent that turns out to be the case.

Suggested Reading

Ackley, Charles Walton. *The Modern Military in American Society: A Study in the Nature of Military Power*. Philadelphia: Westminster Press, 1972.

Agee, Philip. *Inside the Company: CIA Diary*. New York: Stonehill, 1975.

Ball, George W. *Diplomacy for a Crowded World: An American Foreign Policy*. Boston: Little, Brown, 1976.

Barrett, Archie D. *Reappraising Defense Organization: An Analysis Based on the Defense Organization Study of 1977–1980*. Washington, DC: National Defense University Press, 1983.

Briggs, Ellis Ormsbee. *Farewell to Foggy Bottom: The Recollections of a Career Diplomat*. New York: McKay, 1964.

Campbell, John Franklin. *The Foreign Affairs Fudge Factory*. New York: Basic Books, 1971.

Cline, Ray S. *The CIA under Reagan, Bush, and Casey: The Evolution of the Agency from Roosevelt to Reagan*. Washington, DC: Acropolis Books, 1981.

Codevilla, Angelo. *Informing Statecraft: Intelligence for a New Century*. New York: Free Press, 1992.

Cohen, Stephen D. *The Making of United States International Economic Policy: Principles, Problems, and Proposals for Reform*. 5th ed. Westport, CT: Praeger, 2000.

Colby, William Egan, and Peter Forbath. *Honorable Men: My Life in the CIA*. New York: Simon & Schuster, 1978.

Cooper, Richard N. *Economic Policy in an Interdependent World: Essays in World Economics*. Cambridge, MA: MIT Press, 1986.

Craig, Richard B. "Illicit Drug Traffic: Implications for South American Source Countries." *Journal of Interamerican Studies and World Affairs* 29, no. 2 (1987): 1–34.

Destler, I. M. *Making Foreign Economic Policy*. Washington, DC: Brookings Institution, 1980.

Feinberg, Richard E. *The Intemperate Zone: The Third World Challenge to U.S. Foreign Policy*. New York: Norton, 1983.

Feith, Douglas J. *War and Decision: Inside the Pentagon at the Dawn of the War on Terrorism*. New York: HarperCollins Publishers, 2008.

Goldwin, Robert A., ed. *Bureaucrats, Policy Analysts, Statesmen: Who Leads?* Washington, DC: American Enterprise Institute for Public Policy Research, 1980.

Hadley, Arthur Twining. *The Straw Giant: Triumph and Failure, America's Armed Forces: A Report from the Field*. New York: Random House, 1986.

Hilsman, Roger, Laura Gaughran, and Patricia A. Weitsman. *The Politics of Policy Making in Defense and Foreign Affairs: Conceptual Models and Bureaucratic Politics*. 3rd ed. Englewood Cliffs, NJ: Prentice Hall, 1992.

Inderfurth, Karl, and Loch K. Johnson, eds. *Fateful Decisions: Inside the National Security Council*. New York: Oxford University Press, 2004.

Jeffreys-Jones, Rhodri. *The CIA and American Democracy*. 3rd ed. New Haven, CT: Yale University Press, 2003.

Jordan, Amos A., William J. Taylor Jr., and Michael J. Mazarr. *American National Security*. 5th ed. Baltimore, MD: Johns Hopkins University Press, 1999.

Kirkpatrick, Lyman B., Jr. *The U.S. Intelligence Community: Foreign Policy and Domestic Activities*. New York: Hill and Wang, 1973.

Korb, Lawrence J. *The Fall and Rise of the Pentagon: American Defense Policies in the 1970's*. Contributions in Political Science. Westport, CT: Greenwood Press, 1979.

Lake, Anthony. *Somoza Falling*. Boston: Houghton Mifflin, 1989.

Lancaster, Carol. *Foreign Aid: Diplomacy, Development, Domestic Politics*. Chicago: University of Chicago Press, 2007.

Lee, Rensselar. "The Latin American Drug Connection." *Foreign Policy* 61 (1985): 142–59.

Luttwak, Edward. *The Pentagon and the Art of War: The Question of Military Reform*. New York: Simon & Schuster, 1984.

Marchetti, Victor, and John D. Marks. *The CIA and the Cult of Intelligence*. New York: Knopf, 1974.

Mills, James. *The Underground Empire: Where Crime and Governments Embrace*. Garden City, NY: Doubleday, 1986.

Moran, Theodore H. *American Economic Policy and National Security*. New York: Council on Foreign Relations Press, 1993.

Pringle, Robert. "Creeping Irrelevance at Foggy Bottom." *Foreign Policy* 29 (1977): 128–39.

Ransom, Harry Howe. *The Intelligence Establishment*. Rev. ed. Cambridge, MA: Harvard University Press, 1970.

Spero, Joan Edelman, and Jeffrey A. Hart. *The Politics of International Economic Relations*. Belmont, CA: Thomson/Wadsworth, 2003.

Tillema, Herbert K. *Appeal to Force: American Military Intervention in the Era of Containment*. New York: Crowell, 1973.

Weiner, Tim. *Legacy of Ashes: The History of the CIA*. New York: Doubleday, 2007.

Wiarda, Howard J. *Latin America at the Crossroads: Debt, Development, and the Future*. Boulder, CO: Westview Press, 1987.

Wise, David, and Thomas B. Ross. *The Invisible Government*. New York: Random House, 1964.

Woodward, Bob. *Veil: The Secret Wars of the CIA, 1981–1987*. New York: Simon & Schuster, 1987.

Yarmolinsky, Adam. *The Military Establishment: Its Impacts on American Society*. New York: Harper & Row, 1971.

12

The National Security Council: At the Apex of the System

The National Security Council, located in the West Wing of the White House and the White House complex (the neighboring Old and New Executive Office buildings), is a reflection and extension of the president and of the Oval Office. The NSC consists of the president's own, personal foreign policy staff. As such, it is one of the most important foreign policy institutions in Washington—and in the world. Along with the president himself, who is the leading member, the NSC lies at the narrowest point of our decision-making funnel and at the innermost circle of our series of concentric circles (see chapter 3, figures 3.1 and 3.2).

The National Security Council is one of the key agencies—if not *the* key agency—in foreign policy decision making. First, its location brings it physically closer to the president than any other foreign policy agency, and its head, the national security adviser, has an office only a few steps away from the president's own Oval Office. Since proximity to power is power, the NSA is often the most important influence on foreign policy. Second, since it is a presidential staff agency whose appointments do not require congressional approval, the president can appoint his own trusted advisers and loyalists to the NSC. They will undoubtedly carry out his wishes, in contrast to the State Department, DOD, or the CIA, whose career officials may have their own agendas and not necessarily those of the president.

The NSC has also emerged as the president's preferred agency for foreign policy because he can organize and restructure it to his style and personality—again without congressional approval—in ways that he cannot remold the State or Defense departments. Every president since Kennedy, while always paying lip service to the idea that the State Department is in charge of foreign policy, has come around to the view that he would much rather carry out policy through the NSC than through any other agency.

One other thing should be said preliminarily about the NSC, especially for you readers of this book: if you're really interested in foreign policy, the NSC is about the highest position in the U.S. government—unless your ambition is actually to be president someday—that you can attain. The NSC is full of political scientists, foreign policy and international relations specialists, and experts in the comparative politics of different areas and countries of the world who usually have advanced degrees. If you're lucky, the NSC may be the place where you'll end up. Study hard!

Origins

In addition to the Department of Defense, the Joint Chiefs of Staff, and the CIA, the National Security Council was created as part of the momentous reorganization of American security policy contained in the National Security Act of 1947. All these big changes were occasioned by the post–World War II environment that included the rising threat from the Soviet Union and the emerging Cold War. The National Security Act reorganized the structure of American foreign policy to deal with this new threat.

Congress established the National Security Council to correct a problem that began during World War II. The wartime president, Franklin Roosevelt, regularly received numerous lengthy memos from the State Department, departments of the army and navy, the OSS, and other agencies that bombarded him with information. Not all of it was relevant, useful, or even accurate. The memos required presidential decisions, but they were not always in a form conducive to presidential decision making, and sometimes the memos from the different departments were contradictory and competed with each other. Hence was born the idea for the NSC, a small foreign policy staff at the White House level that would collect the input from several foreign policy agencies, separate the wheat from the chaff, summarize it, and present it to the president in a concise, organized format to facilitate decision making.

Sometimes confusion arises about the NSC—specifically about what it is, about its acronyms, and about its makeup. Technically, the formal National Security Council consists only of the president, the vice president, and the secretaries of state and defense. It may, at the president's discretion, include others—the secretary of the treasury, the CIA director, the ambassador to the UN, the chair of the Joint Chiefs, the national security adviser—depending on the particular issues and the president's preferences at the time. But by common usage the NSC refers not just to these high-level decision makers but also to its staff, which usually numbers between 100 and 150 persons. The president chooses the NSC director, referred to as the national security adviser. That position's acronym, NSA, is not to be confused with the government's other NSA, or the National Security Agency, which runs spy satellites and does telephone intercepts.

The National Security Council was originally conceived as a nonpartisan, nonpolitical professional staff office designed to coordinate foreign policy options for the president. The original legislation called on the NSC to "advise the president with respect to the integration of domestic, foreign, and military policies relating to national security." The NSC was supposed to be a summarizer and integrator of foreign policy, not an independent foreign policymaking agency or an implementer of policy. But over the years, the NSC took on increasingly independent, foreign policy decision-making and implementing roles. Every president, while acknowledging the responsibilities of the Department of State, also came around to seeing the advantages of the NSC serving as his foreign policy arm. And predictably, in every administration that discrepancy has led to conflicts between the secretary of state and the national security adviser.

Early Experiences

Harry Truman was the first president (1945–53) to work with this new national security system. He viewed the NSC as a purely advisory body, rarely sat in on its meetings, and insisted that he himself would assume the synthesizing and coordinating roles assigned to the NSC. Largely ignoring the NSC, Truman preferred to implement policy through his able secretaries of state, first George Marshall and then Dean Acheson. This attitude changed, however, with the outbreak of the Korean War in 1950. At that stage Truman, who lacked experience on foreign policy, began to attend all NSC meetings, increased the staff from a few people to twenty, and came to rely on its coordinating role. Then the NSC began to function as the legislation had stipulated.

In keeping with his background as a general and military commander in World War II, President Dwight Eisenhower (1953–61) viewed the NSC as basically a staff agency. He preferred a formal and structured chain of command; hence, the NSC did the lower-level staff work while Ike and his secretary of state, John Foster Dulles, made policy. The president wanted clear lines of authority, with the NSC coordinating policy and he and Dulles making decisions. Robert Cutler, a Boston banker, was Eisenhower's first national security adviser. He was followed by Dillon Anderson and Gordon Gray, with Gen. Andrew Goodpaster working as staff aide. In 1955, midway through Ike's term, the staff increased in size to twenty-eight people.

The Eisenhower system is usually considered a model of how the NSC ought to work. The NSC was nonpolitical; its director, the NSA, did not seek to become a media star; it did its staff work efficiently; and it did not try to dominate the State Department. As the legislation called for, the NSC strictly separated planning and coordination from implementation, which was left to other agencies. The NSC did its work competently and fairly and, unlike other, later NSCs, did not seek to bias the president's decisions. But the NSC under Ike was not without its problems: position papers were often out of date, recommendations to the president were so watered down (Ike read only one-page memos) they suffered from oversimplification, and Secretary of State Dulles often bypassed the NSC.

Nevertheless the basic system, with the staff doing the preparations and Eisenhower and the State Department making most major decisions, worked well. But the Eisenhower system was effectual because (1) Ike knew and understood foreign policy after his years in Europe and position as supreme Allied commander, and (2) he was good at making decisions without hemming and hawing.

Politicizing the NSC

President John F. Kennedy (1961–63) introduced some major changes in the NSC. Kennedy distrusted the State Department, and he was unhappy with the CIA after he felt it misled him about the failed Bay of Pigs invasion of Cuba. He preferred to rely on the NSC as his main foreign policymaking agency, thus shunting the State Department aside and blurring the line between coordination and implementation. He and his NSA, Harvard dean McGeorge Bundy, involved the NSC in operations for the first time. But Bundy was also part of Kennedy's political entourage and a political adviser to the president; consequently, in contrast to Eisenhower's neutral staff operation, Bundy politicized the NSC and doubled its size. Thus Kennedy's NSC differed from Ike's in three major ways: it bypassed the State Department, crossed the line into implementation, and politicized foreign policy.

With its increased size, the NSC came to resemble a miniature State Department. It had a "desk officer" (or two or three) for each area of the world—Africa, Asia, Latin America, the Middle East, and Europe—as well as desks for the main functional issues—disarmament, economic affairs, strategic issues, and so on. Virtually every State Department office and bureau were now mirrored at the NSC. These changes greatly reduced State's power and increased the NSC's. With this concentration of expertise in the White House, Kennedy relied less on the State and Defense departments and the CIA and more on the NSC's own staff. Meanwhile, NSA Bundy was increasingly brought in to serve as a spokesman for the administration, thus bypassing Secretary of State Dean Rusk. Nonetheless, Bundy sought to maintain cordial relations with Rusk. While the NSC had clearly become more activist and politicized, Bundy kept this within bounds, did not engage in power grabs, and fairly presented the options to the president.

The flaws apparent in the Kennedy era changes did not become apparent or even dangerous until Lyndon Johnson's presidency (1963–69). Johnson distrusted not just the State Department but also the NSC he had inherited from the assassinated president, whose staff he regarded as untrustworthy "Kennedy men." So he bypassed the NSC, preferring to make decisions through the "Tuesday lunch bunch," which consisted of Secretary of State Rusk, Secretary of Defense Robert McNamara, the chair of the Joint Chiefs, the CIA director, the president's press secretary, and Bundy. The latter stayed on as NSA until 1966, when he was replaced by his deputy, Walt W. Rostow.

The presence of the president's press secretary guaranteed that the advice the president received and the decisions he made would, more than ever before, be considered in the light of their political implications—another step in politicizing the NSC. In addition, by meeting exclusively with his Tuesday lunch group, Johnson heard only from those persons who supported accelerating the Vietnam War. Even worse, there is reason to believe NSA Rostow was so sure of his own beliefs and agenda that he committed the cardinal sin of giving biased information to the president. Hence, under Johnson the NSC not only was ignored and went into eclipse, but the information the president received did not provide him with sufficient options to deal wisely with the war effort.

The Kissinger System

With the election of Richard Nixon (1969–74), the NSC was reorganized again. An entirely new NSC model came into existence. Nixon chose Henry Kissinger, one of the country's preeminent academic foreign policy analysts, as his national security adviser. Kissinger proved to be a surprisingly adept political and bureaucratic infighter who quickly mastered the ways of Washington and learned how to operate there. Kissinger saw himself as a lone ranger–like manager of American foreign policy who, along with his equally manipulative president, would carry out policy without involving the State or Defense departments or the CIA. Both men distrusted these large bureaucracies and, through the NSC, created a system of decision making personally and politically loyal to themselves. Until the Watergate scandal destroyed Nixon's reputation and led to his resignation, this duo carried out one of the more effective foreign policies in U.S. history, negotiating an end to the Vietnam War, détente with the Soviet Union, arms control, a Middle East peace process, and the opening to China.

The Nixon-Kissinger model involved the nearly complete eclipse of the State Department, the concentration of unprecedented foreign policy power in the White House (the imperial presidency), the complete erasure of the line between the NSC's coordinating and implementing functions, and much greater politicization of the NSC, particularly as the Watergate scandal aired. The NSC took the lead in carrying out policy. It became Nixon's and Kissinger's chief foreign policy tool, and every policy paper and recommendation was filtered through Kissinger's NSC staff. Kissinger insisted on being present whenever the secretaries of state or defense talked to the president. All memos to the president were also channeled through his office so he could then attach his own recommendations to them.

Kissinger, or "Super K" as he was then known, also went public in ways no previous NSA had done. Recently divorced, he was omnipresent on the Washington social circuit, held press conferences and briefings, spoke for the president on many issues, and conducted his own brand of diplomacy while ignoring the hapless secretary of state, William Rogers. All the foreign policy negotiations were Kissinger undertakings; indeed, Secretary of State Rogers was often kept in the dark about all the administration's major initiatives. Kissinger was adept at television interviews and, as an academic, intellectually acute, nimble, and entertaining. For the first time the NSC adviser became visibly more important and powerful than the secretaries of state or defense.[1]

Kissinger brought talented people to the NSC from both academia and government. He increased its size by 50 percent and made it into the hub of American foreign policymaking, keeping himself always in the forefront. The NSC also developed independent sources of information, a huge step that went way beyond its earlier coordinating efforts, when it simply took its information from other agencies. In addition, Kissinger reorganized the NSC's system of interagency committees to give himself greater control.

The Kissinger system had its flaws as well as advantages. Over time, Nixon and Kissinger operated basically as a two-man team, ignoring even the NSC's interagency processes. As Nixon became consumed by Watergate, it became a one-man team, with Kissinger operating alone. Meanwhile, the State Department resented being left out of the process, and other critics faulted Kissinger for being too visible and too public. He was also a hard taskmaster who wore out his own staff. Despite these problems, the innovative Nixon-Kissinger model was creative and produced some of the most significant foreign policy innovations since the 1940s.

In the fall of 1973 Secretary of State Rogers resigned, and Kissinger was named to replace him. He then wore two hats, national security adviser and secretary of state. For the first and only time both positions were held by a single person. He kept his old staff at the NSC, which he continued to direct, while assembling a new staff at the State Department and presiding over its cumbersome bureaucracy. It was not workable to have one person in both jobs, and Kissinger became more aloof and imperious. Then as Nixon got more entangled in Watergate in 1974, Kissinger tried to distance himself from the scandal and maintain continuity in foreign policy at a time of a weakened presidency. When Nixon was forced to resign, a dark cloud settled over the administration's earlier foreign policy accomplishments.

When Vice President Gerald Ford was sworn in, he asked Kissinger to stay. But Kissinger faced increased opposition from both conservative Republicans (Reaganites and neocons) who didn't like his détente policy toward the Soviet Union and liberals who opposed his neglect of human rights. Hence, in 1975 Ford appointed Brent Scowcroft as NSA while keeping Kissinger as secretary of state.

1. Disclosure: The author worked for Kissinger in 1983–84, when he chaired a presidential commission on Central America. Working for Kissinger was perhaps the most intellectually stimulating but personally difficult period of the author's life. Kissinger's a tough boss.

Scowcroft's first, brief period as NSA (he later returned as George H. W. Bush's NSA) is often seen as an attempt, after the flamboyant Kissinger, to return to the neutral, coordinating Eisenhower staff model of the NSC. It was and it wasn't. A former general who also had a doctorate in international relations, Scowcroft was quiet and self-effacing in the Eisenhower staff mode, but he was widely seen as Kissinger's man at the NSC and as subordinate to him. At the same time, while Eisenhower had been experienced in foreign policy, Ford was not; so the model didn't work well on that end either.

Policy Fragmentation

President Jimmy Carter (1977–81) reacted strongly against the Kissinger system. He wanted a new orientation in foreign policy and a low-key NSA who would provide advice and coordination but not be the architect and implementer as Kissinger had been. Carter preferred an idealistic, human rights–oriented foreign policy, not Kissinger's Realpolitik. He also wanted to restore the prestige of the secretary of state's office and make him the main voice on foreign policy. Like Lyndon Johnson, Carter went outside the NSC and had regular weekly lunches with his secretaries of state and defense.

Most analysts consider Carter a failed foreign policy president, with the most fragmentation and lack of coordination since World War II—precisely the kinds of issues the NSC was designed to overcome. Carter's foreign policymaking team encountered several problems. First, his NSA, Zbigniew Brzezinski, was hardly low-key. He did not want to be only a coordinator of foreign policy. Instead, as Kissinger's former colleague (and rival!), Brzezinski saw himself in the Kissinger mold and wanted to have the same kind of highly visible and glamorous presence. Second, Carter's choice as secretary of state, lawyer Cyrus Vance, was a diffident and soft-spoken problem solver and not a "main voice." Soon he and Brzezinski were at odds. Carter wanted to rely on Vance, but he liked Brzezinski. His administration witnessed a running battle between the two until eventually Vance resigned.

The third problem was Carter himself. Idealistic, unable to delegate authority, and not well versed in foreign policy, he was unable to resolve the disputes among his own advisers. Carter's policies were marked by indecision, a disastrous temporizing, and fierce internal battles, both personal and bureaucratic. Another problem was that Carter, a newcomer to Washington, let his secretaries of state and defense pick their own undersecretaries and assistant secretaries rather than coordinating the selections from the White House. The result was that at these policymaking levels many of the appointments came out of the George McGovern wing—the antiwar Left—of the Democratic Party. Soon they were in fierce political and ideological conflicts with the foreign policy professionals and pragmatists in the State Department and other foreign policy agencies. Carter was unable to exert his authority over the feuding factions, which led to a whole series of foreign policy gaffes and missteps and culminated ultimately in the taking of the American embassy personnel as hostages in Iran in 1979. This event and Carter's inability to bring the hostages home cost him the election in 1980.

The Ronald Reagan administration (1981–89) came to office critical of both the Carter administration and the earlier Kissinger approach. Reagan and his advisers quickly issued a set of guidelines that should sound familiar to us by now:

- The administration would speak with one voice on foreign policy.
- The secretary of state would be its chief spokesman.
- The NSC would return to the Eisenhower model.

In practice, the Reagan administration found it hard to follow this plan. First, the administration was torn by political and ideological fault lines— mainly between Reagan "true believers" and the more pragmatic foreign policy professionals at the State Department, DOD, and the CIA—and was unable to speak with one voice. Second, many found the words and deeds of the secretary of state, former general Alexander Haig, ludicrous (particularly his announcement, "I'm in charge here," when Reagan was shot in 1981). Soon the administration replaced him with the more centrist George Shultz. Third, the NSA, conservative ideologue Richard Allen, committed a number of gaffes and then made the ultimate mistake in the administration: he got on the wrong side of the president's wife, Nancy Reagan. He was replaced by Judge William Clark, a Reagan buddy from California who was good at the NSC paperwork but knew little about foreign affairs. Two successive undistinguished (in foreign policy) military officers, Col. Robert MacFarlane and Adm. John Poindexter (one tried to commit suicide, the other was indicted), quickly followed. Like their predecessor, they too knew how to run an office but were terrible at foreign policy.

A fourth problem was that the NSC staffers were selected more for their conservative ideological purity (as "movement conservatives") than for their knowledge or experience in foreign policy. In this regard Reagan's NSC was similar to that of the Carter administration except it was on the opposite side of the political spectrum. Fifth, the NSC under Reagan had high turnover among the staff and six directors in eight years, with only two—Frank Carlucci and Colin Powell—considered competent. Finally Reagan himself was not well informed about the world or analytical, and he often remained detached from the process, trusting his (not very competent) advisers.

So again the system broke down. Remember what had made the now sacrosanct Eisenhower model work: (1) a president who could make decisions and (2) a president knowledgeable about foreign affairs. Reagan could make decisions (although often on the basis of input from friends and cronies), but he was not well versed about foreign affairs. Reagan did, however, have some good instincts. He kept us out of some encounters that might have proved dangerous, and his policies did help undermine the Soviet Union. But looking at both the unhappy and often incompetent Carter and Reagan administrations and the major flaws in their foreign policy machinery, it is quite remarkable that the United States emerged unscathed during these intense Cold War decades.

An NSC that Worked! The Bush I Administration

The George H. W. Bush administration (1989–93) brought back as national security adviser Brent Scowcroft, who had served earlier under Ford. During his four years, Bush had a close working relationship with the NSA, and the NSC and the cabinet departments had no major confrontations. There were no problems either of deep, public ideological clashes within the administration or of different departments going off in their own directions. Bush and Scowcroft ran the smoothest and most effective NSC system since Nixon-Kissinger and maybe since Eisenhower.

What was different? First, though weak on domestic policy and not an effective campaigner, President Bush was knowledgeable and the most experienced president on foreign policy since Nixon. Second, with his nonideological and centrist administration, Bush was able to avoid the extremist positions and partisan conflicts of his two immediate predecessors. Third, Bush's foreign policy team members—NSA Scowcroft, Chairman of the Joint Chiefs Colin Powell, Secretary of State James Baker, Secretary of Defense Richard Cheney—were all experienced in foreign policy, knew how Washington worked, and were used to (from the Nixon, Ford, and Reagan years) working together as a team. Finally, the modest Scowcroft did not grandstand or pursue his own foreign policy as both Kissinger and Brzezinski had done.

Functioning effectively, the Bush team did not come in for the harsh criticisms its predecessors had, and it carried out one of the more successful foreign policies in U.S. history. It presided over the toppling of the Berlin Wall and the reunification of Germany, the dissolution of the Warsaw Pact (the military alliance of the Soviet Union and its Eastern European allies), the democratization of Eastern Europe, and the collapse of the Soviet Union. And all these changes transpired without a shot being fired, let alone a nuclear bomb going off. It was a remarkable achievement. Unfortunately for Bush, presidents are seldom reelected on the basis of their foreign policy accomplishments.

The Clinton NSC: Carter Redux?

After Democrat Bill Clinton's electoral victory in 1992, he selected Anthony Lake as his national security adviser. Lake had served on Kissinger's NSC team but was much more radical than his boss and had resigned in protest over the 1970 bombing of Cambodia, which turned him into an antiwar radical. He had also served in the State Department during the Carter administration; hence, when he became the NSA, he brought back into government many of the Carter era ideologues who were eager to redeem themselves.

As secretary of state, Clinton chose Warren Christopher, another veteran of the Vietnam era antiwar movement and a San Francisco lawyer specializing in trade issues. Christopher had little foreign policy experience, but when there were internal differences in the State Department between the Clinton ideologues and the career Foreign Service officers, Christopher consistently sided with the Clintonites. Determined despite these divisions to avoid the mistakes, bumbling, and discord of the Carter foreign policy era, the Clinton team achieved some notable early successes in helping to stabilize and democratize post-communist Russia, bringing Eastern European countries into NATO, and advancing a Middle East peace process. It also gets high marks for its attention to international economic issues. But it stumbled badly with foreign policy failures in Haiti, Somalia, Rwanda, and the Balkans.

The team had numerous problems: too many ideologues on the NSC left over from the Carter administration, too few people with current foreign policy experience after the twelve Republican years, no coordination among the foreign policy team members, and Lake's inability to articulate a clear, post–Cold War foreign policy strategy. The biggest problem was Clinton himself. Like all recent presidents, Clinton wanted to be his own secretary of state and conduct foreign policy through a subservient, Eisenhower-like NSC, but Clinton was much stronger on domestic politics and policy than on foreign affairs. Thus his NSC system was disorganized and inefficient, and foreign policy discussions often took the form of late-night bull sessions that lacked an agenda and saw nothing decided. That style is perhaps appropriate for university seminars but not for NSC-presidential decision making.

With an inexperienced and indecisive president, an NSC whose members had their own agendas, and an NSA who failed to take the lead, the result was that another NSC system and its foreign policy failed. Hence, in Clinton's second term he got rid of Lake and substituted Sandy Berger. Formerly Lake's deputy, he was also a trade lawyer, a Clinton political crony, and an inexperienced foreign policymaker. Thus Clinton and his new secretary of state, Madeleine Albright, the first woman secretary of state, conducted their own foreign policy while using the NSC as a staff agency. In a disgraceful episode after Clinton had left office that is still not fully explained but probably had to do with protecting the Clinton legacy, Berger was caught stealing documents from the National Archives. He destroyed some of them and then lied about his activities.

Bush II: Reagan Redux?

As these headings imply, certain themes regarding the NSC and foreign policy decision making start to repeat themselves. Just as the Carter administration's foreign policy offered a prelude to Clinton's, so the Reagan era's foreign policy presented a forerunner to that of George W. Bush.

The earliest polls in 1999 showed Bush, an obscure Texas governor, beating Al Gore by twenty percentage points in the upcoming presidential election. For the Clinton-weary Republican Party elite, including its foreign policy leaders, that was all they needed to know in searching for a nominee. No one bothered to look closely at Bush's politics, ideology, or lack of foreign policy experience, for winning against the Democrats was everything. "Besides," the Republican foreign policy establishment (mainly his father's advisers) reasoned, "if he ever gets into trouble on foreign policy, he can call on us to bail him out." Within months of Bush taking office came 9/11 and shortly afterward the wars on terrorism and in Iraq. Unfortunately, Bush did not seek out his father's foreign policy advisers. Instead, he isolated himself from a broader range of views and relied on a narrow coterie of neocon ideologues and close aides who made up the formal NSC.

For his NSA Bush chose Condoleezza Rice, an accomplished academic who was a Russian area expert but lacked a broad background in foreign policy, comparative politics, and international relations. Bush's vice president was Richard Cheney, who had been a successful secretary of defense for Bush's father but who now stood for an especially rigid and hard-line position in the war on terrorism. Donald Rumsfeld, a Cheney ally and also a hard-liner, was secretary of defense. At state was the hapless Colin Powell, a moderate who saluted his commander in chief but was no match for the bureaucratic infighting skills of Cheney and Rumsfeld. As NSA, Rice was supposed to coordinate among the State Department, DOD, and other agencies; she too was no match for the forceful Cheney-Rumsfeld combination. On the most important foreign policy issues this Bush administration faced—namely, the wars in Iraq and Afghanistan—the Cheney-Rumsfeld argument prevailed. The consultative process within the NSC broke down, and other, largely neglected issues and areas (for example, Latin America) were ignored.

In Bush's second term, Powell resigned, Rice moved into the secretary of state's position, and her former deputy, Stephen Hadley, assumed the NSA position. After the 2006 midterm election, Rumsfeld also resigned, and Robert Gates became secretary of defense. With Rumsfeld gone and Rice at the State Department, American foreign policymaking improved somewhat, and issues that had been too long overlooked received renewed attention. But problems persisted at the NSC. Too many leftover, Reagan era ideologues remained on the staff and its work was often undercut by Cheney and his staff. Moreover, the Iraq War (and maybe the intervention in Afghanistan too), under the direction of Bush, his generals, Cheney, Rumsfeld, and the neocons, proved to be a disaster and further undermined other worthwhile initiatives.

The new NSA, Hadley, was a quiet, unassuming lawyer who knew little substantively about international affairs and deferred to Rice and to the other powerful figures in the administration, particularly Cheney and Bush. Here too a pattern emerged: in the Reagan, Clinton, and this Bush administrations, the initial NSA was a person with foreign policy substance (Allen, Lake, Rice) on whom the inexperienced president could rely. Then as the NSA's ideas proved unworkable and the person inadequate to the task, and at the same time as the president gained foreign policy confidence and wanted in his second term to act as his own NSA, the NSA's job went to a manager type, without strong ideas of his or her own, who is usually a lawyer or a military officer (Col. Robert MacFarlane and Adm. John Poindexter under Reagan, Sandy Berger under Clinton, and Hadley under Bush II). That choice, for good or ill, enables the president to run his own foreign policy. Whether it makes for good foreign policy is another matter.

The defining issue for Bush and Hadley was Iraq. As the war continued to go badly, the White House began a search for a czar who could better manage the war's coordination. But that was supposed to be Hadley's job. The White House claimed the new czar would devote full time to Iraq, freeing Hadley for other responsibilities. After a long list of candidates turned the job down, the White House chose only a three-star general for the czar's position. At that rank, which is lower than the other cabinet-level appointments, the czar would not be able to take on (if needed) the secretary of state or defense or the CIA director or the NSA and to coordinate policy and its implementation. Here, then, is what was wrong with this idea: it should have been NSA Hadley's job; creating a new coordinator, or czar, in the White House undermines the NSA; the person chosen did not have sufficiently high rank; and since a resolution in Iraq is ultimately a political matter, a general is the wrong choice for that post.

Conclusion

The NSC lies at the pinnacle of the American system of foreign policymaking. It is the agency closest to the president and therefore more important in many ways than the State or Defense Department, the CIA, and other agencies. Yet its performance over the years and from administration to administration has often been poor. Can the system—and therefore American foreign policy—be improved?

To make the system work, first, the quality of the staff needs to be enhanced. Too often persons are chosen for the staff on the basis of political loyalty rather than for their specialized knowledge. Of course, as president you want your staff to be both loyal and competent, but political credentials should not be allowed to trump knowledge and experience.

Second, the NSC needs greater continuity. Currently (and it's what makes the NSC attractive to a new president), the entire staff changes whenever a new president assumes office. But that turnover causes a lack of continuity from one administration to the next, excessive partisanship on the NSC (with political appointees rather than professionals serving), and a steep learning curve for every new administration, which must relearn (which usually requires a year or more) every lesson from the past.

Third, we must recognize there is no one simple model for an effective NSC. Every aspiring presidential candidate claims to favor an Eisenhower-like model of a neutral and efficient staff operation, but that model presumes the president will be like Nixon, George H. W. Bush, or Ike himself—that is, knowledgeable about foreign policy and able to make decisions. Unhappily most of our modern presidents—Truman, Kennedy, Johnson, Ford, Carter, Reagan, Clinton, Bush II, and now Obama—lacked foreign policy experience. Thus, they required an NSA—Kissinger, Brzezinski, Scowcroft—who had a wide range of foreign policy knowledge and was a forceful advocate. Either of these two options can work well; however, neither works when a president ignores the NSC (as in Johnson's case), when the NSA feuds with other high officials (Carter), or, perhaps worse of all, when both the president is uninformed *and* the NSA is not a foreign policy specialist or is too diffident to express his views forcefully (Reagan, Clinton, Bush II). In all these circumstances, we are likely to see a failed foreign policy.

Fourth, at this level, a great deal depends on personality. Of course, you want a knowledgeable president and a knowledgeable NSA, but they also have to click as a team. Ike and his NSAs, and the Nixon-Kissinger team, while full of tension, worked well together. The Bush-Scowcroft duo presided harmoniously over one of our best periods of foreign policy accomplishments. Other recent administrations were mostly unsuccessful.

As the original legislation called for, the National Security Council has to serve as a neutral referee among contending bureaucratic agencies, and the national security adviser must be able to present these competing perspectives, as well as his or her own recommendations, fairly to the president. But a modern NSA needs to do much more: appear on television talk shows, be a public spokesman for the president, present the White House's case to Congress, undertake missions abroad, and turn the wheels of Washington policymaking. It is not enough to just know foreign policy, the NSA also needs to have the political skills and know-how to get things done in Washington, D.C. Finally, given that most recent presidents have lacked foreign policy experience, the NSA also should be independent and forceful enough to educate the president (whose natural inclination to get himself reelected is to concentrate on domestic issues) and keep him from making mistakes or seeing foreign policy as merely an extension of domestic politics.

It is a daunting set of skills and tasks to master. Unfortunately the United States in recent decades has seldom found the personnel with the right set of intellectual, political, and bureaucratic skills or the right combinations of personalities to make the NSC system work effectively. But remember the challenge: the NSC is probably the highest policymaking level in the U.S. government to which young foreign policy, comparative politics, and international relations specialists can aspire. Of course, you could be president one day. In that case, go on to the next chapter.

Suggested Reading

Bock, Joseph G. *The White House Staff and the National Security Assistant: Friendship and Friction at the Water's Edge.* New York: Greenwood Press, 1987.

Brzezinski, Zbigniew. *Power and Principle: Memoirs of the National Security Advisor, 1977–1981.* New York: Farrar, Straus, Giroux, 1983.

Destler, I. M. "National Security Advice to U.S. Presidents: Some Lessons from Thirty Years." *World Politics* 29, no. 2 (1977): 143–76.

Destler, I. M., Leslie H. Gelb, and Anthony Lake. *Our Own Worst Enemy: The Unmaking of American Foreign Policy.* Rev. ed. New York: Simon & Schuster, 1985.

Hess, Stephen, and James P. Pfiffner. *Organizing the Presidency.* 3rd ed. Washington, DC: Brookings Institution, 2002.

Inderfurth, Karl, and Loch K. Johnson, eds. *Fateful Decisions: Inside the National Security Council.* New York: Oxford University Press, 2004.

Kissinger, Henry. *White House Years.* Boston: Little, Brown, 1979.

Lowenthal, Mark M., and Richard A. Best. *The National Security Council: An Organizational Assessment.* Washington, DC: Library of Congress, 1992.

Menges, Constantine Christopher. *Inside the National Security Council: The True Story of the Making and Unmaking of Reagan's Foreign Policy.* New York: Simon & Schuster, 1988.

Prados, John. *Keepers of the Keys: A History of the National Security Council from Truman to Bush.* New York: Morrow, 1991.

Rothkopf, David J. *Running the World: The Inside Story of the National Security Council and the Architects of American Power.* New York: PublicAffairs, 2005.

Sorensen, Theodore C. *Decision-Making in the White House: The Olive Branch or the Arrows.* New York: Columbia University Press, 2005.

13

The Presidency
and Foreign Policy

The presidency is the focal point, or the epicenter, of the American political and governmental system. It is at the narrowest point of our funnel of foreign policy decision making and at the center of our rings of concentric circles. Especially in wartime (the war in Iraq and the war on terrorism), the president's powers are enhanced, often leading the office to be called an "imperial presidency." To paraphrase former President Harry Truman, the buck still stops in the president's oval office.

Given the American president's immense power and capacity to wage global war and peace, the question needs to be asked: What happens if you have a bad, naive, inexperienced, or dangerous president? The question, of course, applies to President George W. Bush and his conduct of the Iraq War as well as the larger war on terrorism, but it is not meant to be a partisan question. The fact is that almost all presidents over the last half century have been inexperienced on foreign policy. Of the ten presidents during that period, 1950–2008 (Eisenhower, Kennedy, Johnson, Nixon, Ford, Carter, Reagan, Bush I, Clinton, Bush II), only three—Eisenhower, Nixon, and Bush I—could be said to be experienced, adept, and successful at foreign policy.[1] With Obama, we will have to wait and see. But what about the other seven, who represent more than two-thirds of our modern-era presidents? How can the most powerful nation in the world, with awesome global responsibilities and at the same time awesome global reach, afford to have at the helm so many presidents who have had so little foreign policy experience?

1. Note that all three named are Republicans, to dispel any notion that the preceding comment about "W" is partisan.

The Aura of the Oval Office

There is an unmistakable aura, almost a mystique, that surrounds the White House, the presidency, and the person who occupies it. Unlike many European countries where there is both a head of government (prime minister) and a head of state (king, queen, or largely honorary president), in the United States both the governing and the ceremonial functions of the executive branch are gathered in one person and one office, the presidency. The president is both the chief executive and the head of state, both the chief decision maker (or "decider," as George W. Bush liked to say) and the repository of the pomp, glory, and respect lodged in the presidency. That is why, even though they may dislike the occupant of the office personally or politically, audiences (including the media) stand when the president enters the room.

The presidency is the locus of enormous political power domestically but even more so at the international level. The American president has the capability quite literally to make or break nations, to go to war, and to decide the survival or demise of humankind. The president has awesome power that, at least in the short term, may be unchecked by Congress, courts, or public opinion. Because the American president has such enormous power on a global basis, other nations pay close attention to our presidential leadership, applauding when he exercises enlightened leadership but fearful when the vast power of the presidency seems to lead America and the world astray.

The president is both effectively a leader and, in terms of the office's vast trappings (a huge Secret Service detail, Air Force One, Camp David, advance men, and so forth), almost a monarch. One can sense the awe in which the presidency is held by the thousands of tourists who flock to tour the White House's East Wing every day, by the way interest groups and think tanks measure their importance by remarking the number of blocks they are from the White House, by the competition to get invited to White House state dinners or to sleep in the Lincoln bedroom (you'd better be a big donor), and in the glow and murmur that fills a room whenever the president enters. It is striking that Americans' respect for the office of the presidency continues to remain so high even when the incumbent's popularity drops to record lows.

For the White House staff and appointed personnel, the thrill of working at this high level is undiminished. If one works for the president, in the White House, in the Old Executive Office Building next door, or the New Executive Office Building across the street, one feels he or she is doing the most important work in the world. It is a feeling of both immense power and responsibility. The first time one walks into the White House's West Wing (where the presidential offices are), eats in the White House mess, sits in the Situation Room in the deep basement, or walks into the Oval Office, one is liable to be mesmerized, even tongue-tied, by the experience. There is so much history, mystique, and power here that even strong-willed persons are sometimes awed by the experience. It may take you a time or two in the president's presence before you recover your voice and usual articulateness.

There are some reasonable explanations for your awe in the face of the president and the nation's highest office. For the most part, America is not a nation with a natural-born ruling class. There is no natural "right to rule" here. Living in a democratic country and a nation of immigrants, we believe in merit, hard work, and achievement as the way to the top, not reliance on family names or origins. Hence, when Americans make it to the top ranks of the power structure in the White House, they require time to get used to this experience. If you grew up in Peoria, Grand Rapids, Des Moines, or Midland; worked diligently; and with not a little bit of luck made it to a White House position, it's a heady experience. Wow, you've really made it! And the position has some awesome perks: a White House badge, parking space, flattering invitations, access to the White House dining areas, and maybe even some time with the president. Who wouldn't marvel and be temporarily speechless? Once a person has worked in the White House or been the beneficiary of a presidential appointment, no other job seems quite so important.

While the power and importance of the presidency and White House are immense, so are the limits on presidential authority. The American system is one of elaborate checks and balances, and the president is frequently frustrated by his inability to get his agenda through Congress, to change public opinion, or to get the big Washington bureaucracies to follow his lead. The president must constantly work at building and enhancing his power and moving the system along. While the president usually has more power and freedom of action in foreign affairs than he does on his domestic agenda, even here his power is limited. Having access to the best intelligence and availing himself of the reverence in which his office is held, as well as his position as commander in chief, the president has enormous advantages over the other branches. If he makes major mistakes, however, as Johnson and Nixon did in Vietnam or Bush in Iraq, eventually he finds that the electorate, Congress, or the courts begin to hem in his power.

Once the power and majesty of the office have been diminished (think Clinton's impeachment or Bush's handling of Iraq), it is difficult to recapture them. In addition, while most Americans revere the presidency, as compared with other nations the United States remains a country of limited central state power. Most Americans' jobs and lives are affected in limited ways by what goes on in the White House. As a matter of pride and of ultimate national self-survival, of course it matters who occupies the White House, and Americans put enormous trust in the president to run the country correctly and protect them from terrorism and other dangers. But even with all his immense power the president cannot much change other countries in their fundamentals (Russia), create democratic institutions where there is no foundation to build upon (Haiti and Iraq), or stop bloody turmoil in countries where the factions have long been killing each other (Somalia, Rwanda, and Colombia). Every president discovers that, even with all the levers of power at hand, it is difficult to change and manipulate other countries' behavior. Finally, if the president suffers too many failures or maybe one big failure (Iraq), the country that places so much faith and trust in the president may well turn on him and withdraw its support.

History and Background

Although Congress and the White House have long vied for supremacy in foreign policy, the general trend over the country's 220-year history has been toward executive predominance. Even with the reassertion of congressional authority in the last few years as the war in Iraq went badly and the Democrats recaptured control of Congress, the president still leads and directs foreign policy and offers the main initiatives. Congress may check, balance, and sometimes frustrate presidential initiatives, but in almost all cases it is still the president who proposes new directions in policy and provides the leadership while Congress reacts to them. The president, even when he's wrong, remains the main power in the American foreign policymaking matrix.

The Constitution, under Article II, provides that the president is the chief executive and commander in chief of the armed forces. The Constitution also grants the president the power to appoint diplomatic officials and negotiate treaties, although for these actions he may be required to seek the advice and consent of Congress. As chief executive and commander in chief, with broad appointive power, the president has sufficient constitutional authority to prevail in most foreign policy controversies.

Clearly the Founding Fathers intended to enhance the power of the presidency, including on foreign policy. The Constitution of 1787 stood in marked contrast to the earlier Articles of Confederation in which Congress dominated foreign policy through its Committee on Foreign Affairs. But the system that the Articles established quickly proved unworkable, as both the members of Congress and the writers of the new Constitution realized. Hence, in the new Constitution they vested broad powers in the executive branch. As Alexander Hamilton said in *Federalist 70*, the presidency was made into a more powerful office because that way "decision, activity, secrecy, and dispatch" would all be enhanced. The founders associated these qualities with sound government and effective decision making, especially regarding foreign affairs, where quick and clear action was often necessary. The broad constitutional powers granted the president as well as the writings of the founders made it clear the executive was the main branch for carrying out foreign policy. Congress was supposed to check, balance, and oversee his authority and to share in some important responsibilities—particularly, confirmation of appointed officials, appropriations, and declarations of war—but not itself be the leader in this sphere.

In addition, over the course of the next two centuries, the president's power was strengthened even beyond what the Constitution said. At least five factors were involved: new precedents, Supreme Court decisions, congressional delegation and deferment, growth of the executive office, and emergency factors such as war or threats of war.

Some of the initial precedents were set by the first president, George Washington, who made it clear that he would be the one to represent the United States abroad, to negotiate international agreements, to recognize other states, and to initiate the conduct of foreign policy. President Thomas Jefferson later negotiated the Louisiana Purchase without congressional involvement, and President James Polk forced the hand of Congress in declaring war on Mexico. President Abraham Lincoln blockaded the South's port cities during the Civil War, and Presidents William McKinley, Theodore Roosevelt, William Howard Taft, and Woodrow Wilson all sent U.S. military forces abroad without a congressional declaration of war. President Harry Truman similarly sent the U.S. Army into Korea without congressional approval, while Presidents John F. Kennedy and Lyndon Johnson waged the Vietnam War without a congressional declaration of war.

Presidents Carter, Reagan, George H. W. Bush, Clinton, and George W. Bush have all intervened militarily in other countries without a congressional declaration of war but usually, after a time, faced mounting congressional grumbling and opposition. By now we all take it for granted that the president, without legislative branch authorization, can dispatch troops to protect American citizens, restore order in strife-torn countries, feed starving people, patrol international waterways, bomb suspected terrorist hideaways, and engage in nation building. Executive agreements are another way the president can use precedent to negotiate accords with other countries but not call them treaties, which require congressional approval. Over the centuries the magic of precedents has vastly expanded the range of options and actions that a president may take on foreign affairs.

A second factor explaining the enhanced presidential leadership in foreign policy is found in Supreme Court decisions. Over the years the Court has either issued decisions that expand presidential power or remained silent while the president exercised foreign policy initiatives. For example, in *United States v. Curtiss-Wright Export Corporation,* a 1936 case involving a private company's sale of machine guns to Bolivia, the Court ruled that Congress was able to delegate power to the executive, that the president was the representative of U.S. sovereignty in foreign affairs, and that the president's leadership prerogatives in foreign policy went beyond the actual constitutional listing of his powers. In *Missouri v. Holland* (1920) the Court upheld the president's supremacy in foreign policy against the power of the states. In *United States v. Belmont* (1937) the Court held that executive agreements were the law of the land even if, unlike treaties, Congress did not approve them. Numerous other Court decisions have reaffirmed the president's power to spy abroad, to engage in covert activities, and, under the doctrine of executive privilege, to exempt foreign policy officials from being forced to testify before Congress.

A third factor in explaining the president's leading role in foreign affairs is congressional delegation and deference. Recognizing its own limitations in deciding complex foreign policy issues, Congress may delegate or defer its power to the president. For example, in an earlier conflict between (communist) China and (nationalist) Taiwan, Congress delegated to the president the power to defend Taiwan as he saw fit. The famous Gulf of Tonkin Resolution (1964), which passed both houses of Congress virtually unanimously, authorized President Johnson to deploy U.S. forces in Vietnam without a congressional declaration of war, a vote Congress later came to regret. More recently with regard to Iraq, Congress voted to authorize spending for the war but again without declaring war, a vote that tied the Democrats in knots afterward, especially as the war started to go badly and a number of Democrats began to campaign for the presidency. The candidates' dilemma was how to express their distaste for the war and still appear to be supporting those troops fighting the war.

A fourth factor contributing to broad presidential influence in foreign policy is institutional growth within the executive branch. Media attention has focused mainly on how congressional staffs and offices have increased, but in fact growth in the executive branch has been even faster. All the main executive departments—the Departments of State, Defense, Justice, Treasury, and so on—have expanded enormously over the last four decades, which is one key reason why they no longer work well or efficiently. Meanwhile, the White House and presidential staff have similarly experienced major development, with new and greatly expanded offices of national security, polling, liaison, intelligence, public diplomacy, speech writing, travel, politics, media relations, and so on. These increases have given the president an enormous staff and expertise—his own mini State or Defense Department—all of which serve to amplify the executive's knowledge base, political and bureaucratic clout, and operational capacity.

A fifth aspect has to do with the actual practice of foreign policy and its effects on the presidency. Every war the United States has fought for the last two hundred years has served inexorably to increase presidential power in foreign affairs. Wars, including the war on terrorism, are national emergencies, and in such times Americans have felt it necessary to allow presidents broad discretion. War also necessitates quick decisions and flexibility, and only the presidency, not Congress, is thought to have these traits. Thus Presidents Lincoln, Wilson, Franklin Roosevelt, and George W. Bush were able to accumulate such awesome wartime power. In the war on terrorism, for example, Congress, however reluctantly, even acquiesced to wiretapping U.S. citizens, curtailing numerous civil liberties, racial and ethnic profiling, and vastly expanding presidential power, to the extent that the Bush administration, like Nixon's in the past, became an imperial presidency. It is not the case that Congress wanted to cede all this power to the president, but think of our earlier self-aggrandizement and political process models. As a member of Congress, how would you like to have to explain to your constituents at reelection time that terrorist groups were able to get into the country and carry out more attacks because you failed to support telephone intercepts, were overly sensitive about ethnic stereotypes, and opposed strong tactics used against prisoners in Guantánamo? The other interesting question is whether, once the war on terrorism eventually winds down, we'll ever go back to the freer society of the past and a more limited presidency.

Presidential Training for Foreign Policy

Most American presidents have come to office ill equipped for the critical foreign policy responsibilities of the office. They have immense power at their disposal but little training in how to use it. Most European prime ministers have twenty to thirty years' experience in national politics and often have served in several cabinet positions, but the same is not true of American presidents. Lacking either experience at high national political levels or much knowledge of foreign countries or issues, most American presidents assume office entirely inexperienced in foreign affairs. It is not surprising, therefore, that American foreign policy so often produces mistakes and misdirections.

The skills an individual acquires as a politician campaigning for the presidency are not the skills needed to conduct successful foreign policy. Many American presidents have had to learn foreign policy while in office or "on the job"—a very dangerous practice. For instance, most foreign policy experts believe that what saved the United States during the Cold War and enabled us to win was not that our foreign policy was so skillful but that Soviet policy was so inept. Since the end of the Cold War, our presidents (Clinton and George W. Bush) have focused more on domestic policy issues than on foreign policy. The war on terrorism dramatically changed that.

Our presidents' lack of knowledge and experience in foreign countries and foreign affairs, first of all, mirrors that of their constituents. Since most Americans have little capacity in foreign languages, have seldom traveled or lived abroad for extended periods, and know little about other countries and cultures, our leaders usually reflect these same unfortunate traits. Likewise, their attitudes grow out of the public's isolationist, ethnocentric attitudes that have pervaded the American historical experience.

Second, so many of our leading politicians have legal training and lawyer backgrounds. (This is not the usual harangue against lawyers!) While many lawyers do have history or political science backgrounds as undergraduates and may have had an introductory course in international relations, nothing in law school or in the practice of law (wills, divorces, property closings) will give them any more advanced training in the study of world history, comparative politics, foreign policy, or international relations—all the essential fields to being a successful practitioner of foreign affairs. At most, our presidents, with only a couple exceptions, came to office having lived only a few weeks or perhaps one semester abroad and maybe having taken one or two preparatory courses at the undergraduate level. Clearly that level of preparation is not enough to tackle the challenges of today's globalized, interdependent world.

A third factor working against presidential knowledge and experience in foreign affairs is the career patterns of American politicians. Most start out at the local level (school board, town meeting, planning commission, town council, mayor) and then pursue state office (state legislature, governorship), a federal office (House or Senate), and the presidency itself. Nowhere in this career track is foreign affairs experience or the possibility of living abroad included. In fact, interviews with Washington politicians revealed that they believed their careers would have been interrupted and even hurt if they had traveled or lived abroad for a time. The result is that few politicians ever take the opportunity to learn about other countries or foreign policy. Thus, other than perhaps a college-age study abroad program, nothing has ever adequately prepared them for dealing with foreign affairs at serious and sophisticated adult levels.

Parenthetically, let us pause here for a moment to take a look at the opposite but also problematic issue of clientelitis, or what we might also call the "worm's-eye view" of foreign policy. This problem often affects returned Peace Corps volunteers (RPCVs), young missionaries, and others who go abroad at a young age in humanitarian roles. A good example is RPCV and 2008 presidential candidate Senator Christopher Dodd. While serving in the 1960s in the Dominican Republic, Dodd lived in a poor rural village, was often sick from bad water and food, and viewed politics from a worm's-eye (figuratively and literally) view. He grew resentful of the "striped-pants diplomats" in the capital city and of State Department personnel in Washington who only went to fancy cocktail parties and never mingled with real peasants as he did. In crisis situations, he defended the country where he was stationed against his own U.S. government (clientelitis); and when the U.S. militarily intervened in the Dominican Republic in 1965 to turn back a progressive, revolutionary movement that President Lyndon Johnson said was "communist," Dodd condemned the military intervention. So even today, in his mid-sixties, Senator Dodd is still shaped by this early Peace Corps experience, often takes up populist foreign policy positions, is critical of the State Department, condemns U.S. military interventions as in Iraq, and defends other countries against what he sees as his own country's frequently wayward foreign policy.

Reviewing the U.S. presidents since the 1930s, we can gauge the level of foreign affairs experience that each had. Thus, Franklin D. Roosevelt had been secretary of the navy in the early 1920s but had very little foreign policy experience before becoming president in 1932. During the 1930s he failed to involve the United States in foreign affairs and inadequately prepared the country for world war; nevertheless, he successfully guided the country through the war and toward victory in both the European and Pacific theaters. But many observers believe Joseph Stalin of the Soviet Union bested Roosevelt in the Yalta Conference's end-of-war negotiations. Roosevelt also failed to inform his vice president, Harry Truman, about important war matters. Truman had no foreign policy experience before becoming president, yet he managed to pick excellent secretaries of state and made decisions without temporizing. Furthermore, he is credited with major foreign policy accomplishments: NATO, the Marshall Plan, and Point Four, the first major U.S. foreign aid program aimed at the developing countries.

By contrast, Dwight D. Eisenhower, the former commanding general in Europe during World War II and NATO commander in the early 1950s, had lived abroad for many years, knew all the main European leaders and countries, and had seen the issues firsthand. He was perhaps the most experienced foreign policy leader of all recent presidents. It is no accident, therefore, that he is usually considered among the most successful foreign policy presidents.

John F. Kennedy had been a young naval officer in World War II and had briefly lived in Europe as a young man during the late 1930s. But he could not be said to be as experienced in foreign policy or knowledgeable on foreign countries and leaders at high levels as Eisenhower was and, with the possible exception of the expulsion of the Soviet missiles from Cuba in 1962, had few foreign policy triumphs. Kennedy presided over the disastrous attempted Bay of Pigs invasion of Cuba, stood by as the Berlin Wall dividing East and West Germany went up, and began the ill-fated U.S. intervention in Vietnam. Kennedy's successor, Lyndon Johnson, was good on domestic policy but almost completely inexperienced in foreign affairs. Thus, he relied on his advisers, who led him astray in both the Dominican Republic and, even more disastrously, Vietnam. Neither Kennedy nor Johnson could be considered successful foreign policy presidents.

Richard Nixon had little experience with foreign policy before being elected vice president in 1952, but President Eisenhower gave him quite a few foreign affairs responsibilities. In addition, after being defeated by Kennedy in the 1960 election, Nixon traveled extensively abroad, met many world leaders, and hence was one of our most experienced and knowledgeable presidents. With his wily national security adviser (later, secretary of state), Henry Kissinger, Nixon is thought of as one of our shrewdest and most successful foreign policy leaders—until the Watergate scandal forced him to resign.

The vice president who succeeded Nixon, Gerald Ford, was like other vice presidents who had succeeded to the presidency in recent times (Truman and Johnson): strong on domestic policy but woefully inexperienced on foreign policy. Recall it was Ford's goof in the 1976 presidential debates, when he inexplicably said that Poland was not dominated by the Soviet Union, that cost him the election. Ford provided overall balance to the presidency and helped the country recover from the trauma of the Watergate hearings, but his contributions to our foreign policy accomplishments were meager. He was defeated in 1976.

Jimmy Carter was a Naval Academy graduate, but after his navy career he went back to his home state of Georgia, where he expanded the family peanut business and ran for governor. Although he had almost no foreign policy experience prior to being elected president, he nevertheless put forth an ambitious foreign policy agenda based on democracy and human rights. Most foreign policy observers describe the Carter policy as naive, excessively moralistic, and one sided, and they think that it ignored the real threats posed by the Soviet Union and the Iranian revolution of 1979, a forerunner of today's "clash of civilizations" involving the West and the Islamic world. Largely because of his ineffectiveness in resolving the U.S. embassy hostage crisis, Carter was defeated in the 1980 election.

Like Carter, Ronald Reagan had been a governor (California) before becoming president and was inexperienced in foreign policy but nevertheless had strong foreign policy views. More a realist than a Carter-style idealist, though, Reagan wanted to use human rights as a way of embarrassing and bringing down the Soviet Union. He also built up the U.S. military and, in the process, spent the Soviets into the ground. Reagan didn't quite win the Cold War, but his policies contributed to the Soviet Union's bankruptcy and demise, economically, militarily, and politically.

George H. W. Bush was the most knowledgeable and experienced foreign policy president since Nixon and maybe since Eisenhower. He had been a congressman, the head of the Republican National Committee, the director of the CIA, and an ambassador to China, meaning he had lived overseas for long periods. As Reagan's vice president, he had traveled and represented the United States abroad on numerous occasions and specialized in foreign affairs. Following Reagan, Bush presided over the collapse of the Soviet Union, the breakup of the Warsaw Pact, the tearing down of the Berlin Wall and the unification of Germany, and the end of the Cold War. Though better at ending the Cold War than at constructing his "New World Order" to replace it, Bush is considered one of our more successful foreign policy presidents. His foreign policy achievements, however, did not translate into electoral success when he ran for a second term.

Bill Clinton was closer to the Carter tradition. Bright and intelligent, he had traveled and lived abroad as a young postgraduate, but then he spent the next twenty years in his insular home state of Arkansas focused on local and state issues. Inexperienced in foreign policy and a product of the antiwar movement of the 1960s, Clinton was idealistic, antimilitary, and opposed to the use of force. He and his close aides had a romantic, Carter-like faith in democracy promotion and nation building, which proved a failure in Somalia, Haiti, and Bosnia. After these early efforts produced few results, Clinton in his second term described his policy as "pragmatic," but it had no focus, no consistency, and no clear direction.

George W. Bush, like Carter, Reagan, and Clinton, was a former governor who came to the presidency lacking foreign policy credentials. No one paid much serious attention to his background, political beliefs, and inexperience. After years of Clinton, all that mattered to the Republican Party was that polls showed Bush could beat Gore and help the Republicans get back into power. The party counted on a period of normalcy that would allow Bush to concentrate on domestic issues, and the Republican leadership assumed that he could count on his father and his father's experienced foreign policy team should issues arise.

In responding to 9/11, Bush relied on his own gut instincts and not on his father, his father's team, or the serious career analysts in the State Department or the CIA. Lacking foreign affairs experience himself, he depended on his hard-line vice president, Richard Cheney, and on his equally tough-minded secretary of defense, Donald Rumsfeld. But as the shunned professional analysts could have told him, there were no weapons of mass destruction in Iraq, and the effort to build democracy there, after bombing the Taliban in Afghanistan and occupying Iraq militarily, proved unsuccessful. Meanwhile, other programs and other world areas were ignored and stressed for funds. Bush's administration was disastrous for the U.S. image abroad and for U.S. foreign policy in general and proved again how presidential inexperience in foreign policy is especially deleterious for the country.

Barack Obama is an interesting case. On the one hand, because of his unusual family background and early childhood experiences in the third world—Africa, Indonesia, Pakistan—he is especially sensitive to the problems of developing countries. On the other hand, as an adult, Obama's career is not much different from other aspiring politicians' paths—obtaining a law degree, getting involved in local activism, then serving in the state legislature, finally joining the U.S. Senate—but he does not have much further experience in foreign policy or much knowledge of Europe, Asia, Latin America, or the Middle East. Obama therefore fits our pattern of other American presidents who have had little foreign policy experience before coming to office, but his views are likely to be shaped by his background and early experiences.

This brief survey of our most recent presidents does not lead to encouraging conclusions. Of the eleven presidents since World War II, only three—Eisenhower, Nixon, and Bush I—were well prepared for the presidency's foreign policy role. Note, too, that all three men were Republicans, which helps account for the fact that for a long time the public favored Republicans on foreign policy and considered Democrats weak. The rest of our modern presidents were inadequately knowledgeable or often woefully unprepared for their foreign policy roles; however, despite their inexperience, both Truman and Reagan could be said to have been successful foreign policy leaders.

Two interesting corollaries follow from this analysis. The first is that, while the presidency is the focus of the American system of government, the office is often where the least foreign policy expertise lies. Most foreign policy issues (the ones we never hear of) are handled more or less routinely at lower levels of the government—for example, the various regional bureaus of the State Department—where there is real expertise. Only the most important or most politically charged issues (Iraq, Middle East peace, the war on terrorism) get elevated to the White House, but in that office, one finds the least knowledge or in-depth understanding of the issue. Furthermore, domestic political considerations are likely to overwhelm rational foreign policy. Thus foreign policy at the presidential level is often misdirected, produces mistakes, or makes decisions to please a domestic constituency at the cost of good foreign policy. It is a dangerous paradox that only the biggest and most dangerous issues make their way to the White House, and yet that is where the least experience and background—and the most domestic political calculations—are brought to bear on the issue.

The second corollary follows from the first. Because so many presidents lack experience in foreign policy, during election campaigns policy analysts and voters must pay close attention not just to the candidates but also to their teams of foreign policy advisers. These are often the persons appointed subsequently to office as the secretary of state, national security adviser, defense secretary, intelligence chief, and so on. Thus, chapter 8 on think tanks is so important because most of these future officeholders come out of the Washington think tanks, law offices, and "idea shops." In order to articulate their positions clearly, all the presidential candidates now find it necessary to form foreign and domestic policy teams far in advance of the primaries and to announce publicly who is on them. In this way experienced observers can tell, based on the advisers' past records, what to expect from the new administration, even if the candidate is personally inexperienced on foreign policy, and who will occupy what posts. Thus, in this modern, globalized world where so much is at stake for the United States, we need to examine all the details carefully and choose among not just the candidates but the candidates' circle of advisers as well. Increasingly, we are voting for a whole foreign policy team and not just an individual candidate.

The Powers of the Presidency

The president has broad formal power in the area of foreign policymaking. In addition, he has wide informal power that will vary over time depending on personality, political skills, presidential popularity, and the issues and context of the times. The president is similarly limited by both formal, constitutional checks and balances and by informal and dynamic factors.

First, the Constitution states that the president is commander in chief of the Army and Navy. By common consensus it has come to mean the more recently created Air Force and Marine Corps as well. Although there is room for dispute over what precisely the term "commander in chief" means, most presidents as well as Congress and the public have interpreted it broadly to give the president vast power over military mobilization, budgets, deployment strategy, and missions— for example, sending U.S. forces to Iraq or bringing them home.

The president's role as commander in chief is checked by the power of Congress to declare war. But of the 140 instances in our history of serious hostilities and numerous other episodes of near hostilities, Congress has voted to declare war only five times: the War of 1812, the Mexican War of 1846, the Spanish-American War of 1898, and World Wars I and II. All the others, including Vietnam, Iraq, Afghanistan, and the war on terrorism, have been undeclared wars or police actions. The large number of actions in which Congress did not declare war and yet American forces were committed illustrates the president's vast power under the commander in chief clause.

In addition to the power to deploy fighting forces, the position of commander in chief has been interpreted in ways that give the president even stronger power. First, it is the president, along with the Joint Chiefs, the secretary of defense, and military commanders on the ground, who decide military strategy. Second, the president may make decisions and deploy forces in ways that seek to pressure another country (Iran, North Korea) or bluff it into submission. Third, it has been the president's assumed responsibility to plan for the end game of hostilities—that is, to decide on war termination and the withdrawal of troops, what critics say was lacking in the Iraq War. While Congress cannot very well challenge the president as constitutional commander in chief, it has been chipping away at some of these other presidential prerogatives. In today's more politicized context, however, attempts to reduce the president's power usually occur when the opposition controls Congress, and even then Congress is often timid and weak kneed about challenging presidential war-making leadership.

A second major power of the presidency is treaty making. The Constitution gives the president the power to sign treaties "by and with the consent of the Senate, provided two-thirds of the Senators present concur." It is not clear from this language whether the president should seek the advice and consent of the Senate after the treaty is signed or during the negotiations leading up to the treaty. Historically, presidents have sought Senate confirmation after the treaty is signed, but modern presidents have usually seen the wisdom, if they want the treaty to pass, of involving leading senators during the early negotiations. In this more politicized era, whether the issue is arms limitations talks or trade agreements, the president must engage in two negotiations at once: one with the country or countries involved and the other with our own Congress.

Treaty making is not a cut-and-dried process. Usually, much politics is involved in these proceedings as well. First, the treaty is negotiated and signed by the parties themselves, a process that is lengthy, may involve the media as well as strong interest groups, and may be controversial and include numerous compromises both at home and in the other country. Once signed, the treaty is submitted to Congress, where it may be approved, rejected, amended, or approved with reservations. The congressional changes may make the treaty unacceptable to the other country, in which case it will have to be renegotiated and then resubmitted. For example, the 2007 nuclear treaty with India is controversial in both countries, and out on the campaign trail, candidates in the 2008 election called for the renegotiation of NAFTA and other trade agreements.

The president, however, also has extensive power in these negotiations. He may withdraw the treaty from consideration, ask for changes from the other country (an embarrassing situation, since it has already been negotiated), bargain with Congress, or refuse to sign it if it comes back in unacceptable form. While the political process thus unfolds, the treaty may acquire a life of its own. Approval by other nations, such as for the Kyoto Protocol on the environment, may put added pressure on the United States to endorse a treaty, or getting caught up in emotional public opinion (as in the nuclear freeze movement) may oblige a president to sign a treaty with which he is uncomfortable. All these and other complications make it understandable why presidents prefer executive agreements over formal treaties and why presidents prefer fast-track authority in their negotiations: the former does not require congressional approval, and the latter allows no amendments.

A third presidential power involves the appointment of high-level foreign policy officials, including cabinet-level secretaries, the director of the CIA, the national intelligence director, the UN and all other ambassadors, the NSC staff, and the undersecretaries and assistant secretaries of state and defense (where the real decisions are often made). While the national security adviser and NSC staff typically do not require Senate confirmation, all the other positions do; and in recent decades it has also become customary for the NSA to testify and gain approval. In the past, Senate approval of high-level presidential appointments was largely routine, the assumption being that a president is entitled to have the team of his choosing. The Senate rarely rejected a presidential nominee, and even when there was opposition, a determined president could usually have his way.

But now, like everything else, the system of presidential appointments has become more politicized. Even routine appointments are now closely scrutinized and often held up for political or ideological reasons. Evoking "senatorial courtesy," a single senator can hold up an appointment indefinitely and prevent it from coming up for a vote. When Congress is in control of the opposition party and the president is a lame duck (Reagan, Clinton, and Bush in their final two years), it may choose not to confirm any nominations on the assumption that the opposition will win the next presidential race; why should they do anything to help the incumbent party's chances? In this and numerous other ways, partisanship takes precedence over national security and the smooth running of the U.S. government.

The president also has the power to grant, withhold, or withdraw recognition of other nations. This power is derived from the constitutional clause that says the president "shall receive ambassadors and other public ministers." By hallowed custom, the president is head of state and foreign diplomats are accredited to him personally. He has the power to receive them or not, to allow them into the United States, and to ask them to leave.

Recognition of other states has also taken on increasingly political overtones. Most other countries grant or withhold recognition of foreign governments simply on the basis of whether a government is in effective control of its national territory. But the United States has introduced other criteria for recognition. Is the country democratic? What is its human rights record? Is it a terrorist state? Did it come to power by electoral means or through a coup d'état? Is it acceptable to a major domestic lobby—think of the tension over the issue of whether to recognize the Palestinian Authority as a state? These criteria for recognition give the United States leverage over the internal affairs of other nations—we may withhold recognition from a nondemocratic government until it holds elections. But nonrecognition of other states is similar to imposing sanctions: sometimes they work to push another government toward democracy, sometimes they don't. Looking at other nations' domestic behaviors adds new layers of complexity to our own domestic foreign policy debate as well.

Fifth, the president may be said to have certain "inherent powers," or powers that are intrinsic to the job of being president. By common agreement, the president is the chief decision maker on foreign policy as well as domestic policy. The president is also the nation's chief spokesperson on foreign policy and its only official voice. As head of state, he is the person with whom foreign governments have official contacts. When the president travels abroad and represents the United States at summit conferences, the power and image of the United States go with him; when he speaks, the whole world looks for clues to future U.S. policy directions. Both the real and the symbolic power of the presidency have been enhanced in recent decades by modern communication, jet travel (Air Force One), television, and whole phalanxes of advance men and secret service agents.

But the president's vague and changing inherent powers may have been eroded in recent years by uncertain leadership as well as the perception of U.S. weakness and incompetence. Much of the world thought of Reagan and Bush II as cowboys unfit for world leadership; furthermore, the government's inadequate response to Hurricane Katrina and the war in Iraq have especially weakened other countries' faith in U.S. leadership. While Clinton's weaknesses were also recognized, he was still viewed as more intelligent and educable. Domestically, the president's inherent powers have been further eroded by a resurgent Congress often controlled by the other party, by private sector activity that, with the White House preoccupied with Iraq, has moved to supplant the U.S. public sector abroad; and by the hiving off factor discussed in chapter 6, where whole areas of foreign policy are given over to domestic interest groups.

A sixth power of the president is the use of the bully pulpit (speeches and television broadcasts) to dominate the debate and influence the public. But the power of presidential persuasion is limited, increasingly more so among a skeptical electorate. Political scientists' research on public opinion has shown that a major foreign policy speech can change public opinion only by about 5 percent; a concerted White House campaign (repeated speeches and public appearances) may effect at most a 10 percent shift. However, in recent years the president's capacity to move public opinion has eroded. Clinton's speeches on Haiti and Somalia failed to sway public opinion at all, and by this time most people's views on Iraq are already set and cannot be further changed by a presidential pronouncement. Cynicism about the president and skepticism about his ability to lead the nation reached some all-time highs.

In carefully considering the six areas of presidential power listed, one theme stands out—how politicized and contentious the process of presidential foreign policy decision making has become. In every area, politics infuses and is at the heart of the issue. The president cannot just announce new foreign policy initiatives and expect the rest of the country to go along. He must guide, instruct, convince, and cajole. He must meet with members of Congress, go on television, and line up supportive interest groups. He must send his spokespersons out to the universities, town meetings, churches, and synagogues to rally domestic support. The public and Congress, as well as foreign leaders and their constituencies, are now so skeptical that almost no presidential rhetoric will sway them more than marginally. For a president to have a successful foreign policy, he must now become engaged at all levels in the political process and involve himself in lobbying activities that in the past were confined to domestic politics.

This level of involvement is what famed political scientist Richard Neustadt had in mind when he proposed his celebrated, if at the time somewhat demeaning, idea that the president must function essentially as a clerk. All the historic power and majesty of the presidency notwithstanding, Neustadt's research inside the Oval Office indicated that a successful president must bargain, negotiate, twist arms, and compromise. In the American system of checks and balances, the president was never all powerful, but nowadays his authority has been reduced still further. The end of the Cold War, frustrated efforts at nation building, and now Iraq have all eroded trust in the presidency and weakened it. The president can no longer just give marching orders the way a general would and expect Congress and the public to comply. Congress, the public, interest groups, and the big government bureaucracies are all too diverse, independent, and distrusting for that to work. A modern president must now actively pursue allies and support for his policies to succeed, but in the present context of cynicism and intense partisanship, even that effort may no longer be enough.

Presidential Character and Personality

In recent years a new approach to studying the presidency has emerged, the historical study, or psychohistory, of presidential personality and character. A spate of books about each of our recent presidents has probed their early histories, including their relationships with parents, their early conflicts and political experiences, and even their sex lives. The assumption of this approach is that every individual's strengths, weaknesses, and personality traits are derived from early experiences; therefore, from this research, a president's performance in the White House can be explained and perhaps even predicted. Hence, psychohistorians study a president's early life for clues as to how he will respond in the presidency. We should probably be skeptical of some of these efforts, especially as they seek to probe fifty-year-old relationships about which memories may be faulty; documentation, missing; and the context of the times, partially forgotten. Nevertheless, in the right hands, this kind of personality and character analysis can yield rich insights.

One psychohistory approach, for example, has emphasized the distinction between crusaders (those moralistic ones who are set in their ways and have fixed and unyielding views, such as Carter, Reagan, Bush II) and pragmatists (those who value flexibility and choice, such as Johnson, Nixon, Bush I, Clinton). Another approach focuses on authoritarian versus participatory personalities. Is the person collegial or competitive? Is the person a rabble-rouser who likes to stir things up, or a creator and theorist who is often a moralizer, or perhaps a paper-shuffling administrator who lacks creativity and operates according to rigid procedures? Did the person in early life exhibit hostile-aggressive behavior, and what does that characteristic indicate about how the person is likely to behave as president? Does this trait represent a need for power, and do we want such a person in charge? Or is it a desire for achievement and affection? Is the would-be president a loner (Nixon, Carter) or a more social being, at home in the relaxed activity of everyday conversation with friends and colleagues (Reagan, Clinton, Bush II, Obama)? Does the person favor consensus among his advisers (Johnson, Ford), or does he insist on going his own way? These ideas represent only some of the issues and categorizations set forth by different psychohistorians.

Among the more interesting categories directly applicable to the presidency are those devised by political scientist James David Barber. First Barber distinguished between personality types. Positive personalities are those with optimistic, dynamic, and enthusiastic attitudes about life, which often stem from early successes in overcoming adversity. Those folks with negative personalities are lonely, withdrawn, and full of complexes and have chips on their shoulders. Barber then adds a second matrix regarding active or passive attitudes toward public policy. Active public policy, domestic or foreign, is based on the setting of clear goals, the willingness to use White House clout to achieve them, and strong presidential leadership. Passive public policy comes from presidents who are not initiators, who are withdrawn from the political conflict, and who react to others' ideas instead of initiating new programs themselves.

Barber then combines the two matrixes into a table with four boxes and categorizes recent presidents to their corresponding boxes. Thus, using Barber's descriptors, Presidents Roosevelt, Kennedy, and Clinton among Democrats and Reagan among Republicans fall into the positive-active box. By contrast, Eisenhower and Bush I are positive but inactive in a policy sense. The worst presidents, according to Barber, are those negative activists, including Johnson, Nixon, and Bush II. Not only are they complex and quarrelsome, but, as activists, they act compulsively. Witness Johnson with Vietnam, Nixon with Watergate, and Bush with Iraq.

Barber's categories are useful in looking at the relationship between presidential personality and public policy, but many problems remain. First, the approach is politically biased: it favors activists (mainly Democrats) over those who propose a less active government (Republicans). It also runs the risk of engaging in amateurish pop psychology based on incomplete information. Next, the categories are too simple—surely humans have more than two dimensions—and do not allow for mixed types or gradations. Fourth, scholars and others may disagree about into which box our presidents should be placed. Finally, we now know that when he wrote his famous book, Professor Barber was so exorcized about the Vietnam War and Nixon becoming president that he may have designed his categories to portray Nixon in the worst possible light.

Psychohistory and the study of presidential personality, background, and character are useful and suggestive tools of analysis. Because they are easily subject to bias and abuse, one must use them with great care. A useful experiment is to apply these categories to a future crop of presidential candidates.

Dynamic Factors

A great deal of power is concentrated in the office and person of the presidency. Even with the congressional resurgence in influence in recent years, the fragmentation and partisanship in the American polity, and the ebb and flow of presidential popularity, the president remains the leader of American foreign policy decision making. For instance, members of Congress may be more willing to challenge the president but only up to a point, fearing the voters will punish them. Even as criticism of the war in Iraq and Bush's handling of it mounted, television still concentrated mainly on the president and his pronouncements. The White House is able to manipulate the media to its advantage, for the president's perks—the ability to dominate summits and fly off in a gleaming Air Force One—are still impressive. Because the president meets with foreign leaders and dominates foreign policy, the White House becomes a kind of super State Department that can relegate both the real State Department to the sidelines as a courier of presidential messages and Congress to the position of only reacting to presidential initiatives.

Presidents often look to score triumphs in foreign policy issues because the domestic issues—such as Social Security reform and immigration—are often intractable, have little glamour, and cannot be solved within one president's term. Even Clinton, who promised to focus on domestic issues "like a laser," found he could not get his agenda through Congress and, hence, turned increasingly to foreign policy. Reagan standing on the Normandy beach with the World War II soldiers ("the greatest generation"), Bush I ending the Cold War, and Clinton lunching in grand European castles while bringing the former Soviet states into NATO evoked glamour and glory. But Bush II reversed this process: elected as a return-to-normalcy and compassionate conservative president, he opted after 9/11 to become a war president, to increase his presidential powers, and to use his position as commander in chief to cower the Congress into submission on most issues. Unfortunately for Bush, after losing control of Congress in 2006, he had to abandon both his foreign and domestic agenda.

With the attack of 9/11, the war in Iraq, and the war on terrorism, foreign policy has again vaulted to the forefront of American concerns. Yet, ill-prepared by training and background, presidents and their White House staffs cannot deal with fundamental international security issues. The staffs, as well as the presidents they serve, are trained in domestic policy issues. That's how they got to the White House in the first place, by working on the candidate's election campaign and then going with him into high positions in the executive branch. These are persons whose expertise is in elections, primaries, and serving the candidate; they often know little of foreign affairs. Yet they command key White House positions, such as chief of staff, communications director, policy adviser, and so on, while the secretaries of state and defense are across town in separate buildings and do not have the president's ear on an hourly basis.

The problem is further compounded by the fact that the domestic political advisers now routinely participate in National Security Council meetings; therefore, they bring political considerations (reelection possibilities, relations with Congress and public, and so on) into account when discussing security interests. It does not help American presidents, who are often inexperienced in foreign policy, when their key staff people often have little foreign policy understanding as well. As one State Department official told the author, "Karl Rove [in the Bush II administration] was a great political strategist, but I do not want him making foreign policy."

The problem only gets worse as we move down the staff ladder. Many of the persons at lower levels in the White House licked stamps, carried luggage, and stuffed envelopes during the campaign. For their services they were often rewarded with lowly White House jobs. In these appointments, loyalty and service to the president take precedence over competence and expertise. Many of these energetic staffers have only a bachelor's degree—in a city where a master's degree and often a law degree or doctorate are entry-level requirements. Then two things happen: (1) the lowly staffer becomes full of himself and self-important because of his White House position, and (2) his superiors move on to other jobs and he steps into their shoes. The result is a White House often staffed even at high levels by political hacks, or young people too inexperienced to really be running things at high levels, or staffers infused with political loyalty to the president but lacking the knowledge or competence, especially on foreign policy, to be in such high positions. The pattern has repeated itself time after time among our recent presidents.

In all these considerations, what emerges most clearly is an almost perpetual conflict between the political skills and advisers necessary to become president and the knowledge and advisers on foreign policy required to successfully be president. Being president—that is, governing and leading on foreign policy—are far different from being a candidate; the skills required for one are not at all the same as the skills required for the other. While the American system of recruiting candidates from local to state to federal positions prepares candidates to run for office, it does not prepare them to govern or to deal with foreign policy. Hence, the system reinforces in both presidents and staffs the tendency to be woefully inexperienced and ill equipped in foreign policy matters.

Moreover, the time frame in which a president can initiate major new politics, domestic or foreign, is now short. Presidential election or reelection campaigns start three or four years in advance. The all-important funding needs to be secured, loyal advisers lined up, campaigns planned, and staffers hired. Once elected, it starts all over again in planning for reelection; Bill Clinton and his campaign guru James Carville called it "the permanent campaign." But that means the window for new initiatives is largely limited to the president's first year. Afterward, a president's hands are tied by political considerations. During the second year are the congressional midterm elections, the third year has the president usually enjoying less support but already campaigning for reelection, and the fourth year sees nothing getting done because it's an election year. Thus, only during the first year does a president have the power and capability to dominate the system and get his agenda through; otherwise, his initiatives are increasingly unlikely to get congressional approval in succeeding years. But can we afford a political system that functions only one year out of four?

Globalization and the Postmodern Presidency

The world is different now. Because of modern jet travel, electronic money transfers, the Internet, vastly increasing volumes of international trade, and overall globalization, the world is much more connected and interdependent than it used to be. Even the locus of sovereignty and responsibility is now more complicated. How do we deal with pollution or acid rain that comes not from our own smokestacks but from across the ocean? How do we classify cars made in the United States by Japanese companies or those for which the parts are manufactured abroad and only the assembly is done in America? How do we treat multinational corporations that have few or no national loyalties but go only where the markets, taxes, or labor are cheaper or better? We are now in a situation where domestic issues, such as human rights or food inspection violations in China, capital punishment, and natural disasters, quickly spiral into international ones, and where international issues that few paid serious attention to before (immigration and trade negotiations) have become major domestic ones.

Hence, the difference between a modern and a postmodern president is that the postmodern one must live and function as chief executive in this interconnected, vastly more complicated, interdependent, and globalized world. The postmodern president can no longer control and dominate the outside world in the way an American president once could. A postmodern president must not only be skillful in domestic politics but in international relations as well—and in the interconnections between the two. If a postmodern president is unable to adapt and navigate in this new intermestic (combined international and domestic) world, he is likely to fail both at home and abroad. Even more than before, the skills necessary to become president are quite different from the skills necessary to govern as president in this new globalized environment.

If Franklin Roosevelt was the first modern president, then Bill Clinton may be considered the first postmodern president. Clinton, who was also the first post–Cold War president, had to deal not only with various domestic issues but with myriad international ones that impinged on the domestic issues. These problems included global energy needs, human rights, international trade, climate change, refugees, immigration, peacekeeping, nation-building, drugs, terrorism—all of which impacted both domestic and foreign policy–related issues. From 1991 (after the Soviet Union's collapse) to the present, even the world's only superpower learned how vulnerable it was to oil shortages, economic crises, and international terrorism. And we see how limited the United States was in trying to solve these problems alone.

The United States is now much more interdependent with the rest of the world on a host of issues—energy supplies, trade, tourism, investments, labor supplies, immigration, pollution, global warming, nuclear materials, business—as compared with its earlier position of overwhelming dominance. America can no longer dictate solutions to the world's problems; globalization has made everything more complicated. The United States is still the most powerful nation on earth and is still looked to for global leadership, but in this new and interdependent world the United States cannot rule, let alone solve everything, by fiat. Hence, the postmodern president must learn to operate within this new context of global interdependence and make globalization work for the country, not against it. It does not serve the United States well to be on a collision course with other nations or at least not with too many of them—Iraq, Iran, Afghanistan, Russia, China, North Korea, plus our "friends" and allies in Europe—at once. Much as the United States would like to pursue its interests unilaterally, it cannot always go it alone in the world any more. And a skilled postmodern president will have to be able to operate in this new interdependent, globalized, intermestic environment.

The postmodern president must now consider how proposed policies will play not just in Peoria but in Paris, Tokyo, Berlin, Beijing, London, New Delhi, Brasilia, and Mexico City. No longer are most economic or security issues contained within national boundaries; instead, they are international. Thus, the United States has no choice but to compete as well as cooperate in this larger international setting. To succeed in these new arenas and on the new issues, a postmodern president must not only manipulate the power centers and maintain support at home but also direct his policies to influence the international arenas as well.

For good or ill, the standing of a postmodern president is as much influenced by international events as by domestic ones. A postmodern president must be not just a national leader but also a global one judged by both his domestic political skills and his success at international levels. If the postmodern president cannot succeed on both levels, he is likely to be judged a failure. Well-meaning Jimmy Carter was ineffectual at foreign policy while George H. W. Bush was good at foreign policy but clumsy at the domestic level. Bill Clinton vowed to refocus on the domestic economy, but foreign affairs, his weakness, kept interfering with his agenda; likewise, George W. Bush, another ex-governor with little foreign affairs experience, similarly promised a domestic agenda but the 9/11 terrorist attacks forced him into an international role for which he was ill prepared. So far, with the possible exception of Ronald Reagan (who was not knowledgeable but had strong instincts and significant accomplishments), America has not produced the presidential leadership that is strong on both domestic and foreign policy and the connections between them.

The postmodern president requires combinations of skills that recent American presidents have lacked. Brilliance and detailed knowledge of all foreign countries and issues are not necessarily required; those talents can usually be found on the president's staff (which is why it is so important to have a good, not politicized, NSC). But the successful presidency does demand a person who's generally knowledgeable, has integrity and good judgment, has a broad liberal arts education, has traveled or lived abroad, and understands the broad sweep of global and regional events and history. That person must also possess skills in communicating, listening, analyzing, and decision making. Levelheadedness and common sense also help. One would look for these precise talents in the chief executive officer (CEO) of a large company or the president of a university. Multinational corporations call for all these skills plus the experience of extensive living abroad, knowledge of foreign languages and cultures, and an understanding of how the world and its various nations work. It is striking that we require less of the world's greatest CEO (the American president) than we do of heads of private companies.

Perhaps setting less stringent job requirements for our presidents is a major reason why American foreign policy has seldom been successful in recent decades. We have entered a postmodern era of interdependent globalization, but our leadership and the political system, in general, are not yet fully attuned to thinking and operating in those terms. That situation is exceedingly dangerous and harmful for the United States.

Suggested Reading

Barber, James David. *The Presidential Character: Predicting Performance in the White House.* 4th ed. Englewood Cliffs, NJ: Prentice Hall, 1992.

Cronin, Thomas E., ed. *Rethinking the Presidency.* Boston: Little, Brown, 1982.

Cronin, Thomas E., and Michael A. Genovese. *The Paradoxes of the American Presidency.* 2nd ed. New York: Oxford University Press, 2004.

Deibel, Terry L. *Clinton and Congress: The Politics of Foreign Policy*. New York: Foreign Policy Association, 2000.

Hamilton, Lee H., and Jordan Tama. *A Creative Tension: The Foreign Policy Roles of the President and Congress*. Baltimore, MD: Johns Hopkins University Press, 2002.

Hersman, Rebecca K. C. *Friends and Foes: How Congress and the President Really Make Foreign Policy*. Washington, DC: Brookings Institution, 2000.

Hunter, Robert Edwards. *Presidential Control of Foreign Policy: Management or Mishap*. New York: Praeger, 1982.

Kelley, Donald R., ed. *Divided Power: The Presidency, Congress, and the Formation of American Foreign Policy*. Fayetteville: University of Arkansas Press, 2005.

Lehman, John F. *Making War: The 200-Year-Old Battle between the President and Congress over How America Goes to War*. New York: Scribner's, 1992.

Mueller, John E. *War, Presidents, and Public Opinion*. New York: Wiley, 1973.

Neustadt, Richard E. *Presidential Power and the Modern Presidents: The Politics of Leadership from Roosevelt to Reagan*. New York: Free Press, 1990.

Reedy, George E. *The Twilight of the Presidency: From Johnson to Reagan*. Rev. ed. New York: New American Library, 1987.

Rose, Richard. *The Postmodern President: George Bush Meets the World*. London: Chatham House, 1991.

Rossiter, Clinton. *The American Presidency*. Baltimore, MD: Johns Hopkins University Press, 1987.

Schlesinger, Arthur M. *The Imperial Presidency*. Boston: Houghton Mifflin, 2004.

Wildavsky, Aaron B., ed. *Perspectives on the Presidency*. Boston: Little, Brown, 1975.

14

Conclusion:
Broken Governement—
Can It Be Fixed?

American foreign policy is in very bad trouble. It is in much worse shape than it was decades ago when I wrote my first book on foreign policy. The whole system of American government seems to be breaking down. We can't fix our Social Security system, we can't fix health care, and both 9/11 and Hurricane Katrina revealed the inadequacies of the American emergency preparedness and response systems. The wars in Iraq and Afghanistan seem to drag on endlessly with no resolution in sight. Meanwhile, the American economy, in both short- and long-term perspectives, looks dangerously vulnerable. If the American political system, in general, is in crisis, why should we expect our foreign policy to be any more coherent and functioning than the rest of the American system?

Over the years, but especially since the Vietnam War, American foreign policymaking has become deeply divided and fragmented. First of all, American political culture and public opinion are deeply divided. We are no longer certain about who we are as a nation or what we stand for; and when public opinion is deeply divided as it is on Iraq and other issues, we can't expect our leaders to be any clearer than we are. Second, the two political parties, the electorate (red versus blue), interest groups, and Congress are frequently and regularly at loggerheads over Iraq, Afghanistan, climate change, the war on terrorism, and America's place in the world. Third, the media and the country's major think tanks have helped polarize the issues, pitting one group against another and emphasizing the extremes to the detriment of the broad center.

A fourth factor in America's divisive and dysfunctional foreign policy is bureaucratic politics. The State and Defense departments and the CIA fight over turf and budgets, with the State Department's declining over the years as DOD has claimed more and more areas of foreign policy and greater funds. The Treasury, Commerce, and Homeland Security departments, the FBI, and a host of other new agencies have added to the bureaucratic stew. These agencies are all so busy fighting each other that they have little time to deal with serious foreign policy problems originating from abroad. The National Security Council and the president are supposed to be able to knock heads and bring coherence out of this confusion, but they are weak, intensely politicized, and often unable to take on these big bureaucratic interests.

We should not romanticize the earlier periods in our history. Even then there were divisions over World Wars I and II, the Korean War, and the Cold War as well. But there was also an underlying consensus and a belief that, when your country was in trouble and needed you, you supported it wholeheartedly and subsumed your private reservations to its overall patriotic goals. Now most of that consensus is gone, and what is left are the divisions. Moreover, these rifts, played out between members of Congress and on radio and television talk shows, are meaner and nastier than ever before. They are so intense and the conflicts over foreign policy so deep that they produce paralysis, the inability to carry out any successful policy, or what Washingtonians call gridlock.

American foreign policy has become a veritable kaleidoscope of ever-shifting political forces, groups, interests, and bureaucratic rivalries. So many of them are going in so many separate directions that it is difficult to keep track of them all or to forge a coherent and sensible foreign policy. Are we on the right track as a nation, with our economy, in the war on terrorism? Most Americans now answer with a resounding no! It is no longer easy for a president—any president—to weld a workable strategy and set of foreign policy goals out of the myriad of actors and voices now participating, often loudly, in the foreign policy arena. The image that comes to mind is of numerous planets or even whole galaxies of interests and pressures out in the universe that is American foreign policy, often spinning out of orbit, with little attachment to a central core or any center of gravity, and numerous black holes into which foreign policy frequently falls. The sheer number of voices, interest groups, and bureaucratic pressures and the wide gaps between them seem to paralyze our foreign policy and make it all but unworkable.

The Vietnam War was the great turning point, parallel in many ways to Iraq today. Then, too, America was bogged down in an endless war, with obscure goals, and with deep divisions over policy. Discord and fragmentation replaced the earlier consensus that had rallied Americans during World War II and the early years of the Cold War. The Vietnam conflict was terribly polarizing, and since then no American president has been able to put the Humpty Dumpty of American foreign policy back together again. But was Vietnam a cause or an effect? Many commentators have now concluded that the debate over that war, similar to that we hear over the Iraq War today, was really the expression of a great cultural divide already emerging among Americans over religion, race, drugs, politics, the generations, and the future of the country. It is now epitomized by the growing ideological conflict between the parties, between blue and red states, and between Americans, in general. If we are so divided on all these other issues—"the two Americas"—we should not expect our foreign policy to be any more coherent and singular than we ourselves are.

The end of the Cold War in the early 1990s exacerbated rather than resolved these major conflicts. It deprived us of a single enemy, the Soviet Union, whom we could all oppose even though the country was already deeply divided over other issues. Without the Soviet threat, members of Congress, pundits, interest groups, and virtually everyone else could play politics with foreign policy, just as they did with domestic policy, since now there were no associated costs, electoral or otherwise, for making inflammatory comments on foreign policy. We no longer needed that unity of purpose; hence all the passions, partisan politics, and bureaucratic rivalries that the Cold War had kept in check were unleashed. Moreover, in Congress, over the airwaves, and in our political discourse, the disagreements also became nastier and more partisan. It has resulted in many able members of Congress and staffers, as well as high executive branch officials, no longer wanting to work in their respective institutions.

The reasons for these conflicts over foreign policy are many and complex; moreover, there is plenty of blame to go around. The frustrating Vietnam War was one major cause as it sapped American self-confidence and produced heated debate, street demonstrations, and personal and family conflict. The long-term situation of divided and, hence, quasi-paralyzed government, with Congress under the control of one party and the White House under the other, was another major cause. Add to that the rising partisan divide, which was exacerbated by the talk radio and television practice of pitting one extremist spokesperson against another. The great cultural divides among Americans over politics, public prayer, race and gender relations, political correctness, drug use, and other issues also played a major role. It can be said that our government is divided because we ourselves are divided.

The rise of narrow, tunnel-visioned interest groups and greater assertiveness on the part of distinct ethnic groups advocating policy positions toward their country of origin constitute another factor explaining America's recent divisions. At the same time, the media and the think tanks are no longer just neutral reporters and analysts of the news but are themselves participants, and often highly partisan ones, in the process. Meanwhile, the CIA and the FBI are at war with each other over surveillance issues; the State Department has little use for the Defense Department (and vice versa); the economic and trade departments are fighting for recognition; and the Department of Homeland Security and the Directorate of National Intelligence are fighting with just about everyone, including each other. At the level of the general public, moreover, there is less interest in foreign policy and other cultures and countries. Numerous surveys reveal the public's ignorance of geography and other people's languages and customs. Thus, being uninformed the public's common lament now goes, "Why do they [other countries as well as the terrorists] hate us so?"

So what is the matter with America and Americans? Clearly, as we have become more divided than before, we have also grown more self-centered. Have we all become narcissists, interested in ourselves and our own small world but unwilling to sacrifice for the common good? Are we just dumb, as filmmaker Michael Moore maintains, too ignorant of or too lazy to find out about other countries, other cultures, and other people who are different from us? Do we suffer from pride, hubris, and ethnocentrism, convinced that our own ways of doing things are the best and that other countries must always learn from us instead of the other way around? Have our curiosity about celebrities and our leisure activities now substituted for our interest in public affairs and foreign policy? With the decline of religious unity and the rise of "do your own thing," have we also lost our moral values and clear sense of right and wrong? In short, has America lost its way? Is the problem, as Shakespeare said, not in the stars but in ourselves?

Political power in the American system is more diffuse than it used to be, but at the same time the consensus that once supported foreign policy has been badly frayed. There are many more powerful interest groups, think tanks, and lobbying organizations involved in the process; therefore, it is harder for a president to mobilize these groups and public opinion to support his policies.

Now that so many issues are intermestic, more of these groups are brought into the policy discussion, making forging consensus that much more difficult. The public, therefore, often remains confused and uncertain. Should we concentrate on domestic social affairs and pull back from our entangling alliances, or should we continue to serve as the global police and firefighting force, battling injustice and putting out fires wherever they occur?

No one seems certain. As a result, America has faced too much deadlock and lacked cohesion and a sense of common purpose on foreign policy. Most of our foreign policy woes are, in fact, self-inflicted; and we seem unable to address, let alone resolve, our basic problems. Hence, the gridlock and divisiveness that affect both the government and the public are causing the entire political system to become unhinged, quasi-paralyzed, and ineffective.

Iraq is both a cause and an effect of these conditions. At first, in the immediate aftermath of the terrorist attacks of 9/11, President George W. Bush had massive public support—greater than 80 percent—for his actions in Iraq and Afghanistan. But the war went badly; the various rationales for the war—striking al Qaeda, finding WMDs, and establishing democracy in the Middle East—were all shown to be shams; and the mistakes and miscalculations multiplied. Then, it was shown that the war was not the product of a systematic, interagency weighing of the various options (the rational actor model) but of an ideological cabal comprising DOD staff, members from the vice president's office, the president's domestic political advisers, and the president himself, who wanted to rally political support and get reelected as a war president. Support for the war, the president, and his party soon plummeted, and he left the entire American foreign policy apparatus in shambles.

These comments imply that the roots of our foreign policy divisions and problems are deep and will not easily be solved or overcome. The deep fissures in the American political culture and public opinion will not be healed by the simple act of electing a new president and a new Congress. Of course, Bush has been blamed, but he is only one cog in what has become a deeply flawed system. American foreign policy is in such straits because the nation itself is uncertain about the future. Whether it is Iraq, Iran, the war on terrorism, trade, climate change, or other momentous issues, it is hard to find many elements of common consensus on what our policy should be. And as we've said more than once, if the public is confused and divided, in a democracy members of Congress, the

White House, and the federal government are certain to be confused and divided as well.

If the country as a whole cannot agree on what we should do or even in what direction we should be going, we should not expect our leaders in Congress, the Oval Office, or the State or Defense Department to be any more certain and clearheaded than we are. Our foreign policy is divided and fragmented because the country as a whole is divided. Until and unless we reach a new national consensus on goals and identity, we cannot expect our institutions to exhibit some greater singleness of purpose. We expect our political leaders to chart new directions and new initiatives for us, but since they also follow the polls and the fickle shifts of public opinion, they are no more certain about the future than the rest of us.

There are some hopeful signs. Even with all the paralysis, confusion, and gloom and doom, the United States still manages on many issues and in many areas to carry out an effective and more or less consistent foreign policy. First, crises, such as 9/11, force our leaders to act decisively and cut through the often paralyzing barriers of domestic and bureaucratic politics. Crises not only tend to bring issues into focus, they also enable us to set aside—if only temporarily—the partisan acrimony and to act with common purpose. There is no doubt that President Bush acted decisively after 9/11; however, the question is whether in haste, influenced by his more ideological advisers, or calculating his own reelection possibilities, he made the right decisions.

A second hopeful consideration relates to U.S. policy in parts of the world that, unlike Iraq or Afghanistan, do not make headlines and are not on the news every night. In those parts of the world—Russia, Asia, Europe, Latin America, and Africa—U.S. policy is more or less sound. Moreover, there is considerable, even bipartisan, consensus in these areas concerning what needs to be done and how to accomplish it. Our relations with most of these countries and areas, with few exceptions, are normal and (mostly) friendly. Of course, on some issues U.S. relations with individual countries, such as Iran and Venezuela, will continue to be contentious at times, regardless of who or what party is in office, because our interests and theirs may sometimes diverge. Such differences are normal and to be expected; the resolution of these differences or their accommodation is what diplomacy and foreign policy are all about.

Meanwhile, the relatively few contentious issues and countries, of course, get all the news coverage. The most controversial issues in the 1990s were Somalia,

Bosnia, and Haiti, but today, they are mostly out of the headlines and, in the larger scheme of things, do not count for much disagreement. Now the difficult issues are Iraq, Afghanistan, Iran, Israeli-Palestinian relations, North Korea, and, arguably, Venezuela. But U.S. relations with such far more important countries as Great Britain, France, Italy, Canada, China, Japan, Germany, India, Brazil, and Mexico, to say nothing of the other 180-odd countries in the world, are relatively good. As we think about the many flaws in U.S. policymaking, let us also consider that out of this quite imperfect system comes, often by fits and starts, not entirely bad policies.

A third consideration concerning the divisiveness issue is that not all differences over foreign policy are necessarily bad. After all, important differences over policy on such issues as Iraq or counterterrorism need to be thrashed out. In a democracy good policy comes out of such debates. In addition, such institutions as Congress, the State and Defense departments, interest groups, think tanks, and the media all have a legitimate and constitutional right and even an obligation to express their often contrarian views on the issues. Plus, we should remember that expressions of different and dissenting views often help improve the policy. Jimmy Carter, Ronald Reagan, Bill Clinton, and George W. Bush all were obliged to amend their policies, usually for the better, because members of Congress or other agencies of the bureaucracy were naysayers. What frequently seems chaotic and divisive may also be viewed as the working of the democratic process.

The trouble is that on many issues in Washington the policy debates have gone way beyond the normal give-and-take of democratic politics. When the discussion does, in fact, lead to better policy, we need to applaud; but our present divisiveness goes considerably beyond the usual exercise of pluralist politics. It involves unprecedented nastiness and bitterness on some issues, constant backstabbing, and the effort to discredit a position by destroying the character and career of the person who advances it. Some members of Congress call them "scorched earth" or "guerrilla" tactics on the part of various groups, which launch intensely personal attacks that go beyond the issues and subvert policy positions and those who advance them by whatever means necessary. Based on a "take-no-prisoners" mentality, the tactics used to discredit political foes include sneak attacks, lies, deceit, leaking private information, confrontation, and character assassination. These activities go beyond the pale of ethical behavior; they also serve to undermine democracy.

Because the climate has become so nasty and mean spirited, many able persons are no longer willing to work in public policy positions. Thus, many members of Congress and career civil servants have left public service. The same poisonous atmosphere keeps many academic specialists from testifying before Congress or lending their specialized knowledge to government agencies. It would be nice if we could conclude that our fragmentation, quarrels, and gridlock of recent years were just the normal workings of the democratic process, but unfortunately that is not the case. In the long run democracy does often improve our foreign policy, but on too many issues in recent decades America's policymakers have been practicing, not democracy, but the politics of personal destruction.

The causes of our national distemper are many and profound. The economy is floundering, and we are losing manufacturing jobs to China and other emerging countries. Polls show Americans have diminished faith in the future; they believe their children and grandchildren will not live as well as they have. Those same polls indicate most Americans think the country is headed in the wrong direction and they do not have much faith in their leaders or institutions. Public opinion surveys also reveal the United States is more fractious and less civil than it used to be. We yell at each other rather than having polite conversations. There is greater violence, more hard language, and a greater tendency to abuse and lash out at others. Polls tell us that we are also more self-centered and narcissistic. We have less sense of the larger community that is America; instead, we have withdrawn into our own smaller families, circles of friends, and ethnic and other identities. Most Americans would be hard-pressed to name more than two things that they revere and hold in common (other than freedom and the Constitution); hence, to reach a national consensus on almost any issue is nearly impossible. Given all these personal and national tendencies toward fractionalization, it is not surprising that our foreign policy should be open to intense dispute as well.

Recent presidents have recognized the problem but, because the divisions are so deep and intractable, have not been able to do much about it. President George H. W. Bush talked of a "kinder, gentler society," and his foreign policy was the most successful in recent decades, but when Bush foundered on domestic policy, he was rejected for a second term. President Clinton emphasized the need for the country to come together and had a bear hug for everyone, but he was impeached and his presidency ended in a shambles. George W. Bush early on talked of "compassionate conservatism," but his cockiness and mishandling of the war in Iraq made him the most despised president in recent history. As former Senate Majority Leader George Mitchell well put it, government cannot work in a polarized society, one in which deceit and mistrust are widespread.

Since writing my earlier books about foreign policy, I have become increasingly more discouraged about the U.S. political system and the hopes of reforming it. To be personal for just a moment, my first book on American foreign policy laid out what some then called a quite cynical view of partisanship run rampant, of self-interest triumphing over the national interest, and of a political system beginning to pull apart at the seams. In the second edition of that book, I suggested even greater fragmentation and divisiveness were taking place and lamented that America was becoming more partisan, with nastier politics and a diminishing faith in American institutions. My third book about this issue was clear: I used the word "crisis" in the title and showed on the cover a picture of the Liberty Bell, emphasizing its large crack as a way of symbolizing that I thought that America was also dividing and fragmenting.

In this book I go beyond that image. I think America as a nation and as a society is in bad trouble. None of our institutions—Congress, the presidency, CIA, State, Defense, FBI, FEMA, Homeland Security, the economy—seems to be working well or as intended. We cannot seem to get anything right. That is why we chose to include in our title, *Divided* and *Broken Government*. The idea of broken government goes considerably beyond the metaphor of a cracked Liberty Bell, symbolizing a cracked political system. This title reflects my belief that many of our institutions are broken, falling apart, and not functioning well, if at all. No wonder the public is also discouraged about the future and shows so little faith in our institutions. The people are right!

The question now is, what can and should be done about it? I don't believe it is possible for any one person, a new president, to even begin to fix the country's problems in a single term or even two. The long-standing problems are too deep and too difficult for a quick resolution. Instead, Americans' entire culture—their educational system and belief system—will have to change. It is not just a matter of tinkering with our institutions and making piecemeal changes; rather, since the problems also lie within ourselves, wholesale change in how Washington and the country think and work is necessary.

Are we up to it? Frankly, I don't know. I see encouraging signs but have many reasons to be pessimistic. Sometimes, in darker moments, I think the whole political system will have to be scrapped and something else substituted for it. Does that mean the student radicals of the 1960s and '70s were right all along, that the system is so rotten on the inside that it must be abolished? As a nation I fear that we are perilously close to that prospect. But is it possible or realistic to even think of abolishing the present system? What would we substitute for it? Would we then be better off? Not likely.

The alternative to a wholesale overthrow of the system we have is, of course, radical reform. Either we must reform the system fundamentally or, like ripe fruit, it will rot and fall from the tree. The options are stark; it will be up to the younger generations of readers to make the choices and the fundamental reforms called for here. So get involved! Reform the system! Help us prove once again that public policy, foreign policy, and civic responsibility are noble callings.

Suggested Reading

Allison, Graham T., and Gregory F. Treverton. *Rethinking America's Security: Beyond Cold War to New World Order.* New York: Norton, 1992.

Burns, James MacGregor. *The Deadlock of Democracy: Four-Party Politics in America.* Rev. ed. Englewood Cliffs, NJ: Prentice Hall, 1967.

Campbell, Kurt M. *Climatic Cataclysm: The Foreign Policy and National Security Implications of Climate Change.* Washington, DC: Brookings Institution Press, 2008.

Destler, I. M., Leslie H. Gelb, and Anthony Lake. *Our Own Worst Enemy: The Unmaking of American Foreign Policy.* Rev. ed. New York: Simon & Schuster, 1985.

Oye, Kenneth A., Robert J. Lieber, and Donald S. Rothchild. *Eagle in a New World: American Grand Strategy in the Post-Cold War Era.* New York: HarperCollins Publishers, 1992.

Steinbruner, John D. *Restructuring American Foreign Policy.* Washington, DC: Brookings Institution, 1989.

Wiarda, Howard J. *U.S. Foreign and Strategic Policy in the Post-Cold War Era: A Geopolitical Perspective.* Westport, CT: Greenwood Press, 1996.

Zakaria, Fareed. *The Post-American World.* New York: Norton, 2008.

Index

About the Author

Howard J. Wiarda is the Dean Rusk Professor of International Relations and founding head of the Department of International Affairs at the University of Georgia. He is also a senior scholar at the Center for Strategic and International Studies and a public policy scholar at the Woodrow Wilson International Center for Scholars. He is a member of the Council on Foreign Relations in New York, and in 1988 he served on Vice President George H. W. Bush's foreign policy advisory team. A prolific author, Wiarda has published or edited more than seventy books. He lives in Athens, Georgia.